D0213457

Religion, Terror and Violence

In light of the continued shadow cast by 9/11 and the subsequent war on terror, *Religion, Terror and Violence* brings together a group of distinguished scholars to scrutinize the intimate link between religion and violence. A key theme in this collection is that both the violence and the reactions to those events were intimately linked to cultural and social authorizing processes that could be called "religious."

In twenty fascinating contributions, such themes as national identity formation, ritualization of traumatic events, artistic representations, and cultural power contestations are scrutinized, along with reflections on the role of the public intellectual in such situations.

Working from diverse backgrounds and with a range of analytical tools within the field of religious studies, contributors bring together, in surprising ways, the personal and the critical, thereby revealing both the applicability of scholarly tools for understanding religious violence and the engaged role of the scholar in the face of such events. Many of the contributions emerge from the angst created within the classroom setting, while others reflect on the academic profession while under 9/11's shadow, while still others demonstrate the ideological and social implications of such perspectives. Theoretical and methodological diversity shapes this collection, challenging and inviting readers to recognize the necessity for public discourse on issues of religion and violence to engage scholarly approaches to the role of religious phenomena.

Religion, Terror and Violence provides a nuanced but incisive insight into the reaction of the discipline of religious studies to the post-9/11 world.

The editors:

Bryan Rennie is Vira I. Heinz Professor of Religion, and Chair of the Department of Religion, History, Philosophy, and Classics, Westminster College. His publications include *Reconstructing Eliade: Making Sense of Religion* (1996), (editor) *Changing Religious Worlds: The Meaning and End of Mircea Eliade* (2001), (editor) *Mircea Eliade: A Critical Reader* (2006), and (editor) *The International Eliade* (2007).

Philip L. Tite is a Visiting Assistant Professor of Early Christian Literature and History, Department of Religious Studies, Willamette University. His previous publications include *Compositional Transitions in 1 Peter: An Analysis of the Letter-Opening* (1997) and *Conceiving Peace and Violence: A New Testament Legacy* (2004).

Contributors: Martin T. Adam, Jonathan E. Brockopp, Wayne Codling, Michel Desjardins, Joel S. Fetzer, Susan E. Henking, Amir Hussain, Paul Christopher Johnson, Mark Juergensmeyer, Zayn Kassam, Anna S. King, Maureen Korp, Hans Küng, Russell T. McCutcheon, Samuel M. Powell, Caryn D. Riswold, Omid Safi, Robert A. Segal, J. Christopher Soper, Walter Wink.

Religion, Terror and Violence

Religious studies perspectives

Edited by Bryan Rennie and
Philip L. Tite

NEW YORK AND LONDON

First published 2008 by Routledge
270 Madison Ave, New York, NY 1000162

Simultaneously published in the UK by Routledge
Park Square, Milton Park, Abingdon, Oxon OX14 4RN
Routledge is an imprint of the Taylor & Francis Group

© 2008 editorial material and selection Bryan Rennie and Philip L. Tite; individual
contributors their contributions

Typeset in Sabon by The Running Head Limited, Cambridge
Printed and bound in Great Britain by TJ International Ltd, Padstow, Cornwall

All rights reserved. No part of this book may be reprinted or reproduced or utilized in any
form or by any electronic, mechanical, or other means, now known or hereafter invented,
including photocopying and recording, or in any information storage or retrieval system,
without permission in writing from the publishers.

British Library Cataloguing in Publication Data
A catalogue record for this book is available from the British Library

Library of Congress Cataloging in Publication Data
Religion, terror and violence: religious studies perspectives / edited by Bryan Rennie and
Philip L. Tite.
  p. cm.
  Includes bibliographical references and index.
1. Violence—Religious aspects. 2. Terrorism—Religious aspects. I. Rennie, Bryan S.,
1954– II. Tite, Philip L., 1969–
BL65.T47R46 2008
201'.763325—dc22

                                              2007037960

ISBN10 0-415-44230-3 (hbk)
ISBN10 0-415-44231-1 (pbk)
ISBN13 978-0-415-44230-5 (hbk)
ISBN13 978-0-415-44231-2 (pbk)

Contents

Concluding reflections 271

Contributors

Martin T. Adam, Assistant Professor, Religious Studies Program, Department of Pacific and Asian Studies, University of Victoria, Victoria, BC, Canada. He holds a PhD in Religious Studies from McGill University (2003), with a specialization in Indian Buddhism. His recent publications include articles in *Buddhist Studies Review, Journal of Buddhist Ethics, Focus Pragensis,* and *Journal of the American Academy of Religion.*

Jonathan E. Brockopp, Associate Professor of Religious Studies and History, Department of History and Religious Studies, Pennsylvania State University, USA. He holds a PhD from Yale University (1995) and is a specialist in Islamic studies. He is the editor of *Islamic Ethics of Life: Abortion, War and Euthanasia,* Studies in Comparative Religion (University of South Carolina Press, 2003 [reprinted 2005]), and author of *Early Mālikī Law: Ibn 'Abd al-Hakam and his Major Compendium of Jurisprudence,* Studies in Islamic Law and Society 14 (E. J. Brill, 2000), *Judaism and Islam in Practice: A Sourcebook* (co-author with Jacob Neusner and Tamara Sonn; Routledge, 2000), as well as scholarly articles in, for example, *International Journal of Middle East Studies, The Muslim World,* and *Journal of the American Oriental Society.*

Wayne Codling, a Zen meditation teacher, currently lives in Victoria, BC, Canada where he also works with autism. He holds a BA in Religious Studies with an emphasis upon Buddhism from the University of Calgary (1991). He was first introduced to and trained in Zen meditation in 1974 at the San Francisco Zen Center and the Tassajara monastery by Richard Baker (founder Shunryu Suzuki-roshi's successor) and has been an active leader/teacher for the past 30 years.

Michel Desjardins, Professor of Religious Studies, Department of Religion and Culture, Wilfrid Laurier University, ON, Canada. He holds a PhD from the University of Toronto and has research interests in early

Christianity, Gnosticism, issues of peace and violence in religious traditions, and pedagogy. His work with the American Academy of Religion (AAR) includes establishing the online AAR Syllabi Project and he was recently elected Secretary of the AAR. His most recent research and teaching interests include the role of food in religious traditions. His publications include *Sin in Valentinianism* (Scholars Press, 1990), *Peace, Violence and the New Testament* (Sheffield Academic Press, 1997), (co-editor with William Arnal) *Whose Historical Jesus?* (Wilfrid Laurier University Press, 1997), (co-editor with Stephen Wilson) *Text and Artifact in the Religions of Mediterranean Antiquity: Essays in Honour of Peter Richardson* (Wilfrid Laurier University Press, 2000), and numerous articles in various journals including *Studies in Religion, Toronto Journal of Theology, Teaching Theology and Religion, Journal for the Study of the New Testament, Vigilae Christianae,* and *Origini.*

Joel S. Fetzer, Associate Professor of Political Science, Social Science Division, Pepperdine University, Malibu, CA, USA. He holds a PhD in Political Science from Yale University (1996), with research interests in comparative politics, American politics, political methodology, urban politics, immigration politics, religion and politics, political behavior, and ethnic relations. His recent publications include *Muslims and the State in Britain, France, and Germany*, co-authored with J. Christopher Soper (Cambridge University Press, 2004), *Public Attitudes Toward Immigration in the United States, France, and Germany* (Cambridge University Press, 2000), and articles in *Journal of Ethnic and Migration Studies* and *Journal for the Scientific Study of Religion.*

Susan E. Henking, Professor in the Department of Religious Studies, Hobart and William Smith Colleges, Geneva, NY, USA. Her research has centered on religion and psychological studies, and more widely on religion and the social sciences. She is particularly interested in feminist approaches and in links between religion and sexuality. Her teaching is linked with a variety of interdisciplinary programs and she is actively involved in women's studies as well as lesbian, gay, and bisexual studies. She has been an active voice in pedagogical matters in the field of religious studies and is the founding series editor for the AAR Teaching Religious Studies book series. She is co-editor, with Gary David Comstock, of *Que(e)rying Religion: A Critical Anthology* (Continuum, 1997) and of the forthcoming volume *Mourning Religion* (2008) with William Parsons and Diane Jonte Pace, as well as numerous articles and chapters in books.

Amir Hussain, Associate Professor of Theological Studies, Department of Theological Studies, Loyola Marymount University, Los Angeles,

CA, USA. He holds a PhD in Religious Studies from the University of Toronto (2001). His research focuses on Muslim communities in North America. He also teaches about comparative religion and interfaith dialogue. His recent publications include *Oil and Water: Two Faiths One God* (Copper House Publishers, 2006), *Canadian Faces of Islam* (University of Toronto Press, forthcoming), and articles in *Journal of the American Academy of Religion*, *Studies in Religion*, *Journal of Dharma*, *Amerasia Journal*, *Method and Theory in the Study of Religion*, and *Journal of Religion and Film*.

Paul Christopher Johnson, Associate Professor in the Department of History and the Center for Afroamerican and African Studies (CAAS), at the University of Michigan-Ann Arbor, MI, USA, where he is also Director of the Interdisciplinary Doctoral Program in Anthropology and History. He holds a PhD in History of Religions from the University of Chicago (1997), and is the author of *Secrets, Gossip and Gods: The Transformation of Brazilian Candomblé* (Oxford University Press, 2002), and *Diaspora Conversions: Black Carib Religion and the Recovery of Africa* (University of California Press, 2007). Research and teaching interests include history and ethnography of the religions of the African Diaspora in Brazil and the Caribbean, religion and race, migration, ritual studies, and methodological and theoretical perspectives on the comparative study of religion more broadly.

Mark Juergensmeyer, Director of Global and International Studies and Professor of Sociology and Religion Studies at the University of California, Santa Barbara, CA, USA. Beyond holding a PhD in Political Science from the University of California, Berkeley (1974), he has also received an honorary doctorate from Lehigh University (2004). He is an expert on religious violence, conflict resolution, and South Asian religion and politics, and has published more than 200 articles and a dozen books. He was recently elected Vice-President of the American Academy of Religion. Among his more recent books are *Terror in the Mind of God: The Global Rise of Religious Violence* (University of California Press, 2000, now in a third edition 2003), *The New Cold War? Religious Nationalism Confronts the Secular State* (University of California Press, 1993), and (editor) *Religion in Global Civil Society* (Oxford University Press, 2005). Several of his books have been translated into, e.g., Spanish, French, Italian, Japanese, German, and Indonesian.

Zayn Kassam, Associate Professor of Religious Studies at Pomona College, Claremont, CA, USA. She holds a PhD in Religious Studies from McGill University. Her research and teaching interests include

Islamic ethics, gender issues, philosophy, and mysticism. Her recent publications include *Introduction to the World's Major Religions: Islam* (Greenwood Press, 2006), and essays in several books, e.g., *Terrorism and International Justice: A Collection of Philosophical and Political Reflections* (J. Sterba, ed., Oxford University Press, 2003), *Encyclopedia of Islam and the Muslim World* (Macmillan Reference USA, 2004), *A Communion of Subjects: Animals in Religion, Science and Ethics* (P. Waldau and K. Patton, eds, Columbia University Press, 2006), and *Religion, Terrorism and Globalization: Nonviolence: A New Agenda* (K. K. Kuriakose, ed., Nova Science Publishers, 2005).

Anna S. King, Senior Lecturer in Theology and Religious Studies, Faculty of Arts, University of Winchester, UK. Her research and teaching interests include ethics, philosophy, the Indian religious traditions, and subcontinental Islam. She trained as a social anthropologist at the Institute of Social and Cultural Anthropology in Oxford. Recent publications include *The Intimate Other: Love Divine in Indic Religions* edited with John Brockington (Orient Longman, 2005) and *Indian Religions: Renaissance and Renewal* (Equinox, 2006), as well as scholarly articles in, for example, *The Persistent Challenge: Religion, Truth, and Scholarship, Essays in Honour of Klaus Klostermaier* (I. Bocken, W. Dupre, and P. van der Velde, eds, Shaker, 2004) and *The Hare Krishna Movement: Forty Years of Chant and Change* (eds Graham Dwyer and Richard J. Cole, I. B. Tauris, 2007). Her current project is a film collaboration with Jouko Altonem, the Finnish filmmaker, and Graham Dwyer, to be followed by a book on ISKCON's Caitanya Vaisnava tradition (Penguin India). She is editor of *Religions of South Asia (RoSA)* published biannually by Equinox (2007–), and convenor of the annual Oxford Spalding Symposium on Indian Religions.

Maureen Korp, Associate Professor of Architecture and Art History, Beaconhouse National University, Lahore, Pakistan. She holds a doctorate in Religious Studies from the University of Ottawa, Canada. Her scholarly publications and awards are numerous (more than 60 articles, three books), and include contributions to nationally broadcast CBC radio and film documentaries on environmental art and the religious nature of artistic vision. She is currently engaged in a cross-cultural study of twentieth-century war memorials and myth. She has lectured widely in Europe, Asia, and North America on the history of art, architecture, and religions. Her best-known book is *Sacred Art of the Earth: Ancient and Contemporary Earthworks* (Continuum, 1997), now in its fourth printing.

Hans Küng, Professor Emeritus of Theology, University of Tübingen and President of the Global Ethic Foundation. Arguably one of the most significant and controversial Roman Catholic theologians of the last 40 years, he has authored numerous books and articles: e.g., *Justification: The Doctrine of Karl Barth and a Catholic Reflection* (Burns and Oates, 1966), *The Church* (Sheed and Ward, 1968), *Christianity and the World Religions: Paths to Dialogue with Islam, Hinduism, and Buddhism* (Doubleday, 1986), and *Theology for the Third Millennium: An Ecumenical View* (Anchor, 1990). His work on ecumenical theology and his reformist approach to Catholic theology has recently encompassed a more politically oriented theologizing, such as embodied in his *A Global Ethic for Global Politics and Economics* (Oxford University Press, 1997) and *Global Responsibility: In Search of a New World Ethic* (Continuum, 1993).

Russell T. McCutcheon, Professor and Chair, Department of Religious Studies, University of Alabama, USA. He holds a PhD in Religious Studies from the University of Toronto (1995). He is a widely recognized expert in method and theory issues in the academic study of religion, and has published widely in scholarly journals, including *Journal of the American Academy of Religion, Religion, Method and Theory in the Study of Religion, Numen, Culture and Religion,* and *Studies in Religion*. He is the author of *Religious Experience: A Reader* (Equinox, 2007), *Religion and the Domestication of Dissent, Or, How to Live in a Less than Perfect Nation* (Equinox, 2005), *Studying Religion: An Introduction* (Equinox, forthcoming), *The Discipline of Religion: Structure, Meaning, Rhetoric* (Routledge, 2003), *Guide to the Study of Religion*, co-edited with Willi Braun (Cassells, 2000), *Critics Not Caretakers: Redescribing the Public Study of Religion* (SUNY Press, 2001), and *Manufacturing Religion: The Discourse on Sui Generis Religion and the Politics of Nostalgia* (Oxford University Press, 1997).

Samuel M. Powell, Professor of Philosophy and Religion, Point Loma Nazarene University, San Diego, CA, USA. His research and teaching engage philosophy of religion and modern theological trends, especially with regard to Christian spirituality, Trinitarian theology, and Wesleyan theology. His publications include *A Theology of Christian Spirituality* (Abingdon Press, 2005), *Participating in God: Trinity and Creation* (Fortress Press, 2003), *The Trinity in German Thought* (Cambridge University Press, 2001), and (co-editor) *Holiness: Toward a Corporate Theology of Spiritual Growth* (InterVarsity Press, 1999) as well as numerous essays published in books and journals such as *Wesleyan Theological Journal* and *Fides et Historia*.

Bryan Rennie, Vira I. Heinz Professor of Religion, Chair of the Department of Religion, History, Philosophy, and Classics, and President of the local American Association of University Professors (AAUP) at Westminster College, New Wilmington, PA, USA. He holds a PhD in Religious Studies from the University of Edinburgh (1991), and is a specialist in theory and method in the study of religion. His publications include *Reconstructing Eliade: Making Sense of Religion* (SUNY Press, 1996), (editor) *Changing Religious Worlds: The Meaning and End of Mircea Eliade* (SUNY Press, 2001), (editor) *Mircea Eliade: A Critical Reader* (Equinox Press, 2006), and (editor) *The International Eliade* (SUNY Press, 2007), as well as several articles in such journals as *Culture and Religion*, *Method and Theory in the Study of Religion*, *Origini*, *Journal of Religious Studies*, *Jurnalul Literur*, and *Religion*.

Caryn D. Riswold, Associate Professor of Religion, Department of Philosophy and Religion, Illinois College, Jacksonville, IL, USA. She holds a PhD in Theology from Lutheran School of Theology at Chicago (2000). She teaches courses in religion and in gender and women's studies. Her recent publications include *Two Reformers: Martin Luther and Mary Daly as Political Theologians* (Wipf and Stock Publishers, 2007), *Coram Deo: Human Life in the Vision of God* (Wipf and Stock Publishers, 2007), and articles in *Political Theology*, *Dialog: A Journal of Theology*, and *Currents in Theology and Mission*.

Omid Safi, Associate Professor of Religious Studies, Department of Religious Studies, University of North Carolina at Chapel Hill, USA. He holds a PhD in Religious Studies, with a concentration in Islam, from Duke University. His research interests include Islamic mysticism, particularly from a premodern period from the eleventh to the thirteenth centuries; the social and intellectual history of premodern Islam, particularly as it relates to the interaction between political and intellectual institutions; and contemporary progressive Islamic thought, i.e., liberal Muslim intellectuals and activists who seek to engage modernity (and postmodernity) from within an Islamic framework. His recent publications include *The Politics of Knowledge in Premodern Islam* (University of North Carolina Press, 2006), (editor) *Progressive Muslims: On Justice, Gender, and Pluralism* (Oneworld, 2003), (editor) *Voices of Diversity and Change* (Praeger, forthcoming), *Rumi's Life: Wondrous Narratives, Sufi Teachings, and Saintly Lives* (Fons Vitae, forthcoming), *The Tamhidat of 'Ayn al-Qudat al-Hamadani*, translation and commentary by Omid Safi (Paulist Press, forthcoming), *Rumi's Beloved: Shams of Tabriz* (Oneworld, forthcoming), *'Ayn al-Qudat Hamadani* (Oneworld, forthcoming), as well as articles in such journals as *Journal of*

Muhyiddin Ibn 'Arabi Society, Journal of Scriptural Reasoning, and *Muslim World*.

Robert A. Segal, Sixth Century Chair in Religious Studies at the University of Aberdeen, Scotland. He is one of the foremost scholars of mythology and method and theory in the academic study of religion and the author or editor of, among other works, *The Poimandres as Myth* (Mouton de Gruyter, 1986), *Joseph Campbell: An Introduction* (revised edn, Penguin, 1990), *Explaining and Interpreting Religion* (Lang, 1992), *The Gnostic Jung* (Princeton and Routledge, 1992), *Jung on Mythology* (Princeton and Routledge, 1998), *The Myth and Ritual Theory* (Blackwell, 1998), *Theorizing About Myth* (University of Massachusetts Press, 1999), *Myth: A Very Short Introduction* (Oxford, 2004), *The Blackwell Companion to the Study of Religion* (2006), and *Myth: Cultural Concepts in Literary and Cultural Studies* (4 vols) (Routledge, 2007).

J. Christopher Soper, Professor of Political Science and Departmental Chair, Social Science Division, Pepperdine University, Malibu, CA, USA. He holds a PhD in Political Science from Yale University (1992) and has research interests in American politics, comparative politics, and religion and politics. Publications include *Muslims and the State in Britain, France, and Germany*, co-authored with Joel S. Fetzer (Cambridge University Press, 2004), *Equal Treatment of Religion in a Pluralistic Society*, with Stephen V. Monsma (Eerdmans, 1998), *The Challenge of Pluralism: Church and State in Western Democracies*, with Stephen V. Monsma (Rowman and Littlefield Press, 1997), *Evangelical Christianity in the United States and Great Britain: Religious Beliefs, Political Choices* (Macmillan and New York University Presses, 1994), as well as articles in *Journal for the Scientific Study of Religion* and *French Politics*.

Philip L. Tite, Visiting Assistant Professor of Early Christian Literature and History, Department of Religious Studies, Willamette University, Salem, OR, USA. He holds a PhD from McGill University in Religious Studies (2005) and is the author of *Conceiving Peace and Violence: A New Testament Legacy* (University Press of America, 2004) and *Compositional Transitions in 1 Peter: An Analysis of the Letter-Opening* (International Scholars Publications, 1997). He has published numerous scholarly articles in such journals as *Harvard Theological Review, Method and Theory in the Study of Religion, Religion, Culture and Religion*, and *Teaching Theology and Religion*. His research interests include early Christian studies, Gnosticism, and method and theory in the academic study of religion.

Walter Wink, Professor Emeritus of Biblical Interpretation, Auburn Theological Seminary, Sandisfield, MA, USA. He holds a PhD from Auburn
Theological Seminary (1963) and is a leading biblical scholar in the
area of religion and violence. Author of over a dozen books and
over 200 articles, some of his best-known works include *Naming the
Powers: The Language of Power in the New Testament* (Fortress Press,
1984), *Unmasking the Powers: The Invisible Forces That Determine
Human Existence* (Fortress Press, 1986), *Engaging the Powers: Discernment and Resistance in a World of Domination* (Fortress Press,
1992), *When the Powers Fall: Reconciliation in the Healing of Nations*
(Fortress Press, 1998), *Cracking the Gnostic Code: The Powers in
Gnosticism* (Society of Biblical Literature Monograph Series; Schol-
ars Press, 1993), and *Violence and Nonviolence in South Africa* (New
Society Publishers, 1987). More recently, he has published *The Human
Being: Jesus and the Enigma of the Son of the Man* (Fortress Press,
2001), (editor) *Peace Is The Way: Writings on Nonviolence from
the Fellowship of Reconciliation* (Orbis Books, 2000), *The Powers
That Be: Theology for a New Millennium* (Doubleday, 1999), and
*Homosexuality and Christian Faith: Questions of Conscience for the
Churches* (Fortress Press, 1999).

Acknowledgments and permissions

In a collaborative project such as this, thanks and acknowledgments are rightly due to more people than can be mentioned. First, the editors would like to take this opportunity to thank all of the contributors for their thought, honesty, and hard work. The editorial staff at Routledge should also be thanked for their encouragement and patience.

A number of permissions to publish must be acknowledged. Amir Hussain's "Thoughts on Being a Scholar of Islam and a Muslim in America Post-9/11" was published in an earlier version in the tenth anniversary edition of *Subverting Hatred: The Challenge of Nonviolence in Religious Traditions*, edited by Daniel L. Smith-Christopher (Orbis Books, 2007) and appears in the present volume by permission of Orbis Books.

Walter Wink's "Can Love Save the World?" appears with the permission of *YES Magazine*, where it appeared in the Winter 2002 volume.

The chapter by Martin T. Adam and Wayne Codling appears by permission of the editors of *ARC: The Journal of the Faculty of Religious Studies* of McGill University in Montreal, as does "Jihad and Islamic History" by Jonathan E. Brockopp and "Teaching Islam Through and After September 11: Towards a Progressive Muslim Agenda" by Omid Safi.

"The Roots of Public Attitudes Toward State Accommodation of European Muslims' Religious Practices Before and After September 11" by Joel S. Fetzer and J. Christopher Soper originally appeared in the *Journal for the Scientific Study of Religion* (42.2 [2003]: 247–58) and is published with the permission of Blackwell Publishing.

Mark Juergensmeyer's chapter "Religious Terror and Global War" is printed with the permission of the Social Science Research Council.

"Savage Civil Religion" by Paul Christopher Johnson was first published in *Numen* 52.3 (2005): 289–324 and appears here by permission of Brill.

"A New Paradigm of International Relations? Reflections after September 11, 2001" by Hans Küng is a version of an article published in *Justice and Violence*, edited by Allan Eickelmann, Eric Nelson, and Tom

Lansford, Ashgate Publishing Ltd 2005, © 2005 Allan Eickelmann, Eric Nelson, and Tom Lansford.

The images in Maureen Korp's article are reproduced with the permission of the artists: Naz Ikramullah for *City under Siege* and *Lost Dreams*; Marie-France Nitski for *Animal Encounters*; Audrey Churgin for *In Sight Recovered*; Hans Mettler for *Think Different: Power and Decline of the New Economy*; Robin Campbell and Nina Handjeva-Weller for the installation from "The Healing of the World post 9/11"; and William Schick and Meryl Taradash for the photograph of Meryl Taradash's "Detail of Sundial Northeast View."

Introduction

1   Sacred violence and the scholar of religion as public intellectual

Philip L. Tite

When two hijacked planes purposefully crashed into the twin towers of the World Trade Center on September 11, 2001, a series of social and rhetorical processes were set into motion. The political and cultural repercussions were quick and predictable. Although many, both within the United States and in other nations, were horrified by the American government's response of a "war on terrorism," such a response did fit the processes by which great powers remain great powers. The pain and shock of the horrifying events of 9/11 certainly needed an outlet; someone, somewhere—perhaps anyone, anywhere—had to be held accountable for the three thousand innocent lives lost in New York, Washington DC, and Pennsylvania. Grief demands justice; and if not justice, then retribution. Great powers—whether the ancient empires of Egypt, Mesopotamia, or Rome, or the European empires of Britain, France, and Spain—respond to national tragedies by reaffirming their strength, their values, and the privileged moral authority they hold. It is in this sense that both individuals and social bodies affirm, contest, and modify their identity through crisis. Unfortunately, such identity (re-)construction tends to depend upon non-critical (or non-reflective) rhetorical strategies.

The morning of 9/11 I was awakened by a telephone call from my friend, Trevor, informing me that a plane had crashed into the WTC. I watched on live television as the second plane crashed, as a great city was covered in ash and thrown into chaos. I watched as thousands of people died. It was a calm and beautiful day in Montreal, a sharp contrast with the images that every television screen in the city kept replaying throughout the day. I spent most of that day trying to make sense out of what I had just seen. That evening my partner, Colleen, and I listened to President George W. Bush's speech. We witnessed the emergence of a rhetorically powerful discursive act; an act that may have helped direct and shape public discourse on the horrifying events of that day. Rather than offering an exhortation to embody unity and compassion, to embrace each other in suffering, to not take a vigilante stance toward justice against terrorism, we were offered a strong insider–outsider message of war. Even in the major American news media the public discourse was not one of asking serious questions about what factors led to these events and what strategies could be designed to break cycles of violence, but rather a debate over whether George Bush could effectively lead a war against terrorism. When the planes and soldiers poured into Afghanistan and then Iraq, my concern was that without serious reflection on the postcolonial, ideological, and economic reasons for these various acts of violence, only an ongoing perpetuation of violence would occur; cycles of violence driven by superficial constructs of good versus evil typologies; i.e., processes of other-making for the sake of insider identity reaffirmation. A more serious, or, to borrow a category from Clifford Geertz, a "thick" discourse was needed in order to fully appreciate, and more effectively respond to, acts of religious violence.

It was with such a conviction that thick public discourse was necessary, both within the United States and, perhaps more so, within the international community, that this book of essays was first conceived. Both Bryan and I felt that critical reflections were needed within the public sphere, and thus we began to collect and solicit essays for this collection. Since 9/11 and the subsequent events that fall under the label "war on terrorism," several intellectuals, including academics, have offered critical reflections on terrorism, political violence, American foreign policy, and socio-economics. However, one of the most obvious factors not addressed was religion. Indeed, Noam Chomsky, perhaps the most well-known public critic of American foreign policy, though effectively calling into view imperialistic and postcolonial issues, neglected to address religion as a factor even though he clearly recognized Al Qaeda's religious motivation:

> From their point of view, they are defending the Muslims against infidels. And they are very clear about it and that is what they have been doing. (Chomsky 2001a)

> As for the bin Laden network, they have as little concern for globalization and cultural hegemony as they do for the poor and oppressed people of the Middle East who they have been severely harming for years. They tell us what their concerns are loud and clear: they are fighting a Holy War against the corrupt, repressive, and "un-Islamic" regimes of the region, and their supporters, just as they fought a Holy War against the Russians in the 1980s . . . (Chomsky 2001b: 31–2; cf. Chomsky 2003)

For Chomsky, as for other political critics, religion tends to be treated as an aside, or, at worse, an obfuscation of the *real* problems. Religion as a category can serve the dual function of either affirming the purity of "normative" systems from violence, or merely portraying the terrorists as crazy fanatics in contrast to the civilized "us"—thus rendering, in both instances, a rhetorical act of other-making and self-identity construction or reaffirmation (see McCutcheon 2005). What is missing, of course, is an appreciation for the powerful role that ideological valuation plays in social and cultural contestation of power relations. Underlying acts of violence—including acts of physical violence, cultural appropriation, economic exploitation and social stratification—are convictions, values, and conceptual frameworks within which the world is defined in relation to the moral and ethical truths that an individual or social group adheres to. Such underlying valuation, along with attendant devaluation of competing ideological constructs, could be defined as religion.

Not only did religion—a term that is amorphous in definition even, or especially, within the field of religious studies—play a role in the terrorist attack, but so also did religion play a role within the various reactions to those actions. Religious convictions, played out through the usage of language and ritual acts, could be seen not only in a government's rhetoric to support a political policy of violence, but also, perhaps more significantly, in public and private acts of grief. The essays in this book address many of these factors. Caryn Riswold's exploration of the religious rhetoric within the speeches of President George W. Bush, for instance, effectively engages the utilization of religious language within American political reactions to 9/11. Paul Johnson and Maureen Korp both offer insights into the role of religious expression by ordinary people trying to cope with the horror of these events. While Korp offers us an insightful look at an aesthetic appreciation of such expression, Johnson elucidates for us the tension of civil religiosity that emerges from the public utilization of civil religion. Many of the essays in this volume further offer insights into, or are examples of, academic reactions to the events of 9/11 (e.g., Safi, Hussain, Brockopp, and especially McCutcheon's critique of such scholarly reactions). The challenge that we face as contributors to this volume is to ask what role does a religious studies scholar play within the public discourse over the tumultuous events of the past few years? Although not all contributors will agree on such issues as defining "religion," the best or most appropriate methods and theoretical frameworks for a study of religion, or even in what ways a scholar should enter public discourse, I believe each is convinced that a critical perspective on issues of religion and violence can be offered by those who are specialists in the academic study of religion.

We are not, of course, alone in this conviction. Some work on the religious dimensions of 9/11 has already begun to appear, both by several contributors included in this book and by other major scholarly voices in the field. I think in particular of Mark Juergensmeyer's outstanding sociological analysis of terrorism in his *Terror in the Mind of God* (2001; cf. 1997), Bruce Lincoln's *Holy Terrors* (2002), Russell McCutcheon's *Domestication of Dissent* (2005; which developed from his essay in this book), and the book edited by Omid Safi, *Progressive Muslims* (2003;

see also Kassam 2003). Interest in religion and violence is not new (see Segal's essay), though since 9/11 an increase in attention has emerged. This book is one contribution to that scholarly interest, though it is also an attempt at broadening our scholarly discourse to a more public discourse. The recent meeting of the International Association for the History of Religion, held in Tokyo in March 2005, was framed by the theme of "peace and conflict." At that conference, several contributors of *Religion, Terror and Violence* participated in a session, organized by Bryan Rennie, focused on this collection of essays. At that session, disagreement emerged over the role of the scholar within public discourse on religion and violence. Does a scholar need to "bracket out" confessional concerns? Should a scholar speak only to a general public from a secular perspective or is it appropriate to speak from a confessional stance toward diverse publics? Are we critics or caretakers, and what does it mean to be either or both? Should scholars of religion even engage with public discourse, or merely confine their analyses and perspectives to the academy? No consensus emerged, nor does this volume attempt to move toward such a consensus. Indeed, it would not be hyperbole to state that the field of religious studies has no consensus on the public role of the religious studies scholar.

The scholar as public intellectual has been widely debated within the field, though perhaps Russell McCutcheon's now classic 1997 essay has been a lightning rod for furthering the debate (cf. McCutcheon 2000; Henking 2000). In that essay, McCutcheon challenges scholars to cease being caretakers of religious traditions (i.e., simply acting as translators of insider truth claims or *sui generis* ahistorical experiences) and, instead, engage "religion" as a second-order category constructed by scholars for organizing social, cultural, and political acts and ideologies; i.e., to take on the role of cultural critics. As cultural critic, the public intellectual should, according to McCutcheon, be in the business of "expos[ing] the mechanisms whereby these very truths and norms are constructed in the first place, demonstrating the contingency of seemingly necessary conditions and the historical character of ahistorical claims" (1997: 453). With such an agenda for the public intellectual, McCutcheon distances the religious studies scholar from the proactive role of the public intellectual found in the work of Noam Chomsky and Edward Said, as well as the apologetic religious stance of more theologically oriented scholars such as Linell E. Cady (1993), Stephen L. Carter (1993), William Dean (1994), George Marsden (1994), and Martin E. Marty (1989).

What McCutcheon offers is, in part, a helpful call for the scholar of religion to contribute to public discourse as an intellectual and not simply a religious adherent. He certainly sees the importance of the scholar of religion within public discourse, armed with the analytical tools of the profession to assist in our re-describing, for the sake of explaining social and cultural contestations of power that are based upon ideological claims. The essays collected in this book attempt to realize this agenda in various ways, though certainly not within the narrow, secular confines that McCutcheon advocates as "normative" for the field of religious studies. Rather, these essays illustrate that religious studies scholars hold diverse perspectives on the make-up of the "public" within public discourse. Indeed, rather than speaking of a singular, monolithic entity designated "the public," these essays are helpful indices of the diverse "publics" that we as scholars work within. In some cases, our publics will collide, taking on differing masks within changing discursive contexts. For some their public will be found in the classroom setting, thereby raising pedagogical issues of public grief and scholarly explanation. We see such pedagogical concerns emerging with the reflections offered by Safi, Kassam, and Hussain. Some contributors emerge from, and speak to, a confessional body—be that evangelical or Catholic Christian (Wink, Riswold, and Küng), liberal Muslim (Safi, Kassam, Hussain), or North American Buddhist (Adam and Codling). The scholar of religion, furthermore, is no less engaged with the historical processes that she or he attempts to explain than are those whom he or she analyzes. Indeed, the "diaspora" condition of a Canadian Muslim teaching within an American state university is profoundly illustrated by Amir Hussain's reflective essay (cf. Fetzer and Soper on Muslim communities within the European context). For the contributors of this volume, the public from which and to which a scholar as "cultural critic" or "public intellectual" speaks is polymorphic, contingent, and even boundary crossing. Scholars speak across boundaries, linking diverse social spheres while carrying several points of accountability for the various spheres wherein they are located.

Along with the diversity of our publics, scholars of religious traditions are also diverse in their methodological and theoretical perspectives. Along with such diversity come conflicting epistemological valuations and presuppositions. The essays in this book are organized to reflect such variety, allowing readers to engage various scholarly perspectives and concerns. Following the opening survey of scholarly discussions of religion and violence by Segal, the first set of essays offer rhetorical reflections (Johnson, Riswold, and McCutcheon). All three use different tools and address different concerns. Riswold clearly speaks from a theological perspective in order to address ethical concerns over political violence and the rhetoric of "evil"; whereas Johnson's more sociological approach to civil religiosity offers us insights into popular and official religious expressions within material culture; and McCutcheon's critique of religious rhetoric is directed not to religious phenomena, but rather toward the study of such phenomena. The second set of essays offer two very different types of theological reflection on religion and violence. In his special address to the American Academy of Religion, the renowned and controversial Catholic theologian Hans Küng extends his theologizing work to an exhortation to embrace a global ethic for countering political

violence. With a similar concern for constructing an ethical response to violence, Walter Wink, who is well known for his work on biblical peace and
violence, theologizes a response of non-retaliation modeled on the Christian gospels. Both Wink and Küng speak from and primarily to a confessional body, though Küng's call for a minimalist ethic attempts to cross
over to a broader, more secular and international audience.

The third set of essays address historical and social reflections. Juergensmeyer, as a sociologist with a specialization in religion and political violence, challenges us to appreciate the ideological and mythical importance
of terrorist acts for those who perpetrate such acts. Indeed, religious violence, in various traditions and historical contexts, tends to reinforce an
identity construction based on a global war that both transcends and at
the same time encompasses the political, through symbolic acts of perfor-
mative violence. Working as an Islamic scholar, Brockopp reassesses one
of the most potent and, in his view, misunderstood terms in the war on
terrorism: jihad. Through a historical survey of greater and lesser jihad,
Brockopp re-evaluates the "normative" claims of Osama bin Laden.
With Fetzer and Soper we are offered a more quantitative sociological
study of European attitudes toward European Muslims. Their study of
Britain, France, and Germany indicates a shift away from cultural accommodation post-9/11. Following these essays, in the next section, we move
back to North America with Adam and Codling's discussion on Buddhist
perspectives on terrorism. As is typical of Buddhist studies, this essay
avoids the insider/outsider distinction so typical within religious studies by bringing together both a scholar in Buddhist philosophy (Adam),
elucidating Buddhist concepts of nonviolence, and a practicing Buddhist
teacher (Codling) who responds to Adam from personal experience as a
Buddhist adherent.

The fifth set of essays are comprised of three pedagogical reflections by
three Muslim scholars. Each of these essays engages challenges that have
arisen within the classroom and the profession more generally. As was
well recognized within the field post-9/11, Islamic scholars were inun-
dated with demands to speak in response to the terrorist attack, spending much of their time both with students and the media as authoritative
voices who were expected to make sense of these events for listeners or,
at the very least, help the rest of us better understand Islam. Both professionally and personally, such Islamic scholars struggled with the pre-
carious place they found themselves in. Emerging from the AAR Islamic
Studies Group, approximately 80 such scholars signed a "Statement from
Scholars of the Islamic Religion" shortly following 9/11 as an attempt to
counter the violence against American Muslims. Safi offers a powerful
reflection on the uncertainty and concern of a Muslim minority within
a small, elite college. Kassam explores some of the political dynamics
that affected and now challenge the religious studies classroom. Finally,
Hussain, as a Canadian scholar living and working in the United States,

reflects on the difficulties of being Muslim, and an Islamic scholar, in a nation not quite his own. All three of these essays place special emphasis on teaching and researching within higher education, asking what impact religious violence has upon those who enter our classrooms and what we, as teachers, might offer. Pedagogical concerns are also prominent in various other essays in this book, illustrating that religious studies scholars are public intellectuals not only within some general "public," but also, perhaps most often, within the very institutions where we encounter our students and colleagues from other disciplines.

Our final essay delves deeply into religious expression and personal experience. In a powerful and moving discourse, Korp explores themes of ritual expression, physical commemoration, and social memory construction through an aesthetic critique. As a noted scholar of religion and art, with a close working relationship with various artists, she engages a very different public—that of artist. In a sense, the artist is a type of modern mystic or prophet; at the very least, a nexus for drawing together or reflecting upon various publics.

This collection, therefore, offers various scholars voices working with diverse approaches within the field of religious studies. They are not, however, a comprehensive representation of the field nor is this collection meant to offer such representation. Yet they do offer a broad range of perspectives upon which readers may continue discussions of religion and violence. Indeed, it is our hope that this collection will spark rather than close further discussions. In order to encourage an open dialogue on the perspectives raised in this collection, we have invited four scholars to respond to and engage specific sections. Through such discussion pieces by Anna King, Samuel Powell, Michel Desjardins, and Susan Henking, readers are invited to enter into a broader public discourse regarding religion and violence. If such discussion takes place not only within scholarly circles, but also within non-academic circles, our goal as editors will have been accomplished. We firmly believe that issues of violence, peace, and religion are necessary within broader public debates and that, however understood, the religious studies scholar as public intellectual should play an important role within such debates.

References

Cady, Linell E. 1993. *Religion, Theology, and American Public Life*. Albany, NY: State University of New York Press.

Carter, Stephen L. 1993. *The Culture of Disbelief: How American Law and Politics Trivialize Religious Devotion*. Princeton, NJ: Princeton University Press.

Chomsky, Noam. 2001a. "The New War on Terrorism." Special lecture delivered on October 18, 2001 at the Technology and Culture Forum at MIT.

——. 2001b. *9-11*. New York: Seven Stories Press.

——. 2003 "Terror and Just Response." In *Terrorism and International Justice*, edited by James P. Sterba, 69–87. Oxford: Oxford University Press.

Dean, William. 1994. *The Religious Critic in American Culture.* Albany, NY: State University of New York Press.

Henking, Susan E. 2000. "Who is the Public Intellectual? Identity, Marginality, and the Religious Studies Scholar." *ARC: The Journal of the Faculty of Religious Studies, McGill University* 28: 159–71.

Juergensmeyer, Mark. 1997. "Terror Mandated by God." *Terrorism and Political Violence* 9 (2): 16–23.

——. 2001. *Terror in the Mind of God: The Global Rise of Religious Violence.* Paperback edn with new preface. Berkeley, CA: University of California Press.

Kassam, Zayn. 2003. "Can a Muslim Be a Terrorist?" In *Terrorism and International Justice,* edited by James P. Sterba, 114–31. Oxford: Oxford University Press.

Lincoln, Bruce. 2002. *Holy Terrors: Thinking About Religion After September 11.* Chicago: University of Chicago Press.

Marsden, George. 1994. *The Soul of the American University: From Protestant Establishment to Established Non-Belief.* New York: Oxford University Press.

Marty, Martin E. 1989. "Committing the Study of Religion in Public." *Journal of the American Academy of Religion* 57 (1): 1–22.

McCutcheon, Russell T. 1997. "A Default of Critical Intelligence? The Scholar of Religion as Public Intellectual." *Journal of the American Academy of Religion* 65 (2): 443–68.

——. 2000. "Theorizing at the Margins: Religion as Something Ordinary." *ARC: The Journal of the Faculty of Religious Studies, McGill University* 28: 143–57.

——. 2005. *Religion and the Domestication of Dissent: Or, How to Live in a Less than Perfect Nation.* London: Equinox Press.

Safi, Omid, ed. 2003. *Progressive Muslims Speak: Towards a Frank Engagement with Modernity.* Oxford: Oneworld.

Explanatory approaches to violence and religion

2 Violence internal and external

Robert A. Segal

The phrase "religion and violence" does not refer to violence committed *against* religion. It refers to violence committed *in the name of* religion. There are at least two kinds of religious violence: violence committed against fellow members of a religion and violence committed against outsiders. Neither kind of violence need take the form of terror, or random violence against innocents.

Theories, or universal explanations, of religious violence committed against outsiders do not begin with 9/11. The two classic theories of this kind of violence are those of Friedrich Engels and of the French Syndicalist Georges Sorel. In "On the History of Early Christianity" (1894–5) Engels goes beyond Marx to distinguish an initial, brief, revolutionary phase of religion from the subsequent, entrenched, reactionary phase. According to Engels, earliest Christianity, which he compares with modern socialism, was a revolutionary movement. It advocated taking up arms against Rome, the oppressor of Christians. Only later Christianity, which means Christianity from the second century on, espoused loving one's enemies rather than killing them.

For his chronology to work, Engels must make Revelation the first rather than, as for most scholars, the last book of the New Testament. He enlists the arguments of the radical New Testament scholar Bruno Bauer to do so. Of Revelation vis-à-vis the Synoptic Gospels, Engels writes:

> So here it is not yet a question of a "religion of love," of "Love your enemies, bless them that curse you," etc. Here undiluted revenge is preached, sound, honest, revenge on the persecutors of the Christians. So it is in the whole of the book . . . The faith of these early militant communities is quite different from that of the later victorious church: . . . this faith survives only through active propaganda, unrelenting struggle against the internal and external enemy, the proud profession of the revolutionary standpoint before the heathen judges and martyrdom, confident in victory. (Engels [1957] 1964: 337, 345)

For Engels, following Marx, religion always masks economics, so that religious revolt is really economic revolt—against those who oppress adherents economically. Engels' objection to religion in even its revolutionary phase is that it unwittingly masks economic oppression as religious oppression and, worse, strives for an otherworldly, spiritual paradise in heaven rather than a worldly, economic paradise on earth.

In *Reflections on Violence* (1908) Sorel asserts that the only way to establish the socialist ideal is by revolution, which requires both violence and myth. By "violence" he means forceful action, though not mere bloodshed. The key "violent" action is a strike by all workers. By "myth," which for him is often religious myth, he means a guiding ideology, one that preaches an imminent end to present society, advocates a fight to the death with the ruling class, makes rebels heroes, declares the certainty of victory, and espouses a moral standard for the future society. Far from a Marxist, Sorel considers Marxism itself an instance of mythology:

> In the course of this study one thing has always been present in my mind . . .—that men who are participating in a great social movement always picture their coming action as a battle in which their cause is certain to triumph. These constructions . . . I propose to call myths; the syndicalist "general strike" and Marx's catastrophic revolution are such myths . . . Catholics have never been discouraged even in the hardest trials, because they have always pictured the history of the Church as a series of battles between Satan and the hierarchy supported by Christ; every new difficulty which arises is only an episode in a war which must finally end in the victory of Catholicism. (Sorel [1950] 1961: 41–2)

For both Engels and Sorel, violence in the name of religion is a justified means to a nonreligious end.

In my essay I focus not on religious violence against outsiders but on religious violence against fellow adherents. The key theorists I consider are J. G. Frazer, René Girard, and Walter Burkert. There are, of course, other theorists I could consider—most conspicuously, Freud. In *Totem and Taboo* (1950) Freud argues that religion arises as an attempt to alleviate the conscious guilt that the sons who in primordial times killed their father continued to feel. He argues that religion lasts because of the now unconscious guilt that male descendants have, in Lamarckian fashion, felt ever since over their own parricidal wishes, even if rarely acted out, and over their equally murderous wishes towards their father-like god. In addition, male descendants have inherited the guilt felt by the sons who actually did kill their primal father. For Freud, as for Frazer, Girard, and Burkert, religious violence, which for Freud is a mix of wish and deed, is internal, not external.

I use the theories of Frazer, Girard, and Burkert to show that violence in religion has been perpetrated as often against fellow adherents as against outsiders. Violence enacted against outsiders, and especially against innocents on a large scale, is doubtless more shocking than violence against a lone fellow adherent or a small group. But internal violence may reveal as much about religion as external violence.

Theories of any kind purport to apply universally. They acknowledge differences but seek similarities, usually by finding similarities beneath apparent differences. Theories of religious violence, internal or external, thus look for violence in all religions. The issue, then, is not whether Islam is more violent than Christianity or Christianity more violent than Buddhism. The issue is whether all religions sanction violence. If not, the theories must say why not or else prove false.

I begin with Frazer, author of *The Golden Bough*, and then proceed to the contemporary theorists Girard and Burkert, both of whom offer twentieth-century variations on Frazer's nineteenth-century theory. All three theorists concentrate on ancient, not modern, times. Frazer, a professional classicist, focuses on ancient Mediterranean religions. Burkert, also a classicist, focuses on ancient Greece in particular. While Girard is professionally a specialist in modern European literature, he, too, focuses on ancient Greece and, even more, on the Bible.

At the same time all three theorists strive to link the past to the present. Frazer argues that Christianity, even in the modern West, reflects its ancient, indeed "primitive," roots. Christianity, he asserts, was originally a nature religion that functioned to provide food. And so for him it remains, at least for peasants. The spiritual or moral side of Christianity or of Judaism has for him been secondary until modern times.

Burkert argues that religion goes back not merely to the beginnings of farming, as for Frazer, but to the yet earlier stage of hunting. Even after farming replaced hunting as the main source of food, religion remained, for the function it had always served was not, as for Frazer, that of providing food but that of alleviating anxiety and also that of unifying the community. While Burkert does not discuss modern religion, his analysis of ancient religion rests on the views of the ethnologist Konrad Lorenz and of the sociobiologist Edward O. Wilson, for both of whom religion anywhere serves the needs that Burkert finds in ancient Greece.

Girard differs from Frazer and Burkert alike in his stress on the break that takes place within the ancient world between Greece and Rome on the one hand and Judaism and, especially, Christianity on the other. Where Greek religion perpetuated the hoary practice of scapegoating, Israel began the process that culminated in its rejection by the New Testament. The inclination to scapegoating, however, remains in all societies. So, then, too, does the use of religion to excuse scapegoating.

The theories that I present see violence as inherent in religion. For them, violence in religion is neither aberrant nor abhorrent. Yet for them violence is anything but terror. It is not random or unexpected. On the contrary, it is fixed and ritualized. It is religion operating normally, even according to the calendar. Furthermore, the violence occurs within the community and is not the attack of one community on another. Violence is done for the sake of the community and is celebrated by the community. Violence is sacrifice—the sacrifice of one or more lives for the benefit of the community. The "target" of violence may in fact be innocent, as Girard stresses, or may be suffering the fate that goes with the office held, as for Frazer.

For Frazer, Girard, and Burkert, violence is ultimately rooted not in politics but in human nature; yet it is not necessarily rooted in innate aggression. For Frazer, violence is the practical consequence of the sheer need for food. For Girard, violence is rooted in imitativeness and competitiveness, but not in aggression. For Burkert, violence is partly rooted in aggression but is also rooted in fear and guilt, and even aggression is transformed into sociability. None of the three theorists invokes question-begging causes like "evil" or distinctly modern causes like colonialism.

The greatest difference between these theorists and my fellow contributors to this volume is that for the theorists violence serves a positive function. It secures food (Frazer), restores order to society (Girard), or reduces anxiety and binds society together (Burkert). Instead of bemoaning violence, the trio endorses it as an exceedingly useful means to a practical end—even if for Girard the ending of violence is yet more useful.

Although both editors of this volume note that violence in the name of religion is hardly new—Holy War was undertaken by ancient Israelites, for instance—the other contributors limit themselves to the violence of 9/11. That focus is understandable, but the result can be a search for present-day explanations of what in fact is an age-old matter: that religion has long, perhaps forever, been associated with violence.

Frazer

While Frazer, the pioneering Scottish historian of religion, is best known for his tripartite division of all culture into the stages of magic, religion, and science, the bulk of *The Golden Bough* (1900, 1911–15, 1922) is devoted to an intermediate stage between religion and science—a stage of magic and religion combined. In combining magic with religion, this in-between stage also combines ritual with myth. In the stage of sheer magic there are rituals—the routines involved in carrying out the directions—but no myths, for there are no gods. In the stage of sheer religion there are both myths and rituals, but they are barely connected. Myths describe the character and behavior of gods. Rituals, such as sacrifices, seek to curry divine favor. Rituals may presuppose myths, which would suggest what activities would most please the gods, but are otherwise independent of myths.

By contrast, in the following stage of magic and religion combined, rituals and myths work together in what is called "myth-ritualism." Frazer actually presents two versions of myth-ritualism, though he never disentangles them. In the first version the myth provides the biography of the god of vegetation, and the ritual enacts it. More precisely, the ritual enacts that portion of the myth which describes the death and rebirth of the god. The myth constitutes the script of the ritual. The ritual operates on the basis of the magical Law of Similarity, according to which the imitation of an action causes it to happen. The ritual does not manipulate vegetation directly. Rather, it manipulates the god of vegetation. But as the god goes, so goes vegetation. The assumption that vegetation is under the control of a god is the legacy of religion, whereas the assumption that vegetation can be controlled, even if only through the god, is the legacy of magic. The combination of myth with ritual is the combination of religion with magic:

> Thus the old magical theory of the seasons was displaced, or rather supplemented, by a religious theory. For although men now attributed the annual cycle of change primarily to corresponding changes in their deities, they still thought that by performing certain magical rites they could aid the god[,] who was the principle of life, in his struggle with the opposing principle of death. They imagined that they could recruit his failing energies and even raise him from the dead. (Frazer 1922: 377)

In the ritual a human being plays the role of the god and acts out what he magically causes the god to do. Even when the actor is the king, this version of myth-ritualism is not closely tied to kingship.

Insofar as no harm befalls the actor, this first version of myth-ritualism involves no violence. Whoever plays the role of the god of vegetation is not himself killed. The ritual does not cause the death of the god, which, on the contrary, is presupposed as the necessary starting point of the rebirth of the god and thereby of the crops. The ritual causes—magically—the rebirth of the god.

Yet violence is still central to this version of myth-ritualism. For the god has been killed rather than has died a natural death. Frazer's main examples of gods of vegetation are Adonis (Babylonian and Syrian–Greek), also known as Tammuz (Babylonian); Attis (Syrian); Osiris (Egyptian); Dionysus (Greek); and Jesus. Adonis is gored to death by a wild boar while hunting or, worse, is murdered by either a spurned lover, Artemis, or a jealous rival, Ares, "who turned himself into the likeness of a boar in order to compass the death of his rival" (Frazer 1922: 380). Attis, too, is the victim of a spurned lover, Cybele, who in her jealousy drives him to madness and to self-castration and death.

Osiris is killed by his brother Set, who nails him inside a chest that is flung into the Nile. Isis, Osiris' wife (and sister), eventually finds the chest, but Set discovers it and cuts up the body into fourteen pieces, which he then scatters. Isis manages to find all the pieces but one, which has been eaten by fish. Eventually, the body is pieced together, and Osiris is reborn as god of the underworld. To quote Frazer's summary line, "Thus according to what seems to have been the general native tradition Osiris was a good and beloved king of Egypt, who suffered a violent death but rose from the dead and was henceforth worshipped as a deity" (Frazer 1922: 426).

Of Dionysus, Frazer writes, "Like other gods of vegetation Dionysus was believed to have died a violent death, but to have been brought to life again" (Frazer 1922: 450). According to one variant of the myth, "[T]he treacherous Titans," who were enemies of Dionysus' father, Zeus, "attacked him with knives while he was looking at himself in the mirror. For a time he evaded their assaults by turning himself into various shapes . . . Finally, in the form of a bull, he was cut to pieces by the murderous knives of his enemies" (Frazer 1922: 450–1). The Cretan version is even more bestial, for there it is Jupiter's wife, Juno, who sets the Titans against Dionysus, and they "cut him limb from limb, boiled his body with various herbs, and ate it" (Frazer 1922: 451).

In Frazer's second version of myth-ritualism the king is central. In the first version the king may not even participate in the ritual. In the second he must. In the first version the king, even when the actor in the ritual, is merely human: he imitates, not becomes, the god. In the second version the king is divine, by which Frazer means that the god resides in him. Just as the health of vegetation depends on the health of its god, so now the health of the god depends on the health of the king: as the king goes, so goes the god of vegetation, and so in turn goes vegetation itself. Above all, where in the first version the king does not even die, let alone get killed, in the second version he is killed. For to ensure a steady supply of food, the community kills its king while he is still in his prime and thereby safely transfers the soul of the god to his successor:

> For [primitives] believe . . . that the king's life or spirit is so sympathetically bound up with the prosperity of the whole country, that if he fell ill or grew senile the cattle would sicken and cease to multiply, the crops would rot in the fields, and men would perish of widespread disease. Hence, in their opinion, the only way of averting these calamities is to put the king to death while he is still hale and hearty, in order that the divine spirit which he has inherited from his predecessors may be transmitted in turn by him to his successor while it is still in full vigour and has not yet been impaired by the weakness of disease and old age. (Frazer 1922: 312–13)

The king is killed either at the end of a fixed term or at the first sign of infirmity. Doubtless the sudden death of a king can never be precluded, but the killing of the king before his likely passing most nearly guarantees the continuous health of the god and so of vegetation. The aim is to fend off winter. The withering of vegetation during the winter of even a yearlong reign is attributed to the weakening of the king.

This second version of myth-ritualism has proved the more influential by far, but, ironically, it in fact provides only a tenuous link between myth and ritual and in turn between religion and magic. Instead of enacting the myth of the god of vegetation, the ritual simply changes the residence of the god. The king dies not in imitation of the death of the god but as a sacrifice to preserve the health of the god. Myth, hence religion, plays a scant part here. Nor does magic play any part. Instead of reviving the god by magical imitation, the ritual revives the god by substitution. By contrast, in Frazer's first myth-ritualist scenario, one would not ritualistically enact the rebirth of the god of vegetation without the myth of the death and rebirth of that god.

While Frazer presents two distinct and incompatible versions of myth-ritualism, he combines, or tries to combine, them in his description of the myths and rituals of his key gods. Of Adonis, he writes,

> There is some reason to think that in early times Adonis was sometimes personated by a living man who died a violent death in the character of the god. Further, there is evidence which goes to show that among the agricultural peoples of the Eastern Mediterranean, the corn-spirit, by whatever name he was known, was often represented, year by year, by human victims slain on the harvest-field. (Frazer 1922: 394)

Here Frazer tries to combine the imitation of the death and rebirth of the god—"Adonis was sometimes personated by a living man . . . in the character of the god"—with the killing of a human being—"a living man who died a violent death." Yet unless the human victim harbors the god within him, the victim's death duplicates, not imitates, Adonis'. There is no magical efficacy, only emulation. Adonis himself is unaffected. Still, there is conspicuous violence, though not towards any king. Kingship is not even mentioned.

Frazer goes as far as to link the cult of Adonis to an outright cult of death:

> In the summer after the battle of Landen, the most sanguinary battle of the seventeenth century in Europe, the earth, saturated with the blood of twenty thousand slain, broke forth into millions of poppies, and the traveller who passed that vast sheet of scarlet might well fancy that the earth had indeed given up her dead. At Athens the great Commemoration of the Dead fell in early spring about the middle of March, when the early flowers are in bloom. Then the dead were believed to rise from their graves and go about the streets, vainly endeavouring to enter the temples and dwellings, which were barred against these perturbed spirits with ropes, buckthorn, and pitch . . . There may therefore be a measure of truth in the theory of

> Renan, who saw in the Adonis worship a dreamy voluptuous cult of
> death. (Frazer 1922: 395)

Again, there is emulation of Adonis' death but no magical imitation, and
Adonis himself is unaffected. Yet once again, the ritual is still violent.

Furthermore, the emulation here is of Adonis' final death, not of his
annual descent to the land of the dead. Therefore the death here does not
lead to rebirth and so cannot be considered merely a violent means to
renewal. In fact, Frazer splits the myth in two to serve his dual goals. He
focuses on Adonis' annual trip to and from Hades because that trip parallels, and can thereby be said to cause, the annual death and rebirth of the
crops, as Frazer's first version of myth-ritualism requires. Adonis' death
here is wholly irenic: he dies only because he enters—while alive—the
land of the dead. Here Adonis' final, violent death is ignored. Alterna-
tively, Frazer focuses on that violent death, from which there is no return,
because it parallels, though not causes, the death of the king, as Frazer's second version of myth-ritualism requires. Adonis' annual, peaceful
sojourn is ignored.

When Frazer turns to the myths of his other main gods of vegetation,
he does not have the convenience of a dual death to portion out between
his varieties of myth-ritualism. Attis, Osiris, and Dionysus each die only
once. Because all three die violently, their deaths parallel the death of the
king in Frazer's second version of myth-ritualism. However, in order to
make these three gods fit the first version as well, Frazer must argue that
the three were believed to be resurrected annually, so that their seemingly one-time deaths become annual affairs. The myth of at least Osiris
does include his resurrection, but he becomes king of the underworld
and never returns to the world of the living. Some variants of the myth
of Dionysus include his resurrection, but others do not. No variant of
the myth of Attis offers any resurrection. Still, insofar as Frazer fuses a
god's one-time death, which always comes through violence, with a god's
annual death, he is tying both versions of myth-ritualism to violence.

Frazer links the violent rituals of neither Adonis nor Attis to kingship.
He does, however, tie the violent rituals of both Osiris and Dionysus to
kingship. To take the case of Osiris:

> With regard to the ancient Egyptians we have it on the authority of
> Manetho that they used to burn red-haired men and scatter their
> ashes with winnowing fans, and it is highly significant that this bar-
> barous sacrifice was offered by the kings at the grave of Osiris. We
> may conjecture that the victims represented Osiris himself, who was
> annually slain, dismembered, and buried in their persons that he
> might quicken the seed in the earth. Possibly in prehistoric times the
> kings themselves played the part of the god and were slain and dis-
> membered in that character. (Frazer 1922: 439)

Frazer notes a story in which "Romulus, the first king of Rome, was cut in pieces by the senators, who buried the fragments of him in the ground" (Frazer 1922: 439). In fact, Osiris himself was king of Egypt when killed. Still, each subsequent Egyptian king here, while "playing the part" of Osiris, dies in emulation, not magical imitation, of Osiris. Moreover, the king is not said to harbor the god within himself, so that the link between king and god is even more distant. Nevertheless, the death of the king is now a means to rebirth: "that he might quicken the seed in the earth." Yet the rejuvenation of the crops comes from the death, not the resurrection, of the king.

For Frazer, Christianity is just another vegetation cult, indeed the most successful of the lot. Christianity takes over from Judaism the primitive practice of killing a human being, not for the ethereal purpose of atoning for sin but for the mundane purpose of putting food on the table. Jesus was a human king in whom, it was believed, resided the soul of the god of vegetation. The annual spring celebration of Jesus' death and resurrection was a ritual intended to revive the crops, with Jesus the King of the Jews. At work here is Frazer's second myth-ritualist scenario exclusively, not any combination with the first one. Jesus was not an actor imitating the death and rebirth of a god but rather a divine king who was himself killed and replaced, though Frazer never discloses who his successor was.

Trying to account for the "remarkably rapid diffusion of Christianity in Asia Minor," Frazer argues that "the new faith had elements in it which appealed powerfully to the Asiatic mind"—namely, an annual spring ritual of regicide (Frazer 1900, vol. III: 195–6):

> All over Western Asia from time immemorial the mournful death and happy resurrection of a divine being appear to have been annually celebrated with alternative rites of bitter lamentation and exultant joy; and through the veil which mythic fancy has woven round this tragic figure we can still detect the features of those great yearly changes in earth and sky which, under all distinctions of race and religion, must always touch the natural human heart with alternative emotions of gladness and regret, because they exhibit on the vastest scale open to our observation the mysterious struggle between life and death. But man has not always been willing to watch passively this momentous conflict; he has felt that he has too great a stake in its issue to stand by with folded hands while it is being fought out . . . Nowhere do these efforts, vain and pitiful yet pathetic, appear to have been made more persistently and systematically than in Western Asia. In name they varied from place to place, but in substance they were all alike. A man, whom the fond imagination of his worshippers invested with the attributes of a god, gave his life for the life of the world; after infusing from his own body a fresh current of vital energy into the stagnant veins of nature, he was cut off from among the living before

his failing strength should initiate a universal decay, and his place was taken by another who played, like all his predecessors, the ever-recurring drama of the divine resurrection and death. Such a drama, if our interpretation of it is right, was the original story of Esther and Mordecai or, to give them their older names, of Ishtar and Marduk . . . A chain of causes . . . determined that the part of the dying god in this annual play should be thrust upon Jesus of Nazareth, whom the enemies he had made in high places by his outspoken strictures were resolved to put out of the way. (Frazer 1900, vol. III: 196–7)

Frazer demotes Jesus not even to a vegetation god or, worse, to a king but, worse yet, to the temporary substitute for the king. Because the substitute is killed, the king himself is thereby spared and so can be "reborn." By no coincidence the case of Jesus, in the third edition of *The Golden Bough*, falls in the volume (no. 9) entitled "The Scapegoat."[1] To be sure, Frazer does praise Jesus as a moral teacher, but for Frazer it is Jesus' death, not his life, that explains the appeal of Christianity.

Frazer's theory connects religion to violence in the most direct way. Religion is literally about life and death. Humans need food to survive. Crops would continue to grow if they did not die. Their death is not natural, even if recurrent. They die because the god of vegetation dies, and in Frazer's first scenario three of his four main gods die because they have been murdered. Had these gods not been murdered, then in at least these three cases the first myth-ritualist scenario would never have arisen. Religion plus magic arises to undo, usually, a murder. That religion and magic combined restores to life the god and thereby the crops does make this combined stage ultimately life-giving, but again only by reversing a murder or at least a death.

In Frazer's second scenario the king, or a substitute, is killed. His death is anything but natural since he is killed prior to succumbing to a natural cause. Because he is killed as a sacrifice for the community, he cannot be said to be murdered. But killed he still is. He is barred from serving as king all lifelong. "The king must die" is the familiar line. The king is killed so that the god of vegetation residing within him can either retain or regain his health. The death of the crops during the king's reign is somehow attributed to the mere weakening, not the outright death, of the incumbent. But the king is outright killed to ensure that he does not die naturally while still reigning. Were the king to die in office, the god would not himself die but would leave the king's body and no longer be under human control. Regicide is a preventive measure. Abdication is not an option.

In *The Hero* (1936) and other works the English folklorist Lord Raglan adopts the second version of Frazer's myth-ritualism.[2] Hence the king is the god of vegetation rather than plays the part of the god. Consequently, the killing and replacement of the king do not magically cause but physically cause the death and rebirth—better, the weakening and reinvigoration—of that god and therefore of vegetation.[3]

In following Frazer's second scenario, Raglan no more than his mentor finds a place for magic. The health of the god is restored by the sheer transfer of his soul from the body of the incumbent king to that of a successor. There is ritual but no magic. Yet where Frazer, in his second stage, dispenses with myth as well as with magic, Raglan restores myth to the ritual. For him, the myth is not, as in Frazer's first scenario, about the death and rebirth of the god of vegetation. It is about the life and death of the king. While the god still resides in the body of the king, the life of the king, not of the god, is the subject of myth for Raglan.

Going beyond Frazer, Raglan equates the king with the hero. For Frazer, the self-sacrificing king in Frazer's second version may in effect be a hero to his community, but Raglan labels him one. Moreover, Raglan introduces his own detailed hero pattern, which he applies to twenty-one hero myths (see Raglan [1936] 1956: 174–5).

What Raglan considers the core of the myth—the toppling and dying of the king—corresponds to the undeniable core of the ritual: the killing of the king when he either weakens or completes his term. The myth is intended to spur the incumbent to submit to the ritual and thereby be a hero to his subjects. In both the myth and the ritual, heroes are really ideal kings, even if in the myth the king does not voluntarily give up either his throne or his life. For Raglan, just as for Frazer, the community would die without the hero's death. Voluntarily or not, heroes are the saviors of their subjects.

Yet that saving power does not come through control over the world. It comes through death. As for the Frazer of, especially, version two, so for Raglan, the heart of religion is killing. The killing may be ritualistic. It may be obligatory. It may be legal. It therefore may not constitute murder. And it may elevate the victim to heroism. But for Raglan religion still arises and functions to kill the king.

Girard

In *Violence and the Sacred* (1977) and many other works, the French-born literary critic René Girard works out his own theory of myth and ritual. That theory offers an ironic twist to that of Raglan, who himself is never cited. Where Raglan's hero is heroic because he is willing to die for the sake of the community, Girard's hero is killed or exiled by the community for having caused the present ills of the community. Indeed, the figure who subsequently becomes the hero is initially considered to be a criminal, or "transgressor," who deserved to die. Only subsequently is the villain turned into a hero, who, as for Raglan, died selflessly on behalf of the community. The transformation of Oedipus from reviled exile in Sophocles' *Oedipus the King* to revered benefactor in *Oedipus at Colonus* evinces the transformation of outcast into saint.

For Girard, the change from criminal to hero is only the third stage of the process. Violence erupts in the community. The cause is the inclination, innate in human beings, to imitate others and thereby to desire the same objects as those of the imitated. Imitation leads to rivalry, which leads to envy, hatred, and finally violence. Desperate to end the violence, the community chooses an innocent member to blame for the turmoil. This scapegoat can range from the most helpless member of society to the most elevated, including, as with Oedipus, the king. The victim is usually killed, though, as with Oedipus, sometimes exiled. The killing or exile is the ritualistic sacrifice.

Where for Frazer myth directs the killing of the hero, and where for Raglan myth inspires the killing, for Girard myth is created after the killing to excuse it. The myth first turns the scapegoat into a criminal who deserved to die, but then turns the criminal into a hero, who, as for Frazer and Raglan, has died willingly for the good of the community. The scapegoat can even become a criminal and a hero simultaneously. For the figure blamed for the turmoil is also credited with ending it, albeit by death or exile. Yet the criminal can also become even more of a hero thereafter.

As a grand example of his theory, Girard cites the case of Oedipus, who is also Raglan's best example. Far from having caused the plague besetting Thebes during his reign as king, Oedipus, according to Girard, is in fact an arbitrarily selected victim of it. Either there never was a plague, or the plague was not the cause of the upheaval; or the plague is a metaphor for violence, which has spread across society like a contagion. The violence among Thebans is evinced in the tension among the principals of Sophocles' play: Oedipus, Creon, and Teiresias. The only way to end the violence and thereby preserve society is by making a scapegoat of a vulnerable member of society.

Even though he is the king, Oedipus is doubly stigmatized and thereby doubly vulnerable. First, he is an outsider: he is not yet known to be a Theban and has won the throne not by heredity but by the toppling of the Sphinx. Second, he is a cripple—the result of the piercing of his ankles at birth. The myth, which, according to Girard, is created only after Oedipus has been made the scapegoat, serves to absolve the community by "blaming the victim," to use the current lingo. The myth concocted is that Oedipus has killed his father and married his mother and that it is for these deeds that Thebes now endures plague. Or so argues Sophocles' Teiresias:

> If we take Tiresias's reply literally, the terrible charges of patricide and incest that he has just levelled at Oedipus did not stem from any supernatural source of information [and so do not represent the "truth"]. The accusation is simply an act of reprisal arising from the hostile exchange of a tragic debate. Oedipus unintentionally initi-

ates the process by forcing Tiresias to speak. He accuses Tiresias of
having had a part in the murder of [Oedipus' father] Laius; he prods
Tiresias into reprisal, into hurling the accusation back at him . . .
[For each] to accuse the other of Laius's murder is to attribute to him
sole responsibility for the sacrificial crisis; but as we have seen, everybody shares equal responsibility, because everybody participates in
the destruction of a cultural order. (Girard 1977: 71)

In actuality, according to Girard, the Thebans simply decide to accept
Teiresias' and Creon's views rather than Oedipus' view over who is
responsible for the breakdown in society. Only the subsequent myth turns
the victors' opinions into the truth. History—or myth—is written by the
victors, although Oedipus himself accepts the myth and craves punishment to alleviate his guilt.

That collective violence rather than the lone Oedipus is the real cause
of the problem is borne out by ensuing events. True, the plague ends, but
it is soon followed by a fight for the throne between Creon, Oedipus' son
Polyneices, and his other son, Eteocles. According to Girard, Sophocles
challenges the myth, but never explicitly, so that the play can be taken, as
it regularly has been taken, as the dramatized version of the myth rather
than as, for the more astute reader, a challenge to the myth.

The myth, however, which continues with *Oedipus at Colonus*, does
more than blame Oedipus for Theban woes. It proceeds to turn him into
a hero. Even as king, Oedipus is heroic in deeming it his duty to end
the plague that has befallen his subjects, in vowing to discover who the
culprit is, and in insisting on being banished once he discovers that he
himself is the culprit. Yet for Girard the real hero is not the fallen, self-
sacrificing Oedipus, as for Raglan, but the elevated one. Even as culprit,
Oedipus has the power to save Thebes: just as his presence caused the
plague, so his departure ends it. He is a hero even while a criminal. He
already has the god-like power both to bring plague and to end it.

By the time of *Oedipus at Colonus*, Oedipus' stature has grown. Having
arrived, after years of wandering, at Colonus, near Athens, he is now told
to return to Thebes. Just as the welfare of Thebes once depended on Oedipus' exile, so now it depends on his return. Oedipus refuses, for we learn
that Oedipus had wanted to remain at Thebes following the events in
Oedipus the King but had been forcibly exiled by Creon and others. Now
Creon is prepared to take him back to Thebes by force. King Theseus offers
Oedipus asylum. In return, Oedipus declares that his burial spot in Athens
will protect Athens against Thebes. In short, Oedipus, having in *Oedipus
the King* begun as a divine-like King of Thebes, in *Oedipus at Colonus*
ends as the would-be benefactor of Thebes and as almost the divine benefactor of Athens. For Girard, Sophocles' plays, as tragedies, undermine
the myth even while presenting it. Where for Raglan the figure killed is,
as king, simultaneously hero and god, and is simultaneously both from

the start, for Girard the king is in fact first scapegoat—contrary to the myth—and only then criminal and only in turn hero and virtual god—all within the myth.

While Girard never cites Raglan, he does regularly cite Frazer, whom he grudgingly praises for recognizing the key primitive ritual of sacrificing the king but whom he lambastes for missing the real reason for the sacrifice. To Frazer, sacrifice is the neutral application of a benighted, prescientific explanation of the world: the king is killed and replaced so that the soul of the god of vegetation, who resides in the incumbent, either retains or regains his health. The function of the sacrifice is wholly agricultural. There is no hatred of the victim, who simply fulfills his duty as king and, as in the case of Jesus, is celebrated by his followers for that duty at the time of his death. For Girard, Frazer could scarcely be more wrong:

> By interpreting the expression *scapegoat* in the ritual sense only and making a generalization of it, Frazer has done a grave injustice to ethnology. He conceals the most interesting meaning of the expression, which appeared at the beginning of the modern era and which never indicated any kind of rite or theme, or cultural motif, but rather identified the unconscious mechanism . . . for the representation and acts of persecution, the scapegoat mechanism. Frazer turned straight to Leviticus for a Hebrew rite to head the list of a whole nonexistent category of ritual without ever questioning the connection between religion in general and the type of phenomenon alluded to when we say that an individual or a minority group acts as "scapegoat" for the majority. He did not understand that there was something essential in this phenomenon for the understanding of the scapegoat; he did not see that it extended into our own time. He only saw an ignorant superstition that religious disbelief and positivism have served to remove. He perceived in Christianity the remains of and even the ultimate triumph of that superstition. (Girard 1986: 120)

For Frazer, Judaism and, even more, Christianity merely perpetuate primitive myth-ritualism. For Girard, however, Judaism and, far more, Christianity break the myth-ritualist cycle. In Girard's idiosyncratic reading, the Gospels declare Jesus not the innocent victim required by God to be sacrificed for the sake of humanity but the innocent victim who should therefore not be sacrificed:

> There is nothing in the Gospels to suggest that the death of Jesus is a sacrifice, whatever definition (expiation, substitution, etc.) we may give for that sacrifice. At no point in the Gospels is the death of Jesus defined as a sacrifice . . . Certainly the Passion is presented to us in the Gospels as an act that brings salvation to humanity. But

it is in no way presented as a sacrifice. (Girard 1987a: 180; see also
pp. 158–223; Girard 1986: 100–24)

Where Frazer takes the Gospels as just further myths of the death and
resurrection of the king who embodies the god of vegetation, Girard
takes the Gospels as "revelatory texts" rather than as myths at all, expos-
ing as they do the wrongness of scapegoating as the basis of civilization.
The Gospels complete the process of demythicizing that begins with the
Hebrew Bible.

Girard is plainly oblivious to Frazer's differing versions of myth-ritualism, as in truth Frazer himself is. Girard considers just the second version,
which he equates with Frazer's myth-ritualism altogether. What he would
be able to say against the first version, it is not easy to see. For the sacrifice of the king is what spurs Girard's attack on Frazer.[4]

The biggest difference between Girard and Frazer is over the function
of religion. For Frazer, religion, especially in the myth-ritualist stage, is a
scientific-like enterprise: it is an attempt to get the crops to grow. It is the
"primitive" counterpart to agriculture. For Girard, religion is not a natural scientific but a social scientific activity: it is an attempt to control not
nature but human nature. It is a version of socialization. Put another way,
Girard derives religion from aggression rather than from hunger.

Frazer epitomizes the nineteenth-century approach to religion: the first
edition of *The Golden Bough* was published in 1890. As different as the
second (1900) and third (1911–15) editions are, they retain the view of
religion as proto-scientific. Girard's view of religion as sociological and
psychological epitomizes the twentieth-century approach.

Nevertheless, Girard's theory is overwhelmingly beholden to Frazer's.
For all Girard's scorn for Frazer, it is Frazer, the Frazer of the second
version, who provides him with his fundamental claim: that religion
is rooted in violence, that violence actually occurs, and that violence
involves the sacrifice of an innocent on behalf of society—a scapegoat.

Burkert

In *On Aggression* (1966) the famous ethnologist Konrad Lorenz applies
to the case of aggression Sir Julian Huxley's discovery of "the remarkable fact that certain movement patterns [in the courtship behavior of the
Great Crested Grebe] lose, in the course of phylogeny, their original specific function and become purely 'symbolic' ceremonies" (Lorenz 1966:
57–8). Huxley called this process "ritualization" precisely to assert the
similarity between "the cultural processes leading to the development of
human rites" and "the phylogenetic processes giving rise to such remarkable 'ceremonies' in animals" (Lorenz 1966: 58). Lorenz devotes his book
to working out the parallel process in animals and humans of transforming innate aggression into social behavior.

As a staunch evolutionist, Lorenz stresses the descent of humans from animals. Yet instead of arguing the commonplace that humans are as innately aggressive as animals, he argues that human sociability, including morality, stems from the same redirection of innate aggression as animal sociability does. In other words, humans are not innately social. Sociability is learned. But it is learned over endless generations, from situation after situation, and eventually becomes a habit. When Lorenz rejects the "humanistic" view that human behavior is learned where animal behavior is innate, he does so both because human behavior is habituated rather than acquired anew each generation and because animal behavior can change, even if likewise only over millennia. So ingrained does social behavior become in both humans and animals that one can even deem it an "instinct," "just as independent as any of the so-called 'great' drives such as hunger, sex, fear, or aggression" itself (Lorenz 1966: 67). The behavior that "humanists" would attribute to reason or morality Lorenz attributes to instinct, but to an instinct redirected from its opposite: "the drives that have arisen by ritualization . . . are so often called upon . . . to oppose aggression, to divert it into harmless channels, and to inhibit those of its actions that are injurious to the survival of the species" (Lorenz 1966: 67).

Lorenz never denies that parents teach children social behavior, but what they teach amounts to a mechanical, unthinking habit. They teach what to them is self-evident, self-justifying, hence instinctive behavior. For Lorenz, socialization is a two-stage process. First, innate aggression is transformed into sociability. Second, the social behavior often becomes severed from the social function that it arose to serve. Now one acts a certain way simply because that is the way one should act, and to fail to do so is to stir anxiety and to provoke the wrath of society. When parents teach children not to hurt siblings and playmates, they are instilling a sense of morality the benefit of which is obvious. But when, according to Lorenz, Jewish parents teach their children not to eat pork, they are doing so "without being conscious that it was insight into the danger of trichinosis which probably caused . . . lawmakers to impose the prohibition" (Lorenz 1966: 72). (The outdatedness of Lorenz's variety of what William James called "medical materialism" is of no concern here.) Moses, the ancient lawmaker, himself "undergoes an apotheosis, making all his laws seem godly and their infringement a sin" (Lorenz 1966: 72). Parents no more than children know why dietary laws need be obeyed, only that they must. The ritual has become separated from its rationale.

Lorenz's point is not that ritual has lost any function but that it has long since acquired new, if unrecognized, ones. Ritual serves to bolster the bond among members of the group that practices it and to re-channel aggression. The group that eats in the same way, talks in the same way, and dresses in the same way feels camaraderie among its members and hostility towards others. At the same time Lorenz maintains optimistically that rituals can bolster group sociability even without an out-group, not to mention a scapegoat within the group, onto whom to foist aggression.

The German classicist Walter Burkert, who has taught in Zurich for most of his career, has applied Lorenz's theory of ritual to ancient Greek religious ritual.[5] Burkert embraces Lorenz's key claim: that humans are like animals, and in a dual way. On the one hand much human behavior, like much animal behavior, is innate. On the other hand much animal behavior, like much human behavior, is learned. In particular, aggression is at once innate and learned. Aggression, which innately is hostile, can gradually become transformed into its opposite: sociability. Lorenz's assertion that humans are like animals insofar as humans are innately aggressive has provoked the greater reaction,[6] even though Lorenz's bolder assertion is that aggression can be transformed into sociability.

Burkert describes his appropriation of Lorenz:

> In establishing homologies in behavior of different species and deciphering the function of their signals, Lorenz insisted on the positive role of so-called evil behavior, or intraspecific aggression, for the preservation of the balance of life. He showed similarities, analogies, and even continuities between animals and humans in the field of anger, fighting, and war, but in particular he described the establishment of bonds of friendship and solidarity through common aggression, symbolized in aggressive display. By extrapolation it would seem possible to explain the success of religious solidarity on the basis of the aggressive acts of hunt and sacrifice. (Burkert 1996: 9)

An instinct which is redirected—one might say "sublimated"—is for Burkert, exactly following Lorenz, a "ritual." Burkert cites both Lorenz's definition of ritual and his most famous example from the animal world: "Lorenz's standard example is the triumph ceremony of a pair of graylings, consisting in common aggression against a nonexistent interloper; by triumphant cries, these geese assure each other of their friendship and solidarity. In other words, ritual is action redirected for demonstration" (Burkert 1979: 36–7; see also Burkert 1983: 23). The ritualistic function of aggression is the communication of solidarity, not of attack. There is still an enemy, but it is an outsider, real or imagined. Animals no less than humans perform rituals.

Like Girard, Burkert considers the function of ritual sociological and psychological rather than, as for Frazer, physiological. Like Girard, Burkert thus typifies the twentieth-century approach to myth and to ritual alike. For Burkert, the sociological function of ritual is to unify the group: the "message" communicated by ritual "seems to be concerned mainly with the solidarity of the group and the exclusion of others" (Burkert 1979: 48). For Burkert, also following Lorenz (see Burkert 1996: 18), ritual serves a psychological function as well: alleviating anxiety. While the concern with the correct performance of a ritual might seem to stir anxiety, the successful performance of a ritual alleviates anxiety:

> Any omission or alteration of religious ritual is liable to provoke griev-ous anxiety . . . Religious ritual, by producing anxiety, manages to con-trol it. It is just the stereotypy of the sequence which guarantees that the action will not end up in hopelessness, but reach the prescribed end, and thus presents a model of how to overcome. There must be Easter after Good Friday, and the more gloomy the one, the more bril-liant the other. Even feelings of pollution and guilt become manage-able, as highly artificial taboos are set up with expiatory ritual in the background to make up for each transgression. (Burkert 1979: 50)

The sociological and psychological functions work in tandem: "And as anxiety tends to draw a group together, group solidarity is all the more established by the experience and performance of anxiety overcome" (Burkert 1979: 50).

Where Girard dismisses Frazer's derivation of ritual from the quest for food, Burkert roots ritual in exactly that quest. But Burkert takes the quest for food back to a stage prior to agriculture. He takes it back to hunting. "Ritual," as Burkert, following Huxley and Lorenz, uses the term, is not primarily the customs and formalities—the "rituals"—involved in hunting but the transformation of actual hunting into drama-tized hunting. Ritual proper is the dramatization of hunting—in the form of animal killing, or sacrifice. The function is no longer that of securing food, as for Frazer, for the ritual proper arises only in agricultural times, when farming has supplanted hunting as the prime source of food. The ends now served are, as for Girard, sociological and psychological:

> Hunting lost its basic function with the emergence of agriculture some ten thousand years ago. But hunting ritual had become so important that it could not be given up. Stability stayed with those groups who managed to make use of the social and psychological appeal of the ritual by transforming, by redirecting, it until the whole action became a ritual. (Burkert 1979: 55)

Hunting, according to Burkert, stirred feelings of fear and guilt. The fear was not merely of getting killed by the animal hunted but also of kill-ing a fellow hunter and, too, of depleting the food supply:

> Killing to eat was an unalterable commandment, and yet the bloody act must always have been attended with a double danger and a double fear: that the weapon might be turned against a fellow hunter, and that the death of the prey might signal an end with no future, while man must always eat and so must always hunt. (Burkert 1985: 58)

The even deeper fear was of one's own aggression and one's own mortality. The guilt was over the killing of a fellow living creature. Hence "what Karl Meuli called the 'comedy of innocence,' the fiction of the willingness of the victim for sacrifice" (Burkert 1985: 58). It is Meuli (1946) whom Burkert continually credits with first showing the sacrificial nature of hunting (see Burkert 2001: 10–11).

The communal nature of hunting functioned to assuage the individual's fear and guilt, and simultaneously functioned to cement a bond among hunters: "From a psychological and ethological point of view, it is the communally enacted aggression and shared guilt which creates solidarity" (Burkert 1985: 58). Exactly following Lorenz, Burkert maintains that the act of killing an outsider—here the prey—not only redirected aggression outward in a socially acceptable way but also forged group identity: "for it is precisely group demonstration of aggression towards outsiders that creates a sense of close personal community" (Burkert 1983: 20).

Hunting ritual, in contrast to hunting itself, was the dramatization of hunting—first with wild animals, then with domesticated ones. Because domesticated animals were owned, the use of them marked the beginning of sacrifice. In turn, other kinds of food came to be substituted for animals: bread for meat and wine for blood. Eventually, human beings were sacrificed—symbolically—in the form of initiation rituals, in which initiates died as children and were reborn as full members of society.

Burkert relentlessly parallels hunting with animal sacrifice. Not merely was the domesticated animal in sacrifice killed in a blood-letting orgy and then partly eaten, but hunting itself was ritualized. Burkert declares that "for the ancient world, hunting, sacrifice, and war were symbolically interchangeable" (Burkert 1983: 47). Put even more directly: "every slaughter is a sacrifice," and "sacrifice is ritual killing" (Burkert 2001: 21, 31 note 41). By paralleling animal sacrifice with hunting, Burkert can claim that animal sacrifice served sociological and psychological functions: sacrifice still "established cooperation and solidarity by some kind of shared guilt, by traumatic repetition of bloodshed and killing; it tells and visibly demonstrates that Life is unique, but not autonomous; it must accept death in order to perpetuate itself" (Burkert 1979: 56).

The distinctiveness of religious ritual is the presence of gods. Burkert argues that the "turning away from the human has an eminently social function" (Burkert 1985: 54). Burkert seems to be arguing that the invocation of the sacred in ritual arouses an especially high degree of anxiety, a degree that the ritual then alleviates. Religious ritual stirs anxiety over the natural and human phenomena that the gods either control or judge: rain, food, light, sex, and aggression. Ritual "signals and creates situations of anxiety in order to overcome them, it leads from the primal fear of being abandoned to the establishment of society and the reinforcement of status" (Burkert 1985: 54). Burkert combines the psychological function with the sociological one in arguing that ritual somehow arouses the primal fear of abandonment and then alleviates it by offering the security of the group. Presumably, religious rituals for Burkert alleviate anxiety by offering the security of the human group united in its devotion to its gods: "individuals separated from and opposed to one another are joined together, oriented towards the divine" (Burkert 1985: 255).

Burkert's clearest example is the Greek hypochondriac Aelius Aristeides, who in a dream was told by Asclepius, the god of healing, that he was slated to die in a few days but could avert his fate by a journey to the netherworld, by the tossing of coins, by the slaughtering of sheep for a feast with the priests of Asclepius, and above all by the sacrifice of a part of his body—a part to save the whole. Happily, Aristeides was then permitted to sacrifice instead his finger ring, which he readily did. As Burkert summarizes the ritual,

> First, the participant deals with the powers of death and the netherworld; then he crosses the boundary while throwing away money . . . and finally, he achieves integration with a group of celebrants at the god's sanctuary. The dedication of a valuable object, a practice common in all the sanctuaries in the ancient as well as in the modern world, can be interpreted as a substitute for one's own self, *pars pro toto*. Some part would have to be sacrificed to save the whole . . . Aristeides expressly makes his dedication a substitute, a kind of ransom from the threat of death. The coins strewn around at the river evidently serve a similar function: a ransom in cash, a manageable loss in order to gain salvation. (Burkert 1996: 36–7)

The ritual functions "as a defense against life-threatening catastrophe" (Burkert 1996: 36).

As Burkert recognizes, the sacrifice of a part to save the whole might well seem a rational calculation. What, then, makes the act ritualistic? The answer is that the act is symbolic and therefore "displaced." One sacrifices a ring to save one's life—the value of the ring to the god presumably being other than monetary. Burkert grants that the ritual might seem to be "magical"—practical—"in the sense that it seeks to achieve a definite goal by some nonobvious chain of causality" (Burkert 1996: 40). But he maintains that the relationship between cause and effect is so elusive that the ritual is better taken as symbolic rather than magical: "The [causal] pattern is displaced as it loses contact with reality and turns into 'ritual' in its exaggerated and demonstrative character" (Burkert 1996: 40). Once Burkert can show that the function of ritual is not magical, the function for him readily becomes sociological and psychological.

Burkert sharply contrasts the magical, practical, efficacious view of ritual—ritual intended to secure rain, food, or fertility—to the symbolic, expressive one. He dismisses the efficacious view and touts the expressive one. For him, ritual makes a statement rather than carries out an action. The symbolic action that ritual carries out is the dramatization of the practical one. The function thereby served is always social as well as psychological: "Religious ritual is given as a collective institution; the individual participates within the framework of social communication, with the strongest motivating force being the need not to stand apart" (Burkert 1985: 55)—that is, the need not to be alone.

In the history of the myth-ritualist theory, Burkert's chronology of the transformation of initially real action into symbolic, ritual action is ironic. For Frazer and the Cambridge Ritualists (Jane Harrison, F. M. Cornford, and Oxford's Gilbert Murray), myth-ritualism is exactly the magical use of ritual for practical ends. Myth-ritualism means the use of both myth and ritual to secure food and other physical necessities. For Frazer and the Ritualists, ritual is dead when it is no longer believed to deliver the goods.

For Harrison in particular, ritual that is no longer believed to work continues to be practiced, but now as an end in itself rather than as a means to securing crops. Ritual for its own sake becomes art, of which her paramount example is drama (see Harrison 1913). For her, ritual no longer taken seriously is mere drama. For Burkert, ritual taken seriously is drama.

Put another way, ritual for Burkert is "as if" behavior. Ritual is make-believe. Because the ritual is merely "as if" action, it requires myth to make it real. Myth ties ritual to actual events. Myth and ritual work together:

> The defect of ritual . . . is the apparent nonsense inherent in its redirection of activity, the "as-if" element; here a tale may supply a plausible context and fill the vacant places. The defect of the traditional tale is its lack of seriousness and stability; here ritual may supply a basis; for the serious character of ritual is guaranteed by the role of anxiety controlled by it, and its stability is secured even by explicit sanctions. (Burkert 1979: 57)

Myth and ritual do not merely work together, as for Frazer and Raglan, but reinforce each other, though not, as for Girard, in collusion. Each confers on the other a weightiness that neither alone would possess. The two do not merely parallel each other, as for Frazer and Raglan, but strengthen each other.

Where Girard dismisses Frazer's theory of myth and ritual, Burkert assesses it, even though he, too, fails to disentangle the versions of myth-ritualism. Beginning with the second version, Burkert grants that some kings might have been killed annually in order to secure crops, and he acknowledges "clear examples of kings being sacrificed to assuage drought and famine" (Burkert 1979: 68). But he rightly asks "how old and widespread the institution of 'magical kingship' really was" (Burkert

1979: 68). Furthermore, he maintains that Frazer's own best case for regicide—Babylonian and Hittite—is in fact not an annual festival but "a special procedure, seldom performed, to save the king from evil portended by omens: the king retired for a while, and the substitute had to take his fate" (Burkert 1979: 69). The problem for Frazer here is not the substitution of someone for the king but the infrequency of the event.

Against the first version of Frazer's myth-ritualism, Burkert observes that the interpretation of Adonis and the other figures as gods of vegetation is found not in classical Greek religion but only in "post-classical allegory," and "we may leave it to rhetoric and poetry from whence it sprang" (Burkert 1979: 100). Worse, the "central feature of the cult" of Frazer's would-be gods of vegetation turns out to be not death and rebirth but sheer death: "The evidence for resurrection is late and tenuous in the case of Adonis, and practically nonexistent in the case of Attis; not even Osiris returns to real life, but instead attains transcendent life beyond death" (Burkert 1979: 101).[7] Even if Burkert accepted Frazer's interpretation of the myths of Adonis and Attis, neither would abet Burkert's argument since both figures are solitary, not group, hunters.

Yet for all Burkert's refutation of Frazer's theory, he retains the heart of it: that religion originates in violence. Initially, the violence is hunting itself: the killing of an animal for the sake of the community. The animal is a sacrifice—not to god but for the community. Only subsequently does violence become religion proper—with ritualized hunting. Where Girard, like Frazer, derives religion from actual acts of violence, Burkert derives it from merely dramatized, symbolic violence. Still, the violence dramatized is that of the sacrifice of one living thing for the sake of others, and the redirection of aggression outwards means the killing of other human beings.

Where for Frazer religion arises and functions to tame the physical world, for Girard and Burkert religion arises and functions to tame human beings. Religion for Girard and Burkert arises to cope with aggression and in turn with guilt. Religion arises to cope with human reactions to violence.

Bloch

None of the three theories of violence within a religion can be extended to encompass violence outside a religion. The three cannot, therefore, account for events like 9/11. Is there a theory that does link internal violence to external? In *Prey into Hunter* (1992) the English Marxist anthropologist Maurice Bloch comes closest to doing so (see also Bloch 1986). Building on the theories of Arnold van Gennep and of Victor Turner, both of whom deem rituals of initiation paradigmatic for rituals generally, Bloch divides rituals into three stages: separation, initiation, and return.

Bloch begins with the initiation ritual of the Orokaiva of Papua New

Guinea. The Orokaiva raise pigs alongside their children. Pigs are treated like children and symbolize the physical, mortal side of human beings. In stage one of the ritual, the children about to be initiated are rounded up like pigs by adults dressed like birds. The initiates are hunted, though not killed, and are herded to a platform like the one where pigs are killed. Symbolically killed as pigs, the initiates are reborn as birds, who are considered immortal and are associated with the spirits of the ancestors: "If they are to be born as spirits the initiates must first die as pigs so that their post-mortal existence as spirits, that is as members of the clan, can begin" (Bloch 1992: 14).[8]

Once the hunted, the initiates return to their village as hunters. Symbolically and even literally, they now hunt pigs, with which they had formerly been paired:

> Previously . . . the children had been ritually killed at the hands of the masked adults as though they were pigs. Now, after their sojourn in the initiation hut, the initiates, who have partly become spirits themselves, return not as prey but as hunters of pigs, shouting the same formula which had been addressed to them: Bite, bite, bite. (Bloch 1992: 10)

The initiates return as "a mixture of pig and spirit, but now the spirit or clan or bird element dominates the pig element" (Bloch 1992: 16). At death, they will lose their bodies and so will become sheer spirits.

Following Durkheim, Bloch parallels society, which is permanent, with the sacred and the "transcendental," and parallels individual members, who are mortal, with the everyday. Initiation into the transcendental is initiation into the social. Initiates "become part of permanent institutions" (Bloch 1992: 5). The function of ritual for Bloch is, as for Girard and Burkert, socialization, but not through the taming of anti-social impulses, which Bloch equates with aggression. Rather, as classically for Durkheim, socialization comes through the experience of society:

> Such a conclusion may seem close to that reached by such writers as Girard (1972) and Burkert (1973), who see an indissoluble link between violence and religion, but it does so for totally different reasons. These writers assume an innate aggressiveness in humans which is expressed, and to a certain extent purged, by ritual. In contrast, I do not base myself on some innate propensity to violence but argue that violence is itself a result of the attempt to create the transcendental in religion and politics. (Bloch 1992: 6–7)

For Bloch, violence occurs at two stages of the ritual: in stage two, the initiation stage, when the bodily, "native vitality" is replaced, or "conquered," by the transcendental spirit, and in stage three, the return stage, when the native, "home-grown" vitality discarded in stage two is replaced by a "conquered vitality obtained from *outside* beings, usually animals, but sometimes plants, other peoples or women" (Bloch 1992: 5). "This second violence can therefore be considered as the consequence of the first," for "the elimination of ordinary vitality" is what "necessitates its replacement by a new, plundered vitality," and "contact with the transcendental" is what "provides the impetus for this forced substitution" (Bloch 1992: 6).

The "second violence" can be directed against animals, against neighbors, and even against oneself, but it can also be directed against outsiders: "Orokaiva initiation concludes with an open-ended menace to outsiders which can in certain circumstances be the beginning of serious hostility" (Bloch 1992: 17). The hunting of pigs—the internal violence of the return—is preparation for any ensuing external violence.

Bloch's theory seems to provide the "missing link" between internal and external violence. Still, it does so only secondarily, for Bloch, like Girard and Burkert, is primarily concerned with the way religion, through ritual, regulates society—that is, internally. Violence can be directed as frequently at insiders and at oneself as at outsiders, and even when it is directed externally, the goal is the strengthening, not the expanding, of society.

Conclusion

The theories of Frazer, Girard, and Burkert have lessons to teach even those preoccupied with external religious violence. The first lesson they teach is that religious violence, like religion as a whole, does not explain itself. Rather, it itself must be explained. Attributing religious violence to the teachings of a religion raises, if not begs, the question: why does religion preach violence?

The second lesson the theories of Frazer, Girard, and Burkert teach is that violence in religion is natural rather than unnatural. Violence occurs regularly rather than *in extremis*, is controlled rather than uncontrolled, operates as part of the normal functioning of religion rather than only with the radicalization of religion, and can be beneficial rather than harmful. Seen from the standpoint of these theories, religious violence need be neither bemoaned nor excused. It is simply the way religion works.

Notes

1   Frazer takes the section on Jesus from the second edition of *The Golden Bough* and puts it as an appendix to volume 9 of the third edition.
2   See Raglan 1956 [1936], part II; 1945; 1949, especially chs 9–10.
3   Strictly, the chief god for Raglan is of the sky rather than, as for Frazer, of vegetation.
4   Against Frazer, see Girard 1977: 28–30, 96, 121–3, 316–18; 1986: 120–1; 1987a: 168–9; 1987b: 75–8, 81, 93, 111–12.

5   On Burkert's beholdenness to Lorenz, see Burkert 1983, especially pp. xiv, 1, 20, 35, 41; 1996: 9–10, 18; 2001: 14, 15. More recently, Burkert has taken his inspiration from sociobiology: see Burkert 1996: 8–12.

6   Burkert himself cites, for example, the devastating rejoinders to Lorenz as well as to Robert Ardrey and Desmond Morris by Ashley Montagu and others, who assert that Lorenz fails to prove that human aggression is innate rather than acquired: see Montagu 1968. Yet Burkert is somehow not fazed by these criticisms: see Burkert 1983: 1, note 1.

7   Against Frazer, see Burkert 1979: 68–9, 99–101, 139; 1985: 2–3, 12, 176–7, 266; 1987a: 75–6; 1987b: 161.

8   Against Bloch's analysis of the Orokaiva initiation ritual, see Whitehouse 1996.

References

Bloch, M. 1986. *From Blessing to Violence*. Cambridge: Cambridge University Press.

——. 1992. *Prey into Hunter*. Cambridge: Cambridge University Press.

Burkert, W. 1979. *Structure and History in Greek Mythology and Ritual*. Berkeley, CA: University of California Press.

——. 1983. *Homo Necans*. Trans. P. Bing. Berkeley, CA: University of California Press.

——. 1985. *Greek Religion*. Trans. J. Raffan. Cambridge, MA: Harvard University Press.

——. 1987a. *Ancient Mystery Cults*. Cambridge, MA: Harvard University Press.

——. 1987b. "The Problem of Ritual Killing." In *Violent Origins*, edited by R. G. Hamerton-Kelly, 149–76. Stanford, CA: Stanford University Press.

——. 1996. *Creation of the Sacred*. Cambridge, MA: Harvard University Press.

——. 2001. *Savage Energies*. Trans. P. Bing. Chicago: University of Chicago Press.

Engels, F. [1957] 1964. "On the History of Early Christianity" [1894–5]. In *On Religion*, edited by K. Marx and F. Engels, 316–47. New York: Schocken Books.

Frazer, J. G. 1890. *The Golden Bough*. 1st edn. 2 vols. London: Macmillan.

——. 1900. *The Golden Bough*. 2nd edn. 3 vols. London: Macmillan.

——. 1911–15. *The Golden Bough*. 3rd edn. 12 vols. London: Macmillan.

——. 1922. *The Golden Bough*. 1-vol. abridgment. London: Macmillan.

Freud, S. [1913] 1950. *Totem and Taboo*. Trans. J. Strachey. New York: Norton.

Girard, R. 1977. *Violence and the Sacred*. Trans. P. Gregory. London: Athlone Press; Baltimore, MD: Johns Hopkins University Press.

——. 1986. *The Scapegoat*. Trans. Y. Freccero. London: Athlone Press; Baltimore, MD: Johns Hopkins University Press.

——. 1987a. *Things Hidden since the Foundation of the World*. Trans. S. Bann and M. Metteer. London: Athlone Press; Baltimore, MD: Johns Hopkins University Press.

——. 1987b. "Generative Scapegoating." In *Violent Origins*, edited by R. G. Hamerton-Kelly, 73–105. Stanford, CA: Stanford University Press.

Harrison, J. E. 1913. *Ancient Art and Ritual*. New York: Holt; London: Williams and Norgate.

Lorenz, K. 1966. *On Aggression*. Trans. M. K. Wilson. New York: Harcourt, Brace.

Meuli, K. 1946. "Griechische Opferbräuche." In *Phyllobolia (Festschrift für Peter von der Mühll)*, 185–288. Basel: Benno Schwabe and Co.

Montagu, M. F. A., ed. 1968. *Man and Aggression*. Oxford: Oxford University Press.

Raglan, Lord. 1945. *Death and Rebirth*. London: Watts.

——. 1949. *The Origins of Religion*. London: Watts.

——. [1936] 1956. *The Hero*. New York: Vintage Books.

Sorel, G. A. [1950] 1961. *Reflections on Violence* [1908]. Trans. T. E. Hulme and J. Roth. New York: Collier Books; London: Collier-Macmillan.

Whitehouse, H. 1996. "Rites of Terror: Emotion, Metaphor and Memory in Melanesian Initiation Cults." *Journal of the Royal Anthropological Institute* 2: 703–15.

Rhetorical reflections

3 Savage civil religion

Paul Christopher Johnson

Il est impossible de vivre en paix avec des gens qu'on croit damnés.

Jean-Jacques Rousseau

Truth or fantasy-truth? Did this state-making-thing really exist outside of its representations? What is certain is the accuracy of the idea shooting forth in its second and repeated comings following the originary act of spirit possession by the state arising from the ashes of war. And this war is ceaseless.

Michael Taussig, *The Magic of the State*

Despite the horrific violence perpetrated in the attacks of September 11, 2001, the decision to begin the war against Iraq one and a half years later cannot be seen as an automatic or natural response. That it finally did appear inevitable and that its announcement evoked little dissent or critique within the US, despite the absence of evidence linking the Al Qaeda organization to the state of Iraq, testifies not to its aptness but to the strategic success of agents of the state in generating terms of reality, or acceptance frames, that made it appear so. Within these acceptance frames, war was not only tolerable but finally even seemed required. What follows is an analysis and critique of how such a consensus was achieved, by way of a theoretical tour of a refurbished concept of civil religion.

It may already be difficult to recall the patriotic unanimity within the US that was generated out of a shared sentiment of victimization in fall 2001. After the torture-photos from Abu Ghraib, and in face of a steadily increasing death toll (3,382 US soldiers, and a conservatively estimated 63,610 Iraqi civilians as of May 15, 2007 [www.iraqbodycount. org]), a clear US majority now views the war in Iraq as separate from the war on terrorism (a key transformation first marked by the USA Today/CNN/Gallup poll of June 24–26, 2005). Still, even recent speeches by President Bush held firmly to the original line: "On September the 11th, 2001, we saw what a refuge for extremists on the other side of the world could bring to the streets of our own cities. For the safety of our people, America must succeed in Iraq" (January 10, 2007). The rhetorical attempt anecdotally suggests the very mechanism this chapter seeks to clarify: the attempt to channel or divert the force of the unclouded sanctity of the event of "9/11" and the sacred space of "Ground Zero" toward murky and contested political ends. At this point it is worth reassessing how the very same process of symbolic hijacking that today rings of desperation was so utterly effective just a few years past; and as we do so, worth reconsidering the spontaneous memorials that filled the space where the towers of the World Trade Center once stood. What can they teach us as we again open the issue of civil religion?

I. Introduction

At 8:30 p.m., less than twelve hours after Flight 11 hit the north tower of the World Trade Center, President Bush gave a prime-time television address from the Oval Office fixing the terms of a clear plot and structure, and transforming a complex sequence of happenings, and a wide range of possible significations, into a clearly defined "event" that soldered a set of as-yet opaque "happenings" to a structure and narrative of interpretation (Sahlins 1985; Feldman 1991). As an event, those terms were widely reproduced in the press and sedimented within days.[1] "Today our nation saw evil," the President said on the 11th, later in the speech reciting part of Psalm 23. On the 14th, from the National Cathedral, he upped the ante: "God's signs are not always our own. We ask Almighty God to watch over our nation. We pray that He will comfort and console those who walk in sorrow." By the 16th, the discursive shift from mourning to military action was realized: "We will rid the world of the evildoers . . . This crusade, this war on terrorism, is going to take a while."

This was the incipient form of one sort of civil religious response, which I will call *instrumental civil religion*: national political events were narrated in religious terms by the most powerful speaker in the world, whose words were designed to accomplish calculated political objectives. It was an expression of power in that it attempted to control, by virtue of the "sheer redundancy of ideological communications" (Wolf in Palmié 2002: 144), as well as through the censorship of possible rival communications, such as Osama bin Laden's actual discourse and stated motives (Lincoln 2003: 19). Discussion of additional and wider frames of interpretation—the role of oil or the presence of US soldiers in Saudi Arabia, or indeed the competing definitions of "terror" itself (Williams 1976: 329; Lincoln 2003: 27)—were obfuscated.[2] This was accomplished with enormous success: a complex set of occurrences ceased to exist, eclipsed by the narrative monolith, "9/11," as an artifact of popular consciousness. It occurred so rapidly and with such force that it was as if by magic—state magic, as it happens (Bourdieu 1996: 3, 376; Taussig 1997; Coronil 1997). The magic had the effect of people becoming *possessed*

(Taussig 1997: 99–108), possessed by narratives presented flawlessly and with such authority as to bury the inchoate, "senseless" violence with a massive outpouring of nationalist fervor and solidarity. Durkheim's reference to collective effervescence as feeling possessed (1995: 220), or to the flag as totem, never seemed so timely as at that time. The possession was not only by the spirit of the state, however, which the second epigraph struggles to convey, but by the spirit of the state read against religious myth, such that the possessing spirits' powers were doubled.

And yet the speed of semiotic doubling, the making of this "event" by way of narrative transfer and ideological redundancy in mass media, did not wholly contain the response. Another kind of response erupted coevally with the words crafted in the West Wing, which I will call *organic civil religion*.[3] This second form had no official spokespersons and was not orchestrated from above, but rather had a character of bricolage, as New Yorkers and visitors adapted whatever objects were at hand—T-shirts, caps, boots, buttons, balloons, and teddy bears—to respond to a crisis of memorialization and mourning at hand. It proffered no specific political objective, and religiously was relatively ecumenical. It entailed the spontaneous practice of erecting memorial altars at various sites around the smoking site of the World Trade Center, where collections of objects were placed, visited, touched, added to, and improved upon. I refer to such organic civil religion as "savage" in the title, with a nod to Marett's (1914) or Lévi-Strauss' (1966) notion of "meaning" that becomes explicit only secondarily, in so far as it is danced, dressed, eaten, or built into existence, but which is nevertheless structured, and for that reason communicates something of its builders' sentiments and motivations. But "savage" refers not only to the materiality of the altar-building, comprised as it was of modern fetishes—common objects endowed with strange and extraordinary powers, and treated as sacred in the Durkheimian sense—but also to the altars' semiotic resistance to modern closure and disclosure. The altars were never completed, but remained works-in-progress, nor did they "speak" coherently to declare their significance.[4] The very point of the spontaneous altars, rather, was to express something that could not be placed into words: to express, commune, and communicate with objects and through practice.

The altar-building process continued to gain force with the pilgrimage of many non-New Yorkers to Ground Zero over the next year, and became a key feature of the site and its sanctity. "Sanctity" is not a term I impose as an analytical term here, but like "sacred," became a common term of practice in public debates about Ground Zero. Legislation proposed by the city on May 6, 2003, for example, sought to prohibit vendors around Ground Zero, "in recognition of the sanctity of the site," even as Governor Pataki intoned his concern about the state, and fate, of the "hallowed ground." On that ground and around it, the very same materials that in another context would have been the mere flotsam and jetsam of tourist traffic trucked upstate for disposal, were here transformed into sacred indices of an organic civil religious moment. By winter 2002 that spontaneous moment was already passed, as most of the spontaneous memorials were dismantled—though some were affixed in a permanent exhibit within St. Paul's Chapel adjacent to the site—and the collective enthusiasm they had crystallized was hijacked by instrumental civil religion, the drumbeat of the march toward widespread public support for war in Afghanistan and then Iraq.[5]

This essay (an "attempt," *essai*) considers the question of how organic civil religion was hijacked by instrumental civil religion: how the relatively inclusive material practices of altar-building typical of the first civil religious expression were swallowed by the exclusive us/them discourse of instrumental civil religion as momentum for war gathered. Taking a phrase of Pierre Bourdieu as axiomatic (2000: 185), the "symbolic hijacking that occurs in the move from praxis to logos," I argue that organic civil religion, though emotionally powerful, was compact in its signifying range—it remained mute in its capacity for social mobilization toward specific political objectives. Indeed, it was because the improvised practices of mourning and memorializing entailed little specifically political content that it carried the emotional force of a relatively pristine representation of social unity. Instrumental civil religion, by contrast, was strategically designed with precise ends in view. Its strident us/them discourse had dramatic effects in mobilizing popular support for specific actions, namely the invasion/liberation/occupation of Iraq. However, instrumental civil religion carried enormous risks of splintering the very consensus on which collective national action depended. That is why its speakers sought and continue to seek to appropriate the social force of organic civil religion. If this sounds overly abstract, simply consider the site, time, and key images used in the Republican National Convention that re-nominated Bush for re-election in November 2004. It was orchestrated to take place in New York City as near to the anniversary of 9/11, as near to the space of Ground Zero, and with as much of its tragic and heroic imagery as possible. This would magically (by contact) transfer the immediate post-9/11 moment when Bush enjoyed enormous popular approval ratings—topping out at 89 percent on October 12, 2001 (CNN/Gallup)—to the viciously contested presidential race. Translated into the analytic terms of my argument, the political strategy was to harness the social force of organic civil religion and attempt to transfer it to the ideologically more specific program of the Bush campaign.

After attempting to clear a theoretical space for reevaluating civil religion in part two, the third and fourth parts of the essay empirically describe organic and instrumental forms of civil religion. My method in those sections is to compare the spontaneous altars erected around the wreckage site with official presidential speeches. The former were observed during four separate visits to the Ground Zero area, in October and November

2001, January 2002, on the anniversary date of September 11, 2002, and in the days surrounding September 11, 2003; the latter are readily available in the public domain. The conclusion assesses the relation between them as one of symbolic hijacking toward the destination of the national rationalization (in both commonsensical and Weberian senses of, on one hand, justification, and on the other, systematization and normalization) of state-sanctioned violence.

I begin with the definitional problem of "civil religion" as a whole, before moving to empirical descriptions of the two types of civil religious response to September 11.

II. A short critique of "civil religion"

Civil religion—the idea if not always the exact phrase—has always been formulated as an interested intervention in a moment of perceived crisis (Hughey 1983: 160–4): the social unrest and declining authority of the *ancien régime* leading up to the French Revolution (Rousseau), the anomie of industrialized urbanization at the turn of the twentieth century (Durkheim), the fascist transformation of Italy (Gramsci), or the Viet Nam War (Bellah).[6] The aftermath of September 11, 2001, presents another propitious moment for its invocation, having produced the most dramatic display of civil religion in the US since a half-century ago— the Cold War and McCarthyist moment when "In God We Trust" was inscribed on paper currency, and "Under God" was added to the Pledge of Allegiance.[7] Yet just when we most need the analytical category of civil religion, it lies spent on the sideline, exhausted both from overuse and the lack of any consistent theoretical regimen. Civil religion needs to tone its legs again before being taken out for any further exercise.

Civil religion in Rousseau

When "civil religion" appeared in *The Social Contract* (1762), it carried the marks of the simultaneous publication by Rousseau of his idea of "natural religion," as articulated in the mouth of Vicar Savoyard in Book Four of *Emile*. The place of natural religion in a child's education, wrote Rousseau, should remain unspecified before age fifteen; a child's religion ought to be no more, but no less, then "a matter of geography." It ought to be intuited, experienced in the world, and imaginatively created. Rousseau's notion of natural religion rejected revelation, and rejected the particularism and provincialism of specific religions. Natural religion should be the "religion of man," of humanity as a whole.

The problem civil religion addressed was that this idea of "natural religion" creates no political bond. In Chapter Eight of the fourth volume of *The Social Contract*, "civil religion" makes its first and all too brief appearance, introduced by Rousseau as he considered internal national bonds in relation to external neighbors. If natural religion generated no political bond, the religion of established churches like Catholicism was worse; it actively divided citizens from the nation-state. The religion of the citizen (*religion de citoyen*), meanwhile, could generate the requisite loyalty, but has the liability of falseness and empty ceremonialism. The challenge of civil religion, then, was to be both genuine and universal. But the requirements of the nation take clear priority. The public dimension of descriptions of gods and their attendant rituals must generate social and political bonds. The citizen must have a religion that makes him love his duty; the question of precisely which religion, as Eisenhower quipped two centuries later, is immaterial (cited in Bellah 1967).[8] Societies of antiquity like the Spartans or the Romans, which Rousseau took as models of communitarian-religious spirit, were superior in this sense (Bloom 1987: 299)—hence Rousseau's enthusiastic citations of Montesquieu, Hobbes, and Machiavelli.

The "positive dogmas" were articulated in simple and concise fashion: the existence of an all-powerful, good, and intelligent divinity, the afterlife to come, the belief in justice or the good, the punishment of evildoers, and the sanctity of the social contract and its laws. The only sin for civil religion was intolerance, wrote Rousseau (1968 [1762]: 335) in a passage that was not quite forthcoming, since catalyzing *intolerance* for political outsiders was a key part of the desired outcome.

Now, considering the ink spilled over the notion of "civil religion" after Robert Bellah's appropriation of Rousseau's phrase in 1967, this is hardly a well-developed theory. But the link between Rousseau and the United States is larger, and more material, than the fact of Bellah's appropriation of him in the sixties. *The Social Contract* was on the bookshelves of George Washington, Ben Franklin, John Adams, Thomas Jefferson, and many other foundational figures in the American narrative of the nation-state (Spurlin 1969). It informed, moreover, De Tocqueville's record of America's popular democratic spirit, and thus crept into the canon of descriptions Americans[9] used to understand and talk about themselves in the nineteeth and twentieth centuries.

Civil religion and Bellah

Robert Bellah's 1967 essay brought Rousseau's concept into contemporary currency. He expanded the concept from Rousseau to include not only "dogmas" but also national temporal orders, mythic narratives, and places—Washington's establishment of Thanksgiving Day in 1789 (p. 7), the view of America as the "new Israel" with Washington as its Moses and Lincoln's Gettysburg Address as its "New Testament" (p. 10), and Kennedy as its messianic sacrifice (p. 13). The real force of Bellah's essay, though, derived from its empirical focus on presidential inaugural addresses in the United States. As Bellah reported, all but one presidential address invoked a generic god, Providence, or a higher power, terms to which an overwhelming number of Americans assented and continue to assent. Later in this essay, I follow Bellah's lead by examining presidential addresses between September 11, 2001 and 2004 to uncover new trends.

The period since Bellah's 1967 intervention witnessed a proliferation of studies that lacked Bellah's initial empirical focus, exhausting many scholars' patience.[10] One problem was civil religion's close imbrication with the normative functionalism of Durkheim, such that it was analytically construed as an ever-present social quality—the human sacralization of the symbols of the community, whatever they might be—rather than a particular *content* of discourse.[11] But as José Casanova indicated, the fallacy of a strict Durkheimian argument for civil religion is that there is no reason for assuming the necessary presence of religion to anchor social solidarity. Subjective individualism, not religion *per se*, provides the collective force of industrialized states (Casanova 1994: 37–8, 58–60), which depend at least officially on "minimalist" constructions of religion (Lincoln 2003: 58–60). Though it is possible to open the consideration of the discourse of "religion" widely enough to consider many features of modernity, notably the exchange of commodities, as Marx made clear in conceptualizations like commodity fetishism, as "religious"—sacrosanct, unquestionable, circumscribed by taboos, larger than life, the very ground of being, and so forth—Casanova's point is that since all such ontologies are in the contemporary moment elective rather than ascribed or required, it is that very quality of subjective selectivity that unites modern societies. Unless we want to say that individualism itself can be totemic—but thereby remove all possible circumscriptions of "religion" as a topic of scholarly investigation—we must be prepared to state that some societies are simply not religious. Religiosity, including civil religiosity, depends on a particular kind of legitimation, one invoking transcendent powers and eternal sources of authority (Lincoln 2003: 5–7).

Just so with regard to the question of violence. Though some might claim that violence always entails ultimate and therefore religious claims, transcendent authority is not always applied to justify violence. As Talal Asad (2003: 10) notes, men like General Haidar of Syria, Saddam Hussein of Iraq, and Ariel Sharon of Israel have executed widespread violence extraordinarily well without any need of invoking the Qur'an or Torah to legitimate it. As with religion in general, so with civil religion, which is not always or by necessity present. From the perspective of a content-based definition, which I am advocating here, civil religion is not inevitably present but rather occurs when nation-state narratives are fused with religious narratives—often themselves regarded as timelessly authoritative—of transcendent beings like gods, spirits, and ancestors.

The interpretation of some scholars, of the State as more or less sacred, elides the question of what that "more or less" depends upon, namely the conditions and discourses of the State's representation. In this essay, then, civil religion refers to a specific kind of human discourse relating state histories to extra-historical forces—gods, spirits of the dead, ancestors, saints, and to a lesser extent larger-than-life figures, documents and institutions, "forefathers" and constitutions, to the degree that they are ascribed transcendent statuses (cf. Lincoln 2003: 5–7).

In regard to its discursive content, civil religion entails neither the absolute fusion of national and religious identities, as in the frequently invoked limit-cases of Shinto or the Roman imperial cult, nor the sort of public religion articulated by Casanova. Public religions are initiated from a sectarian religious group that enters the public sphere to influence the relative arrangement of religious pluralism. By contrast, as Phillip Hammond (Hammond and Bellah 1980: 121–2) argued, the conditions for civil religion's presence are that (1) religious pluralism prevents any one religion being used by all people as a source of generalized meaning, but (2) a need for religious meanings that invest activity yet exists, so that (3) a substitute meaning system is sought and, if found, exalted by those whose activities it facilitates. Civil religions are empirical religions that are distinct from either traditional religions or the state, possessing their own moral codes, ritual forms, and truth claims (Albanese 1992).

Yet this is not quite sufficient either, however, for it is not the case that civil religion is produced from outside all traditional religions. It rather partakes of extant signs and symbols that are already loaded with tradition, and detaches them from their specifically religious venues for recycling in political symbols, speeches, and spectacles (Zubrzycki 2002). The process of recycling traditional religious signs and symbols into civil religious ones is not an egalitarian contest conducted on a level field. In the US, for instance, there is little possibility that witnesses in court might be asked to swear truthfulness by placing a hand on the Qur'an, or by wrapping themselves in an Iroquois *wampum* belt. The religious field of "neutral" words and symbols is already highly circumscribed by what has become known, following Bourdieu above all, as symbolic violence (Long 1986; Comaroff and Comaroff 1991; Deloria 1992; Bourdieu 1977, 1996, 2000). As some sectarian religious groups' discourses, symbols, and rituals are roughly approximated in civil settings, thereby naturalizing those religions as marked parts of the civil landscape, other sectarian religions are elided or suppressed. However much transcendent appeals may appear to present a legitimate social consensus—naturalized as what goes without saying, or hegemony (Williams 1976; Gramsci 1992; Comaroff and Comaroff 1991)—civil religion has in fact a fluid boundary that is, and always has been, contested and debated, though that instability is usually occluded in narratives of American religious history.[12]

Top-down or bottom-up: Ideological and organic forms of civil religion

Some scholars have refined the definition by distinguishing "high" from "low" civil religion (e.g., Novak 1974; Hammond 1976). Though taking a cue from this distinction, here I favor the opposition between *organic* and *instrumental* expressions of civil religion.[13] Organic expressions of civil religion are based on lived practices and are *relatively* spontaneous, whereas instrumental civil religion is composed of speeches and ceremonies calculated for political effect, entailing relatively less improvisation. Antonio Gramsci made a similar distinction between "religion of the people" and "religion of intellectuals." These do not comprise distinct traditions, but rather distinct applications and practical experiences of even the same religion. The religion of the people is "crassly materialistic" (Gramsci 1992: Q1862) and spontaneous in that it is a direct response in religious terms to the needs of everyday experience. What the religion of intellectuals sacrifices in the immediacy and force of such material practice, however, it gains in integrative potential exercised in writing, speeches, and other official forms. Despite any aversions one may have to denominating the Bush speeches in the wake of 9/11 as "the religion of intellectuals," there can be no doubt that such speeches were calculated to articulate a cogent message in a way that spontaneous material practices, like altar-building, were not.

Yet organic civil religion, precisely through its crass materialism, holds within it a philosophy (per Gramsci, "spontaneous philosophy"), a "sense of things" in relation to one another, albeit an implicit one of practice (Gramsci 1992: Q1375). Lévi-Strauss made an analogous point in his opposition between the bricoleur's knowledge and that of the engineer (1966: 16–36). The bricoleur acts in the world through the science of the concrete, organizing through the exploitation of the "sensible world in sensible terms" (1966: 16). The bricoleur (in contradistinction to the engineer) creates structures of meaning only secondarily through the arrangement of a finite set of objects used to solve a given problem. It is not conscious, meditated action, though something like reflection—taken broadly as the capacity to evoke critical revision—may occur out of, through, or following, the action's performance.

Instrumental civil religion seeks to fill in polysemic space. Deriving in part from the bricolage of organic civil religious practice, it transposes an implicit language of objects, a science of the concrete, to an explicitly mythic discourse, discourse that is not only transcendent but also hierarchic in the terms it affixes (Lincoln 1999). In the transition from civil religion as a science of the concrete—the altar-building process surrounding Ground Zero—to civil religion as mythic discourse—the us/them binary division rendered transcendent when molded in biblical tropes—instrumental civil religion becomes a total system able to direct public opinion and mobilize group action in the public sphere. Civil religion as organic practice has no conceptual coherence. Only instrumental civil religion presents such coherence, though it is inevitably, for Gramsci, a distorted one—"a purely mechanical contact, an external unity based in particular on the liturgy and on a cult visually imposing to the crowd" (Q1862). What is key here is Gramsci's observation that official (instrumental) civil religion tries to disguise and repress the fact of religious multiplicity, which would undermine universalizing claims (e.g., good/evil, "You're either with us or against us," etc.). It attempts to reconfigure what "goes without saying," and in so far as it is successful in this mission, to return from the public discourse of explicit ideology to implicit hegemony (Comaroff and Comaroff 1991: 19–32).

The question that must be asked is, to whom are the effect of religio-national "unity" and the erasure of political debate useful, and why? Civil religion is always an ideological construct that is always and necessarily interested or motivated.[14] Any articulation of collective will—whether Gramsci's "national-popular" or Rousseau's *volonté générale*—is not merely imposed, nor does it emerge spontaneously. It is, rather, legitimated (naturalized, reified, routinized, primordialized) through the political strategies of forging and delimiting the field of possible identifying distinctions, and by making such meanings stick (Eagleton 1991: 126, 195; Asad 2003: 3).

My argument, however, is that under rare circumstances like the crisis of 9/11, something like a moment of "collective will" may occur that is *relatively* unstructured, and *relatively* innocent of political strategy. To claim that such moments are wholly non-ideological is obviously an unfounded utopianism. The more modest claim is simply that there are more and less instrumental, more and less organic, kinds of civil religious enactments. The altar-building movement, a *relatively* organic civil religious moment, was rapidly coopted and assumed civil religion's second, *more* instrumental form.

Let's now consider empirical examples of two distinct responses to 9/11 using the refurbished construct of civil religion.

III. Organic civil religion at Ground Zero

The entire site where the World Trade Center Towers stood became in a certain sense an altar, a collection of material objects in space assembled and treated with specific techniques so as to evoke memory, disclose meaning, and present sites of exchange with deities and with the dead. Within this picture of the overall "hallowed ground" of Ground Zero, however, were developed specific sites as occasions for focused action, exchange, memorialization, and reflection.

Along Broadway in front of St. Paul's Chapel, the most public memorial site was shaped in the weeks following the attack. A block-long row of banners ("Jacksonville Loves New York"; "This is God's War Now") hung

on a fence. The banners expressed the solidarity of towns, civic organizations, unions, and countries with New York. The fence was additionally
lined with baseball caps and T-shirts from manifold places and organizations, each with a message: "University of Virginia," "Toledo Lutheran
Youth," "God Bless America," "Union 825, Albany." Underneath were
glass-cased candles, deflated Mickey Mouse balloons, wilted flowers, and
ragged teddy bears.

Several blocks away, at the corner of Park Place and Vesey, an altar
was built onto the wooden barricade wall that bordered Ground Zero.
Above it was erected a wooden cross hung with a wreath. Below the cross
was a red, white, and blue banner emblazoned with "God Bless America"
and silhouettes of the Towers. A large plastic angel had been placed under
each tower. Under the angel, the altar's shelf was covered with Jewish
Jahrzeit candles, and other candles devoted to multiple Catholic saints. A
Christian nativity scene and a Hindu image of Ganesa were prominent,
as was a Yankee baseball cap.

The firefighters' and police officers' memorial was erected in November 2001 on the Hudson River side of Ground Zero, and protected by a
canopy erected by the city. Here were gathered collections of photos and
lists of the lost firefighters and police officers, as well as individual shrines
built by families, friends, and strangers. Lists of the deceased from different stations were embellished with notes inscribed next to individual
names: "devoted brother," "loving husband." By the first anniversary
of the event, on September 11, 2002, the memorial had been filled with
actual belongings of the dead: compact disks of Irish music and empty
bottles of Killian's beer, ash-laden rubber boots, helmets, patches, and in
several cases the actual jackets that had been worn by firefighters when
the towers fell around them. Items salvaged from the wreckage had been
incorporated as well, including two chains hung in the form of a cross.
Candles were periodically lit alongside pieces of clothing that carried
traces of the last physical contact with the deceased. These rendered the
altars places of tactile as well as visual remembering. On September 11,
2002, as police officers and firefighters stood in groups recounting where
they were in the year prior when the towers fell, several visitors wept as
they ran their hands over the jackets, helmets, and boots. Others mouthed
silent words as they placed their hands on the garments. Still other visitors wrote notes and added them to the altar.

Under a nearby but separate canopy, many of the deceased flight attendants were materially remembered. Between September and November
2001, hundreds of teddy bears had been formed into a neat pile. Indeed,
teddy bears were omnipresent at improvised altars throughout the city.
Verbal explanations I received about the bears were predictably vague:
"showing affection," "paying respects," "an expression of love." This
flight attendants' memorial site was already dismantled by spring 2002.

Elsewhere in the city, memorials that were both planned and then improvised upon took form as well. In Grand Central Station at 42nd Street, to mention just one, a set of bulletin boards was erected in October 2001, labeled "The Wailing Wall," and left to be filled with names, pictures, and notes. In Battery Park, an "eternal flame" was dedicated on the one-year anniversary, in September of 2002, and this immediately became a new site of material displays, with the first day after its inauguration bringing candles, a hand-written translation of several paragraphs from the *Bhagavad Gita*, balloons, the ubiquitous teddy bears, and photos of deceased victims.

The sites were always unfinished, uncensored, and in porous process. On the one-year anniversary (September 11, 2002), a group of girls from London added a British flag to the fence in front of St. Paul's and scribbled a note of condolence. A group of young men from the Midwest signed an "I (heart) NY" T-shirt and hung it nearby. A child added a cardboard box with cut-out angelic action-figures glued to the sides. An official delegation from Hawaii distributed thousands of magnificent purple orchid lais near the site, and these became part of the unfolding process of altar-building, as they appeared on many of the shrines in the days that followed. The same occurred with the arrival of origami birds shipped from well-wishers in Nagasaki, Japan.

By the second anniversary of 9/11, in fall 2003, all altars were gone, and that particular form of memorializing had given way to others. The displays in front of St. Paul's had been photographed for exhibit within the church walls, and some retained for a permanent exhibit, but many of the actual objects were simply removed. The firefighters' altar along the Hudson was likewise dismantled and moved elsewhere in the city, allegedly for permanent storage. At the police officers' memorial wall nearby, only a single altar was erected for the 2003 anniversary. While scattered notes and bouquets again punctuated the fences surrounding Ground Zero, the period of conjoining such offerings into flashpoints of ritual action had passed. What remained was an endless stream of tourists snapping photographs of themselves waving, posed before the void of the world's most famous hole in the ground, a semantic gap ready to be resignified by any and all. These included Daniel Libeskind, the (then) knighted architect of the coming "Park of Heroes," "Wedge of Light" and "Freedom Tower," who wrote that "The foundations . . . stand as eloquent as the Constitution itself, asserting the durability of Democracy and the value of individual life" (mounted on the wall of the World Financial Center's lobby).

Interpretation

What could be read in these altars? As bricolage, a science of the concrete, was there a structure generated out of the objects? Lévi-Strauss argued that the process of bricolage occurs as objects are detached from one context of use and recycled into new chains of signification (1966: 150). So,

for example, Mickey Mouse balloons were detached from Disney amuse-
ment parks or the world of children's entertainment and reattached at
Ground Zero as something else. T-shirts communicating local rivalries
and allegiances in towns in Kentucky or Minnesota were detached from
that original context of use and submitted to a new one on the altars of
9/11. The objects appear to be interchangeable indices of pop-Americana:
Mickey Mouse balloons, plastic spinners, baseball-caps, T-shirts, flags,
and teddy bears. Perhaps such objects expressed the persistence of a
vulgar American vernacular, an unsightly but muscular material lingua
franca. Quite apart from the homage paid to individuals and corporate
groups, there was a eulogy to the nation, here presented in its most trashy
manifestations, an insistence—whether warranted or not—on its continued urgent vitality.

But was anything being "said" through the objects beyond the obvious one of co-presence: I (or my group) was at Ground Zero, as marked
by this object now contacted both by myself and the place, the object
now representing our meeting and passing co-presence? At best, any such
structure remains opaque, open-ended, and highly interpretive. Perhaps
we might hazard—testing the dark hermeneutic waters—that the caps,
shirts, buttons, and signs that formerly were designed to foment local
identities, distinctions, and rivalries were here submitted to the broader
identity of the nation.

At this first level of civil religion—civil religion as organic bricolage—
the submission of local distinctions to the national one condensed at
Ground Zero took shape as a relatively inclusive ideal. The altars expressed a dramatic national religious pluralism: candles inscribed in
Hebrew, Christian crosses, Hindu deities, Native American "four directions" circles, Latin American spiritualist texts, popular Catholic saints'
icons, and fanatical sports allegiances, all found a place there and were
left, untouched by official authorities, as coequal symbols.[15] Noteworthy
was the conspicuous absence—at least in my reconnaissance—of any
Muslim symbols or citations in Lower Manhattan, suggesting the limits
of inclusion in the organic civil religion I am describing.[16] As will be presented in the next section, this physical absence in the spontaneous altars
is all the more striking when juxtaposed with the dramatic inclusion of
Islam in presidential speeches after 9/11, for strategic reasons, rendering
the comparison more complex.

Next, the altars gave structure to the tension between remembering
and forgetting, of rendering present in one place so as to have some relief
from the constant burden of presence elsewhere. The problem in the case
of Ground Zero was particularly acute because of the absence of almost
all of the bodies.[17] The long delays and likely impossibility of recovering most bodies in recognizable form presented a serious problem for
mourning. The mass media's tact in not revealing specific bodies falling
or jumping, a deliberate filtering of *too much* presence, was here inverted

for the loved ones of the dead. The need for initial tact was replaced by the need for the tactile, the flesh-and-blood presence of bodies that might allow for emotionally rich leave-taking. The diverse objects assembled on altars compensated for the lack of physical corpses with photos, favorite objects, clothing, and other synechdochic pointers—parts of a life gesturing to, and temporarily recalling, its wholeness despite the body's absence. Perhaps most importantly, the altars served to locate loss within greater narratives, religious, cultural, and political, in many cases all three at once, as a form of practical history-making.

That the spontaneous altars surrounding the former towers were regarded as "sacred" again became clear in debates about when and how to remove the accumulated debris. The city acted to remove the altars along Broadway in fall 2002. Michael Wilson, writing in the *New York Times*, narrated the removal as follows: "The job is delicate, both physically and symbolically. Two men in windbreakers worked in silence yesterday, peeling worn T-shirts like layers of skin from the iron bars . . . [one of them] folds every item carefully and lays it inside a cardboard box, pausing to shake the dust out of a cap or a frayed flag" (November 7, 2002). They cleared just ten feet of fence per week so as not to shock passersby too abruptly with the absence. Yet the void felt in lower Manhattan by the removal of the assemblage of multivocal symbols was quickly filled by words, the most consequential of which were spoken by the President, and which were far less open either to spontaneous adaptation or to interpretation.[18]

IV. Presidential speeches as instrumental civil religion

In the consideration of official presidential speeches, the questions of actual authorship or personal intent are bracketed. It has been much commented upon that the lead speechwriter, Michael Gerson, is a graduate of a fervently evangelical institution located in the suburbs of Chicago, Wheaton College, and is therefore personally responsible for many of the religious references of speeches—both overtly religious phrases like "placing our confidence in the loving God behind all of life and all of history" and covertly religious phrases recognizable only to the evangelically attuned, like "there is power, wonder-working power in the goodness and idealism and faith of the American people," referring to Baptist hymnody familiar to certain churched adepts (both quotations are from the State of the Union address, January 28, 2003). Here the perspective taken is that major official speeches reflect neither the personal views of Bush nor of Gerson, but are rather collective efforts, vetted by multiple members of White House staff and advisory groups at multiple levels of bureaucratic hierarchy (Lincoln 2003: 24). They can, therefore, be critiqued as ideology, as official representations in a way that ad-hoc improvisations, which may or may not reflect a considered political platform, cannot be.

An examination of Bush's speeches does not suggest the absence of regard for the kind of inclusiveness of expressions I have called organic civil religion. To the contrary, beginning with his inaugural address, Bush's speeches were the first in presidential history to include the word "mosques" in stock phrases about places of worship. On the newly proclaimed National Day of Prayer (May 1, 2003[19]), the same day that the "end of combat operations" in Iraq was declared, for example, Bush said, "In this hour of history's calling, Americans are bowing humbly in churches, synagogues, temples, mosques and in their own homes in the presence of the Almighty." The inclusion of "mosques" in such statements presented a novel recognition of American religious pluralism in official presidential discourse.

Moreover, the speeches explicitly recognized, and applauded, the kind of initial impulse represented in the altar-building process. The discursive recognition of unity amidst diversity in practices and beliefs, however, was in most speeches rapidly shifted to statements indicating the collective action that should naturally follow. For example, immediately following the recognition of what I have called organic civil religion in the address of September 20, 2001, the President's discourse initiated a strategic shift to a more ideological and instrumental tone: "Tonight we are a country awakened to danger and called to defend freedom. Our grief has turned to anger, and anger to resolution." Even within the context of the National Day of Prayer speech in the National Cathedral (September 14, 2001), where a sustained focus on the organic civil religious phenomenon of grieving might have been expected, a similar dramatic shift obtained. On the one hand there was an acknowledgment of a collective state of mourning—"God's signs are not always the ones we look for. We learn in tragedy that his purposes are not always our own"—and on the other hand, the channeling of that diffuse state of collective mourning toward a clear political meaning—"Just three days removed from these events, Americans do not yet have the distance of history. But our responsibility to history is already clear: to answer these attacks and rid the world of evil."

The fight against evil, cast in apocalyptic terms, became a leitmotiv of official speeches in the ensuing years and continues to the present. Only two weeks after the attack, citizens were informed to "not expect one battle, but a lengthy campaign, unlike any other we have ever seen"; the world was likewise warned, "every nation, in every region, now has a decision to make. Either you are with us, or you are with the terrorists" (September 20, 2001). The same speech referred to America's "calling," in a mission divinely mandated and with ultimate consequences: "Freedom and fear, justice and cruelty, have always been at war, and we know that God is not neutral between them" (September 20, 2001). The showdown between good and the "axis of evil" was invoked in the State of the Union address several months later (September 29, 2002).

To support the invocation of evil in an absolute, ontological sense, that to which the US must reply, Bush's speeches likened Al Qaeda repeatedly to the standard-bearer for unequivocal evil, Nazism (e.g., November 9, 2001, September 11, 2002, January 20, 2003, and May 1, 2003). Since the US played a key role in the defeat of "evil" on that occasion, Bush's words exhorted, it had to again take up arms, now again "to save civilization itself" (November 8, 2001).

If America was "called by history" (January 28, 2003), that history was one of divine intervention ("an angel still rides in the whirlwind and directs this storm," January 20, 2001) for which the US was the earthly representative: "The liberty we prize is not America's gift to the world; it is God's gift to humanity" (January 28, 2003); *ergo*, America is the giver of God's gift of liberty to the world. This was a large task, to be sure, but one Americans had to be willing to shoulder: "Once again, we are called to defend the safety of our people and the hopes of all mankind" (January 28, 2003). In the address that prematurely declared the alleged end of combat in Iraq, Bush added, "All of you, all in this generation of our military, have taken up the highest calling of history" (May 1, 2003). The calling was repeatedly affirmed as divinely mandated.

The "calling" to save the world was cast in increasingly biblical, and increasingly bilious language in the period approaching Operation Iraqi Freedom (March 19–May 1, 2003). On September 11, 2002, the anniversary of the attacks and the eve of Bush's pitch to the United Nations for action against Iraq, Bush's discourse presented a shift from the recognition of an organic civil religiosity to an ideological claim upon it. In words uttered from a carefully positioned stage just below the Statue of Liberty, the speech moved from statements like "Yet we do know that God has placed us together in this moment," to a clarion call, "This ideal of America is the hope of all mankind . . . and the light shines in the darkness. And the darkness will not overcome it. May God bless America." In the speech marking the (putative) conclusion of combat operations in Iraq of May 1, 2003, Bush's remarks, spoken on the deck of an aircraft carrier whose tower advertised "Mission Accomplished!," again invoked the apocalyptic theme: "We do not know the day of final victory, but we have seen the turning of the tide." Here "day of final victory" does double duty, communicating to evangelical Christians that the war with Iraq is embedded in an eschatological sequence of events leading to the "end times," but to non-evangelicals merely that this is only one battle in a longer engagement. The speech ended by citing the Hebrew Bible: "In the words of the prophet Isaiah, 'To the captives, "come out"—and to those in darkness, "Be free".'" (The Book of Isaiah was a favored source for speeches of this president, and was also quoted following the explosion of the Columbia space shuttle [February 1, 2003]).

An additional rhetorical device employed was the distinction between practitioners of true religion and those who practice false religion. The speech of September 20, 2001 disparaged the "fringe form of Islamic extremism . . . that perverts the peaceful teachings of Islam"; "Its teachings are good and peaceful, and those who commit evil in the name of Allah blaspheme the name of Allah." The speech from October 7, 2001 derided the "barbaric criminals who profane a great religion," as did succeeding speeches (November 8, 2001, September 11, 2002). Practically speaking, the statements were crucial to avoiding a public anti-Islam backlash. But they also conveyed an ideological distinction consistently drawn in the Bush speeches: there is true religion and false religion, and thus also "true" and "false" Islam, the latter represented by the Taliban and Al Qaeda.

In sum, the post-9/11 Bush speeches often began by invoking the immediacy and force of organic civil religion, before then casting the world in the strongest possible binary terms: us/them, good/evil, civilization/barbarism, real religion/blasphemy. The binary terms were discursively linked either obliquely or explicitly to transcendent authority. In these strategic discursive shifts, organic civil religion, the shared repertoire of practices that actually presented something approximating a collective will in the need to give tangible form to memorialization and the sentiment of loss, was hijacked. It was hijacked by instrumental civil religion, the top-down form of civil religion in which a powerful leader harnessed contingent political objectives to transcendent authority. This helps account for why Bush's nomination for the coming presidential election took place in New York City, and as close to September 11 as possible: by returning spatially and temporally to a vital source of organic civil religion, and symbolically to a moment of genuine national-popular collective enthusiasm—a move depending, following Frazer's classic formulation, on the magic of contagion—political power could then be discursively transferred to ideologically more specific ends, most immediately that of reelection. That strategy was successful in November of 2004, as Bush won reelection over contender John Kerry by stridently linking the war in Iraq to imagery of the sacred space of Ground Zero and to the memory of his own leadership in the days immediately following. By far the most used campaign image was that of Bush standing heroically on the rubble, shouting encouragement through a bullhorn.

V. Conclusion

The official speeches were a symbolic hijacking of a genuine social consensus built around mourning and memorializing, for politically divisive instrumental ends. Perhaps such hijacking is even inevitable in the transition from popular practice to official speech, since the latter is denotative and propositional, while the former is not. The key question is not whether such hijackings will occur, but toward which ends. For example, the move from practice to discourse, from organic to instrumental civil religion, need not in every case imply a politically conservative or bellicose shift. Yet in the vast majority of cases of discourse presented by agents of the US state since 9/11, the process of ideological distillation was devoted to military objectives, and its strategic objective was the instrumental one of generating popular support for the President and his war. This redirecting of the social force generated by organic civil religion for instrumental ends was a form of symbolic violence; it controlled representations and directed the collective emotional force they evoked—their national *effervescence*, if you will—toward particular military objectives.

That civil religion is usually contained by symbolic or actual violence is not surprising, and rather suggests the rarity of organic civil religious episodes. That civil religion is most typically made and maintained by coercion or the threat of it was clear even in the phrase's initial articulation by Rousseau, though the passage is infrequently cited:

> While not having the ability to obligate anyone to believe them [the articles of the civil religion], the sovereign can banish from the state anyone who does not believe them. It can banish him not for being impious but for being unsociable, for being incapable of sincerely loving the laws and justice, and of sacrificing his life, if necessary, for his duty. If, after having publicly acknowledged these same dogmas, a person acts as if he does not believe them, he should be put to death . . . ([1762] 1968: 102)

There was no such dramatic coercion levied against citizens, though such force was certainly used against non-citizens at Abu Ghraib, at Guantanamo in Cuba, and at Camps Bucca and Cropper in Iraq. Rather, the hijacking of organic civil religious force occurred through the formation of a discourse community about the war, within which the President's official speeches were only the most disseminated and influential part, which made the war appear as an inevitable chapter of the United States' national destiny.

Acts of actual physical violence in military actions were detached and fetishized in sanitized news reports filed by "embedded" and therefore partisan reporters. These became magnets that drew additional narratives—of individual heroic acts, of soldiers' leavings and homecomings, and of public displays of support—that generated their own logic and system of symbolic capital (Feldman 1991: 5, 7; Palmié 2002) and, once commodified, economic value as well (Coronil and Skurski 1991: 333). Old national mythologies, especially those of World War II and its comfortingly clear evil of Nazism, were burnished to promote heroic events and figures which, when successfully imitated, yielded further symbolic capital within that mytho-logic (Apter 1997: 10–15). Hummer-brand automobile sales exploded as Operation Iraqi Freedom unfolded, as a civilian mimesis of the war's daily broadcasts,[20] even as the market for positive cinematic depictions of the military mushroomed through a series of movies produced with Pentagon or official military help (e.g., *Black Hawk Down*, *Tears of the Sun*, *War of the Worlds*).[21]

As the discourse community of war grew, the practice of viewing the military imagery transmitted "live" on television became itself a kind of ritual practice, a symbolic and interpretive discourse, or "semio-technique" (Feldman 1991: 261), through which "Iraq" was interpellated into the US cultural repertoire precisely through its destruction. To be sure, the destruction was a sanitized version, with actual images of dead Iraqi civilians, their numbers or names, edited out. Watered by the stream of edited images, an imagined community flowered, as each American came to view him- or herself as a member of a vast army of viewers and readers simultaneously consuming the same images, and reacting to them similarly (Anderson 1991). The event of "9/11" and the "war on terror" became a meta-fictional funnel through which all information was siphoned. The world was remade as a field of endless battles, reproduced in state spectacles, cinema, and urgent television updates where, larger than life, its truth value was rendered nearly irresistible (Apter 1997: 14).

Nearly, but not quite. The narrative chain linking 9/11 to the war was not immune to rust. As the death toll of US soldiers rose and as Iraq's alleged weapons of mass destruction that provided the stated justification for the war remained undiscovered, and as the public's attention span was stretched thin, by the spring of 2005 Bush's approval rating for his handling of Iraq sagged below 40 percent. As expected, President Bush and other officials continued to revisit Ground Zero and "9/11" as often as possible, either physically or discursively, to attempt to recharge the batteries of instrumental civil religion by plugging it into the site of organic civil religion—"to traverse the circuitous route from abstraction to concrete particularity and return with *more*—just as the person possessed by a spirit of the dead returns with more . . ." (Taussig 1997: 137–8; italic mine).

This, I hope, is at least a plausible interpretation of the difference between organic civil religion and instrumental civil religion, and how the latter relies for its creation on the legitimacy of the former. Civil religion can undergird a social contract by arising out of a shared repertoire of bodily action taken in response to a shared crisis, as it did in the altar building that was indexical of organic civil religion. But it can also provide the set of strategies and discursive tools for the fundamental ideological move, the absolute distinction between "me" and "other" (Eagleton 1991: 126) by which war is justified. If organic civil religion is "savage" in its materiality, instrumental civil religion savages, in so far as it creates and then naturalizes rigid binary social classifications, affixes such classifications to transcendent terms, and spectacularizes and mythologizes war as salvific drama.

Notes

1 The morning headlines on September 12 were astonishingly uniform. "'Our Nation Saw Evil'" (Austin, Texas: *American-Statesman*; Kalamazoo, Michigan: *Kalamazoo Gazette*), "'Freedom Itself was Attacked This Morning'" (Allentown, Pennsylvania: *The Morning Call*), "'Evil Acts'" (Miami, Florida: *Miami Herald*; Loveland, Colorado: *Reporter-Herald*). I offer merely typical examples of what was a universal pattern. There were, to be sure, variations. The *Washington Post* and the *Boston Globe* posted Osama bin Laden's name on the front page the morning of September 12, while others, like the *New York Times*, were more circumspect. While most papers focused on the tragedy and loss of life, the *Wall Street Journal* also lamented the seemingly inevitable economic recession. *El Universal*, from Mexico City, and *O Dia*, from Rio de Janeiro, both showed photos of recognizable bodies falling or leaping from the towers, while all North American papers censured such disturbing images.

2 Not to mention (it goes without saying) any notion of more economic or social-structural interpretations of the "everyday violence" (Scheper-Hughes 1992: 20), "terror as usual" (Taussig in Scheper-Hughes 1992: 220), or "hidden violence" of postmodern empires (Coronil and Skurski 1991: 334) inflicted routinely on the poor, in part as a result of US policies past and present.

3 "Organic" draws not only on the legacy of the Gramscian lexicon, but also on Lévi-Strauss' characterization of ritual bricolage as bringing about an organic relation between initially separate groups (Lévi-Strauss 1966: 32).

4 Trying to interpret such improvised ritualizations, of course, has the feel of throwing darts in the dark. When one asks those placing objects on what I am calling altars about why they perform the actions, as I have, he quickly learns the question's futility, receiving answers like "to show respect," "to remember," "to honor," "to not forget." But why in this form, with these things? The response to such a question is beyond the pale of what is speakable. But then, what shall we do when faced with the aporia, or at least inadequacy, of actors' words—can we say nothing, or only repeat the forced phrases altar-builders uttered under duress? How do we "read" mute, or jumbled, practice? At the least, in hazarding an interpretation, though we may not hit a bullseye—which in any case would depend on the kind of board hung on the wall—we will probably stick some theoretical nerves. This alone makes it worthwhile.

5 On March 22, 2003, three days after the bombing had begun, 72 percent of US citizens supported the war, compared with 26 percent who opposed it (CNN/Gallup). That support later climaxed at 89 percent. By June 2005, that unanimity disappeared, with 53 percent of respondents agreeing with the statement that "the U.S. made a mistake in sending troops to Iraq" (USA Today/CNN/Gallup June 24–26, 2005).

6 Most notoriously, Bellah invokes civil religion at a specific historical point, a "third moment of crisis" (1967: 16). The first moment was the question of independence, the second that of the Civil War, the third, the moment of his writing, 1967. The third crisis is "the problem of responsible action in a revolutionary world, a world seeking to attain many of the things, material and spiritual, that we have already attained" (16). Prophetically, Bellah anticipates the need for symbols that will reflect the civil religion of a genuine transnational sovereignty: of American civil religion becoming merely one part of a new *civil religion of the world* (18). The interjection of civil religion as a crisis response entails a claim to authenticity, though, that is in part

derived from empirical cues, and in part constructed by its very invocation. His is not merely a description and interpretation, then, but concomitantly a normative call.

7 "In God We Trust" was added to paper currency following a bill passed in 1955, proposed by a Florida Democrat in the House of Representatives, Charles E. Bennett. In 1956, the phrase became the national motto. To quote the *New York Times* obituary of September 9, 2003 (Bennett died on September 6), "Mr. Bennett said America had to distinguish itself from other world superpowers. 'In these days when imperialistic and materialistic communism seeks to attack and destroy freedom, we should continuously look for ways to strengthen the foundations of our freedom,' he said of his bill from the House floor in April 1955. 'At the base of our freedom is our faith in God and the desire of Americans to live by his will and his guidance. As long as this country trusts in God, it will prevail.'"

8 Here we see most clearly the link between Rousseau, Durkheim (who equates sectarian religion and civil religion in function) and more recent Durkheim-influenced theorists like the late Victor Turner and Pierre Bourdieu, for whom the function of ritual was (among other things) to make social obligations desirable.

9 I use "America" advisedly in keeping with presidential discourse, conscious that this appropriation of the name of two continents for a single nation-state is a discursive power play. Properly, of course, the referent is the United States of America.

10 Bellah himself declared the topic moribund in 1975's *The Broken Covenant*, and had offered his "swan song" by 1980 in the volume co-authored with Phillip Hammond.

11 Wuthnow (1994) refers to these competing analytical uses as broad versus narrow constructs of civil religion, which roughly echo differences in the use of "religion" in general. An additional problem in the decades after Bellah's essay derived from attempts to sieve "authentic" American civil religion from its distortions into "civil idolatry" (e.g., Marty 1987: 72), a normative hierarchy that further mired civil religion in a definitional bog.

12 Consider Philip Hamburger's recent (2002) *Separation of Church and State*, for example. Hamburger argues that the infamous "wall" separating church and state is nowhere in the US Constitution, but derives from Thomas Jefferson's correspondence with Baptists seeking legal aid for a specific, local grievance in relation to a Congregationalist majority. The metaphor of the separating "wall" only became canonical as a result of nineteenth-century efforts by the Protestant majority to restrict Catholic efforts to acquire civil benefits; and even more stridently when the Ku Klux Klan appropriated anti-Catholic rhetoric into its nativist-racialist revival. Hamburger shows the dense, confusing ideological networks in which a cause primarily embraced by the "Left," a strict separation between church and state, gained force as rhetoric of the extreme Right.

13 My use is idiosyncratic: More common is to describe "high" civil religion as "priestly," devoted to maintaining and reproducing social stability. "Low" civil religion, by contrast, we might expect to be "prophetic," dissatisfied with mere social reproduction and is concerned with change. The problem is that one might argue the opposite, based on an idea of massification and false consciousness: "low" civil religion is likely to simply reproduce ruling ideas assimilated through television. It is likely to uncritically accept political discourse without question, and more likely to submit to military training and propaganda.

14 To invoke ideology does not of necessity cast a villainous shadow, or imply

the fleecing of some by others. It can also be a utopian vision inspiring collective action. It is in this sense that Sidney Meade recalled that "the ideal 'Republic' dreamed by the founders never existed in actuality. It was a vision, an artist-people's creative idea . . ." (Meade in Hammond 1980: 204). Rousseau's or Habermas' conditions for communicative, rather than instrumental or strategic action, ideal conditions that probably cannot be met empirically (Althusser 1972: 149–50; Habermas 1984: 285–6; Eagleton 1991: 130), could also be named "positive ideologies." As Gramsci stipulated, there are socially progressive as well as retrograde forms of ideology.

15   It is plausible, moreover, that this kind of inclusive civil religion was correlated with inclusive social effects in other domains of civil society, such as "race." In a survey conducted by the *New York Times* between June 4 and 9, 2002, for example, 53 percent of African-Americans reported that relations between races are "generally good," compared with only 16 percent of African-Americans offering a similar response in 2000. Whether the organic, bricolage form of civil religion was a cause or consequence of such reports of the submission of identity groups to the city of New York and to the nation is unknowable. Sufficient here is to note their temporal, and probably temporary, correlation. Robert Putnam (2002), to wit, argued that the attacks bonded Americans in a way unseen since World War II, with greater religious and racial tolerance, greater faith in public institutions, and an overall "public spiritedness" that contradicted the observations made in his book, *Bowling Alone*.

16   Consider this example of the limits of American civil religion. During the first week of January, Florida pilot and sky-writer Jerry Stephens "wrote" in giant letters across the sky, "GOD IS GREAT." On the face of it, this was a distinctly American sort of act and message. Though it is hard to imagine another country where the notion of flying an airplane to advertise for God would seem normal, here it would barely draw a second glance, ordinarily. This time, though, the response was more pronounced. The phrasing sounded too "Muslim," and set off a minor panic around Boca Raton that it heralded a possible terrorist attack. Interviewed on National Public Radio, Stephens said that next time he would exercise more caution, and more clearly specify that "JESUS IS GREAT," a message he felt sure could not possibly be mistaken or arouse fear. The anecdote is suggestive for the trends it points toward. Stephens aimed to present a civil religious sort of message, but discovered that some kinds of civil religion were, at that moment, "too Muslim." American civil religion, that set of religious discourses and symbols that goes without saying, needed to be more clearly marked and distinguished as *Judeo-Christian*.

17   The final tally of morbidity at Ground Zero was 2,752. The number of bodies actually issued death certificates as of mid-January 2001 was just 622. A further 1,962 death certificates had been issued at the request of families, even without the bodies. One solution to this problem of the lack of bodies was to give family members pieces of rubble as ciphers to help focus memory and mourning. On this score, I am not at all sure how to consider the teddy bears, which were perhaps, along with flags, the dominant symbol present. Why should teddy bears play so important a part in altars devoted almost exclusively to the memory of adults? My suspicion is that they had something to do with the problem of the absence of the corporeal dead; that they gave tangible form to the loss which otherwise has no trace. The bears no doubt communicated comfort, tenderness, and security, the sort of comfort many of them devoted to their families while they were alive. Perhaps the teddy bears laid at the altars gave comfort to the living, to those left as bereft

and uncomprehending by the sudden attack as lost children. If so, it is not that the victims were made symbolic "children" as rendered present at their altars, but rather that those they left behind were now become "children" in their absence.

18 To be fair, even this site I have named the epicenter of relatively inclusive organic civil religion was hotly contested and the subject of frequent ideological debate. To wit, on November 2, 2001, the heroes of September, police officers and firefighters with 366 dead between them, squared off in fisticuffs over Mayor Giuliani's decision to reduce the number of firefighters working at the site from 64 to 25. To firefighters, the reduction was an attempt to turn the sacred burial site of their brothers into a mere clean-up zone, a "full-time construction scoop and dump operation" (*The New York Times*, November 3, 2001). In early January 2002, conflict again arose, this time over the issue of Ground Zero and tourism. As the city built the first of a projected four viewing ramps from where visitors could survey the site, street vendors set up tables to hawk "F.D.N.Y." T-shirts and "Ground Zero" caps and pins. This evoked protests from relatives of the deceased against the cheap exploitation of a sacred site for capital gain, complete with comparisons to Jesus' overturning of moneychanger's tables in the temple. The same basic issue of whether, and how, to combine commercial with sacred uses, and the assumption that they are antithetical, oriented these (ongoing) heated exchanges. These sallies were exchanged especially between the (then) winning architect for the redesign of "Ground Zero," Daniel Libeskind, who defended his design's appeal to the families of the deceased, and Larry Silverstein, the territory's leaseholder and most promising financier, who defended the need to restore lower Manhattan's capital viability.

Also notable in this very public debate was the progressive shrinkage of the site consecrated as "hallowed ground," such that by summer 2003 some actors' discourses had restricted that denomination only to the towers' footprints, or actual foundations. Other debates focused on how deep the sacredness of the site extends: whether to the level of the buildings' foundations, or to the lowest level of human loss of life. The precise dimensions of Ground Zero as sacred space are constantly shifting.

19 Also May Day, the International Worker's Day. The symbolism of the "Day of Prayer" eclipsing the primary international labor celebration could not be more obvious.

20 For two years after the war's onset, the Hummer "H2" was among the best-selling large SUVs in the US. Commented Rick Schmidt, founder of the International Hummer Owners Group, "In my humble opinion, the H2 is an American icon . . . it's a symbol of what we all hold so dearly above all else, the fact that we have the freedom of choice, the freedom of happiness, the freedom of adventure and discovery, and the ultimate freedom of expression . . . Those who deface a Hummer in words or deed deface the American flag and what it stands for." Added Travis Patterson, "To me the Hummer, the H2, is the most American vehicle on the planet. It oozes patriotism. You put some flags on the Hummer and drive down the road and everyone is honking and waving at you" (*The New York Times*, April 5, 2003).

21 *Black Hawk Down* was reportedly used both as a "pep rally" before going into battle for troops stationed in Iraq, and as a "how-to" manual by Iraqi resistance.

64   *Paul Christopher Johnson*

References and further reading

Albanese, Catherine. 1992. "Dominant and Public Center: Reflections on the One Religion of the United States." *South Atlantic Quarterly* 81 (1): 14–29.

Althusser, Louis. 1972. *Politics and History: Montesquieu, Rousseau, Hegel and Marx*. Trans. Ben Brewster. London: NLB.

Anderson, Benedict. 1991. *Imagined Communities: Reflections on the Origin and Spread of Nationalism*. London: Verso.

Apter, David E., ed. 1997. *The Legitimization of Violence*. Washington Square, NY: New York University Press.

Asad, Talal. 2003. *Formations of the Secular*. Stanford, CA: Stanford University Press.

Bellah, Robert. 1967. "Civil Religion in America." *Daedalus* 96 (1): 1–21.

——. [1975] 1992. *The Broken Covenant: American Civil Religion in a Time of Trial*. Chicago: University of Chicago Press.

Bloom, Allan David. 1987. *The Closing of the American Mind*. New York: Simon and Schuster.

Bourdieu, Pierre. 1977. *Outline of a Theory of Practice*. Trans. Richard Nice. New York: Cambridge University Press.

——. 1996. *The State Nobility: Elite Schools in the Field of Power*. Trans. Lauretta Clough. Oxford: Polity.

——. 2000. *Pascalian Meditations*. Cambridge: Cambridge University Press.

Bush, George W. 2003. *State of the Union Address*. http://www.whitehouse.gov/news/releases/2003/01/20030128-19.html.

Casanova, José. 1994. *Public Religions in the Modern World*. Chicago: University of Chicago Press.

Comaroff, Jean and John Comaroff. 1991. *Of Revelation and Revolution: Christianity, Colonialism, and Consciousness in South Africa, Volume One*. Chicago: University of Chicago Press.

Coronil, Fernando. 1997. *The Magical State: Nature, Money and Modernity in Venezuela*. Chicago: University of Chicago Press.

Coronil, Fernando and Julie Skurski. 1991. "Dismembering and Remembering the Nation: The Semantics of Political Violence in Venezuela." *Comparative Studies in Society and History* 33 (2): 288–337.

Deloria, Vine. 1992. "Secularism, Civil Religion and the Religious Freedom of American Indians." *American Indian Culture and Research Journal* 16 (2): 9–20.

Durkheim, Emile. 1995. *The Elementary Forms of the Religious Life*. Trans. Karen E. Fields. New York: The Free Press.

Eagleton, Terry. 1991. *Ideology*. London: Verso.

Elias, Norbert. 1988. *The Civilizing Process*. London: Blackwell.

Fanon, Frantz. 1965. *A Dying Colonialism*. Trans. Haakon Chevalier. New York: Grove Press.

Feldman, Allen. 1991. *Formations of Violence*. Chicago: University of Chicago Press.

Girard, René. 1977. *Violence and the Sacred*. Trans. Patrick Gregory. Baltimore, MD: Johns Hopkins University Press.

Gramsci, Antonio. 1992. *Prison Notebooks*. New York: Columbia University Press.

Habermas, Jürgen. 1984. *The Theory of Communicative Action.* Trans. Thomas McCarthy. Boston, MA: Beacon Press.

Hamburger, Philip. 2002. *Separation of Church and State.* Cambridge, MA: Harvard University Press.

Hammond, Phillip E. 1976. "The Sociology of American Civil Religion: A Bibliographic Essay." *Sociological Analysis* 37 (2): 169–82.

Hammond, Phillip E. and Robert Bellah. 1980. *Varieties of Civil Religion.* San Francisco: Harper and Row.

Hughey, Michael W. 1983. *Civil Religion and Moral Order.* Westport, CN: Greenwood Press.

Lévi-Strauss, Claude. 1966. *The Savage Mind.* Chicago: University of Chicago Press.

Lincoln, Bruce. 1999. *Theorizing Myth: Narrative, Ideology and Scholarship.* Chicago: University of Chicago Press.

——. 2003. *Holy Terror.* Chicago: University of Chicago Press.

Long, Charles H. 1986. *Significations: Signs, Symbols and Images in the Interpretation of Religion.* Philadelphia: Fortress Press.

Marett, R. R. 1914. *The Threshold of Religion.* New York: Macmillan.

Marty, Martin. 1987. *Religion and Republic: The American Circumstance.* Boston, MA: Beacon Press.

Marvin, Carolyn and David Ingle. 1999. *Blood Sacrifice and the Nation: Totem Rituals and the American Flag.* Cambridge: Cambridge University Press.

Novak, Michael. 1974. *Choosing Our King: Powerful Symbols in Presidential Politics.* New York: Macmillan.

Palmié, Stephan. 2002. *Wizards and Scientists: Explorations in Afro-Cuban Modernity and Tradition.* Durham, NC: Duke University Press.

Putnam, Robert. 2002. "Bowling Together." *The American Prospect Online.* February 11.

Rousseau, Jean-Jacques. 1762. *Émile, ou De l'éducation.* Amsterdam: Néaulme.

——. [1762] 1968. *The Social Contract: Or, Principles of Political Right.* Trans. Maurice Cranston. New York: Penguin Books.

Sahlins, Marshall. 1985. *Islands of History.* Chicago: University of Chicago Press.

Scheper-Hughes, Nancy. 1992. *Death Without Weeping: The Violence of Everyday Life in Brazil.* Berkeley, CA: University of California Press.

Spurlin, Paul M. 1969. *Rousseau in America: 1760–1809.* Tuscaloosa, AL: University of Alabama Press.

Taussig, Michael. 1987. *Shamanism, Colonialism and the Wild Man: A Study in Terror and Healing.* Chicago: University of Chicago Press.

——. 1997. *The Magic of the State.* New York: Routledge.

Williams, Raymond. 1976. *Keywords.* New York: Oxford University Press.

Wuthnow, Robert. 1994. *Producing the Sacred.* Urbana, IL: University of Illinois Press.

Zubrzycki, Geneviève. 2002. "With or Without the Cross? Nationalism and Religion in Post-Communist Poland." PhD dissertation. Department of Sociology, University of Chicago.

4   The rhetoric of evil and eradicating terrorism

Caryn D. Riswold

On September 20, 2001, President George W. Bush delivered a speech in response to unprecedented terrorist attacks on the United States that shifted US foreign policy and reasserted the power of theology over political ideology. It is that power of theology with which this essay is concerned. It is also the implications of such a religious position for the work of resisting evil in the world with which we will wrestle here. When the President asserts that "you are with us, or you are with the terrorists" and that "freedom and fear have always been at war . . . we know that God is not neutral between them," he assumes and suggests that struggles against evil are clear-cut, easily distinguished from the good, and able to be simply resolved.

When it comes to the present "war on terrorism," this rhetoric is not satisfactory. This essay will first examine the President's rhetoric about evil to reveal what it is that he is saying. Because this rhetoric describes and discusses evil and God in matter-of-fact, clear-cut ways, the essay will move on to explore the complex nature of evil to show why this presidential language is unsatisfactory. The specific evil found in the complex ideology of terrorism will then be analyzed—if terrorism is what this war is against, then we need to attempt to understand what it is in order to presume to defeat it. Finally, the essay will conclude by suggesting that our response to evil lies not in certainty but in humble awareness of the specific roles that we play in struggles of resistance.

Two basic questions guide this essay: Why is President George W. Bush's rhetoric inadequate to address the reality of evil in the world? What then must we do?

The rhetoric of evil

The rhetorical character of President George W. Bush's speeches and statements since September 11, 2001 reflects his personal faith commitments, and reinforces a worldview of clear-cut examples of right and wrong, good and evil. This is problematic when confronting the complex reality of evil in the world. In this section, I will briefly examine some of that rhetoric—

what does he say? what are the theological assumptions and implications of these positions? As a theologian, I am aware that the President is a politician and commander-in-chief, and thus when he speaks there are specific intentions, audiences, and outcomes in mind that should have little to do with theology. However, it has become clear that this president speaks of God and evil in very specific ways that need to be revealed and examined because of the assumptions and dangerous implications of his rhetoric.

While one could go back to the President's inaugural address for examples of the ways that his Christian faith affects his politics and policies,[1] I choose to begin this study with the more dramatic speech delivered to a joint session of Congress on September 20, 2001, just nine days after transformative terrorist attacks on the United States. The President's assertions about matters of justice, God, and evil have continued since then and can be further seen in his State of the Union address on January 28, 2003. This section will focus on what these two rhetorical moments reveal.

On September 20, 2001, the President delivered a masterful speech crafted to both comfort Americans and to convince them along with the rest of the world that the United States had been violated and that someone was going to have to be punished. The truth of this was never disputed. However, the way in which President Bush began making his case against the declared enemies provides a stunning example of his interweaving of political and military activity with the will of God.[2] The words and images employed in this particular speech convey a presidential appeal to the divine, a presentation of retribution theology in the context of a political response, and ultimately, they communicate the arrogance of a president certain that he is carrying out the will of God.

In this speech, the President spoke clearly of "enemies of freedom" who attacked the United States. He named Al Qaeda as the culprit behind the September 11 attacks for the first time in public, and likened them to other members of "murderous ideologies of the 20th century" like "fascism, Nazism, and totalitarianism." The applause-line of this section of the speech reads poetically: "And they will follow that path all the way, to where it ends: in history's unmarked grave of discarded lies" (Bush 2001: 12). The remark that then shifted US foreign policy and opened the way for future military activity follows:

> Every nation, in every region, now has a decision to make. Either you are with us, or you are with the terrorists. From this day forward, any nation that continues to harbor or support terrorism will be regarded by the United States as a hostile regime. (Bush 2001: 13–14)

The President offers his vision for what needs to be done: "[T]he only way to defeat terrorism as a threat to our way of life is to stop it, eliminate it, and destroy it where it grows" (Bush 2001: 15).

Ultimately, the President claims to possess three things: chosen rightness,

And in our grief and anger we have found our mission and our moment. Freedom and fear are at war. The advance of human freedom—the great achievement of our time, and the great hope of every time—now depends on us.

certainty,

Our nation—this generation—will lift the dark threat of violence from our people and our future. We will rally the world to this cause by our efforts, by our courage. We will not tire, we will not falter, and we will not fail.

and the will of God:

The course of this conflict is not known, yet its outcome is certain. Freedom and fear, justice and cruelty, have always been at war, and we know that God is not neutral between them. (Bush 2001: 23)

The combination of these elements and the decidedly theological bent of all of the above language turned this speech into doctrine. Freedom is lifted up as the highest good, as something that the United States possesses, something that is under attack by this nebulous enemy, and something that Americans are called on by God to defend, protect, and expand.

The claims about God's position and favor, coupled with the stated *certainty* of the outcome of whatever military action might follow, speak to the presumed power and privilege of the United States. In a statement at the very end of the speech, Bush claims the now divinely sanctioned "rightness of our cause" and his confidence "of the victories to come" (Bush 2001: 24). Problems begin to emerge when considering basic questions: Is it that easy? Can evil be defeated? Is the President of the United States God's chosen savior? Is it really certain that we, the good free Americans, are going to win?

Before we turn to an analysis of evil to understand more thoroughly the inadequacy of this presidential rhetoric, a few more examples are in order. In early 2003, as the United States moved closer to a war with Iraq, the President stood before a joint session of Congress again to deliver the State of the Union address. He remarked about the ongoing war on terrorism:

We have the terrorists on the run. We're keeping them on the run. One by one, the terrorists are learning the meaning of American justice . . . Our war on terror is a contest of will in which perseverance is power . . . Whatever the duration of this struggle, and whatever the difficulties, we will not permit the triumph of violence in the affairs of men—free people will set the course of history. (Bush 2003)

Noting the presumption that "perseverance is power," we see this section of the speech flowing into the next, to connect the present war on terrorism, an outgrowth of the September 11 terrorist attacks, with the problem of the dictatorial regime of Saddam Hussein and the atrocities committed under his guidance.

> International human rights groups have catalogued other methods used in the torture chambers of Iraq: electric shock, burning with hot irons, dripping acid on the skin, mutilation with electric drills, cutting out tongues, and rape. If this is not evil, then evil has no meaning. (Bush 2003)

And finally the President reminds the American people once again of the three elements noted above—chosen rightness, certainty, and the will of God:

> Americans are a free people, who know that freedom is the right of every person and the future of every nation. The liberty we prize is not America's gift to the world, it is God's gift to humanity. (Bush 2003).

These remarks inextricably link the privilege of American freedom to the will of God, and place the United States in the position of the bearer of God's gift (freedom) to the rest of the world. The proposal is something like this: We have it, God gave it to us, everyone deserves it, our war against this dictator is therefore the intention of God, and so we know that God is on our side. The logic of this rhetoric is seductive, but is it appropriate? In assuming the favor of God, it implies that whatever military activity in which the country engages is thereby sanctioned by God.

Aside from the following philosophical and theological analysis of the nature of evil which points toward problems in this language, a few basic problems with this rhetoric ought to be briefly noted. Howard Fineman notes in his "faith portrait" of the President that "Bush is dwelling on faith-based foreign policy of the most explosive kind: a potential war in the name of civil freedom" (Fineman 2003: 30). In addition to the already volatile nature of this approach, the will of vast numbers of Americans and significant groups of citizens is not taken into account. Fineman further notes that "the president is facing a mighty force of religious leaders on the other side. They include the Pope, the Council of Bishops, the National Council of Churches, many Jewish groups, and most Muslim leaders" (Fineman 2003: 30). In fact, a letter from the National Council of Churches to its constituents reads in part:

> We have been warmly received in every county—except our own. We have repeatedly asked to meet with President Bush, a fellow man

of faith, and a committed United Methodist. We have been rebuffed or ignored. (National Council of the Churches of Christ in the USA 2003)

This emerging faith-based foreign policy comes from the Bush administration's own narrow Christian views of God, good and evil, and American privilege. It does not draw on universally accepted religious views, as evidenced in part by the opposition of the groups noted above.

In terms of secular impact, the Bush doctrine has led to numerous examples of columnists, entertainers, and anyone opposed to, critical of, or even asking questions about the war on terrorism being labeled as un-American, even heretical. Early critics after September 11 faced the immediate wrath of the public, witness Bill Maher, Susan Sontag, and Barbara Kingsolver.[3] The wrath continued as the country moved toward the war with Iraq. Entertainers Tim Robbins and Susan Sarandon found themselves held hostage by their own critical statements when the Baseball Hall of Fame canceled an innocuous event set to celebrate the fifteenth anniversary of the movie *Bull Durham* in April 2003. Dale Petroskey, president of the Baseball Hall of Fame, sent a letter to Robbins and Sarandon criticizing them for speaking out against the impending war in Iraq:

> In a free country such as ours, every American has the right to his or her own opinions, and to express them. Public figures, such as you, have platforms much larger than the average American's, which provides you an extraordinary opportunity to have your views heard—and an equally large obligation to act and speak responsibly. (Associated Press 2003)

The stunning presumption of this statement is that acting and speaking "responsibly" *necessarily* means that you support the President and his administration's position. That this follows on the statement about American rights to freedom is ironic.

However, the problems with President George W. Bush's rhetoric of evil, war, and terrorism, go far beyond the ostracizing of celebrities, and it is to the depth of the complexity of evil that we must turn in order to appreciate the inadequacies of the approach presented in this rhetoric of evil.

The nature of evil

To judge by his rhetoric, the President believes God has chosen him to lead the U.S. in a war against "Evil"; beside that eschatological assignment, NATO, the UN, our allies, Arab opinion, world opinion, the war on terror, the budget, are as nothing . . . The "moral clarity" Bush's publicists salute him for gives fearful permissions. Against evil, all means are sanctified. (Beatty 2003)

What is the reality of evil in our world? This is what the President claims to be fighting, and presumes to defeat. Is this possible? The rhetoric examined thus far shows a president who is certain that he is right about what is good and what is evil, and that he is doing the will of God. His personal faith inextricably defines his political position and guides his military decisions. As Howard Fineman notes, this is not necessarily a wholly new phenomenon: all presidents invoke God, ask for a divine blessing, and are guided by moral principles often informed by their religion. The difference here is the clarity that Bush claims to possess, giving him "fearful permissions" according to Beatty above. The claims of chosen rightness, certainty, and the will of God appear repeatedly in not only his rhetoric, but in his decisions. His background might provide a clue: "A frat man at Yale in an increasingly radical time—the late 1960s—he came to loathe intellectual avatars of complexity and doubt . . . As he describes it, his faith is not complex" (Fineman 2003: 29). In this section of the essay, I will briefly examine the nature of evil and show how the complex nature of its reality in the world demands nuanced and complicated responses, ill-served by this president and his theological presumptions. Faith must be complex in response to this world.

Susan Neiman provides a thorough analysis of modern philosophy and struggles with defining evil and understanding the role that intentions play in activity labeled as evil. Her work highlights the ambiguous nature of the discourse overall. Wendy Farley develops a theodicy of compassion, built around a tragic vision of the world, wherein creation is ruptured and the world is characterized by brokenness. She invokes the power of divine love and compassion to understand the struggle that defines human life in the world. These two contemporary approaches will be explored as they highlight the complicated nature of the issues surrounding the ancient problem of evil.

First, Neiman's analysis of evil as the central concern of modern philosophy hinges on her analysis of responses to two catastrophic events: the Lisbon earthquake in 1755 and the concentration camps at Auschwitz in 1945. Identifying these two events as the beginning and end of the modern, she asks the question which responses to the events share: "what threatens our sense of the sense of the world?" (Neiman 2002: 2). If the earth beneath our feet is not to be taken for granted, then what is? If the leader of a nation can confidently seek the decimation of a people he deems undesirable, what does this suggest about being human? The task of theodicy grows out of the sense that things are not as they should be: "Every time we make the judgment *this ought not to have happened*, we are stepping onto a path that leads straight to the problem of evil" (Neiman 2002: 5). The problem of evil, as ancient as human reflection itself, is generally stated in the form of a question like this: If God is all-good and all-powerful, then why does evil exist? The connection between the existence of God and the existence of evil becomes a problem when one asks the simple question, "why?"

Two issues that emerge from Neiman's extensive analysis are important here: the nature of intentions, and the ambiguous definition of evil. Neiman states in her analysis of intentions as related to evil: "What counts is not what your road is paved with, but whether it leads to hell" (Neiman 2002: 275). This is what she describes as a feature unique to contemporary evil: "individuals' intentions rarely correspond to the magnitude of evil individuals are able to cause" (Neiman 2002: 273). Hannah Arendt's work *Eichmann in Jerusalem* highlights this very point, with Neiman focusing on the claim that this man working for the Nazi party on trial for war crimes "was moved by nothing worse than the desire to please his superiors by doing his job well" (Neiman 2002: 272). The argument is that harmless or banal intentions do not lessen responsibility for the outcome of one's actions: what matters is the outcome of actions. As the notion of intent is central to much Western jurisprudence, this is somewhat of a radical idea with far reaching implications.

Along with questioning the role of intentions in creating evil, Neiman insists that she will not offer a definition of evil: "There may be no general principle that proves torture or genocide wrong, but this does not prevent us from taking them to be paradigmatic of evil" (Neiman 2002: 9). What is evil? How can we define it? Neiman's is somewhat of a you-know-it-when-you-see-it approach. Does this approach create problems for the discussion or solve them? When confronted with the question, "are earthquakes evil?" most people will now tend to say no, because earthquakes are natural events, products of a series of geological and physical conditions. But when asked, "was the Holocaust evil?" most people will answer yes. Once that step is taken, however, we inevitably ask, "why?" We then can move through a list of responses that have rejoinders, qualifiers, and exceptions. "Nearly anyone who ever taught a humanities course will have met students who discovered that words like *good* and *evil* are out of date, since used by different cultures in different ways" (Neiman 2002: 9). Does this mean that everything is relative, and therefore there is no such thing as evil? Not necessarily. Remarkably, we might draw on the words of President Bush when he said in the 2003 State of the Union address, "If this is not evil, then evil has no meaning." What is the meaning of evil? Neiman sufficiently complicates the discourse and notes that, "the problem of evil began by trying to penetrate God's intentions. Now it appears we cannot make sense of our own" (Neiman 2002: 281). This is one devastating result that she focuses on—the way that the Lisbon earthquake exhausted conceptual resources at the time (the earth is not stable or unqualifiedly good), and the way that Auschwitz now does the same (intentions may not dictate the outcome of our actions).

With regard to terrorism, Neiman includes a brief section written after September 11, that, while it feels somewhat like an editorial afterthought, proposes an interesting response: "September 11 provided an instance of evil that was old-fashioned in structure . . . Malice and forethought, the classic components of evil intention, have rarely been so well combined" (Neiman 2002: 284). Given the above understanding of contemporary evil as no longer defined by intentions, the overwhelming intentionality of flying particular fuel-loaded planes into specific symbolic buildings sure to be shown on television becomes described as old-fashioned. While terrorism as a form of evil will be considered more at length later, it is worth noting here that Neiman again emphasizes the ambiguous nature of evil:

> Evils can be acknowledged as evils without insisting that evil has an essence. Our inability to find something deep that is common to the mass murders committed by terrorists and the starvation furthered by corporate interests does not prevent us from condemning both. Thinking clearly is crucial; finding formulas is not. (Neiman 2002: 287)

We take the following complications from Neiman: Evil cannot be fully defined. Sometimes intentions are clearly evil, sometimes they are good; often they are simply banal. Nevertheless, we clearly live in a world that has evil as part of its nature—how are we to understand our role in this world?

Wendy Farley develops a theodicy built on an understanding of the tragic nature of the world, and the role of divine compassion in the midst of it. This broad view of the world and God's relation to it will bring our discussion of the nature of evil to a close, and perhaps provide some theological responses to Neiman's philosophical position. The key element to Farley's theodicy is that tragedy is constitutive of the cosmos:

> I am drawn to tragedy because it retains the sharp edge of anger at the unfairness and destructiveness of suffering. I explore a tragic vision in order to find categories for evil that do not justify or explain suffering . . . Tragedy is driven by a desire for justice. (Farley 1990: 13)

Farley is concerned with understanding the world, seeking some explanations for evil without allowing justifications, and continuing to work for justice with an understanding of divine compassion. Farley's tragic vision offers an understanding of the world as a complex mix of good and evil: "Tragedy recognizes something in the world order recalcitrant to human freedom and well-being, which qualifies and even corrupts obligation" (Farley 1990: 25). Finitude, diversity, and embodiment are part of the nature of the world, can be occasions for life and joy, but are often themselves the sources of conflict, irreconcilable obligations, and unfulfillable desires:

> Creation is tragically structured, but tragedy is neither the barrenness of nothingness nor the wickedness of evil. Tragedy is the price paid for existence—but the fecund grace of nature makes it appear that the price is not too high. (Farley 1990: 61).

Tragedy and grace exist together in the nature of the world. Farley maintains that the sources of life, growth, development, and change can be both gift and burden. The burden can often be a crushing one, and therefore brokenness lies at the heart of reality. Creation is ruptured.

If the goodness of creation is violated, and this is the nature of the world, then where is the hope? Farley develops a phenomenology of divine love to provide some resources and remedies. She is very clear, however, that nothing justifies this fundamental brokenness. The fact of it should not lead to acceptance of it. Farley chooses compassion as the language best suited to address this reality: "Compassion resists suffering rather than tries to justify it" (Farley 1990: 69). This is the struggle, therefore, that is fundamental to human life. There are perhaps no answers, and never any satisfactory explanations, but there is always the struggle: "Compassion remains the ground and power of resistance, of hope, of a transformation of the future and a recovery of the past: fragments of liberation and a return to the center" (Farley 1990: 132). This is how new life continues to emerge, how freedoms are won, and how in the midst of unimaginable suffering, human communities flourish and grow. The purpose of Farley's work is not, she says, to "explain away evil or make evil into any good." Rather, it is to "illuminate the radical love of God that is not overcome by evil" (Farley 1990: 133).

We take the following complications from Farley: the world is tragically structured, evil is an inevitable part of the world, radical suffering is never justified, and we are left to struggle in concert with a compassionate God, continuously resisting evil as it emerges.

With the complex analyses provided by this philosopher and this theologian, we return to the problem with President Bush's rhetoric. Recall the characteristics that are weaved through his speeches: chosen rightness, certainty, and the will of God. With Neiman, we can now say that chosen rightness is not so easily determined. The President claims to be right and to have good intentions, but does that justify his call to arms and move to war? He also claims to be certain of the outcome of whatever conflict will come. With Farley, we can now say that the nature of the world is such that evil and suffering sometimes tragically overpower the good. This is not to say that we ought not continue eternally to struggle against evil, for that is precisely the function of divine compassion. Rather, the point to be noted here is that the struggle is ongoing, and to presume that it will end, and that evil can be defeated, rings impossible given the tragic structure of the world in its multiplicity, finitude, and vulnerability. We should not be so arrogant as to presume that our victory is certain. We may need to *act as if* we can win, but assuming that we *will* win can be a problem. Wendell Berry notes that "A government, committing its nation to rid the world of evil, is assuming necessarily that it and its nation are good" (Berry 2003). This is one serious implication of Bush's mingling of politics, theology, and military action: presumption of rightness and goodness sanctions *any* action the nation may take. Finally, discerning the will of God as evidenced in Neiman and in Farley remains the ultimate unlikely task. The concept of God as a god of justice is nearly universally embraced, but what is justice in contexts such as the one in which we live? Who is defining the good in this case?

We must turn briefly to examining the ideology of terrorism. If what we are concerned about here is the rhetoric of evil and eradicating terrorism, we need to see if terrorism can be eradicated, or if it may tragically be a part of the fabric of the complex world: something that is to be resisted, but may never be completely overcome.

The evil of terrorism

Susan Neiman suggests above that terrorism returns us to an old-fashioned form of evil: with malice and forethought abundant. Mark Juergensmeyer offers several insights in his study of religious terrorism that further our study here. He notes, at the outset, that these acts can be "forms of public performance rather than aspects of political strategy. These are symbolic statements aimed at providing a sense of empowerment to desperate communities" (Juergensmeyer 2001: xi). After the dramatically horrifying collapse of the World Trade Center's twin towers on television, the images of crumbling and flaming walls at the Pentagon, and the video footage of a scorched hole in the earth in Pennsylvania, we know too well the symbolic power of such destruction. The world was terrified. Therefore, in defining terrorism, Juergensmeyer notes the retrospective nature of the term:

> Hence the public response to the violence—the trembling that terrorism effects—is part of the meaning of the term. It is appropriate, then, that the definition of a terrorist act is provided by us, the witnesses—the ones terrified—and not by the party committing the act. (Juergensmeyer 2001: 5)

In this section of the essay, we will narrow the study of the nature of evil to examine what is the nature of this specific evil of terrorism. With Neiman, I am not prepared to say why exactly terrorism is evil. Juergensmeyer notes that it is not the perpetrators who intend evil, but rather it is the witnesses who define it as such. This perspective on defining terrorism underscores its ambiguous definition. For this study, I will simply assert that terrorism is an evil. The United States is engaged in a war on terrorism, the President is certain that we will prevail, but from our brief study of the nature of evil, it is problematic to assume that a war on evil is certain to be won. What is the nature of terrorism that challenges the rhetoric of universal rightness, certainty, and sense of the will of God asserted by President Bush?

Wendell Berry asks difficult questions about terrorism in his study of the National Security Strategy of the United States: "There is, however, no acknowledgement in The National Security Strategy that terrorism might have a cause that could possibly be discovered and possibly remedied. '*The embittered few*,' it seems, are merely '*evil*'" (Berry 2003). We have seen that there seems to be no such thing as "merely evil," so a brief examination of the nature of terrorism is in order. Juergensmeyer's study of religious terrorism provides good resources here. After some initial attempts at defining terrorism, his five sets of case studies of terrorism from five distinct religious settings lead to some reflection on features shared across the boundaries of culture and religion.[4]

As noted above, one feature raised in this study is the performance dimension to such violence: "They have a secondary impact. By their demonstrative nature, they elicit feelings of revulsion and anger in those who witness them" (Juergensmeyer 2001: 122). The intent of terrorism lies more in the secondary impact than in the actual violence done. This is tied to the second feature identified, the sense of the perpetrators that they are engaged in a cosmic battle: ". . . the notion of cosmic war provides the script being played out in the violent performances of militant religious activists and is linked to notions of conquest and failure, martyrdom and sacrifice" (Juergensmeyer 2001: 148). In this setting, then, the next feature of death as victory, a twisted form of martyrdom, comes into play. With regard to the individual warrior, Juergensmeyer next examines how the sense of empowerment resulting from the violent action is out of proportion to the actual damage caused. He calls this "symbolic empowerment" and concludes that one effect of this is to make "a daring claim of power on behalf of the powerless . . . [showing] how fragile public order actually is" (Juergensmeyer 2001: 188, 215). Finally, Juergensmeyer indicates the variety of ways that leaders and activists in a multitude of religions "go about the business of killing with the certainty that they were following the logic of God" (Juergensmeyer 2001: 218).

These five dimensions of the ideology of terrorism as revealed in the case studies provided begin to reveal the complexity of rationalizations found in cultures of violence. They are embedded in religious beliefs as certain as those of President George W. Bush. Terrorism, like the broader concept of evil itself, is not easily defined nor is it easily located. Questions about intentions and definitions that accompanied Neiman's study of evil in modern philosophy are relevant here as well. If we, the witnesses, are the ones defining terror, what is our criterion? Perhaps we will resort to the you-know-it-when-you-see-it approach that can be taken when defining evil. However, greater qualification may be necessary when US foreign policy and military decisions are made based on these definitions.

The ultimate question with which this study is concerned is this: can terrorism be defeated? Can the United States win its war on terrorism, as the President is certain that it will? According to the President, this means that the United States is going to single-handedly defeat evil in the world. Bush sees this as his imperative as the leader, noted by Berry's incorporation of "President Bush's speech made at the National Cathedral on September 14, 2001: '*But our responsibility to history is already clear: to answer these attacks and rid the world of evil*'" (Berry 2003). If terrorism is the specific form of evil with which we are presently concerned, can it be eradicated?

The danger of course is this: what if we say no? What if Berry is right, that:

> ... we must suppose a new supply of villains to be always in the making, we can expect the war on terrorism to be more or less endless, endlessly costly and endlessly supporting of a thriving bureaucracy. (Berry 2003)

If we affirm that ideologies of violence, like religious terrorism, are part of the tragic nature of the world, a feature of a ruptured creation in Farley's terms, then are we admitting defeat? If, as Neiman suggests, terrorism as it appeared on that sunny September morning is as old-fashioned as evil can be, then what progress has been made in human history? If the President's certainty about his chosen rightness and sense of the will of God is misguided, what then must we do?

What then must we do?

Based on the previous section, it seems as if this essay is moving toward hopelessness. Quite the contrary. By understanding the dangerous and complex nature of the world, we become better equipped to confront it, to transform it, and to resist it. We also gain the humility necessary to engage in struggles against evil in a tragic world. It is this humility that is missing from the presidential rhetoric at the center of this study. I appreciate as much as anyone the necessity for clear and decisive speeches to rally a nation in a time of tragedy and confusion. However, when the clarity and decisiveness leads to the President sounding more like a fanatic than a true leader, then problems emerge.

Understanding President Bush's ideology is the first step. That the leader of the United States has beliefs is in essence a good thing. Rogers M. Smith calls this an "ethically constitutive account" and maintains that communities of people inevitably have stories that define and unite them. However, members of the populace have a responsibility: "Those who disagree with stories like Bush's must contest those narratives with, among other things, rival ethically constitutive stories of their own" (Smith 2003: B10). What President Bush is doing through his rhetoric is important, and is powerful. If it were not, this essay would not exist. The task, then, is this: "Since ethically constitutive stories, like factions, cannot be eliminated, we should instead seek to multiply and diversify them and set them against one another" (Smith 2003: B11). This is the work begun in this essay, and it is the work attempted by anyone who questions and challenges the President's positions as expressed in his major speeches. How do we do this? Where do we do this?

One specific community concerns me, and many others: the community of learners in the college classroom. By way of concluding this essay, and providing some concrete examples to bring the theoretical discussion to a close, I will offer some reflection on how teaching is one kind of work that enables the creation and transformation of ethically constitutive stories.

If one thing that we must do is multiply and diversify the stories that constitute who we are as a human community, then we must continue to produce individuals who are able to do just that. Higher education is one concrete way in which this can take place. Mary Rose O'Reilley asks the question posed to her when she was a new teaching assistant: "Is it possible to teach English so that people stop killing each other?" (O'Reilley 1993: 9). Through her engaging discussion of her own career in classrooms, she refers at first to the banal hope of most teachers, to create "a certain kind of human being: compassionate, balanced, and inwardly mobile" (O'Reilley 1993: 39). However, the work of teaching goes beyond that, and O'Reilley identifies a key element:

> But finding voice—let's be clear—is a political act. It defines a moment of presence, of being awake to transmit that self-understanding to others. Learning to write so that you will be read, therefore, vitalizes both the self and the community. (O'Reilley 1993: 58)

If one of the things that we must do in response to the nature of the world and the complex reality of evil as seen in terrorism is to multiply and diversify our ethically constitutive stories, we must engage in work that enables others to do just that. "And helping someone to find voice demands a spiritual partnership with that seeker. It's an exercise of compassion" (O'Reilley 1993: 62). This suggests that the work of teaching is an integral part to the ongoing struggle against the brokenness inherent in this world.

An autobiographical conclusion: I teach religion in a way that centers on the questions—much as this essay is driven by questions and raises new and difficult ones. In my religion classroom, the point of study is not to find the answers but to find the questions, the ways that various people have answered them, and to discern new questions in response to those answers. Once we lose the questions, we lose the transformative power of learning. This is the approach that Smith calls for above, and is perhaps one way that the teaching of religion may help people to stop killing each other. It may not be so much what we teach (English, religion, biology, or economics), but *that* we teach—that we empower others to be critically constructive members of a body politic. This is the exercise of compassion that echoes Wendy Farley's theodicy of divine compassion as the crucial element of hope in the midst of tragedy. It builds on humility, and challenges any claims of chosen rightness, senses of certainty, and knowledge about the favor of God.

Conclusion

The rhetoric of evil in which President George W. Bush engages is inadequate and inappropriate for the work of eradicating terrorism. Discourse about evil must be complicated, as the nature of evil is complicated. We need more questions, answers, and leaders capable of engaging in the "intellectual avatars of complexity and doubt" (Fineman 2003: 29) that this president seems to loathe. Understanding the complex nature of the reality of evil leads not to a cynical abandonment of hope, but rather to honest assessment of the enormous tasks involved in fighting evil, in waging a war on terrorism, and in discerning the will of a gracious God. It leaves us to find real means by which we can humbly engage in the work of resistance in places as mundane as the college classroom.

> We can no longer afford to confuse peaceability with passivity. Authentic peace is no more passive than war. Like war, it calls for discipline and intelligence and strength of character . . . If we are serious about peace, then we must work for it as ardently, seriously, continuously, carefully, and bravely as we now prepare for war. (Berry 2003)

Notes

1 Howard Fineman does just this in his "faith portrait" of the President in *Newsweek* (2003).
2 My analysis of this speech, summarily noted here, is more thoroughly developed and explained in Riswold 2004.
3 The ostracizing and professional snubbing of Maher, Kingsolver, and Sontag is discussed in Riswold 2004.
4 The study examines terrorists embracing their own forms of Christianity, Judaism, Islam, Sikhism, and Buddhism.

References

Associated Press. 2003. "A load of *Bull*." http://sportsillustrated.cnn.com/base-ball/news/2003/04/09/hall_bulldurham_ap.

Beatty, Jack. 2003. "In the Name of God." http://www.theatlantic.com/unbound/polipro/pp2003-03-05.htm.

Berry, Wendell. 2003. "A Citizen's Response to the National Security Strategy of the United States of America." http://www.commondreams.org/views03/0209-11.htm. Also published February 9, 2003, in the *New York Times* as a full page advertisement placed by *Orion Magazine*.

Bush, George W. 2001. *Our Mission and Our Moment: President George W. Bush's Address to the Nation Before a Joint Session of Congress, September 20, 2001*. New York: Newmarket Press.

——. 2003. *State of the Union Address*. http://www.whitehouse.gov/news/releases/2003/01/20030128-19.html.

Farley, Wendy. 1990. *Tragic Vision and Divine Compassion: A Contemporary Theodicy*. Louisville, KY: Westminster/John Knox Press.

Fineman, Howard. 2003. "Bush and God." *Newsweek*, March 10, 22.

Juergensmeyer, Mark. 2001. *Terror in the Mind of God: The Global Rise of Religious Violence*. Berkeley, CA: University of California Press.

National Council of the Churches of Christ in the USA, Office of the General Secretary, Rev. Bob Edgar. 2003. Letter to constituents, April.

Neiman, Susan. 2002. *Evil in Modern Thought: An Alternative History of Philosophy*. Princeton, NJ: Princeton University Press.

O'Reilley, Mary Rose. 1993. *The Peaceable Classroom*. Portsmouth, NH: Boynton/Cook.

Riswold, Caryn D. 2004. "A Religious Response Veiled in a Presidential Address." *Political Theology* 5 (1): 39–46.

Smith, Rogers M. 2003. "The Next Chapter of the American Story." *Chronicle of Higher Education*, July 11: B10–11.

5 The tricks and treats of classification

Searching for the heart of authentic Islam

Russell T. McCutcheon

Given that an estimated 30,000 Russians die of alcohol poisoning each year (a statistic reported in Erofeyev 2002: 56), it is somewhat difficult to understand why anyone would disagree with Mikhail Gorbachev's judgment that "vodka has done more harm than good to the Russian people."[1] Instead, Evgeny Popov—a contemporary Russian author—was recently quoted, in an article on the history of the 500-year-old, odorless, colorless, and tasteless drink, to believe nonetheless that it has performed a crucial social function.

> Vodka has provided access to a private life that is closed to the state, a place where it is possible to relax, to forget your troubles, to engage in sex with the illusion of free choice. (Erofeyev 2002: 61)

Vodka—the drink whose quality is linked directly to its apparent lack of qualities—has helped the Russian people to, in his words, "counter the stress of living in a less than perfect nation."

Taking a thoroughly historical approach to the study of society means that a basic issue in need of examination is how it is that large-scale groups comprised of competing—and often contradictory—interests can generate, then reproduce, the impression of uniformity and continuity often over long periods of time and across vastly changing political and material conditions. In other words, if we all live in the midst of what the Austrian novelist Robert Musil (1880–1942) in his novel *The Man Without Qualities* once called "the old storyline of the contradictions, the inconsistency, and the imperfection of life" ([1952] 1996: 23), then how do we reproduce the illusion of consistency and perfection so successfully? Although it may sound flippant, for Popov a virtually invisible elixir offers at least one explanation; vodka has provided, in his words, the illusion of free choice, making possible access to a private life that is seemingly closed to the state. I say "seemingly" for a reason, of course; as scholars we ought to assume that, despite claims to the contrary among the people whose cultural products comprise our data, there is no escape from the historical (i.e., the contingent, the *ad hoc*), the public, and the collective. For example, consider the fact that in the 1970s the profits from state-controlled domestic vodka sales injected 170 billion rubles into the Soviet treasury; using conversion rates for the mid-1970s, and accounting for inflation, that is roughly equivalent to 804 billion US dollars today.[2] This apparent sense of isolation and privacy brought about by consuming a drink with virtually no detectable qualities turns out to have been one of the financial engines that helped to make the idea of one particular collectivity possible and persuasive.

The lesson we learn from vodka's social effects is that the means by which we invent and then assert the limits of privacy are public, political, and economic acts through and through; they are techniques for making an invariably imperfect social group seem to work by disengaging some of its participants from a storyline that makes certain forms of collective life possible and others utterly unthinkable. This assists us to see claims to privacy not in some realist fashion—as a self-evident thing or essential state of being—but, instead, as ways of negotiating the limits of fundamentally contestable public space, making the rhetoric and techniques for establishing and monitoring the limits of the group highly effective social regulatory mechanisms. In fact, with Musil's notion of living out a storyline in mind, we can see that it is a regulatory process remarkably similar to the sort of picking, choosing, discarding, and ignoring that goes into all acts of narrative. Defined minimally as a story with a beginning, a middle, and an end, narrative structure results from the skill of ignoring countless historical moments, overlooking events, and marginalizing interactions, all in the effort to frame, exclude, enhance, isolate, and thereby raise yet others to a level of significance they could not have possessed if they were left merely as part of the continual background noise that surrounds us all. Narratives of careers, lives, and social groups therefore result from what Jonathan Z. Smith has aptly termed an economy of signification (1982: 56) whereby just some events get to count—an economy that is, as Smith argued, negotiated by means of those behaviors we call rituals that simultaneously focus and distract attention, all in the service of establishing limits in terms of which significance can be judged, thereby making comparisons, and thus meaning and identity, possible. If narrative and ritual declare significance by arranging moments that appear tactically disengaged from their inevitably competitive and imperfect context, then vodka (at least according to Popov) creates social groups by tactically disengaging people from their inevitably collective and imperfect lives by opening for them a passage of retreat into the seemingly inner, private self: the opiate of the people, indeed.

I'm hoping that readers can begin to see what all this has to do with the topic at hand: the manner in which difference, disagreement, and dissent in the homeland have been efficiently domesticated by means of a discourse on private experience, faith, principle, and homogenous tradition—in a word, religion. Simply put, just as vodka's apparent lack of qualities is no indication of its effects at both a personal and a societal level, so too there is nothing private about the rhetoric of faith.

For example, consider the January 2003 workshop my university sponsored for students on the basic beliefs and history of Islam. Prompted by the widespread interest in (and, many would no doubt hasten to add, the widespread misunderstanding of[3]) Islam that quickly became evident throughout the US soon after the September 11 attacks, the planning committee carefully considered how to structure this event. At one point early in its planning, the committee—of which I was a member, along with representatives of the local Muslim community (a number of whom are professors at the university), representatives from various academic departments, and assorted student organizations on campus—considered presenting Islam in terms of its role as a social movement, or in common parlance, as a "civilization," rather than as a "religion." Made by a member of the committee who happened also to be Muslim, this suggestion (whether intentionally or not, on the part of my colleague) echoed a distinction commonly found in the current literature on Islam. A well-known representative of this position is the former Princeton University Near Eastern studies professor and the oft-cited pundit, Bernard Lewis, as in when he attempts to define Islam in the opening chapter of his recent book, *The Crisis of Islam*. "To begin with," he writes,

> the word [Islam] itself is commonly used with two related but distinct meanings, as the equivalents both of Christianity and of Christendom. In the one sense it denotes a religion, a system of belief and worship; in the other, the civilization that grew up and flourished under the aegis of that religion. ([2003] 2004: 3)

Perhaps because, Lewis informs his readers, religions are concerned with matters of private belief expressed in worship (i.e., rituals that give voice to people's inner beliefs), and not with overt forms of political behavior, Lewis primarily concerns himself with Islam as a civilization.[4] "While generalizing about Islamic civilization may be difficult and at times in a sense dangerous," he warns his reader, "it is not impossible and may in some ways be useful" (2004: 4). But since utility is a relational term— table saws are useful to carpenters but not to diamond cutters—we should ask: Useful to whom? And for what purpose?

The utility of the private religion/public civilization distinction was apparent in our workshop. My colleague's classificatory suggestion seemed to have been prompted by a desire not to affront the sensibilities of local, conservative Christians (a number of whom are evangelical Protestants) who, quite predictably, are represented in fairly large numbers in our part of the US. For example, not long before the initial meeting early in the autumn of 2002 to plan our workshop, the University of North Carolina at Chapel Hill had been thrust into the national headlines for, of all things, having incoming undergraduate students read Michael Sells' annotated selection of excerpts from the Qur'an (1999)—a curricular decision that was troubling enough to some North Carolina residents that a lawsuit was filed against the school by the Virginia-based Family Policy Network on behalf of three anonymous UNC students who apparently felt that the school was proselytizing. (The case was thrown out by a Federal appellate court.) Perhaps approaching our topic as the study of a "civilization," so the reasoning could have gone, might help the public to understand the event better, and thereby get something important out of it, and thereby prevent some of the problems experienced in North Carolina.

Despite this suggested classification, this was not in fact how the event was billed; instead, it was an introduction to the "religion" of Islam, with students preparing by reading in advance chapters from the works of such standard authors on religions as Huston Smith and John Esposito, and with two scholars of religion speaking (one of whom was myself, who opened the event with a brief comment on the requirements of the publicly funded study of religion), along with a historian and a political scientist. Most interesting was that, shortly before the event, it became apparent that, despite the complete silence of the local conservative Christians, a small group of politically engaged, pro-Israeli students voiced concern regarding the possible tone of the event and whether such topics as, for example, the current Israeli–Palestinian conflict would be on the table. If so, then they requested representation at the event so that, as it was put to me by a rather impassioned young lady, both sides could be represented, thus giving the attendees more "balanced" information.

Anyone even partially familiar with the flood of popular information on Islam that is now available to the curious reader will see that this anecdote of a small conference on Islam in the southern US has surprising relevance for the topic at hand. Inasmuch as the mass movement once known across Europe as Mohammadism, and now as Islam, was portrayed as a religion—which is, as Lewis informed his readers, a matter of personal belief expressed in forms of private behavior we call ritual and worship—these potential critics were quite comfortable with the event, for its exotic content would, they must have reasoned, necessarily be far removed from contemporary politics, studying instead disembodied sets of beliefs, antique origins, esoteric doctrines, etc. However, if Islam was classified as a socio-political movement, as a "civilization," then this would make the event necessarily political and thus controversial due to its potential conflict with other civilizations—notably Israeli, or so the young lady led me to believe.

At the heart of this debate over naming lies our topic: the politics of privatization and the socio-political utility of the modern taxon "religion."

From the outset it was obvious to everyone on our planning committee that there was something significant at stake (for those attending? for those sponsoring? for those participating?), depending on how the one-day workshop was conceived, structured, and advertised; what was particularly interesting was that so much hinged on the category "religion"—whether anticipating possible evangelical Christian responses or addressing pro-Israeli student concerns. But surely it comes as no surprise that much hangs on the question of classification—what Pierre Bourdieu simply but significantly termed the struggle to have power over words (1987: 14). For classification matters; as recently observed by the US humorist, David Sedaris, recalling how his childhood neighbors, who had been away for Halloween one year, arrived at their door in costumes asking for treats a day late: "Asking for candy on Halloween was called trick or treating, but asking for candy on November 1st was called begging" (2003: 51).

For example, consider how Islam—much like every other world religion, by the way—was portrayed in an introductory book that was suggested for the students in our workshop to read:

> If the *principles of Islam* were followed, every Muslim would treat every other Muslim like a brother; in fact, they have been attacking one another almost since the founding of the faith. (Lippman [1982] 1995: ix; emphasis added)

Or, as Frederick Denny observes in the concluding lines to his introductory textbook:

> Muslims *true to their calling* should continue to invite others to the Straight Path and to hope for a day when all humans will celebrate their brother- and sisterhood in a worldwide *Umma*, reflecting God's Unity in human religious unity and harmony . . . (1987: 127; emphasis added)

It is obvious from the above quotations that a stable, authentic, and thus supremely normative, originary point exists—the heart of Islam, as some books refer to it—presumably communicated across the chasms of historical change through the mediation of disembodied meanings encoded within scripture and commentary (in a word, tradition). Such tradition—when read closely and interpreted correctly—serves as a criterion by which to judge contemporary, fractious cultural practices. In this way, one can accomplish the trick of distinguishing peaceful and authentic orthodoxy ("principles" or a "calling") from dangerous, contemporary aberrations.

And just what does this essence, the principle, of Islam end up looking like? As stated clearly in the preface to Lippman's book, his aim is to distinguish the inclusivist and quietist principles of Islam conceived as a faith from the common "misconceptions and misinformation" ([1982] 1995: x), so as to counter the daily images we see in the US of so-called militants, guerrillas, terrorists, and extremists. Denny's closing words clearly advocate recovering the supposed origin's unambiguous drive toward a similarly liberal, inclusive tradition that outlives all so-called parochial differences. Is it merely a coincidence that authentic Islam ends up looking an awful lot like yet another personal choice in the so-called free market? As phrased by one commentator: "The challenge of the future can only be faced by an Islamic worldview that embraces diversity, equality of the sexes, and the freedom, not only to be right, but also to be wrong"—so writes Vincent Cornell, himself a Muslim and the Director of the King Fahd Center for Middle East and Islamic Studies at the University of Arkansas, in a post-September 11 essay collection entitled *Dissent from the Homeland*. "Failure to meet the challenges of a diverse, multicentered, and religiously pluralistic world," he adds, "will ultimately lead to an Islam that is irrelevant to contemporary life, and might even herald the decline of Islam as a world religion" (2003: 93). After all, as he concludes: "People who appear uncivilized do not get invited into the community of nations" (2003: 92).

Because our workshop seems to have called its object of study the right thing—a religion—unlike asking for candy on the wrong day, our public event went off without a hitch. In fact, it was quite successful; despite this Latin-based term ("religion") and its modern derivations not really being at home in the context of a social movement that arose on the Arabian peninsula some 1,500 years ago, Islam was nonetheless a religion for us. And because of this, the presenters could utilize the well-known distinction between its timeless *principles*, on the one hand, and its sadly degraded forms of subsequent *practice*, on the other—what amounts to the old essence/manifestation distinction long favored by phenomenologists of religion, but applied in this case to chronological time. In this way a specific sort of Islam was presented to the participants as normative while all others were easily relegated to the status of either aberration or degradation. The task for scholars who employ such devices, then, is to explain reasons for this deviance, rather than account for how they concocted the normative standard by means of which they categorized certain behaviors *as* deviant.

For instance, consider whether the September 11 hijackers—as suggested by at least one scholar of religion, Ivan Strenski—"behave[d] according to very different rules of rationality than those who are profit or power maximizing in a cost–benefit calculus of a political or economic sort" (2002: 429). On one level, this line of argumentation—which presupposes that so-called religious people operate by means of some set apart rationality—seems perfectly sensible; yet, as argued by the French scholar of religion Daniel Dubuisson, "the principles of this 'religious reason' [that scholars try to understand in their cross-cultural studies] are obvious only because they previously shaped an important part of our own intellectual instrumentation and our most intimate ways of thinking. The notions that we so willingly see as transcendental, aprioristic, or original are almost always those that are most deeply buried in our own cultural memory" ([1998] 2003: 198)—which makes such principles of explanation particularly appealing to trot out when trying to account for what strikes us as other people's anomalous behaviors. However, on another level, such explanations, when such explanations are offered by scholars, leave me utterly puzzled, for I do not understand how a scholar can see any human behaviors as *not* part of a complex, historically based calculus concerning how actors understand negotiations over power and privilege (i.e., politics) to be connected to the manner in which people negotiate clashes between systems of value and exchange (i.e., economics), as well as organization (sociology), and the manner in which they authorize this series of connections by appeals to rhetorics that involve such invisible agents as gods, destiny, the free market, rationality, common sense, or human nature. To my way of thinking, one need have no sympathy or affinity whatsoever for such actors' motives or actions to be able to understand that calling their actions religious, guided by principles and faith, and thus the result of "different rules of rationality," is merely a form of obscurantism that shelves, rather than addresses, the matters of most importance in the study of how matters of difference are negotiated and contested in daily life.

Instead, why not shift the ground a bit and study this and other such conflicts in terms of how historically situated groups draw on competing sets of discursive markers to authorize their all too practical and obviously conflicting socio-political interests? Such a shift entails seeing such classificatory tools as sacred/secular or Church/State as ways some groups make it possible to plot, delineate, demarcate, and rank membership, all of which are some of the many ways that human beings make habitable cognitive and social worlds possible and—to their peers, at least—persuasive. As the anthropologist Mary Douglas phrased it in the introduction to her influential study of classification, a basic presumption of this alternative approach is that such systems of distinction, and the punishments that attend their transgression, "have as their main function to impose system on an inherently untidy experience" ([1966] 1991: 4).

Before proceeding further, an important point needs to be made explicit regarding the metaphysics of presence entailed in groups' efforts to tidy up their collective experiences and realize their various interests. The specific effort to tidy experience that I have in mind is our widespread scholarly use of the term "religion," and the common presumption that it designates a private site of inner experience and sentiment. For example, that our Latin-based classification "religion" finds no equivalent in Arabic seems not to prevent well-meaning scholars—who otherwise lament the way some scholars trample over what they consider to be authentic, indigenous meanings that require respectful treatment—from calling Islam a religion. In fact, the Arabic term *dīn* is routinely translated as religion. But, as argued in *The Encyclopaedia of Islam*, the etymology of *dīn* involves three separate lines: (1) a Hebraeo-Arabic origin meaning "judgment" or "retribution"; (2) an Arabic root meaning "a debt" or "money owing" that comes to mean "custom" or "usage"; and, finally (3) a Pahlevi (i.e., Middle Persian) linguistic origin meaning "revelation" that is therefore translatable as "religion." Disagreeing with the first and third etymologies, the article's author makes a persuasive case for considering *dīn* to develop from the notion of a debt that must be settled on a specific date, which in turn leads to such successive usages as: the idea of properly following an established custom of settling debts; the act of guiding one in a prescribed direction; the act of judging whether such a prescription has in fact been followed; visiting retribution upon one who has failed to follow the required path (see Lewis, Pellat, and Schacht 1965: 293–6). As such, *yawm al-dīn*, or "Day of Judgment," therefore comes to signify the day when Allah gives direction to all human beings. So, much as with the relation between the geographic and prescriptive senses of such English words as "direction" and "directive," we see here a gradual conflation of social exchange and social status with geographic movement and, eventually, with rules of propriety. Accordingly, *dīn* eventually moves from the more narrow sense of a debt to be discharged to being a term that stands in for "the body of obligatory prescriptions to which one must submit" (Lewis et al. 1965: 293).[5]

Therefore, it is rather misleading to suggest, as does one reference resource, that *dīn* is "*employed to mean* a religion together with its practices in general" (Glassé 1989: 99; emphasis added). Although italicizing this suggestion of intentionality may be too fine a nuance, *dīn* is not "employed to mean a religion"—as if early Arabic users were hunting for a local equivalent for what some of us now take to be the obviously universal concept that lurks deep within the human heart; instead, it is translated by contemporary English speakers by means of their local word, religion. What's more, if the above etymology is persuasive, then there is a great deal lost in this translation, for "the concept indicated by *dīn* does not exactly coincide with the ordinary concept of 'religion' precisely because of the semantic conception of the word" (Lewis et al. 1965: 293).

Just what is lost is significant. For instance, consider a modern translation of the Qur'an's famous *Sura 5.3*:

> Today I have perfected your system of belief
> and bestowed My favours upon you in full,
> and have chosen submission (al-Islam) as the creed for you. (Ali [1984] 1988: 98)

Or, as phrased in another popular translation of the Qur'an:

> The day I have perfected your religion for you and completed My

favour to you. I have chosen Islam to be your faith. (Dawood [1956]
1983: 387)

Both "system of belief" and "creed" in the first, and "religion" and "faith"
in the second, are, it turns out, English renderings of *dīn*, locking the
Arabic term within a discourse on inner sentiment and individual choice
concerning a series of systematically related propositions (i.e., a creed that
expresses a meaning with which one either does or does not agree). Nothing could be further from the complex social, transactional basis of the
concept.

But perhaps such problems with translation are to be expected, at least
with N. J. Dawood's popular edition of the English language Qur'an—the
first translation of the Arabic text into English idiom which, according to
its publisher, has sold over one million copies since it was first published
in 1956. (This sales figure alone should suffice to quiet those readers who
might dismiss my use of this edition as one of the above examples, since
they might see it as not being scholarly enough to take seriously.[6]) After
all, in the earlier editions of this translation, "the traditional arrangement
[of its chapters] has been abandoned" (1956: 11; more recent editions
have reverted to the so-called traditional order of revelations), since it
is aimed at the "uninitiated [i.e., Christian?] reader." Therefore, his version places the "more Biblical and poetic revelations" at the beginning
and then ends with "the much longer, and often more topical, chapters."
Given the uproar with which some Christians greeted inclusive language
Bibles, one can only imagine how many Christians would react to a version of the Bible that had its chapters rearranged, to make it easier on
novice readers.[7] Perhaps this is analogous to the understandable ways in
which Jewish people respond to being told by Christians that their text is
the "old testament" that has been fulfilled and thereby supplanted by one
that is new and improved.

Although "[t]hese few remarks cast some light on and perhaps over-
simplify the difficulties encountered in translating the *dīn* of Kur'anic
[sic] verses into Western languages" (Lewis et al. 1965: 293–4), we see
that, much like the ancient Greek concept *eusebia*, or the later Latin
pietas—terms that once signified a social value in antiquity that one was
thought to possess if one properly negotiated a complex social world of
differing ranks and competing entitlements—a concept of obvious public
rank and social relationship (i.e., being in another's debt) has eventually
come to be sentimentalized as a matter of inner faith, belief, opinion, and
judgment. Because other authors have drawn attention to this process—
what we might call the modernist sentimentalization of classical piety
(e.g., see Smith 1998: 271)—it should suffice for me simply to present
only one additional example of how historically situated relationships of
contest and difference are easily minimized by means of this rhetoric of
individual belief and experience along with the metaphysics that attends

"religion" discourses. So, consider the nifty tricks that we find in the opening pages of a recent co-written textbook, *World Religions Today* (Esposito, Fasching, and Lewis 2002). In a section of the Introduction entitled "Understanding Religious Experience and its Expressions," the authors draw attention to the etymology of the technical term, "religion," by asking readers to picture themselves time traveling to ancient Rome and asking someone on the street: "What religion are you?" Although the spirits of some authors might be dampened after acknowledging that people in antiquity did not talk like this at all, much less speak English, they nonetheless press on with their thought experiment: "Frustrated, you try rephrasing your question and ask: 'Are you religious?' Suddenly their faces light up and they smile and say, 'Of course, isn't everyone?'" (2002: 5).

Despite this example striking me as having something remarkably in common with the stereotypical paternalism of some English speakers who think that if they merely spoke loudly and slowly enough foreigners would understand them (i.e., "Are you R-E-L-I-G-I-O-U-S?"), there is something more that we can take away from this story of time travel. For in the process of granting the inevitable historicity, contingency, and thus contestability of our terminology (i.e., demonstrating that the modern word religion derives from ancient Latin words, though the precise etymology is unclear; these authors favor *religare*, meaning to bind or tie something, along with the root *ligere*, meaning to act with great care or pay particularly close attention[8]), they nonetheless presuppose that the adjectival form of the modern word—which names not "something you join" but, instead, "a way of seeing, acting, and *experiencing* things" (2002: 5; emphasis added)—is necessarily a universal signifier. For, in concluding that "people [in antiquity or outside the orbit of Latin-influenced modern languages and cultures] did not think of what they did as 'a religion'—a separate reality one had to choose over against another" (2002: 5), the authors yet presume that the words "religion" and "religious" name some deeply human(e), interior disposition. In fact, it is not just any old disposition but, quite possibly, the most authentically human thing of all. For, as they conclude:

> Religion as a form of human experience and behavior, therefore, is not just about purely "spiritual" things. Religion is not just about gods or God. People's religiousness is as diverse as the forms of power they believe govern their destiny, whether it be the gods as forces of nature, or wealth, or political power, or the forces of history. Religious attitudes in the modern world can be discerned in what many people would consider purely secular and very "unspiritual" attitudes and behaviors in relation to power. Hence, whatever powers we believe govern our destiny will elicit a religious response from us and inspire us to wish "to tie or bind" ourselves to these powers . . . (2002: 7)

Apparently, everyone is religious—much as everyone apparently understands English if spoken slowly enough—whether they know it or not, and whether or not "religion" is part of their conceptual tool box.

The trick here is akin to what hucksters once called the old "bait and switch"; for in the midst of acknowledging the historicity of their terminology these authors nonetheless assert that behind the changeable word there lurks an enduring, universal presence or meaning that transcends time and place. What they offer with one hand (i.e., careful scholarly attention to the historicity of our objects of study) is swiftly removed by the other (i.e., the presumption that words correspond to timeless concepts and universal meanings); understandably, their readers are left confident that behind the merely transitory appearances of their mundane, daily lives there resides an enduring permanence that is not only theirs, for it is lodged deep within the immutable confines of trans-human experience. (It is difficult not to read in this the kind of self-importance that we find both on US bumper stickers, in which everyone's child is now apparently on their school's honor roll, as well as in the so-called New Age penchant for recovering past lives in which everyone was undoubtedly someone far more important than they are in this life.)

Unfortunately, due to their philosophically idealist presumptions, such writers do not take seriously that words *and* concepts (i.e., signifiers *and* signifieds) are both arbitrary, and thus changeable, historical artifacts; they therefore give the lie to the historian of antiquity Peter Brown's thoughtful words: "A little history puts one firmly back in one's place." For in their case, doing only *a little history* apparently frees them significantly *from* their place! As Brown goes on to remark in his American Council of Learned Societies (ACLS) 2003 Haskins Lecture, taking history seriously

> counters the amiable tendency of learned persons to think of themselves as if they were hang-gliders, hovering silently and with Olympian ease above their field, as it has come to spread out beneath them over the years. But real life, one knows, has not been like this. We are not hang-gliders. We are in no way different from the historical figures whom we study in the distant past: we are embodied human beings caught in the unrelenting particularity of space and time. (2003: 3)

That the terrain mapped by such amiable, high-flying scholars ends up looking an awful lot like what they either need it to look like or assumed it would look like long before donning their flight suits—a point convincingly demonstrated by Berg (2000) in his study of scholarly efforts to ascertain the authenticity of hadith (i.e., the authoritative collection of sayings attributed to the Prophet) as well as the above survey of scholarship on authentic Islam—is therefore not a coincidence. Such scholars would therefore be wise to consider the caution of Dubuisson, writing on the history of the classification "religion":

> Although it is fortunate that cultures mutually translate themselves and try in this fashion to understand one another somewhat better, we should not conclude that what we translate into European languages, and because we translate it without any too great difficulty, refers back to universals to which we have the key. ([1998] 2003: 197)

Somewhat reminiscent of Jonathan Z. Smith, who advises scholars of religion to be "relentlessly self-conscious" of their choices and analytic tools—going so far as to suggest that "this self-consciousness constitutes his primary expertise, his foremost object of study" (1982: xi)—Dubuisson concludes: "All scientific study today ought to have as its sine qua non the critical uncompromising study of its own language" ([1998] 2003: 197).

Apart from sheer assertion, I am not sure how one would ever provide evidence to mount a persuasive argument concerning the fact that elements of one's own conceptual framework are universal or that one specific set of elements from a complex, worldwide mass movement is its authentic heart. Failing to recognize that one can never get outside language and conventions, many authors are playing with loaded dice, since they set up their argument by presupposing that English is a universal language, that time travel exists, or that one aspect of a mass movement is any more authoritative than another—all of which are forms of historical hang-gliding that bypass taking historical difference and contest seriously.

Yet as troubling as such forms of argumentation are—if "argumentation" is even the right word to describe them—it was precisely this asserted metaphysics of enduring presence that helped to make our workshop in Tuscaloosa an uncontroversial success. For it confirmed everyone's presumptions concerning the normalcy of their world and the exoticness of all others who failed to play by the free market's commonsense rules. Much like the apparently private sphere created by vodka, it is just this metaphysic that enables members of competing social formations to concoct compliant allies who keep their differences buried deeply within their voluntary organizations where they are free to give voice to their faiths; and it is just this metaphysic that enables us to understand those who fail to have the good manners to disengage their seemingly private beliefs from their public actions as dangerous enemies who commit the unforgivable sin of expressing their dissent in organized action.

Pick up virtually any of the post-September 11 books on Islam and you will find the rhetorics of faith and privacy doing this trick, providing a treat for readers who are looking for an authentic heart that does not collide with their own interests.[9]

Notes

1   According to Nemtsov (2002), the mid- to late-1980s anti-alcohol campaign of Gorbachev's Soviet government reduced annual per capita alcohol consumption and decreased all mortalities due to alcohol (e.g., not just poisoning but also accidents caused by impairment, etc.) from 1161.6 per 100,000 people to 1054. Despite estimating that, between 1986 and 1991, 1.22 million lives were therefore saved, in 1994 alone there was a total of 751,000 alcohol-related deaths.

2   As reported by Erofeyev; to determine the contemporary value in dollars I have used *Comecon Data*, produced by the Vienna Institute for Comparative Economic Studies (London: Macmillan, 1989), 383; according to this resource, the conversion factor for imports/exports lists one ruble in 1975 as being equivalent to US \$1.3862. I also used the *Consumer Price Index* for 1975 (http://oregonstate.edu/Dept/pol_sci/fac/sahr/cv2003.pdf), which uses a factor of 0.293 to convert US\$1 in 1975 to \$3.413 in 2003.

3   Of course, just what gets to constitute normative Islam (let alone the normative form of any mass movement) and hence the standard against which any particular understanding can be judged a *mis*-understanding, is *the* question.

4   Lewis certainly follows Samuel Huntington in this regard. For instance, in Lewis' *What Went Wrong? The Clash Between Islam and Modernity in the Middle East* ([2002] 2003) there are only three page references under "religion" in the index (though four appear under "persecution, religious"). In fact, the trouble with this civilization, at least according to such overly ambitious writers as Lewis, is that the religion/politics distinction that apparently lies at the heart of Christianity—"render unto Caesar the things which are Caesar's; and unto God the things which are God's" (Matthew 22:21)—is absent in Islam (see Lewis [2003] 2004: 5–7; see also [2002] 2003: 97). In assuming that the spheres named as religion and politics are ontologically distinct realms, writers such as Lewis fail to entertain that such Bible passages provide the social theorist with artifacts that constitute what I have elsewhere described as "a fascinating study in tactical, emergent social engineering" whereby "marginal or emergent social formations . . . carve out a zone in which to exist" ([2002] 2003: 272).

5   Although he argues that *dīn* refers to "the external forms this religion [i.e., Islam] took in combining worldly action with religious inspiration and thought" (2003: 106), Waardenburg's survey of the historical uses of the term is worth considering (2003: 101–7).

6   In fact, this is the manner in which *dīn* is almost always translated—in older as well as modern editions. See, for example, the English translation by Fakhry ([2000] 2002) and the French translation by Blanchère (1966).

7   Despite its mission to spread the word of the Christian God to the nations, I assume that the American Bible Society (ABS) seeks merely to translate the Bible into foreign languages and not to reorganize the text in a fashion more appealing to novice readers.

8   Although his work is but another example of the troublesome metaphysics of presence we find in this field, those interested in the etymology of religion would do well to consult chapter 2 of Wilfred Cantwell Smith's 1962 classic, *The Meaning and End of Religion* ([1962] 1991; notably, chapter 2, "'Religion' in the West"). Other relevant English language resources on the history of "religion" range from W. Warde Fowler's early work (e.g., 1908: 169–75 and [1909] 1933: 319–52) to Toomey (1954) and Smith (1998).

9   This chapter is based on chapter 3 of McCutcheon 2004a, which draws upon work published in McCutcheon 2004b.

References and further reading

Ali, Ahmed, trans. [1984] 1988. *Al-Qur'ān: A Contemporary Translation*. Princeton, NJ: Princeton University Press.

Berg, Herbert. 2000. *The Development of Exegesis in Early Islam: The Authenticity of Muslim Literature from the Formative Period*. Richmond, Surrey: Curzon.

Blanchère, Régis, trans. 1966. *Le Coran (al-Qor'ân)*. Paris: G.-P. Maisonneuve & Larose.

Bourdieu, Pierre. 1987. "What Makes a Social Class? On the Theoretical and Practical Existence of Groups." *Berkeley Journal of Sociology* 37: 1–17.

Brown, Peter. 2003. *A Life of Learning*. American Council of Learned Societies Occasional Paper Series, no. 55. New York: ACLS.

Cornell, Vincent J. 2003. "A Muslim to Muslims: Reflections after September 11." In Hauerwas, Stanley and Frank Lentricchia, *Dissent from the Homeland: Essays After September 11*, 83–94. Durham, NC: Duke University Press.

Dawood, N. J., trans. [1956] 1983. *The Koran*. London and New York: Penguin Books.

Denny, Frederick M. 1987. *Islam and the Muslim Community*. San Francisco: Harper San Francisco.

Douglas, Mary. [1966] 1991. *Purity and Danger: An Analysis of the Concepts of Pollution and Taboo*. London and New York: Routledge.

Dubuisson, Daniel. [1998] 2003. *The Western Construction of Religion: Myths, Knowledge, and Ideology*. Trans. William Sayers. Baltimore, MD and London: Johns Hopkins University Press.

Erofeyev, Victor. 2002. "The Russian God." *The New Yorker*, December 16: 56–63.

Esposito, John L., Darrell J. Fasching, and Todd Lewis. 2002. *World Religions Today*. New York: Oxford University Press.

Fakhry, Majid, trans. [2000] 2002. *An Interpretation of the Qur'an. English Translation of the Meaning. A Bilingual Edition*. Washington Square, NY: New York University Press.

Fowler, W. Warde. 1908. "The Latin History of the Word 'Religio'." In *Transactions of the Third International Congress for the History of Religions*, vol. 2, 169–75. Oxford: The Clarendon Press.

——. [1909] 1933. *Social Life at Rome in the Age of Cicero*. New York: The Macmillan Company.

Glassé, Cyril. 1989. *The Concise Encyclopedia of Islam*. Intro. by Huston Smith. San Francisco: Harper and Row.

Lewis, Bernard. [2002] 2003. *What Went Wrong? The Clash Between Islam and Modernity in the Middle East*. New York: Perennial.

——. [2003] 2004. *The Crisis of Islam: Holy War and Unholy Terror*. New York: Random House.

Lewis, B., Ch. Pellat, and J. Schacht, eds. 1965. *The Encyclopaedia of Islam*. New edn. Vol. II, C–G. Leiden: E. J. Brill.

Lippman, Thomas W. [1982] 1995. *Understanding Islam: An Introduction to the Muslim World*. New York: Meridian.

McCutcheon, Russell T. 2003. *The Discipline of Religion: Structure, Meaning, Rhetoric*. London and New York: Routledge.

——. 2004a. *"Religion" and the Domestication of Dissent, or How to Live in a Less than Perfect Nation*. London: Equinox Publishing.

——. 2004b. "'Religion' and the Governable Self." *Method & Theory in the Study of Religion* 16 (2): 164–81.

Musil, Robert. [1952] 1996 . *The Man Without Qualities*. Vol. 1. Trans. Sophie Wilkins. New York: Vintage International.

Nemtsov, A. V. 2002. "Alcohol-related Human Losses in Russia in the 1980s and 1990s." *Addiction* 97 (11): 1413–25.

Sedaris, David. 2003. "Tricked." *The New Yorker*, November 3: 50–3.

Sells, Michael, trans. and intro. 1999. *Approaching the Qur'an: The Early Revelations*. Ashland, OR: White Cloud.

Smith, Jonathan Z. 1982. *Imagining Religion: From Babylon to Jonestown*. Chicago: University of Chicago Press.

——. 1998. "Religion, Religions, Religious." In *Critical Terms for Religious Studies*, edited by Mark C. Taylor, 269–84. Chicago: University of Chicago Press.

Smith, Wilfred Cantwell. [1962] 1991. *The Meaning and End of Religion*. Foreword by John Hick. Minneapolis, MN: Fortress Press.

Strenski, Ivan. 2002. "Review of R. McCutcheon, *Critics Not Caretakers*." *Journal of the American Academy of Religion* 70 (2): 427–30.

Toomey, Wilt Henry. 1954. *Religio: A Semantic Study of the Pre-Christian Use of the Terms Religio and Religiosus*. PhD dissertation, Columbia University. Ann Arbor, MI: UMI Dissertation Services.

Waardenburg, Jacques. 2003. *Muslims and Others: Relations in Context*. Berlin and New York: Walter de Gruyter.

6 Discussion

Rhetorical reflections

Anna S. King

The authors in this section are concerned with public discourse post-9/11 —not with the neo-colonialist policies of the USA or the self-perceptions of hijackers or the wider Muslim world, but with the power of rhetoric to justify and distort, and above all to aid the pursuit of self-interest. These chapters, therefore, act as counterpoint to a growing literature which focuses on militarist and extremist versions of Islam. The authors challenge particularly the framework and binary language within which American public religious discourse constructs reality. Highlighting the centrality of narrative to all human activity and communication, they seek to sensitize the reader to the very rapid emergence of manipulative, violent, and coercive narratives in the USA in the post-September 11 context. The common theme is an uncompromising critique of hegemonic religious/theological narratives; narratives which, when deconstructed, are shown to obfuscate, contain, marginalize, and destroy alternative narratives. The authors concur that American religious public utterances in the wake of 9/11 are specifically designed to marginalize active political dissent and opposition. They also agree that religious rhetoric can become the vehicle of state ideology, and that the political rhetorics of "religion" and "faith" can be understood as forms of social engineering and techniques of governance. Paul Johnson's critique focuses on the violence of American instrumental civil religion, revisioned as ideology which reduces internal dissent by directing symbolic and actual violence against national and religious "outsiders." Caryn Riswold analyzes the nature of evil and the failure of President George W. Bush's rhetoric to understand or adequately address its complexity. Russell T. McCutcheon in the final chapter attacks as dangerous the academic and media privatization and domestication of "religion." "There is nothing private about the rhetoric of faith." McCutcheon tells us the parable of Russian vodka, a "virtually invisible elixir," which appears to provide access to a private life that is closed to the state, but turns out to have huge public and collective consequences. Religion, like vodka, offers no escape from the historical, the public, and the collective.

The authors come from very different perspectives and disciplines.

Paul Johnson's chapter is the longest, possibly the most complex and certainly the most challenging to summarize. He begins with the sobering reflection that the decision to wage war against Iraq was not inevitable, and the fact that it came to seem so was due to the strategic success of agents of the state. He asks how that consensus was achieved, and his whole chapter is a quest for answers.

Part one provides an introduction to the chapter as a whole. It begins with a critique of the concept of civil religion "in order to resurrect it as a particularly powerful form of ideology." Readers are introduced to two forms of civil religious response to the events of 9/11. The first, which Johnson calls *instrumental civil religion*, emerges in the narrations of President George W. Bush; the second, *organic civil religion*, emerges in the ashes and mud of Ground Zero. Johnson, with a nod to Marett and Lévi-Strauss, refers to such organic civil religion as "savage" in the sense that meaning becomes explicit only secondarily, in so far as it is danced, dressed, eaten or built into existence. Following Lévi-Strauss, Johnson refers to it as bricolage, the science of the concrete. As a response to 9/11 it manifests an undetermined quality as spontaneous practice.

Part two traces the history of the idea of civil religion from Rousseau to Durkheim, Gramsci, Lévi-Strauss, and Bellah. The definition Johnson advocates melds politics and religion: "[C]ivil religion is not inevitably present but rather occurs when nation-state narratives are fused with religious narratives—often themselves regarded as timelessly authoritative—of transcendent beings like gods, spirits and ancestors." Parts three and four deal with empirical case studies which manifest the distinction between civil religion as popular practice and civil religion as spectacle. Johnson's method here is to compare the spontaneous and inclusive altars erected around Ground Zero with official presidential speeches. Johnson's analysis of the President's speeches as instrumental civil religion is acute. He observes that the post-9/11 Bush speeches often began by invoking the immediacy and force of organic civil religion, then casting the world in the strongest possible binary terms: us/them, good/evil, civilization/barbarism, real religion/blasphemy, which were discursively linked either obliquely or explicitly to transcendent authority. The fight against evil, cast in apocalyptic terms, became a leitmotiv of official speeches. The showdown between good and evil, with the "axis of evil" invoked in the State of the Union address several months later (January 29, 2002), was America's calling, in a mission divinely mandated and with ultimate consequences.

Part five assesses the relation between the two forms of civil religion as one of "symbolic hijacking toward the destination of the national rationalization . . . of state-sanctioned violence." Johnson observes that the transition from popular practice to official speech, from organic to instrumental religion, need not have implied a politically conservative or bellicose shift. Yet, he comes to the conclusion that in the vast majority of cases of discourse presented by agents of the US state since 9/11, the process of ideological distillation *was* violent, and its strategic objective was the instrumental one of generating popular support for war. Civil religion assumed violent forms. Johnson claims that the key narratives of American instrumental civil religion in the wake of "9/11 comprised a discourse community of violence": "As the discourse of violence grew, physical violence became itself a kind of ritual practice, a symbolic and interpretative discourse, a 'semio-technique' through which 'Iraq' was represented and interpolated into the US cultural repertoire precisely through its destruction." American spectators and readers became members of an imagined community, consuming the same edited images and reacting to them similarly. The event of 9/11 and the "war on terrorism" became a "meta-fictional funnel" through which all information was siphoned. The world was revisioned "as a field of endless battles, reproduced in state spectacles, cinema and endless television updates where, larger than life, its truth value was rendered nearly irresistible."

Johnson ends with a powerful restatement of his argument. Civil religion *can* "undergird the social contract" (organic civil religion), but it can also legitimate violence. It can provide the set of strategies and discursive tools for what Johnson calls "the fundamental ideological move": the rigid distinction between "me" and "other." "If organic religion is 'savage' in its materiality, instrumental civil religion savages, in so far as it promulgates and naturalizes binary social classifications, affixes such classifications to transcendent terms, and spectacularizes and mythologizes state policy as salvific drama."

Caryn Riswold's more theological chapter, "The Rhetoric of Evil and Eradicating Terrorism," similarly employs critical discourse analysis of President George W. Bush's presidential addresses after 9/11. She argues that in George Bush's public discourses and elsewhere we find selectiveness in representing the Christian tradition and an intolerance of contrary voices. She asserts that the addresses shaped by George W. Bush's narrow Christian views of God, good and evil, and American privilege, led to a dangerous mingling of politics, theology, and military action. Bush's claims to chosen rightness, certainty, and the will of God make the assumption that the war against terror was sanctioned by God. Yet such rhetoric ignored the will of vast numbers of fellow American citizens and the mighty force of religious leaders on the other side. It failed to draw on "universally accepted religious views."

In the second section of her essay Riswold argues that the reality of evil in the world is complex, and that the White House responses to the evil of 9/11 were deeply problematic and misguided. From Susan Neiman she learns that evil cannot be fully defined. Sometimes intentions are clearly evil, sometimes they are good; often they are simply banal. From Wendy Farley she understands that the world is tragically structured, evil is an inevitable part of the world, radical suffering is never justified, and we are left to struggle in concert with a compassionate God, continuously resisting evil as it emerges. Armed with these resources, Riswold turns again to consider President Bush's rhetoric. She now confidently asserts that chosen rightness is not so easily determined, that certainty of success cannot be assumed and that discerning the will of God is the ultimate unlikely task.

Riswold argues that it is in fact only by understanding the dangerous and complex nature of the world that we become equipped to confront it, to transform it, and to resist it. What then should we do? The first step is to understand President Bush's ideology. The greater task is to multiply and diversify our ethically constitutive stories and engage in work that enables others to do just that. Riswold concludes by arguing that the rhetoric of evil in which President George W. Bush engages is inadequate and inappropriate for the work of eradicating terrorism: "We need more questions, answers, and leaders capable of engaging in the 'intellectual avatars of complexity and doubt' (Fineman 2003: 29) that this president seems to loathe. Understanding the complex nature of the reality of evil leads not to a cynical abandonment of hope, rather to honest assessment of the enormous task involved in fighting evil, in waging war on terrorism, and in discerning the will of a gracious God. It leaves us to find real means by which we can humbly engage in the work of resistance to it in places as mundane as the college classroom."

McCutcheon's chapter is a clarion call for heightened awareness of the power of language, of the arbitrariness of words and concepts, and of the selectivity involved in all acts of narration. It is a powerful critique of all those who would relegate "religion" to the domain of private interiority and "essence." It offers a hard-hitting exposé of the tricksy ways in which the category "religion" with all its other binary pairings (sacred/secular, faith/doctrine, Church/State, etc.) is employed by "amiable, high-flying scholars" and others to prop up particular worldviews and de-authorize others. At the heart of his chapter is the deconstruction of "religion" as a category or taxon; a category which enables scholars and others to make the distinction between private religion/public civilization, and to portray Islam as a religion, a private site of inner experience and sentiment. "Religion" is used to domesticate, to tidy experience, and to divorce private beliefs from public actions. Thus McCutcheon finds that the humane intentions of scholars give rise to obscurantism—failure to understand that all human behaviors are part of a complex, humanly based calculus concerning how actors understand negotiations over power and privilege, clashes between systems of exchange as well as organization, and the manner in which they authorize this series of connections by appeal to rhetorics that involve invisible agents.

McCutcheon refers then, with mock bewilderment, to scholars who assume that a stable, authentic, and thus supremely normative, originary point exists which serves as a criterion by which to judge "contemporary, fractious cultural practices." He critiques the language of those scholars and media pundits who assume that words correspond to timeless concepts and universal meanings: "Failing to recognize that one can never get outside language and conventions, many authors are playing with loaded dice, since they set up their argument by presupposing that English is a universal language, that time travel exists, or that one aspect of a mass movement is any more authoritative than another . . . all of which are forms of historical hang-gliding that bypass taking historical difference and contest seriously." McCutcheon thus challenges all those who aim to distinguish the inclusivist and quietist principles of Islam conceived as a faith in order to counter the daily images seen in the United States of so-called militants, guerrillas, terrorists, and extremists. Their apparently liberal language is "tricky" precisely because it has the effect of categorizing certain behaviors as deviant. It normalizes one particular form of religion and distinguishes "peaceful" and "civil" from "dangerous" and "aberrant" forms of social organization. Islamic principles and "faith" are understood to be in opposition to so-called militant forms of Islam. Those who do not disengage their seemingly private beliefs from their public actions are classified as dangerous enemies who "commit the unforgivable sin of expressing their dissent in organized action." McCutcheon concludes with the words, "Pick up virtually any of the post-September 11 books on Islam and you will find the rhetorics of faith and privacy doing this trick, providing a treat for readers who are looking for an authentic heart that does not collide with their own interests."

This entire section therefore vividly warns us of the power of religious rhetoric to persuade with its oversimplified characterization of the battle of good against evil to the acceptance of inevitably violent responses to the catastrophic occurrences of 9/11. By its use of popular slogans and vivid images, and by tying its worldview to superficial evocations of Christian belief, such rhetoric allows no space for the exploration of alternative perspectives nor for the acknowledgment of the complexities of Islamic thought. This is not just a caution against the beguiling power of unexamined language, but also a warning that when this is itself tied to the authority and persuasiveness of state power, it can mislead us into accepting paths that will entail unpredictable and unpalatable consequences.

Theological reflections

7   A new paradigm of international relations?

Reflections after September 11, 2001[*]

Hans Küng

Many readers of my earlier books may be surprised by the present topic. I have chosen it *not only because* of the present political situation, but because it reflects the ultimate phase of my long odyssey in theology. It started in the fifties with *Justification*—the problems of Christian existence. Then it went on, in a rather consistent way:

- in the sixties with *The Church, The Council: Reform and Reunion* and *Infallible? An Inquiry*;
- in the seventies the new foundation of a Christian theology with *On being a Christian, Does God Exist?, Eternal Life?*;
- in the eighties (after the big clash with the Vatican) *Christianity and World Religions* and *World Peace*;
- culminating in the nineties with *Global Responsibility* and *Global Ethic for Global Politics and Economics* and in the first years of the new century with the new paradigm of international relations. I did not give up anything I have written, e.g., on being a Christian, but I *expanded constantly* the fields of my research.

Let me introduce my present topic by a little story:

Before I started my first American lecture tour in 1963, a Jewish colleague from America visited me in Tübingen and asked me: "What is the topic of your lectures?" My answer: "The Church and Freedom." "Very interesting," he said, with a charming smile. "I know that there's

---

[*] *Editors' note*: This essay was originally a special address given at the American Academy of Religion's annual meeting in Toronto, Ontario on November 25, 2002. We are pleased to include this special address, which was overwhelmingly attended and well received, in this volume. The importance of such a significant address by one of the world's leading theologians to the largest professional association of religious studies scholars warrants both its preservation and thus its inclusion in this volume. At Professor Küng's request we have kept the oral nature of the lecture and have not attempted to update the material addressed (which, obviously, only covers political developments up to November 2002).

a Church, and I know that there's freedom, but I didn't know that you could have the Church and freedom together!"

But now, nearly 40 years later, when I prepared my lectures for the United States this time, I was also asked about the topic and said: "America and the New Paradigm of International Relations." And the answer in Europe was: "We know that there is a new American President, and we know that there is a new paradigm, but we didn't know that you could have the American President and the new paradigm *together!*" And people asked me: "Why do you want to enter the lion's den?" But I survived a few weeks ago in Washington DC so I hope to survive also in Toronto, Canada.

In 1963 I was able to convince a few people that the church and freedom can go together. And I hope that in 2002 I shall also convince you that America and the new paradigm can go together. But let me now start in a very un-American way: from history.

I. Paradigm change in international relations

Let me begin with three symbolic dates that signal the new paradigm in international relations that is slowly and laboriously establishing itself: its announcement (1918), its realization (1945), and finally its breakthrough (1989).

First opportunity: 1918, the First World War ended with a net result of around 10 million dead, the collapse of the German Empire, the Habsburg Empire, the Tzarist Empire and the Ottoman Empire. The Chinese Empire had collapsed earlier. Now there were for the first time American troops on European soil and, on the other side, the Soviet Empire was in the making. This marked the beginning of the end of the Eurocentric-imperialistic paradigm of modernity and the dawning of a new paradigm. That new paradigm had not yet been defined, but had been foreseen by the far-sighted and enlightened thinkers, and was first set forth in the arena of international relations by the United States of America. With his "Fourteen Points," President Woodrow Wilson wanted to achieve a "just peace" and the "self-determination of the nations," without the annexations and demands for reparations which some in Congress wanted. President Wilson has been ignored too much in the United States and even denigrated by Henry Kissinger who often polemized against "Wilsonianism."

The Versailles Treaty of Clemenceau and Lloyd George prevented the immediate realization of the new paradigm. That was the *Realpolitik*, a word used first by Bismarck, but its ideology was developed by Machiavelli and it was for the first time put into political practice by Cardinal Richelieu. Instead of a just peace, there emerged a dictated peace in which the defeated nations took no part. The consequences of this approach are well known to you: Fascism and Nazism (backed up in the Far East by Japanese militarism) are the catastrophic reactionary errors which two decades later led to the Second World War, which was far worse than any previous war in world history.

Second opportunity: 1945 saw the end of the Second World War with a net result of around 50 million dead and many more million exiled. Fascism and Nazism had been defeated, but Soviet Communism appeared stronger and more formidable than ever to the international community, even though internally it was already experiencing a political, economic, and social crisis because of Stalin's policy.

Again, the initiative for a new paradigm came from the USA. In 1945 the United Nations was founded in San Francisco, and the Bretton Woods Agreement on the reordering of the global economy was signed (the foundation of the International Monetary Fund and the World Bank). Then in 1948 came the Universal Declaration of Human Rights, along with American economic aid (the Marshall Plan) for the rebuilding of Europe and its incorporation into a free trade system. But Stalinism blocked this paradigm for its sphere of influence and led to the division of the world into East and West.

Third opportunity: 1989 saw the successful peaceful revolution in Eastern Europe and the collapse of Soviet Communism. After the Gulf War it was again an American president who announced a new paradigm, a "new world order," and found enthusiastic acceptance all over the world with this slogan. But in contrast to his predecessor, Woodrow Wilson, President George H. W. Bush felt embarrassed when he had to explain what this "vision thing" for the international order should look like. No change in Iraq, no democracy in Kuwait, no solution for the Israeli–Palestinian conflict, no democratic change in other Arabian States. And in the present moment the doubts also in the United States increase that the so-called "war on terrorism" can be our vision for the future. So today the question arises: over the last decade, have we again forfeited the opportunity for a "new world order," a new paradigm?

I do not share this opinion. After all, despite the wars, massacres, and streams of refugees in the twentieth century, despite the Gulag archipelago, the Holocaust, the most inhuman crime in the history of humanity, and the atomic bomb, we must not overlook some major changes for the better. After 1945, not only has humanity seen numerous grandiose scientific and technological achievements, but many ideas set forth in 1918 that had been pressing for a new, postmodern and overall global constellation were able to better establish themselves. The peace movement, the women's rights movement, the environmental movement and the ecumenical movement all began to make considerable progress. There emerged a new attitude to war and disarmament, to the partnership of men and women, to the relationship between economy and ecology, among the Christian churches and the world religions. After 1989, following the end of the enforced division of the world into West and East and the definitive demystification of both the evolutionary and now also of the revolutionary ideology of progress, concrete possibilities for a pacified and cooperative world have begun to take shape. In contrast to European modernity, these possibilities are no longer Eurocentric but polycentric. Despite all the monstrous defects and conflicts still plaguing the international community, this new paradigm is post-imperialistic and postcolonial, with the ideals of an eco-social market economy and truly united nations at its core.

Despite the terrors of the twentieth century, there is "still perhaps something like a hesitant historical progress." Over the last century, the formerly dominant political orientations have been banished for good. For one, imperialism has no scope in global politics after de-colonialization. Moreover, since the end of the South African apartheid regime, racism, a consistent policy of racial privilege and racial discrimination, is no longer the explicit political strategy in any state. Likewise, in the lands of Western Europe from which it originated, nationalism has become a non-word and for many people is being replaced by "European integration."

II. The new paradigm for international relations

The movement now is toward a novel political model of regional cooperation and integration, and is attempting to peacefully overcome centuries of confrontation. The result, not only between Germany and France first, not only in the European Union, but in the whole area of the OECD (Organization for Economic Cooperation and Development, founded in 1948 and developed in 1960), including all of the Western industrialized countries (the European countries, the USA, Canada, Mexico, Australia, New Zealand and Japan), is half a century of democratic peace. That truly is a successful paradigm change! There are wars in Asia, Africa, South America and in the Islamic world (e.g., El Salvador, Guatemala, Nicaragua, Colombia, Israel–Palestine, Sudan, Yemen, Algeria, Persian Gulf, Bosnia, and Kosovo), but nobody could anymore imagine a war between Germany and France or the United States and Japan.

So after this all too brief historical tour I want to move to the fundamental definition of the new paradigm of international relations. I have received much stimulation and support in a discussion within the small international "group of eminent persons" which was convened by UN Secretary-General Kofi Annan for the UN year of "Dialogue of the Civilizations" 2001,[1] an endeavor which produced a report for the UN General Assembly, *Crossing the Divide. Dialogue Among Civilizations* (Aboulmagd et al. 2001).

On the basis of the experiences in the EU and the OECD, the new overall political constellation can be sketched briefly as follows. Here, ethical categories cannot be avoided. In principle, the new paradigm means policies of regional reconciliation, understanding, and cooperation instead of the modern national politics of self-interest, power, and prestige. Specifically, the exercise of political action now calls for reciprocal cooperation, compromise, and integration instead of the former confrontation, aggression, and revenge. This new overall political constellation manifestly presupposes a change of mentality, which goes far beyond the politics of the present day. For this new overall political constellation to hold, new approaches to international politics are needed.

For one, new international organizations are not enough here; what is needed is a new mindset. National, ethnic, and religious differences must no longer be understood, in principle, as a threat but rather as possible sources of enrichment. Whereas the old paradigm always presupposed an enemy, indeed a traditional enemy, the new paradigm no longer envisions or needs such an enemy. Rather, it seeks partners, rivals, and economic opponents for competition instead of military confrontation, and uses "soft" power (diplomatic influence and political persuasion, cultural influence and prestige) instead of "hard" military power.

This is so because it has been proven that in the long run national prosperity is not furthered by war but only by peace, not in opposition or confrontation but in cooperation. And because the different interests that exist are satisfied in collaboration, a policy is possible which is no longer a zero-sum game where one wins at the expense of the other, but a positive-sum game in which all win.

Of course this does not mean that politics has become easier in the new paradigm. It remains the "art of the possible," though it has now become nonviolent. If it is to be able to function, it cannot be based on a random "postmodernist" pluralism, where anything goes and anything is allowed. Rather, it presupposes a social consensus on particular basic values, basic rights, and basic responsibilities. All social groups and all nations must contribute to this basic social consensus, including religious believers and non-believers and members of the different philosophies or ideologies. In other words, this social consensus, which cannot be imposed by a democratic system but has to be presupposed, does not mean a specific ethical system, but a common minimum of ethical standards, a common ethic, an ethic of humankind. This global ethic is not a new ideology or "superstructure," imposed by the West on the "rest," but gathers together the common religious and philosophical resources of all of humankind, for instance the Golden Rule you find already in the Analects of Confucius: "What you do not wish done to yourself, do not do to others." And a few very basic directives you find everywhere in humanity: Not to murder, not to steal, not to lie, not to abuse sexuality.

A global ethic should not be imposed by law but be brought to public awareness. A global ethic is simultaneously oriented on persons, institutions, and results. To this degree, a global ethic does not just focus on the collective responsibility to the relief of any responsibility the individual may hold (as if only the social "conditions," "history," and the "system" were to blame for specific abuses and crimes). Instead, it is focused in a particular way on the responsibility of each individual in his or her place in society and specifically on the individual responsibility of political leaders.

Free commitment to a common ethic does not of course exclude the support of law but rather includes it, and can in some circumstances appeal to law. Such circumstances include cases of genocide, crimes against humanity, war crimes and aggression contrary to international law, as recently in former Yugoslavia. Meanwhile, following the ratification by more than 60 nations, the International Criminal Court (ICC) is now established to which such violations can be brought, specifically when a treaty state is unable or unwilling to inflict legal penalties for atrocities committed on its territory.

As you know, the United States, which was always in favor of international agreements and especially of the International Criminal Court, tried to sabotage it, together with Israel, China, and Russia. And therefore I come now to my third and for your ears probably the most delicate part, and I could easily and comfortably stop my lecture here or evade in my third part in generalities. I know of course that I am a foreigner, but I am not a stranger, having taught many semesters in American universities. I also know that I have not to give you advice on foreign policy but that you expect me to express my personal concerns, which are certainly shared by more and more American men and women and also by more and more columnists in the *New York Times* and the *Washington Post*. So I hope you will forgive me my frankness!

III. Opportunities after September 11

It is notorious that it is the new Bush administration which also opposes other important international agreements like the Kyoto agreement to reduce global warming, the Comprehensive Test Ban Treaty, the Anti-Ballistic Missile Treaty, the implementation of the Biological Weapons Treaty, etc. These are sad facts for all admirers of American democracy. The present administration of the only remaining superpower seems to many people not only in the Islamic world, but also in the Asian and African worlds and in Europe, to disrupt a policy in the new paradigm. So I cannot avoid comparing the new paradigm with the political reality after September 11, 2001, given that beyond any doubt the fight against terrorism had to be started and the monstrous crime in New York and in Washington could not remain un-atoned for. I had initially intended to entitle this part "Critical Questions after September 11," but I decided to reverse the perspective with the more hopeful title "Opportunities after September 11."

I shall not dwell on the question whether after September 11 there was a possible alternative to the Afghanistan scenario that we experienced. Let me make it clear: I was never and I shall never be an absolute pacifist. But on the other side also the fundamentalists of the Christian Right should know that, in the Christian tradition, war can never be the *ratio proxima*, but only the *ratio ultima* which needs a just cause (change of a dictatorial regime?), legitimate authority (the UN or US?), a reasonable chance for success, and a proportionate amount of force. Today pacifists and "just warriors" share a common moral assumption against a preemptive war on Iraq by the US; it undermines the civilized world's consensus against unprovoked trans-border aggression.

But now that we have this very questionable war, we must not allow anyone to forbid us to ask some questions. We have:

- A war which after more than one year has still not attained its primary objectives ("Osama bin Laden dead or alive"): the master terrorist is probably alive and plotting, and Afghanistan risks a descent into chaos—new tribal conflicts, the rule of the war lords, and banditry as in the period before Taliban rule; no, there is no peace in Afghanistan, nor the promised reconstruction. Many reasonable people all over the world doubt the value of invading Afghanistan, not to mention the wisdom of invading Iraq in the name of regime change. Indeed, attacking Iraq is likely to worsen the terrorist threat to Western countries. America is not threatened by nuclear, biological or chemical weapons of Iraqi origin, but by an Islamic radicalism which will be intensified by war with Iraq. Because no Arab country wants a totally US-dominated Middle East and a "friendly" Iraq under an American oil imperialism.
- A war in which European soldiers, too, become increasingly entangled in actions on the basis of "unlimited solidarity" and are possibly condemned to years of maintaining a presence and getting involved in clashes in the Hindukush with responsibility for the capital, Kabul; the battle against Islamic extremism is far from being over. Is it therefore good foreign policy to focus on Iraq before having finished the fight against Al Qaeda?

After the most recent experiences, the decisive question is more than ever: what international commitment are we to make? And should we simply continue the fight against terrorism in this style? Can armed forces solve the terrorist problem? Can a bigger NATO stop terrorism? And should European nations now furnish and finance what would amount to a "foreign legion" in the Pentagon service? My concern is not the alternatives of the past, but the alternatives of the future. Have we any alternatives at all, as long as foreign policy is above all military policy and billions are being spent on sinfully expensive new weapon systems and transport planes instead of on kindergartens, schools, healthcare, public services at home, and on fighting against poverty, hunger, and misery in the world? Are there still any opportunities at all for the new paradigm outside the OECD world as well?

I think that there are, and I want to indicate them cautiously: not with apparently certain predictions, but in the mode of "It could be that . . ." I shall do this in full awareness of all the real uncertainties of the future, which today often bring about fundamental changes more quickly than before, changes which are, however, not always for the worst—as we have seen in the changed attitude of the Bush administration regarding the United Nations. I shall adopt, so to speak, the realistic anti-Murphy principle: "What can go wrong need not always go wrong . . ." And as an admirer of the great American tradition of democracy and the demand for human rights, I would plead for peace—even in face of the campaign against terrorism which has to be not only a military, but also a political, economic, and cultural fight.

It could be that the present American administration, too, will realize that those who think that they can win the fight against evil all over the world are self-righteously condemning themselves to eternal war; that even the sole remaining superpower and a self-designated police force of the world can carry out a successful policy only if it does not act unilaterally in a high-handed way, but has real partners and friends, not satellites, practicing therefore the "humility" in dealing with other nations that George W. Bush promised before his election.

It could be that the United States, more shrewdly than former empires, will not over-extend its power and come to grief through megalomania, but will preserve its position of predominance by taking into account not only its own interest but also the interests of its partners. The attempt to organize a messy world to our liking, is hubris; and also for empires— remember the French, the British, the German, the Japanese, and the Russian empires—pride goes before the fall.

It could be that President Bush realizes that a US attempt to go to war—in the case of Iraq not a war of self-defense, but a war of free choice—on a flimsy basis, would jeopardize the domestic and international consensus so painstakingly assembled; the UN Security Council in the world of a single dominant superpower obviously became even more important, not less.

It could be that the Bush administration recognizes that the peace in Bosnia after seven years continues to depend on 12,000 foreign troops, and that peace-building in Iraq will be much harder and take much longer—a long-term occupation and nation-building that cannot be effectively pursued alone or under an exclusively US umbrella. Terrorism, not Iraq, remains the great fear of the moment.

It could be that Saddam Hussein swallows his pride and complies with the Security Council's decision, and in that case George W. Bush declares victory and calls off his invasion; he could show himself proud of a policy that ended with the nonviolent disarming of Iraq.

It could be that the American President, whose budget surplus has decreased in the past year by four trillion dollars and who in the future must again reckon with deficits, will once again reorient his budgetary policy and instead of being primarily concerned with military policy and oil, will be concerned with a more successful economic policy, which also has in view the potential for further Enron-style bankruptcies, Arthur Andersen crimes, stock market disasters and a recession and Wall Street crash which is still possible.

It could be that the present American administration, because it does not want to alienate the whole Islamic world, will take more interest in the causes of Arab and Muslim resentment toward the West and the United States in particular; that instead of being concerned only with the symptoms it will be more concerned with therapy for the social, economic, and political roots of terror; that instead of spending yet more billions for military and policing purposes it will devote more means to improving the social situation of the masses in its own country and those who lose out all over the world as a result of globalization.

It could be that the superpower USA would also act out of enlightened self-interest to prevent the international sense of law from being shaken, as it is when the only superpower sets different standards from those which apply generally in international law. By doing this it helps those powers which do not want to observe the standards of international law and precisely in this way encourages terrorism and the breakdown of international rules governing the use of force.

It could be—to say only one word on the Israeli–Palestinian conflict as the main source of terrorism—that a new majority of the Israeli people replaces leaders who provided Israelis with neither peace nor security but with an economy which teeters on ruin, and will elect more peace-minded political leaders with the vision and ability to lead the country out of the morass and—not without American pressure—take up the peace proposal put forward by the Saudi Arabian Crown Prince Abdullah, supported by the US, the EU, the UN and Russia: withdrawal from all occupied territories and recognition of the State of Israel by all Arab states, with normal political and economic relations. This would make possible an autonomous and viable (not dismembered) state of Palestine, preferably in an economic union with Israel and Jordan, which could be a real blessing for the whole region and especially for Israel.

Indeed, it could be that then even the radical Palestinians, who applied the same logic of violence, will stop their bloody terrorist activities, and that the Palestinians will realistically restrict their "right to return" to symbolic return for some particularly hard cases—in exchange for new settlements and financial compensation. In the long run, only the recognition by Israel will lead to a less authoritarian and corrupt and more democratic administration in Palestine.

Here particular demands would be made on the three prophetic religions, Judaism, Christianity, and Islam, not to support uncritically the official politics of their respective governments but to show their prophetic role:

- "Recompense no one evil with evil" (Romans 12:17). This New Testament saying is today addressed to those Christian crusaders in America and elsewhere who look for evil only in the other, thinking that a crusade hallows any military means and justifies all humanitarian "collateral damage."
- "An eye for an eye, a tooth for a tooth" (Exodus 21:24): this saying from the Hebrew Bible on the limitation of damage is addressed to those Israeli fanatics who prefer to take two eyes from their opponent instead of just one, and would like to knock out several teeth, forgetting that the perpetuation of "an eye for an eye makes the world go blind" (Gandhi).
- "And if they incline to peace, do thou incline to it" (*Sura* 8.61): this saying from the Qur'an is addressed to those Palestinian warriors of God who today would still like most of all to blot out the state of Israel from the map and try to sabotage all peace initiatives.

Conclusion

Peace among the religions is a presupposition of peace among the nations. Let me therefore conclude with a few elementary remarks on a Global Ethic, which in the age of globalization is more urgent than ever. Indeed, the globalization of the economy, technology, and communication needs also the globalization of ethic in coping with global problems. The two fundamental demands of the 1993 Chicago Declaration, confirmed by the third Parliament of the World's Religions in Cape Town 1999 and taken up in the manifesto *Crossing the Divide* for the United Nations Year of Dialogue among Civilizations, are the most elementary ones that can be made in this regard, yet it is by no means a matter of course.

The first is the Humanity Principle: the demand for true humanity. Now as before, women and men are treated inhumanly all over the world. "They are robbed of their opportunities and their freedom; their human rights are trampled underfoot; their dignity is disregarded. But might does not make right! In the face of all inhumanity our religious and ethical convictions demand that 'every human being must be treated humanly'" (Beversluis 2000: 177). This means that every human being—man or woman, white or colored, young or old, American or Afghan—has to be treated not in an inhuman, even bestial way, but in a truly human way.

The second fundamental demand is the Golden Rule: "There is a principle which is found and has persisted in many religious and ethical traditions of humankind for thousands of years: What you do not wish done to yourself, do not do to others . . . This should be the irrevocable, unconditional norm for all areas of life, for families and communities, for races, nations, and religions" (Beversluis 2000: 177).

On the basis of these two fundamental principles, four ethical directives, found in all the great traditions of humanity, have to be remembered:

- You shall not murder, torture, torment, wound; in positive terms: have reverence for life; a committment to a culture of nonviolence and reverence for life.
- You shall not lie, deceive, forge, manipulate; in positive terms: speak and act truthfully; a committment to a culture of truthfulness and tolerance.
- You shall not steal, exploit, bribe, corrupt; in positive terms: deal honestly and fairly; a commitment to a culture of fairness and a just economic order.
- You shall not abuse sexuality, cheat, humiliate, dishonor; in positive terms: respect and love one another; a commitment to a culture of partnership and equal dignity of men and women.

But let me conclude now: I started with the lack of vision after 1989. I hope it became clear what this vision really could be. It is not a vision of war—"Sweet is war only to those who do not know it" (Erasmus of Rotterdam, sixteenth-century humanist)—but a vision of peace. And I may summarize it in the following four propositions:

- There will be no peace among the nations without peace among the religions. There will be no peace among the religions without dialogue among the religions.
- There will be no dialogue among the religions without global ethical standards.
- There will therefore be no survival of this globe without a global ethic.

Note

1 Dr. A. Kamal Aboulmagd, Egypt; Dr. Lourdes Arizpe, Mexico; Dr. Hanan Ashrawi, Palestine; Dr. Ruth Cardoso, Brazil; The Honorable Jacques Delors, France; Dr. Leslie Gelb, United States of America; Nadine Gordimer, South Africa; His Royal Highness Prince El Hassan bin Talal, Jordan; Prof. Sergey Kapitza, Russia; Prof. Hayao Kawai, Japan; Prof. Tommy Koh, Singapore; Prof. Hans Küng, Switzerland; Graça Machel, Mozambique; Prof. Amartya Sen, India; Dr. Song Jian, China; Dick Spring, TD, Ireland; Prof. Tu Weiming, China; The Honorable Richard von Weizsäcker, Germany; Dr. Javad Zarif, Iran; Giandomenico Picco, Italy (Personal Representative of Secretary-General Kofi Annan for the United Nations Year of Dialogue among Civilizations).

References and further reading

Aboulmagd, A. Kamal et al. 2001. *Crossing the Divide: Dialogue Among Civilizations*. South Orange, NJ: Seton Hall University.

Beversluis, Joel. 2000. *Sourcebook of the World's Religions: An Interfaith Guide to Religion and Spirituality*. 3rd edition. Novato, CA: New World Library.

Küng, Hans. 1991. "Global Responsibility." In *In Search of a New World Ethic*. New York: Crossroad; London: SCM Press.

——. 1997. *A Global Ethic for Global Politics and Economics*. New York: Oxford University Press.

Küng, Hans and Helmut Schmidt. 1998. *A Global Ethic and Global Responsibilities. Two Declarations*. London: SCM Press.

8 Can love save the world?

Walter Wink

Michael Kelly thinks he has killed pacifism. In an op-ed editorial in the *Washington Post* of September 26, 2001, he cites George Orwell's 1944 description of pacifism as "objectively pro-Fascist." "If you hamper the war effort on one side you automatically help out that of the other," Orwell reasoned. Applied to "America's New War," Kelly finds the logic irrefutable. "Organized terrorist groups have attacked America. These groups wish the Americans to not fight. The American pacifists wish the Americans to not fight. If the Americans do not fight, the terrorists will attack America again. And now we know such attacks can kill many thousands of Americans. The American pacifists, therefore, are on the side of future mass murders of Americans. They are objectively pro-terrorist." Hence the pacifist position is "evil."

Would that life were so logical! For what Mr. Kelly overlooks is a third way, neither passive nor aggressive. For millions of years his error has been endlessly repeated. It is the fight/flight response. But that third way has occasionally been tried, and, wonder of wonders, it has frequently succeeded. Religions pioneered the third way as a nonviolent protest against those two invidious alternatives. Starting with the Hebrew midwives, nonviolence was elaborated by Jainism and Buddhism, given political bite by Jews like the prophets and Jesus, articulated by Christians like St. Francis and Martin Luther King, Jr., and made programmatic and practical by the Hindu Gandhi and the Muslim Badshah Khan.

Nevertheless, I agree with Mr. Kelly that pacifism must go. It is endlessly confused with passivity. In the nations in which Christianity has predominated, Jesus' teaching on nonviolence has been perverted into injunctions to passive nonresistance, which, as we shall see, is the very opposite of active nonviolence. Jesus had said, "You have heard that it was said, 'An eye for an eye and a tooth for a tooth.' But I say to you, Do not resist an evildoer. But if anyone strikes you on the right cheek, turn the other also; and if anyone wants to sue you and take your outer garment, give your undergarment as well; and if one of the occupation troops forces you to carry his pack one mile, go two" (Matthew 5:38–41). As it stands, this saying seems to counsel supine surrender. If you are a woman and you are struck by your spouse on one cheek, turn the other; let him pulverize you. If you are sued for a piece of clothing, give all your clothes voluntarily, as an act of pious renunciation. And if a Roman soldier forces you to carry his pack one mile, be a chump: carry it two. And the crowning blow: don't resist evil at all.

For centuries, readers of this advice have instinctively known something was wrong with that interpretation. Jesus always resisted evil. Why would he tell us to behave in ways he himself refused? And that's where the trouble starts. The Greek word translated as "resist" (*antistenai*) is literally "to stand (*stenai*) against (*anti*)." The term is taken from warfare. When two armies collided, they were said to "stand against" each other. The correct translation is given in the new Scholars Bible: "Don't react violently against the one who is evil." The meaning is clear: don't react in kind, don't mirror your enemy, don't turn into the very thing you hate. Jesus is not telling us not to resist evil, but only not to resist it violently.

Jesus gives three examples to explain his point. The first is: "If anyone strikes you on the right cheek, turn the other also." Most people picture a blow with the right fist. But that would land on the left cheek, and Jesus specifies the right cheek. A left hook wouldn't fit the bill either, since the left hand was used only for unclean tasks, and even to gesture with it brought shame on the one gesturing. The only option, then, is a back-handed strike with the right hand against the right cheek. This was not a blow to injure. It was symbolic. The back-handed blow was intended to humiliate, to put an inferior in his or her place. It was always given by a master to a slave, a husband to a wife, a parent to a child, or a Roman to a Jew. The message of the powerful to their subjects was clear: You are a nobody, get back down where you belong.

It is to those accustomed to being struck thus that Jesus speaks ("if anyone strikes *you*"). By turning the other cheek, the person struck puts the striker in an untenable spot. He cannot repeat the backhand, because the other's nose is now in the way. The left cheek makes a fine target, but only persons who are equals fight with fists, and the last thing the master wants is for the slave to assert equality (see the *Mishnah, Baba Kamma* 8:6). This is, of course, no way to avoid trouble; the master might have the slave flogged to within an inch of her life. But the point has been irrevocably made: the "inferior" is saying, in no uncertain terms, "I won't take such treatment anymore. I am your equal. I am a child of God." By turning the other cheek, the oppressed person is saying that she refuses to submit to further humiliation. This is not submission, as the churches have insisted. It is defiance. That may sound a bit idealistic, but people all over the globe of late have been taking their courage in their hands this way and resisting, nonviolently, those who have treated them thus.

Jesus' second example deals with indebtedness, the most onerous social problem in first-century Palestine. The wealthy of the Empire sought ways to avoid taxes. The best way was to buy land on the fringes of the Empire. But the poor didn't want to sell. So the rich jacked up the interest rate from 25 to 250 percent! When the poor couldn't repay, first their moveable property was seized, then their lands, and finally the very clothes on their backs. Scripture allowed the destitute to sleep in their long robes, but they had to surrender them to the creditor by day (Deuteronomy 24:10–13).

It is to that situation that Jesus speaks. Look, he says, you can't win when they take you to court. But here is something you can do: when they demand your outer garment, give your undergarment as well. That was all they wore. The poor man, then, is standing stark naked in court! And in Israel, nakedness usually brought shame, not on the naked party, but on the one viewing his nakedness. (See the story of Noah, Genesis 9.) Jesus is not asking those already defrauded of their possessions to submit to further indignity. He is enjoining them to guerrilla theater.

Imagine the debtor walking out of the court. When onlookers ask what happened, he tells them that the creditor got all his clothes. People come pouring out of the streets and alleys and join the little procession to his home. It will be a while before creditors in that village take a poor man to court!

But, of course, the Powers That Be are shrewd, and within weeks new laws will be in place making nakedness in court punishable by fines or incarceration. So the poor need to keep inventing new forms of resistance. Jesus is advocating a kind of Jujitsu or Aikido, where the momentum of the oppressor is used to throw the oppressor and make him the laughing stock of the community. Jesus is not averse to using shame to kindle a moral sense in the creditor.

Jesus' third example refers to the *angeria*, the law that permitted a Roman soldier to force a civilian to carry his 65 to 85 pound pack. But the law stipulated one mile only. At the second marker the soldier was required to retrieve his pack. By carrying the pack more than the prescribed mile, the peasant makes the soldier culpable for violation of military law. Again, Jesus is not just "extending himself" by going the second mile, as the popular platitude puts it. He is putting the soldier in jeopardy of punishment.

So you can see why I agree with Mr. Kelly's objections to pacifism. The examples Jesus gives are something more than nonresistance. They are gutsy, courageous, even defiant. So I don't regard myself as a pacifist. I see myself rather as a violent person trying to become nonviolent. Mr. Kelly and I concur that the "flight" option is usually cowardly, irresponsible, and ineffective (though there are times when flight is the only alternative). But whereas he is still mired in the "fight" option, I am prepared to risk active, even militant, nonviolence—a third way.

Far from proving impractical, nonviolence has been about the only thing that has been working of late. With the possible exception of the

Bush Wars, I cannot think of any other instances where violence prevailed. And our actions during and after the Bush Wars are at the root of the hatred felt by so many in the Middle East toward the US. By contrast, in 1989–90 alone, seventeen nations involving 1.7 billion people underwent nonviolent revolutions, all but one (China) successfully. During the twentieth century, 3.4 billion people were involved in nonviolent struggle. Yet most churches and their members since the time of St. Augustine have embraced the Roman "just war theory," convinced that nonviolence won't work, that only violence can save us.

Little wonder that people have begun to conclude that someone is not telling the truth. First we were told that we were going to war to capture Osama bin Laden. But that meant destroying the Taliban, which meant destroying Afghanistan. When that strategy didn't turn up Osama bin Laden, they decided to destroy Iraq. But Saddam and bin Laden loathed each other, and there was no hard evidence of any collaboration between the two. So they changed the story once again. Now Iraq had to be destroyed in order to rid the world of Iraq's weapons of mass destruction. When these weapons failed to turn up, it became clear that what we wanted in Afghanistan and Iraq was not related to the "war on terrorism" at all. It was oil, in the form of an oil pipeline in Afghanistan and oil reserves in Iraq that constitute the second largest supply in the world. Iraq had signed contracts to drill with other nations in the region; Big Oil needed to conquer Iraq in order to nullify those contracts so new ones could be drawn up with Bush's buddies, the American oil companies.

But it wasn't just Big Oil: it was also Big Militarism. Iraq's destruction was necessary so we could use it as a staging area for insinuating American military control of the region. Already we have permanent access to four bases in Iraq that will serve that purpose for the indefinite future. Whatever military adventurism the Bush people decide to engage in, it will originate at those bases.

But not just Big Oil and Big Militarism: Big Empire. The Bush cabal has its eyes on complete world hegemony. The most blatant emblem of this lust for power is "Joint Vision 2010," published by the United States Space Command, which is the dream of complete control of space against both our enemies and our friends. The goal is to achieve what the Space Command calls "Full Spectrum Dominance." (Available from the US Space Command, Director of Plans, Peterson AFB. CO 80914-3110, DSN 692-3498, Comm (719) 554-3498.) Meanwhile, back on earth, the United States has stationed soldiers in 156 countries. Its military expenditures alone total more than the next 15 powers combined. In the absence of real enemies, one may fairly ask on whom we intend to use these weapons. The answer is clear: anyone who gets in our way. Who's next? Iran? Syria? Saudi Arabia?

In response to the attack on America, Attorney General John Ashcroft created secret military tribunals in which suspects were detained without their identities being made public or charges brought against them. The USA Patriot Acts I and II allow law enforcement authorities to enter a home, office, or other private place without a warrant and conduct a search, take photographs, and download computer files without notifying the person whose property is being searched until sometime *after* the search is conducted. Most troubling, this authority is not limited to anti-terrorism investigations, but also extends to supposed criminal ones. Wiretapping has virtually been removed from the discretion of judges, and Internet communications can be intercepted. Student records will be made accessible to a variety of governmental agencies, thus stifling dissent (this includes participation in demonstrations). Furthermore, the agencies receiving this and other private information have virtually unlimited use of it, thus resurrecting the specter of the government spying on its own citizens and using that power to limit free speech. This is not an empty threat. The Pentagon is proceeding with plans to open a dossier on every American citizen, despite the expression of outrage by the public. This erosion of civil liberties may land us in the very "objectively pro-Fascist" situation of which the unwitting Mr. Kelly warns and which the Bill of Rights was intended to prevent.

This is not a brief for exonerating terrorists. The rationale of terrorists is terror, and reasons given today may shift tomorrow. The terrorist who regretted being caught before he could kill 250,000 Americans betrayed the game when he admitted that his goal was simply to kill Americans. What we have here is a massive projection of a fundamentalist Muslim shadow on the United States. We no doubt deserve censure, but not the murder of our innocents. No pretext can ever excuse the slaughter of innocents, whether Americans in the twin towers or Afghan or Iraqi civilians in the Middle East.

One of the most lucid reflections on the crisis of September 11, 2001, was made three years before the event by Lt Col. Robert M. Bowman, Ret., who flew 101 combat missions in Vietnam and directed all the "Star Wars" programs under Presidents Ford and Carter. We are the target of terrorists, he said, not because we stand for democracy, freedom, and human rights, as President Bush has alleged, but because, in much of the world, our government stands for dictatorship, bondage, and human exploitation. "We are the target of terrorists because we are hated. And we are hated because our government has done hateful things" (Bowman 2001). We are hated because our government denies democracy, freedom, and human rights to people in Third World countries whose resources are coveted by our multinational corporations. We are hated because we have been involved in the overthrow of democratic regimes in Iran, Chile, Vietnam, the Congo, and much of Central America, in the case of the last, many times over. We have bombed 22 nations since 1946, not one of which, out of gratitude for being "softened up" from the air, became a democratic government respectful of human rights.

Lt Col. Bowman concludes, "Only one thing has ever ended a terrorist campaign—denying the terrorist organization the support of the larger community it represents. And the only way to do that is to listen to and alleviate the legitimate grievances of the people." As Uri Avnery, founder of the Israeli peace group Gush Shalom put it, "One can kill a million mosquitoes, and millions more will take their place. In order to get rid of them, one has to dry the swamp that breeds them" (Avnery 2001). Doing justice in the Middle East will not mollify true terrorists. But it could remove the source of much outrage, and thus dry up the reservoir of recruits for holy war.

It is natural to react defensively when attacked, as we were in 9/11. But retaliation will not work, else Israel would be the safest nation in the world. An Israeli cab driver unwittingly exposed the impotence of revenge when he said, "We have to beat and beat and beat the Palestinians until they learn to love us." Nicholas Lemann (2001) shows how our massive military reaction unwittingly played right into bin Laden's hands. Using the Spanish Basque's "action–reprisal–action cycle," the Al Qaeda terrorists carried out a spectacular act of aggression that made the insurgency appear to be powerful and exciting. The most powerful nation in the history of the world could be humbled by only 19 men. This action was then calculated to create a savage over-reaction by the US that would gain international sympathy for the terrorists' cause and lead to massive enlistments among daring and angry young men. We could scarcely have cooperated with the terrorists better. Unless we use our power to institute real justice, we will find ourselves with the "endless enemies" of whom Jonathan Kwitny (1984) so eloquently wrote.

President Bush wants us to believe in a final violence that will eradicate evil once and for all and make future violence unnecessary. But the violence we use creates new evil, no matter how just the cause. It inculcates the longing for revenge, and for what the losers call "justice." And they will have learned from our example how to use violence more efficiently. *Violence can never stop violence because its very success leads others to imitate it.* Paradoxically, violence is most dangerous when it *succeeds*.

The problem is not merely to gain justice but to end the system of domination that prevents justice from being achieved. In the struggle against oppression, every new increment of violence simply extends the life of that system and deepens faith in violence as redemptive. You cannot free people from the Domination System by using its own methods. You cannot construct the City of Life with the weapons of death. You cannot make peace—real peace—with war. As Gandhi observed, "The only people on earth who do not see Christ and His teachings as nonviolent are Christians."

The church is called to nonviolence not in order to preserve its purity, but to express its fidelity. It is not a law but a gift. It is simply offered to those who seek what God has in store for the world. The gospel is not in the least concerned with our anxiety to *be* right; it wants to *see right done*. Those who today renounce the kingdom of death do so not because they are trying to please a deity who demands obedience, but because they have committed themselves to the realm of life. They refrain from killing, not because they are ordered to, but because they recognize something of God in everyone, and realize that what we do to the least of these—our enemies—we do to God.

For Christians, in the final analysis, nonviolence is not a matter of legalism but of discipleship. It is the way God has chosen to overthrow evil in the world. Therefore, Jesus does not advocate a perfectionist ethic in which our salvation depends on being nonviolent. God can forgive our failures to be nonviolent. It is not a "work" which one must achieve in order to be counted righteous. We cannot even say that nonviolent actions are in every circumstance the will of God. How can I know, in any given situation, whether my nonviolence is not a heinous crime, or a total miscalculation of what God desires? I cannot presume on the judgment of God. I can only say that nonviolence is at the very heart of the gospel, and that the church's task is to attempt to spread this leaven into the life of the world. I can only believe that history will finally vindicate the power of truth and love over the power of violence and death.

References and further reading

Avnery, Uri. 2001. "Twin Towers." *Peacework*, October 10, http://www.peace workmagazine.org/pwork/0110/011010.htm.

Bowman, Robert M. 2001. "What Can We Do About Terrorism?" *North Coast Xpress*, Winter. http://www.sonic.net/~doretk/ (full text available at: http://www.forwriters.com/archive/writers_archive132.html).

The Friends Committee on National Legislation's Washington Newsletter. 2001. October, no. 659: 7, 8.

Kwitny, Jonathan. 1984. *Endless Enemies: The Making of an Unfriendly World.* New York: St. Martin's Press.

Lemann, Nicholas. 2001. "What Terrorists Want." *The New Yorker*, October 29: 36–41.

Wink, Walter. 1992. *Engaging the Powers: Discernment and Resistance in a World of Domination.* Minneapolis, MN: Fortress Press.

9 Discussion
Theological reflections

Samuel M. Powell

Religion has a long relationship with terror. The fear of the Lord, after all, is the beginning of wisdom and the experience of the *mysterium tremendum* is a well-attested theme in religious literature of many traditions.

However, not all terror is induced by an encounter with God. The human race has its own demonic capacity for creating terror. Sadly, religion has often abetted this capacity and found itself a willing partner in human evil.

In light of religion's complicity in violence and terror, it is not an idle pastime to ask whether the world's religious communities can respond constructively to human terror and violence. Can they respond in ways that promote peace and well-being? Can their members truly become peace-makers?

Of course, it is not only religion that has generated terror and violence; political communities likewise have a history of terror-inducing behavior. Consequently, we can ask of them the same question we ask of religious communities, namely whether they can respond constructively to terror and violence. Do national governments have the moral resources needed to bring about peace?

In their contributions to this volume, Hans Küng and Walter Wink address these questions in the course of setting forth theological ideas that are simultaneously simple to state and seemingly difficult to practice. The simplicity of the ideas means that they can be set forth briefly: A better world is possible.

- This better world can be attained if we, individually and collectively, undergo conversion—a change of thinking and behavior.
- Conversion especially summons us to find alternatives to violence.
- Nonviolent solutions to human political problems are the only practical solutions.

In spite of the fact that nonviolent solutions to political problems are eminently practical—they are, in fact, the only solutions that can actually bring about a better world—putting these practical nonviolent solutions

into practice is daunting. It is tempting to attribute this daunting character to original sin but there are more proximate reasons that deserve
attention.

One reason, adduced by Wink, is Christians' confusions about the moral
demands of the gospel. There is perplexity enough when these demands are
considered from a hermeneutical perspective. Everyone with even a cursory knowledge of the New Testament knows that Jesus commended us
not to resist evil people and to turn the other cheek when struck. Our problem is that all we have are the bare words of the gospel and not the social
context in which they were uttered. This is a recipe for hermeneutical
mischief, as it encourages us to load our assumptions onto the words.
The result, Wink argues, is that Jesus' words routinely incite us to passivity toward evil. In the face of evil, we tend to believe that our duty is to
suffer its harm. We intuitively know that this passivity is a poor strategy
for overcoming evil, so we turn to a more familiar strategy with proven
results—violence. The alternative that Wink proposes is that we see Jesus
as commanding an active (although nonviolent) resistance to evil. Evil,
then, is not something to be tolerated but is instead something to be overcome and eliminated. Wink thus argues that the gospels show us how to
respond constructively to terror and violence in a way that breaks the
cycle of retaliation.

But the challenge of interpreting gospel sayings is not the only reason
for the difficulty of finding and implementing nonviolent solutions to
political problems. Another reason is that Christians today (perhaps especially Protestants in America) are collectively a bit confused about their
role in politics and their relation to the nation. In the optimistic days of
the nineteenth century, many Protestants—conservative and liberal—in
America agreed that their efforts at evangelism and social reform were
preparing the way for the millennial kingdom of God. History and human
deeds within history, in other words, were continuous with the work of
God and with the eschatological kingdom. However, in the twentieth
century an increasingly apocalyptic eschatology seized the imagination of
conservative Protestants, with the result that they increasingly regarded
history and human effort as *dis*continuous with the kingdom of God.
Politics was seen as at best useless, for nothing that humans could do
would alter the eschatological timetable that God had set. In the mean-
time, theologically liberal Protestants, now enjoying leadership of many
of the largest denominations, turned politics into a major preoccupation,
especially in the reform-minded 1960s and 1970s. But, with America
turning more conservative in the 1980s, liberal Christians found themselves seriously out of step with America's political direction. To add to
their woes, by the 1990s worriers emerged among the liberals, crying out
that the liberal denominations had sold their souls to the nation and its
agendas. The church's only hope, they declared, was to distinguish the
church from the nation-state and its politics and from the nation's people

and their morality. The church must be true to its own ethos and heritage. It must be a culture within a culture. While liberals were thus engaged in internecine debate, conservatives, now called evangelicals, were by the 1980s wondering why they were missing out on the fun of politics and came to believe that politics could be an instrument of God's righteousness. Consequently, they threw themselves into local and national politics with great gusto, convinced that America's political problems could be fixed by correcting its moral failures and that moral failures could be remedied by political means. However, the collapse of the Moral Majority has thrown cold water on that party.

So, in the first decade of the twenty-first century, Protestants find themselves in a state of confusion about their relation to politics and the nation. In this post-Christian context, where both evangelicals and liberals feel that the aims of the nation are at variance with the aims of the church, one thing Christians could use is a vision of the nation and its politics that is simultaneously realistic about the moral failings of nations and hopeful about the prospects for nations undergoing genuine conversion. Hans Küng proposes the outlines of such a vision in his contribution. In the morally ambivalent history of international politics, Küng finds hope in the power of ideas to change politics, especially as these ideas find concrete expression in international treaties and agreements. Although discouraged by the policies of the current American president, he believes that a better world, characterized by reconciliation, understanding, and cooperation, is appearing. The way toward this better world is, Küng argues, peace among the religions. The religious impulse is vital for an improved world because the major religious traditions affirm exactly what is required: basic moral injunctions such as the Golden Rule and moral ideals about the way in which human beings ought to be treated.

Wink's and Küng's essays offer a vision of religion liberated from violence. But the vision is more than the possibility of a freedom from violence. It is also the vision of religions freed to be communities of peace-makers. In this way religion can be true to its calling of serving God and God's purposes. Of course, this requires religious communities to pursue peace not only in the world but also among their members and between themselves. In other words, they will have to set a good example of peacefulness in order to be effective at peace-making.

The vision that Wink and Küng set forth implies as well a healthy attitude toward political involvement by religious people. Protestants in America perpetually face a two-fold temptation: either to identify the kingdom of God with a political party (and thus to believe in a maximum of continuity between the kingdom and human political action) or to abandon political involvement (and thus to believe in a maximum of discontinuity between the kingdom and human political action). What is needed is a view of politics as the "art of the possible" (Küng). With this view, we can commit ourselves wholeheartedly and in good faith to the political process in the hope of achieving concrete good. At the same time, we will recognize that politics is the art of what is *humanly* possible and will recognize that some problems can be solved only by God's grace. This is not to deny that grace is effective within the political process; however, as Wink and Küng argue, the reduction of violence and terror in the world requires conversion—the change of thoughts, attitudes, and behaviors. Although political processes can curb violence, only God's grace can change the heart. But it is also true that the conversion of the heart is insufficient to solve the problem of terror and violence. This is because humans are social and political beings and because we need political structures to give shape to our moral lives. The religious and moral impulse that happens in conversion requires nurturing in and by social communities.

Wink's and Küng's essays call upon those of us who dwell in religious communities to turn our backs on whatever violence lies in our past and to take up the life of active peace-making. For Wink, this is the clear implication of the gospel, when it is properly understood. For Küng, it is required if our world is to become a humane world in which everyone is treated with dignity and in which peace reigns. These are surely worthy considerations. Although politics cannot bring about God's kingdom, Wink and Küng help us remember that it can actualize anticipations of that kingdom. Accordingly, politics can be a holy vocation for those whose calling is to be peace-makers.

Historical and
social reflections

10 Religious terror and global war

Mark Juergensmeyer

Though the horrific images of the aerial assaults on the World Trade Center and the Pentagon on September 11, 2001 were shocking, the headlines of American newspapers on September 12 contained another surprise: how quickly the rhetoric of warfare entered into public consciousness. "The world at war," pronounced one headline. "The first war of the twenty-first century," President George W. Bush proclaimed. The September 11, 2001 assaults were in fact the most spectacular of a decade-long series of attempts by Osama bin Laden's Al Qaeda network to bring the rest of the world into his view of global war. An earlier, less devastating attack on the World Trade Center in 1993 received scarcely a shrug from the American populace. But in 2001 he was more successful, both in the enormity of the event and the change in America's mindset that it created.

Yet even though it seemed palpably to be an act of war, it was not clear what kind of war it was. The instant comparisons to Pearl Harbor seemed forced. The Japanese attack that signaled America's entry into World War II was, after all, the military act of a sovereign state. Osama bin Laden's Al Qaeda network was essentially a rogue band of transnational activists based in distant caves but spread throughout the world. What united them was neither a state-centered organization nor a political ideology, but the ties of a certain form of politicized religion and the riveting image of an evil secular foe.

The Al Qaeda network has not been alone in the religious assault on the secular state. In the last fifteen years of the post-Cold War world, religion seems to have been connected with violence everywhere: from the World Trade Center bombings to suicide attacks in Israel and Palestine; assassinations in India, Israel, Egypt, and Algeria; nerve gas in the Tokyo subways; abortion clinic killings in Florida; and the bombing of Oklahoma City's federal building. What unites these disparate acts of violence is their perpetrators' hatred of the global reach of the modern secular state.

Thus in many ways the September 11 attacks were a part of a global confrontation. In the minds of many on both sides this confrontation is increasingly viewed as a war—though the enemies in this engagement are less like the axis of powers engaged in World War II than the ideological foes of the Cold War (see Juergensmeyer 1993). Like the old Cold War, the confrontation between these new forms of culture-based politics and the secular state is global in its scope, binary in its opposition, occasionally violent, and essentially a difference of ideologies; and, like the old Cold War, each side tends to stereotype the other. The image of war mobilizes the animosities of both sides. The major differences between the old Cold War and the new one is that the present war is in a sense imaginary—it entails very little state support—and the various forms of religious opposition are scarcely united. Yet when they do lash out in acts of terrorism, as September 11 demonstrated, the results can be as awesome as they are destructive.

The role of religion

What is odd about this new global war is not only the difficulty in defining it and the non-state, transnational character of the opposition, but also the opponents' ascription to ideologies based on religion. The tradition of secular politics from the time of the Enlightenment has comfortably ignored religion, marginalized its role in public life, and frequently coopted it for its own civil religion of public religiosity. No one in the secular world could have predicted that the first confrontations of the twenty-first century would involve, of all things, religion—secularism's old, long-banished foe.

Religious activists are puzzling anomalies in the secular world. Most religious people and their organizations are either firmly supportive of the secular state or quiescently uninterested in it. Osama bin Laden's Al Qaeda network, like most of the new religious activists, comprises a small group at the extreme end of a hostile subculture that itself is a small minority within the larger world of its religious culture. Osama bin Laden is no more representative of Islam than Timothy McVeigh is of Christianity, or Japan's Shoko Asahara is of Buddhism.

Still one cannot deny that the ideals and ideas of activists like bin Laden are authentically and thoroughly religious and could conceivably become popular among their religious compatriots. The authority of religion has given bin Laden's cadres the moral legitimacy of employing violence in their assault on the very symbol of global economic power. It has also provided the metaphor of cosmic war, an image of spiritual struggle that every religion has within its repository of symbols—the fight between good and bad, truth and evil. In this sense, then, the attack on the World Trade Center was very religious. It was meant to be catastrophic, an act of biblical proportions.

Though the World Trade Center assault and many other recent acts of religious terrorism have no obvious military goal, they are meant to make a powerful impact on the public consciousness. These are acts meant for television. They are a kind of perverse performance of power meant to ennoble the perpetrators' views of the world and to draw us into their notions of cosmic war. In my comparative study of cases of religious terrorism around the world I have found a strikingly familiar pattern (Juergensmeyer 2001).[1] In all of these cases, concepts of cosmic war are accompanied by strong claims of moral justification and an enduring absolutism that transforms worldly struggles into sacred battles. It is not so much that religion has become politicized, but that politics have become religionized. Worldly struggles have been lifted into the high proscenium of sacred battle.

This is what makes religious warfare so difficult to combat. Its enemies have become satanized—one cannot negotiate with them or easily compromise. The rewards for those who fight for the cause are transtemporal, and the time lines of their struggles are vast. Most social and political struggles look for conclusions within the lifetimes of their participants, but religious struggles can take generations to succeed. When I pointed out to political leaders of the Hamas movement in Palestine that Israel's military force was such that a Palestinian military effort could never succeed, I was told that "Palestine was occupied before, for two hundred years." The Hamas official assured me that he and his Palestinian comrades "can wait again—at least that long," for the struggles of God can endure for eons.[2] Ultimately, however, they knew they would succeed.

Insofar as the US public and its leaders embraced the image of war following the September 11 attacks, America's view of this war was also prone to religionization. "God Bless America" became the country's unofficial national anthem. President George W. Bush spoke of the defense of America's "righteous cause," and the "absolute evil" of its enemies. Still, the US military engagement in the months following September 11 was primarily a secular commitment to a definable goal and largely restricted to limited objectives in which civil liberties and moral rules of engagement, for the most part, still applied.

In purely religious battles, waged in divine time and with heaven's rewards, there is no need to compromise one's goals. There is no need, also, to contend with society's laws and limitations when one is obeying a higher authority. In spiritualizing violence, therefore, religion gives the resources of violence a remarkable power.

Ironically, the reverse is also true: terrorism can give religion power. Although sporadic acts of terrorism do not lead to the establishment of new religious states, they make the political potency of religious ideology impossible to ignore. The first wave of religious activism, from the Islamic revolution in Iran in 1978 to the emergence of Hamas during the Palestinian intifada in the early 1990s, was focused on religious nationalism and the vision of individual religious states. Increasingly, religious activism has a more global vision. Such disparate groups as the Christian militia, the Japanese Aum Shinrikyo, and the Al Qaeda network all target what their supporters regard as a repressive and secular form of global culture and control.

Global war

The September 11 attack and many other recent acts of religious terrorism are skirmishes in what their perpetrators conceive to be a global war. This battle is global in three senses. The choices of targets have often been transnational. The World Trade Center employees killed in the September 11 assault were citizens of 86 nations. The network of perpetrators was also transnational: the Al Qaeda network that was implicated in the attack—though consisting mostly of Saudis—is also actively supported by Pakistanis, Egyptians, Palestinians, Sudanese, Algerians, Indonesians, Malaysians, Filipinos, and a smattering of British, French, Germans, Spanish, and Americans. The incident was global in its impact, in large part because of the worldwide and instantaneous coverage of transnational news media. This was terrorism meant not only for television, but also for global news networks such as CNN—and especially for al Jazeera, the Qatar-based news channel that beams its talk-show format throughout the Middle East.

Increasingly terrorism has been performed for a televised audience around the world. In that sense it has been as real a global event as the transnational activities of the global economy and as vivid as the globalized forms of entertainment and information that crowd satellite television channels and the Internet. Ironically, terrorism has become a more efficient global force than the organized political efforts to control and contain it. No single entity, including the United Nations, possesses the military capability and intelligence-gathering capacities to deal with worldwide terrorism. Instead, consortia of nations have been formed to handle the information-sharing and joint operations required to deal with forces of violence on an international scale.

This global dimension of terrorism's organization and audience, and the transnational responses to it, gives special significance to the understanding of terrorism as a public performance of violence—as a social event that has both real and symbolic aspects. As the late French sociologist Pierre Bourdieu observed, our public life is shaped by symbols as much as by institutions. For this reason, symbolic acts—the "rites of institution"—help to demarcate public space and indicate what is meaningful in the social world (Bourdieu 1991: 117). In a striking imitation of such rites, terrorism has provided its own dramatic events. These rites of violence have signaled alternative views of public reality: not just a single society in transition, but a world challenged by strident religious visions of transforming change.

What is extraordinary about such performances is their success in bringing the rest of the world into their worldview—specifically their view of the world at war. War is an enticing conceptual construct, an all-embracing view of the world that contains much more than the notion of forceful contestation. It points to a dichotomous opposition on an absolute scale. War suggests an all-or-nothing struggle against an enemy who is determined to destroy. No compromise is deemed possible. The very existence of the opponent is a threat, and until the enemy is either crushed or contained, one's own existence cannot be secure. What is striking about a martial attitude is the certainty of one's position and the willingness to defend it, or impose it on others, to the end.

Such certitude may be regarded as noble by those whose sympathies lie with it and dangerous by those who do not agree with it. But either way it is not civil. One of the first rules of conflict resolution is the willingness to accept the notion that there are flaws on one's own side as well as on the opponent's side. This is the sensible stand to take if one's goal is to get along with others and avoid violence.[3] But often that is not the goal. In fact, a warring attitude implies that the one who holds it no longer thinks compromise is possible or—just as likely—did not want an accommodating solution to the conflict in the first place. In fact, if one's goals are not harmony but the empowerment that comes with using violence, it is in one's interest to be in a state of war. In such cases, war is not only the context for violence but also the excuse for it. This reasoning holds true even if the worldly issues that are at heart in the dispute do not seem to warrant such an extreme and ferocious position.

This logic may explain why acts of terrorism seem so puzzling to people outside the movements that perpetrate them and entirely understandable to those within them. The absolutism of war makes compromise unlikely, and those who suggest a negotiated settlement can be excoriated as the enemy. In the Palestinian situation, the extreme religious positions on both sides loathed the carefully negotiated compromise once promised by Israel's Yitzhak Rabin and Palestine's Yasir Arafat. "There is no such thing as co-existence," a Jewish activist in Israel told me, explaining that there was a biblical requirement for Jews to possess and live on biblical land. This was why he despised the Oslo and Wye River accords and regarded Rabin and Netanyahu as treasonous for signing them.[4] Hamas leaders told me essentially the same thing about the necessity for Arab Muslims to occupy what they regarded as their homeland. They expressed anger towards their own secular leader—Yasir Arafat—for having entered into what both Jewish and Muslim extremists regarded as a dangerous and futile path towards an accommodation deemed by them to be impossible.[5] The extremes on both sides preferred war over peace.

One of the reasons why a state of war is often preferable to peace is that it gives moral justification for acts of violence. Violence, in turn, offers the illusion of power. The idea of warfare implies more than an attitude; ultimately it is a worldview and an assertion of identity. To live in a state of war is to live in a world in which individuals know who they are, why they have suffered, by whose hand they have been humiliated, and at what expense they have persevered. It provides cosmology, history, and eschatology, and offers the reins of political control. Perhaps most importantly, it holds out the hope of victory and the means to achieve it. In the images of religious war this victorious triumph is a grand moment of social and personal transformation, transcending all worldly limitations. One does not easily abandon such expectations. To be without such images of war is almost to be without hope itself.

The idea of warfare has had an eerie and intimate relationship with religion. History has been studded with overtly religious conflicts such as the Crusades, the Muslim conquests, and the Wars of Religion that dominated the politics of France in the sixteenth century. These have usually been characterized as wars in the name of religion, rather than wars conducted in a religious way. However, the historian Natalie Zemon Davis has uncovered what she calls "rites of violence" in her study of religious riots in sixteenth-century France. These constituted "a repertory of actions, derived from the Bible, from the liturgy, from the action of political authority, or from the traditions of popular folk practices, intended to purify the religious community and humiliate the enemy and thus make him less harmful." Davis observed that the violence was "aimed at defined targets and selected from a repertory of traditional punishments and forms of destruction" (Davis 1973: 52–3). According to Davis, "even the extreme ways of defiling corpses—dragging bodies through the streets and throwing them to the dogs, dismembering genitalia and selling them in mock commerce—and desecrating religious objects," had what she called "perverse connections" with religious concepts of pollution and purification, heresy and blasphemy (1973: 81–2).

Anthropologist Stanley Tambiah showed how the same "rites of violence" were present in the religious riots of South Asia (Tambiah 1996: 310–11). In some instances innocent bystanders would be snatched up by a crowd and burned alive. According to Tambiah, these horrifying murders of defenseless and terrified victims were done in a ritual manner, in "mock imitation of both the self-immolation of conscientious objectors and the terminal rite of cremation" (1996: 311). In a macabre way, the riotous battles described by Davis and Tambiah were religious events. But given the prominence of the rhetoric of warfare in religious vocabulary, both traditional and modern, one could also turn this point around and say that religious events often involve the invocation of violence. One could argue that the task of creating a vicarious experience of warfare— albeit one usually imagined as residing on a spiritual plane—is one of the main businesses of religion.

Virtually all cultural traditions have contained martial metaphors in their symbols, myths, and legendary histories. Ideas such as the Salvation Army in Christianity or a Dal Khalsa ("army of the faithful") in Sikhism characterize disciplined religious organizations. Images of spiritual warfare are even more common. The Muslim notion of jihad is the most notable example, but even in Buddhist legends great wars abound. In Sri Lankan culture, for instance, virtually canonical status is accorded the legendary history recorded in the Pali Chronicles, the Dipavamsa and the Mahavamsa, that related the triumphs of battles waged by Buddhist kings. In India, warfare contributes to the grandeur of the great epics, the Ramayana and the Mahabharata, which are tales of seemingly unending conflict and military intrigue. More than the Vedic rituals, these martial epics defined subsequent Hindu culture. Whole books of the Hebrew Bible are devoted to the military exploits of great kings, their contests related in gory detail. Though the New Testament does not take up the battle cry, the later history of the Church does, supplying Christianity with a bloody record of crusades and religious wars.

What is unusual about contemporary acts of terrorism is that the vision of religious war is not confined to history and symbols but is a contemporary reality. Politics have become religionized as struggles in the real world become baptized with the absolutism of religious fervor. Acts of violence are conducted not so much to wage a military campaign as to demonstrate the reality of the war to an unknowing public. In such cases, the message is the medium in which it is sent: the bombings provide moments of chaos, warfare, and victimage that the perpetrators want a slumbering society to experience. These acts make the point that war is at hand by providing a bloody scene of battle in one's own quiet neighborhoods and everyday urban streets.

What is buttressed in these acts of symbolic empowerment is not only the credibility of their cause. These acts, for the moment, place the perpetrators on a par with the leaders of governments that they target, and equate the legitimacy of the secular state with their own vision of religious social order. Through the currency of violence they draw attention to what they believe to be significant and true about the social arena around them. In the language of Bourdieu they are creating a perverse "habitus," a dark world of social reality, and forcing everyone to take stock of their perception of the world (Bourdieu and Wacquant 1992: 131). Thus the very act of performing violence in public is a political act: it announces that the power of the group is equal or superior to that of the state. In most cases this is exactly the message that the group wants to convey.

The establishment of political rule based on religious law is the primary aim of many Muslim groups. Members of Hamas regarded this as the main difference between their organization and the secular ideology of Fateh and other groups associated with Yasir Arafat's Palestinian Authority. A similar argument was made by activists associated with Egyptian groups. Mahmud Abouhalima told me that President Hosni Mubarak could not be a true Muslim because he did not make shari'a—

Islamic law—the law of the land.[6] A cleric in Cairo's conservative Al-Azhar theological school told me he resented his government's preference for Western law. "Why should we obey Western laws when Muslim laws are better?" he asked me.[7] It was this position that was assumed by many Muslim activists: that Western political institutions and the ideology on which they were based should be banished from their territories. They wanted to rebuild their societies on Islamic foundations.

Yet the images of political order that these activists yearned to create have been deliberately fuzzy. Sometimes the goals have appeared to be democratic, sometimes socialist, sometimes a sort of religious oligarchy. Sometimes the goals have been nationalist, at other times international in scope. A Hamas leader told me that what distinguished his organization from Yasir Arafat's Fateh movement was that Fateh was waging a "national struggle" whereas Hamas was "transnational."[8] The Al Qaeda network of Osama bin Laden is especially striking in its global reach and curious in its lack of a specific political program. It is as if the idea of global struggle was sufficient, its own reward. Although it is clear who the supporters of Al Qaeda hate, nowhere have they given a design for a political entity—Islamic or otherwise—that could actually administrate the results of a victory over American and secular rule and the emergence of a religious revolution, should they achieve it.

My conclusion is that acts of religious terrorism are largely devices for symbolic empowerment in wars that cannot be won and for goals that cannot be achieved. The very absence of thought about what the activists would do if they were victorious is sufficient indication that they do not expect to win, nor perhaps even want to do so. They illustrate a peculiar corollary to the advice of the French theorist, Frantz Fanon, during Algeria's war of independence some years ago when he advocated terrorism as the Algerians' mobilizing weapon. Fanon reasoned that even a small display of violence could have immense symbolic power by jolting the masses into an awareness of their own potency (Fanon 1963). What Fanon did not realize is that for some activist groups the awareness of their potency would be all that they desired.

Yet these acts of symbolic empowerment have had an effect beyond whatever personal satisfaction and feelings of potency they have imparted to those who supported and conducted them. The very act of killing on behalf of a moral code is a political statement. Such acts break the state's monopoly on morally sanctioned killing. By putting the right to take life in their own hands, the perpetrators of religious violence have made a daring claim of power on behalf of the powerless, a basis of legitimacy for public order other than that upon which the secular state relies. In doing so, they have demonstrated to everyone how fragile public order actually is, and how fickle can be the populace's assent to the moral authority of power.

Empowering religion

Such religious warfare not only gives individuals who have engaged in it the illusion of empowerment, it also gives religious organizations and ideas a public attention and importance that they have not enjoyed for many years. In modern America and Europe, warfare has given religion a prominence in public life that it has not held since before the Enlightenment, more than two centuries ago.

Although each of the violent religious movements around the world has its own distinctive culture and history, I have found that they have three things in common regarding their attitudes towards religion in society. First, they reject the compromises with liberal values and secular institutions that most mainstream religions have made, be it Christian, Muslim, Jewish, Hindu, Sikh, or Buddhist. Second, radical religious movements refuse to observe the boundaries that secular society has set around religion—keeping it private rather than allowing it to intrude into public spaces. And third, these movements try to create a new form of religiosity that rejects what they regard as weak modern substitutes for the more vibrant and demanding forms of religion that they imagine to be essential to their religion's origins.

During a prison interview, one of the men accused of bombing the World Trade Center in 1993 told me that the critical moment in his religious life came when he realized that he could not compromise his Islamic integrity with the easy vices offered by modern society. The convicted terrorist, Mahmud Abouhalima, claimed that the early part of his life was spent running away from himself. Although involved in radical Egyptian Islamic movements since his college years in Alexandria, he felt there was no place where he could settle down. He told me that the low point came when he was in Germany, trying to live the way that he imagined Europeans and Americans carried on: one where the superficial comforts of sex and inebriation masked an internal emptiness and despair. Abouhalima said his return to Islam as the center of his life carried with it a renewed sense of obligation to make Islamic society truly Islamic—to "struggle against oppression and injustice" wherever it existed. What was now constant, Abouhalima said, was his family and his faith. Islam was both "a rock and a pillar of mercy."[9] But it was not the Islam of liberal, modern Muslims: they, he felt, had compromised the tough and disciplined life the faith demanded. In Abouhalima's case, he wanted his religion to be hard, not soft like the humiliating, mind-numbing comforts of secular modernity. Activists such as Abouhalima—and for that matter, Osama bin Laden—have imagined themselves to be defenders of ancient faiths. But in fact they have created new forms of religiosity: like many present-day religious leaders they have used the language of traditional religion in order to build bulwarks around aspects of modernity that have threatened them, and to suggest ways out of the mindless humiliation of modern life. It was vital to their image of religion, however, that it be perceived as ancient.

The need for religion—a "hard" religion as Abouhalima called it— was a response to the soft treachery they had observed in the new societies around them. The modern secular world that Abouhalima and the others inhabited was a dangerous and chaotic sea, in which religion was a harbor of calm. At a deep level of their consciousnesses they sensed their lives slipping out of control, and they felt both responsible for the disarray and a victim of it. To be abandoned by religion in such a world would mean a loss of their own individual locations and identities. In fashioning a "traditional religion" of their own making they exposed their concerns not so much with their religious, ethnic, or national communities, but with their own personal, perilous selves.

These intimate concerns have been prompted by the perceived failures of public institutions. As Pierre Bourdieu has observed, social structures never have a disembodied reality; they are always negotiated by individuals in their own strategies for maintaining self-identity and success in life. Such institutions are legitimized by the "symbolic capital" they accrue through the collective trust of many individuals (Bourdieu 1991: 72–6; see also Bourdieu 1977: 171–83). When that symbolic capital is devalued, when political and religious institutions undergo what the German social philosopher Jürgen Habermas has called a "crisis of legitimacy," this devaluation of authority is experienced not only as a political problem but as an intensely personal one, as a loss of agency (Habermas 1975).

It is this sense of a personal loss of power in the face of chaotic political and religious authorities that is common, and I believe critical, to Osama bin Laden's Al Qaeda group and most other movements for Christian, Muslim, Jewish, Sikh, Buddhist, and Hindu nationalism around the world. The syndrome begins with the perception that the public world has gone awry, and the suspicion that behind this social confusion lies a great spiritual and moral conflict, a cosmic battle between the forces of order and chaos, good and evil. The government—already delegitimized—is perceived to be in league with the forces of chaos and evil.

Secular government is easily labeled as the enemy of religion, because to some degree it is. By its nature, the secular state is opposed to the idea that religion should have a role in public life. From the time that modern secular nationalism emerged in the eighteenth century as a product of the European Enlightenment's political values it did so with a distinctly anti-religious, or at least anti-clerical, posture. The ideas of John Locke about the origins of a civil community, and the "social contract" theories of Jean-Jacques Rousseau required very little commitment to religious belief. Although they allowed for a divine order that made the rights of humans possible, their ideas had the effect of taking religion—at least Church religion—out of public life. At the time, religious "enemies of the Enlightenment" protested religion's public demise.[10] But their views were submerged in a wave of approval for a new view of social order in which secular nationalism was thought to be virtually a natural law, universally applicable and morally right.

Post-Enlightenment modernity proclaimed the death of religion. Modernity signaled not only the demise of the Church's institutional authority and clerical control, but also the loosening of religion's ideological and intellectual grip on society. Scientific reasoning and the moral claims of the secular social contract replaced theology and the Church as the bases for truth and social identity. The result of religion's devaluation has been "a general crisis of religious belief," as Bourdieu has put it (1977: 116).

In countering this disintegration, resurgent religious activists have proclaimed the death of secularism. They have dismissed the efforts of secular culture and its forms of nationalism to replace religion. They have challenged the notion that secular society and the modern nation-state are able to provide the moral fiber that unites national communities, or give it the ideological strength to sustain states buffeted by ethical, economic, and military failures. Their message has been easy to believe and has been widely received, because the failures of the secular state have been so real.

The moral leadership of the secular state was increasingly challenged in the last decade of the twentieth century following the breakup of the Cold War and the rise of a global economy. The Cold War provided contesting models of moral politics—communism and democracy—that were replaced with a global market that weakened national sovereignty and was conspicuously devoid of political ideals. The global economy became controlled by transnational businesses accountable to no single governmental authority and with no clear ideological or moral standards of behavior. But while both Christian and Enlightenment values were left behind, transnational commerce did transport aspects of Westernized popular culture to the rest of the world. American and European music, videos, and films were beamed across national boundaries, where they threatened to obliterate local and traditional forms of artistic expression. Added to this social confusion were convulsive shifts in political power that followed the breakup of the Soviet Union and the collapse of Asian economies at the end of the twentieth century.

The public sense of insecurity that came in the wake of these cataclysmic global changes was felt not only in the societies of those nations that were economically devastated by them—especially countries in the former Soviet Union—but also in economically stronger industrialized societies. The United States, for example, saw a remarkable degree of disaffection with its political leaders and witnessed the rise of right-wing religious movements that fed on the public's perception of the inherent immorality of government.

Is the rise of religious terrorism related to these global changes? We know that some groups associated with violence in industrialized societies have had an anti-modernist political agenda. At the extreme end of this religious rejection in the United States were members of the American anti-abortion group, Defensive Action; the Christian militia and Christian Identity movement; and isolated groups such as the Branch Davidian sect in Waco, Texas. Similar attitudes towards secular government emerged in Israel—the religious nationalist ideology of the Kach party was an extreme example—and, as the Aum Shinrikyo movement has demonstrated, in Japan. As in the United States, contentious groups within these countries were disillusioned about the ability of secular leaders to guide their countries' destinies. They identified government as the enemy.

The global shifts that have given rise to anti-modernist movements have also affected less-developed nations. India's Jawaharlal Nehru, Egypt's Gamal Abdel Nasser, and Iran's Riza Shah Pahlavi once were committed to creating versions of America—or a kind of cross between America and the Soviet Union—in their own countries. But new generations of leaders no longer believe in the Westernized visions of Nehru, Nasser, or the Shah. Rather, they are eager to complete the process of de-colonialization and build new, indigenous nationalisms.

When activists in Algeria who demonstrated against the crackdown against the Islamic Salvation Front in 1991 proclaimed that they were continuing the war of liberation against French colonialism, they had the ideological rather than political reach of European influence in mind. Religious activists such as the Algerian leaders, the Ayatollah Khomeini in Iran, Sheik Ahmed Yassin in Palestine, Sayyid Qutb and his disciple, Sheik Omar Abdul Rahman, in Egypt, L. K. Advani in India, and Sant Jarnail Singh Bhindranwale in India's Punjab have asserted the legitimacy of a postcolonial national identity based on traditional culture (for a forceful treatment of this thesis, see Chatterjee 1993).

The result of this disaffection with the values of the modern West has been a "loss of faith" in the ideological form of that culture—secular nationalism, or the idea that the nation is rooted in a secular compact rather than religious or ethnic identity.[11] Although a few years ago it would have been a startling notion, the idea has now become virtually commonplace that secular nationalism is in crisis. In many parts of the world it is seen as an alien cultural construction, one closely linked with what has been called "the project of modernity" (Habermas 1987: 148). In such cases, religious alternatives to secular ideologies have had extraordinary appeal.

This uncertainty about what constitutes a valid basis for national identity is a political form of postmodernism. In Iran it has resulted in the rejection of a modern Western political regime and the creation of a successful religious state. Increasingly, even secular scholars in the West have recognized that religious ideologies might offer an alternative to modernity in the political sphere (see, for instance, Friedland 1999). Yet, what lies beyond modernity is not necessarily a new form of political order, religious or not. In nations formerly under Soviet control, for example, the specter of the future beyond the socialist form of modernity has been one of cultural anarchism.

The Al Qaeda network associated with Osama bin Laden takes the challenge to secularism to yet another level. The implicit attacks on global economic and political systems that are leveled by religious nationalists from Algeria to Indonesia are made explicit: America is the enemy. Moreover, it is a war waged not on a national plane but a transnational one. Their agenda is not for any specific form of religious nation-state, but an inchoate vision of a global rule of religious law. Rather than religious nationalists, transnational activists like bin Laden are guerilla antiglobalists.

Postmodern terror

Bin Laden and his vicious acts have credibility in some quarters of the world because of the uncertainties of this moment in global history. The fear that there will be a spiritual as well as a political collapse at modernity's center has, in many parts of the world, led to terror. Both violence and religion have appeared at times when authority is in question, since they are both ways of challenging and replacing authority. One gains its power from force and the other from its claims to ultimate order. The combination of the two in acts of religious terrorism has been a potent assertion indeed. Regardless of whether the perpetrators consciously intend them to be political acts, all public acts of violence have political consequences. Insofar as they have been attempts to reshape the public order, these acts have been examples of what José Casanova has called the increasing "deprivatization" of religion (1994: 211). In various parts of the world where attempts have been made by defenders of religion to reclaim the center of public attention and authority, religious terrorism is often the violent face of these attempts.

The postmodern religious rebels such as those who rally to the side of Osama bin Laden are therefore neither anomalies nor anachronisms. From Algeria to Idaho, they are small but potent groups of violent activists who represent masses of potential supporters, and they exemplify currents of thinking and cultures of commitment that have risen to counter the prevailing modernism. The enemies of these groups have seemed to most people to be both benign and banal: such symbols of prosperity and authority as the World Trade Center. The logic of this kind of militant religiosity has therefore been difficult for many people to comprehend. Yet its challenge has been profound, for it has contained a fundamental critique of the world's post-Enlightenment secular culture and politics.

Acts of religious terrorism have thus been attempts to use violence to purchase public recognition of the legitimacy of this view of the world at war. Since religious authority can provide a ready-made replacement for secular leadership, it is no surprise that when secular authority has been deemed morally insufficient, the challenges to its legitimacy and the attempts to gain support for its rivals have often been based in religion. When the proponents of religion have asserted their claim to be the moral force undergirding public order, they sometimes have done so with the kind of power that even a confused society can graphically recognize: the force of terror.

What the perpetrators of such acts of terror expect—and indeed welcome—is a response as vicious as the acts themselves. By goading secular authorities into responding to terror with terror, they hope to accomplish two things. First, they want tangible evidence for their claim that the secular enemy is a monster. Second, they hope to bring to the surface the great war—a war that they have told their potential supporters was hidden, but real. When the American missiles began to fall in Afghanistan on October 2, less than three weeks after the September 11 attacks, the Al Qaeda forces must initially have been exhilarated, for the war they had anticipated for so long had finally arrived. Its outcome, however, likely gave them less satisfaction: their bases were routed, their leadership demolished, and the Muslim world did not rise up in support in the numbers and enthusiasm they had expected. Yet the time line of religious warfare is long, and the remnant forces of Al Qaeda most likely still yearn for the final confrontation. They are assured that the glorious victory will ultimately be achieved, for they are certain that it is, after all, God's war, not theirs.

Notes

1 Excerpts from this book are utilized in this essay.
2 Author's interview with Dr. Abdul Aziz Rantisi, cofounder and political leader of Hamas, Khan Yunis, Gaza, March 1, 1998.
3 One interpretation of the basic rules of nonviolent conflict resolution may be found in my book, *Gandhi's Way* (Juergensmeyer 2002).
4 Author's interview with Yoel Lerner, Director of the Sannhedrin Institute, Jerusalem, March 2, 1998.
5 Interview with Dr. Rantisi, March 2, 1998.
6 Author's interview with Mahmud Abouhalima, convicted codefendant in bombing of the World Trade Center, United States Penitentiary, Lompoc California, August 19, 1997.
7 Author's interview with Dr. Muhammad Ibraheem el-Geyoushi, Dean of the Faculty of Dawah, Al-Azhar University, Cairo, May 30, 1990.
8 Interview with Dr. Rantisi, March 1, 1998.
9 Interview with Abouhalima, September 30, 1997.
10 The phrase originates with historian Darrin McMahon, in his fascinating book on the religious roots of the far right, *Enemies of the Enlightenment* (2001).
11 I describe this "loss of faith" at length in Juergensmeyer 1993: 11–25.

References

Bourdieu, Pierre. 1977. *Outline of a Theory of Practice*. Trans. Richard Nice. Cambridge: Cambridge University Press.

——. 1991. *Language and Symbolic Power*. Trans. Gino Raymond and Matthew Adamson. Cambridge, MA: Harvard University Press.

Bourdieu, Pierre and Loic J. D. Wacquant. 1992. *An Invitation to Reflexive Sociology*. Chicago: University of Chicago Press.

Casanova, José. 1994. *Public Religions in the Modern World*. Chicago: University of Chicago Press.

Chatterjee, Partha. 1993. *The Nation and Its Fragments: Colonial and Postcolonial Histories*. Princeton, NJ: Princeton University Press.

Davis, Natalie Zemon. 1973. "Rites of Violence: Religious Riots in Sixteenth Century France." *Past and Present* 59: 51–91.

Fanon, F. 1963. *The Wretched of the Earth*. New York: Grove Press.

Friedland, Roger. 1999. "When God Walks in History: The Institutional Politics of Religious Nationalism." *International Sociology* 14 (3): 301–19.

Habermas, Jürgen. 1975. *Legitimation Crisis*. Trans. Thomas McCarthy. Boston, MA: Beacon Press.

——. 1987. "Modernity—An Incomplete Project." Reprinted in *Interpretive Social Science: A Second Look*, edited by Paul Rabinow and William M. Sullivan, 141–56. Berkeley, CA: University of California Press.

Juergensmeyer, Mark. 1993. *The New Cold War? Religious Nationalism Confronts the Secular State*. Berkeley, CA: University of California Press.

——. 2001. *Terror in the Mind of God: The Global Rise of Religious Violence*. Berkeley, CA: University of California Press.

——. 2002. *Gandhi's Way: A Handbook of Conflict Resolution*. Berkeley, CA: University of California Press.

McMahon, Darrin. 2001. *Enemies of the Enlightenment: The French Counter-Enlightenment and the Making of Modernity*. New York: Oxford University Press.

Tambiah, Stanley. 1996. *Leveling Crowds: Ethnonationalist Conflicts and Collective Violence in South Asia*. Berkeley, CA: University of California Press.

11 Jihad and Islamic history

Jonathan E. Brockopp

On September 11, 2001, I was teaching at a small college in New York State. Like many people around the country, I immediately reached out to my Muslim neighbors, fearful of vigilante attacks. My colleague, Salahuddin Muhammad, the Imam (prayer leader) of a small mosque in Newburgh, New York, assured me he and his congregation were fine, but he also told me that some members were worried enough to change the name of their mosque, called "Masjid al-Jihad al-Akbar" or the "Mosque of the Greater Jihad." He understood their concern, but initially refused, insisting on using misconceptions about the word jihad as a chance to teach others about Islam.

Like many religious terms, jihad has a whole array of meanings all centered on the root concept of struggle. The "greater jihad" is understood as the *jihad al-nafs*, or the struggle with one's own evil inclinations, and it is based on a story that goes back to the Prophet of Islam, Muhammad. It seems that Muhammad was returning to his home after a significant campaign, where the Muslim forces had prevailed. But instead of giving a victory speech to his followers, he said: "Now we have returned from the lesser jihad in order to take up the greater jihad," in essence, devaluing the whole place of warfare in the Islamic tradition.[1]

This is just one of many stories that portray Muhammad as a peaceful, deeply spiritual person, one who was quite reluctant to take up the ways of warfare. In naming their mosque after the Greater Jihad, the Muslims of Newburgh were not menacing their neighbors with the threat of war, but rather exhorting their fellow Muslims to devote themselves more fully to God, pray five times daily and come together at noon prayers on Fridays. They were evoking a sense of Islamic history quite different from the one that extremists like Osama bin Laden imagine in their calls to "kill Americans everywhere."

The six years since 9/11 have witnessed many changes in the world. As a patriot, I weep as I watch my country sink deeper into the morass of an unjustified and unwinnable war. The reputation of my country has been permanently damaged by our new policies of torture and extraordinary rendition, and our blatant disregard for the lives of American

soldiers and Iraqi citizens alike. As an educator, I see young people growing increasingly skeptical of their government, convinced either that all
Muslims are potential terrorists, bent on destroying the United States, or
that the whole system of government is corrupt. My job is to keep them
from both these extremes, and to teach them to see knowledge as a tool
to move beyond soundbites.

I wrote this essay because I am convinced that the only way to understand the debate over the meaning of jihad is to explore Islamic history for
ourselves. Such a task involves far more than recounting a series of places,
names, and dates, though these are important too; it also means understanding the ways that religions construct history to make their authoritative statements. These are difficult tasks, but note that I am making a
distinction between: (1) history as a discrete set of events that happened
in the past; and (2) the meaning of those events for religious traditions.
For religious people, there can be no dispassionate or objective retelling of
certain facts and events; rather those events are both descriptive of God's
involvement in the world and also prescriptive of correct human action.
Religious history therefore takes events and constructs meaning out of
them in a dynamic dialogue between past events and present concerns.[2]

Further, the recording and rehearsing of past events is one of the most
important jobs of the religious adherent. By remembering and retelling
the originating stories, they claim sacred history for themselves and are
actively involved in its reconstruction. This retelling may be an actual
reading of history, but it can also be found in rituals that put the believer
back at that very moment in time when God was most closely involved
in human events. For Christians, approaching the table for communion
re-enacts the Last Supper when Jesus foretold his death and commanded
his disciples, saying: "Do this in remembrance of me" (Luke 22:19).
For Jews, eating unleavened bread during the Passover meal is a similar
reminder of God's deliverance from slavery in Egypt. What is at issue here
is not the historical fact of the matter, but rather the meaning of those
facts for these religions.[3]

In this essay, I analyze four constructions of the "lesser jihad," that
is jihad as warfare. The classical positions I describe first (those of legal
scholars and historians) dominate the Islamic tradition even today, and
many modern jurists and historians would give much the same account
as that of their medieval counterparts;[4] as one example of such a modern
jurist, I have chosen Muhammad Abduh (d. 1905). But in some ways
the point of this essay is to provide a context for understanding extremist voices, such as that of Osama bin Laden. As I hope to demonstrate,
extremists like bin Laden are marked by their rejection of the pluralism
embedded in the Islamic tradition. They argue that their version of history
is the only one that preserves the heart of the tradition. As a result, they
must be both highly selective in representing this tradition and also intol-
erant of contrary voices. To my mind, it is this intolerance that identifies

them as extremists, purposefully living on the edge of a tradition that loves discussion and disagreement.[5]

Beginnings

The basic stuff of Islamic history has become widely known: a charismatic Prophet appears in Arabia in the seventh century, preaches a monotheistic faith and builds the initial Muslim community; his revelations from God are then collected in the Qur'an. The meaning of these events was obvious to those who experienced them. For the following generations, conquests and empire-building occupied their time and prevented serious reflection on these events. It was only 200 years later, when scholars faced a broad, diverse Muslim community, that the construction of history began in earnest as a way of reconciling the present with the exemplary past. Surprisingly, Muslim historians achieved this reconciliation by developing an almost postmodern view of the past: preserving multiple perspectives on key events; presenting them side-by-side; and proclaiming that God alone could know the truth of the matter.

This method of writing history was mirrored in similar methods for extracting legal and ethical action from the Qur'an; the commonest method became known as the doctrine of abrogation. The great legal scholar Muhammad b. Idris al-Shafi'i (d. 820) summarized his method of abrogation when addressing the question of the prayer direction. In al-Shafi'i's day all Muslims prayed facing Mecca, just as they do today, but in the earliest community they prayed facing Jerusalem. Al-Shafi'i writes:

> God [initially] turned his messenger to the direction of the holy temple [of Jerusalem] in prayer. This was the direction of prayer, and it was not permitted to turn in any other direction before its abrogation. But then God abrogated prayer in the direction of the holy temple and turned [Muhammad] in the direction of the House [in Mecca]. Then it was no longer permitted, as written, to turn in the direction of the holy temple, nor was it permitted to turn to any other direction than that of the Sacred House . . . The same applies every time God has abrogated, for the meaning of "abrogate" is to abandon His command. It was right in its time, but its abandonment is right, too, since God abrogated it. (al-Shafi'i 1979: 121–2)

In this text al-Shafi'i tries to explain how two subsequent commands from God can each be right in their own time. By using the sequencing of history, al-Shafi'i is able to organize verses and dismiss false interpretations. For example, the Qur'an commands believers "do not come to prayer when you are drunk" (4:46), which seems to suggest a tolerance of moderate drinking. However, another verse contains a more complete prohibition of wine (Qur'an 5:93), and legal scholars understood 5:93 to have been revealed after 4:46, thereby abrogating it. The first verse remains in the Qur'an and is still considered revelation from God, a part of His holy Qur'an. By emphasizing this doctrine of abrogation, Muslim jurists recognize the diversity of God's commands while organizing them to the benefit of the community.

As important as it is as a source for correct human actions, such as jihad, the Qur'an contains only some 600 verses that have direct legal import. Therefore scholars must consult other sources, such as Muhammad's Sunna or his general "way of doing things." The Prophet's words and deeds were preserved and passed on from generation to generation in a form of oral transmission known as hadith. The Arabic word hadith means "narrative," and a typical hadith begins with a list of those from whom the story was received, going back in time to the Prophet. Following this list is the story itself, often an account of the Prophet's actions in a particular situation or the Prophet's advice on a certain problem. The list of transmitters is an integral part of the hadith and connects the story to an authoritative history of scholarship.

The need to organize contradictory hadith was even greater than for verses of the Qur'an, since hadith continued to be collected, and in some cases created, until long after the Prophet's death. When the Prophet's Sunna seems to contradict the Qur'an, their relationship must be clarified. The difficulty of this task was also recognized by al-Shafi'i, who flatly denies that any such contradiction is possible:

> [The Prophet] never says anything except by a judgment from God ... Were it permissible for it to be said that the Messenger of God laid down a Sunna and then abrogated his Sunna by the Qur'an ... it would also be permissible for it to be said that the cutting off of the hand of the thief should not be dropped even if the stolen article were kept securely or if its value were less than a quarter dinar. (al-Shafi'i 1979: 111–12)

What al-Shafi'i is referring to is the fact that an important Prophetic Sunna clarified, but did not contradict, the stark command of the Qur'an to cut off the hand of a thief. In actual practice, the punishment for theft was never administered unless the value of the stolen goods exceeded one-quarter of a gold dinar and the item could not be recovered. But if one simply read the Qur'an literally, without this historical context, then even stealing a loaf of bread could be cause for amputation.

Here the history of the early community is cited to guide interpretation, but al-Shafi'i appeals to more than simple chronology. Rather, the role of the Prophet as bearer of the revelation is invoked. As God's chosen Prophet, he knew best what was meant by the Qur'anic text, so in some cases his interpretations are taken as more authoritative than the apparent meaning of the Qur'an. How one remembers the history of that Prophetic moment, those 22 years of revelation and the early community of Muslims, is key to identifying and interpreting sacred text in Islam.

As influential as it was, not everyone accepted al-Shafi'i's construction of history, but most everyone seemed to agree that it is not possible simply to extract meaning from the Qur'an directly. Rather that text must be read within several historical constructs: the correct order of the revealed verses; the interpretive words of the Prophet and his companions; and the practice of the Muslim community. With these tools of history and abrogation in hand, we can now turn to classical and modern views of the lesser jihad. The classical genres of legal and historical writings each stake a claim to authority, and in those different constructs of jihad we will see the effects of different rememberings of history.

Classical views

As we think back to the American Revolution, it is hard for us to imagine anyone fighting that sort of war. Two hundred years ago, British navies fired guns on our port cities, and their armies marched across our fields and forests. Both sides commandeered supplies from local farmers and most every family had someone fighting in the war, on one side or the other. Today we are comparatively distant from war; most of us could hardly handle a combat rifle, much less fly a B-2 bomber. The same must have been true for our legal scholar al-Shafi'i (d. 820) as he struggled to make sense out of the prescriptions for war in the Qur'an, written almost 200 years before his time.

Al-Shafi'i wrote his books from within a rich and stable Islamic empire, one whose enemies remained hundreds and even thousands of miles from the capital in Baghdad. Professional armies fought campaigns from year to year, but so meager was the popular interest in these campaigns that the government had to hire mercenaries and slaves to fill the ranks. Trade flourished (coins from this period have been found as far away as Scandinavia), schools and hospitals were built, and increasing numbers of people devoted themselves to the study of philosophy, theology, and the sources of religious law.

Part of al-Shafi'i's problem was how to square these new realities with the history of warfare in the Qur'anic period. Clearly the Qur'an could not be irrelevant, since God states directly: "We have sent down to you the Book as a clarification for everything and as a guidance and a mercy" (Qur'an 16:91). But then how was it relevant? Al-Shafi'i begins his discussion by quoting the theological basis for warfare in the Qur'an:

> God has imposed the duty of jihad as laid down in His book and uttered by His Prophet's tongue. He stressed the calling of the jihad as follows: "God has bought from the believers their selves and their possessions against the gift of Paradise. They fight in the way of God;

they kill, and are killed; that is a promise binding upon God in the Torah and Gospel and the Qur'an; and who fulfils his covenant better than God? So rejoice in the bargain you have made with Him." (al-Shafi'i 1979: 82–3; the quotation from the Qur'an is *Sura* 9.112)

It is instructive to note that the Qur'an sees this duty of war as continuous with that imposed by God on Christians and Jews. Al-Shafi'i continues to quote several other verses from the Qur'an along with statements from the Prophet that seem to suggest, however, that taking part in war is required of all able-bodied believers at all times, just as with other religious duties such as the giving of alms or the performance of prayer. He even admits that "the literal meaning of this communication is that the duty is obligatory on all men (*rijal*)" (al-Shafi'i 1979: 84). But in al-Shafi'i's understanding, the literal meaning, taken out of historical context, does not yield an accurate interpretation. Using other Qur'an verses, as well as Prophetic example, he demonstrates that jihad was not imposed on everyone at all times even during the Prophet's lifetime.

God said [in the Qur'an]: "It is not for the believers to go forth all together, but why should not a part of every section of them go forth . . ." [Qur'an 9:123]. [Al-Shafi'i explained:] When the Apostle went to battle he was accompanied by some of his companions while others stayed at home; for Ali b. Abi Talib stayed at home during the battle of Tabuk. Nor did God ordain that all Muslims were under obligation to go to battle, for He said: "Why should not a part of every section of them go forth?" So He made it known that going into battle was obligatory on some, but not all, just as knowledge of the law is not obligatory on all but on some . . . If some go forth [into battle], so that a sufficient number fulfils the collective duty, the others do not fall into error. (al-Shafi'i 1979: 85–6)

As we will see below, this distinction between a "collective duty" and an "individual duty" will be completely reversed by Osama bin Laden, but what I find important here is the construction of a historical narrative to interpret texts and the fact that a "literal" reading may be misleading.

Al-Shafi'i's concern to make sense out of Qur'anic commands was not widely shared in the classical period. Legal texts by other authors were far less concerned with the Qur'an, taking instead the practice of the community as the primary issue. In most every legal text, one chapter is devoted to jihad, usually clustered with chapters on funerals, oaths, and international relations. It is rarely connected to the chapters on the duties of faith: prayer, pilgrimage, fasting, and charity. The *Muwatta'* of Malik b. Anas (d. 795), for example, cites very few verses from the Qur'an and has only a short section on issues of going to war. Even the question of how to wage war receives little space, though Malik does cite a statement of Abu Bakr (d. 634): "I advise you ten things: Do not kill women or children or an aged, infirm person. Do not cut down fruit-bearing trees. Do not destroy an inhabited place. Do not slaughter sheep or camels except for food. Do not burn bees and do not scatter them. Do not steal from the booty, and do not be cowardly" (Malik b. Anas 1951: 448). The vast majority of Malik's chapter is devoted to what to do after war: how to bury the dead, how to divide the spoils of war, and how to treat the conquered peoples. In this text, emphasis is much more on practical rules, not on jihad as a religious duty.

In a sense, both al-Shafi'i and Malik were addressing the same problem. While the sacred history of the early community has an undeniable religious authority, it is hard to gain clear rules from a period marked by so much change. Whereas al-Shafi'i attempts to deal with this by developing logical rules of order and primacy, Malik simply pays more attention to the pragmatic needs of the community. Another way of resolving the issue, however, is to homogenize the history itself, and cite those events that fit a narrative of salvation. The author of one of the grandest of narratives was Abu Ja'far al-Tabari (d. 923).[6]

While there is no single, official history of Islam, al-Tabari's *History of Prophets and Kings* is one of the most highly regarded accounts. He begins not with the birth of Muhammad, but with the creation of the world, demonstrating God's active involvement in every moment. Only after 1,000 pages of history is Muhammad's birth recorded, and his early life is filled with signs of his coming mission. In one of these stories, two angels come and place him on a scale, weighing him against ten, then one hundred, then one thousand of his people, but Muhammad outweighs them all. His breast is then opened and his heart removed; al-Tabari purports to record Muhammad's own account of this event:

> He opened my heart, and took out from it the pollution of Satan and the clot of blood, and threw them away. Then one said to the other, "Wash his breast as you would a receptacle—or, wash his heart as you would a covering." [. . .] Then they sewed up my breast and placed the seal between my shoulders. No sooner had they done this than they turned away from me. While this was happening I was watching it as though I were a bystander. (Watt and McDonald 1988: 75)

This spiritual cleansing is just one of the many such stories that al-Tabari cites in order to emphasize God's special favor toward his chosen Prophet. Al-Tabari then recounts the Prophet's trials in his hometown of Mecca, recalling incident after incident of persecution by the Meccan polytheists. This persecution eventually forced Muhammad and his followers to flee Mecca for Medina, where the clans of the Khazraj tribe willingly protected him and his community. Al-Tabari records this account of their pledge, as one of their leaders addressed them:

"People of the Khazraj, do you know what you are pledging your-selves to in swearing allegiance to this man?" "Yes," they said. He continued, "In swearing allegiance to him you are pledging your-selves to wage war against all mankind. If you think that when your wealth is exhausted by misfortune and your nobles are depleted by death you will give him up, then stop now, for, by God, it is disgrace in this world and the next if you later give him up. But if you think that you will be faithful to the promises which you made in invit-ing him, even if your wealth is exhausted and your nobles killed, then take him, for, by God, he is the best thing for you in this world and the next." They answered, "We shall take him even if it brings the loss of our wealth and the killing of our nobles. What shall we gain for this, O Messenger of God, if we are faithful?" He answered, "Paradise." (Watt and McDonald 1988: 134)

Thus, with prophecy and apocalyptic references, al-Tabari lays the foun-dation for a singular interpretation of this history. In contrast, several verses in the Qur'an suggest that Muhammad's early followers were much more equivocal about the prospects of war. For example, the Qur'an states: "Fighting is prescribed for you, though it be hateful to you. Yet it may be that you will hate a thing that is better for you, just as you may love a thing that is worse for you" (Qur'an 2:215). Other Qur'an verses speak of the many Muslims who preferred staying at home to fighting. Even al-Tabari records a variant version of this pledge in which para-dise is gained by the following terms: "that we should not associate any-thing with God, should not steal, should not commit adultery, should not kill our children, should not produce any lie . . . and should not disobey [Muhammad] in what was proper." Warfare does not appear at all in this pledge, but al-Tabari dates it to the previous year, claiming that it was superceded (El-Hibri 1999: 127).

Classical Islamic texts therefore offer at least two competing narratives about jihad and Islamic history. In the legal texts, jihad is seen as a lim-ited venture that need concern only one part of the community. Just as the community as a whole must support and train religious scholars, so also the community must see that there is a sufficient army available to defend Islamic territory; in no way does the duty of jihad approach the duties of prayer, pilgrimage, fasting, or charity so far as the individual Muslim is concerned. In contrast, many history texts glorify the role of jihad in the early community. More than simply a series of local skirmishes, these early battles are seen as signs of God's direct guidance of his community. Both sorts of text depend on the same set of events, but they each construct a his-torical narrative that responds to issues of contemporary importance. For the legal scholars, a pragmatic approach was taken; the apocalyptic nature of war in the early community was clearly irrelevant and warfare needed to be routinized into a functioning government. For historians, emphasis on a glorious past was a way of making up for an overall decline in the empire, and the re-telling of the sacred history could itself be a pious act.

Modern responses

Medieval manipulation of historical events lays the groundwork for understanding modern interpretations. Today, in a manner quite similar to al-Tabari and al-Shafi'i, reformers, feminists, and militant extremists all turn to the early history of Islam to support their interpretations. The Moroccan sociologist Fatima Mernissi has written about this process with extraordinary clarity:

> Delving into memory, slipping into the past, is an activity that these days is closely supervised . . . The act of recollecting, like acts of black magic, really only has an effect on the present. And this works through strict manipulation of its opposite—the time of the dead, of those who are absent, the silent time that could tell us everything. (Mernissi 1991: 9–10)

In her study, Mernissi returns to the classical history texts, mining them for new information and making them respond to modern concerns. In this process, Mernissi discovers that

> Ample historical evidence portrays women in the Prophet's Medina raising their heads from slavery and violence to claim their right to join, as equal participants, in the making of their Arab history . . . Muslims can take pride that . . . women enjoyed the right to enter into the councils of the Muslim *umma* [community], to speak freely to its Prophet-leader, to dispute with the men, to fight for their happiness, and to be involved in the management of military and political affairs. The evidence is there in the works of religious history [of the women] who built Muslim society side by side with their male counterparts. (El-Hibri 1999: viii)

Some may find Mernissi's reading to be surprising, even misleading.[7] Islam, she claims, is not a religion built on violence and war, but rather a revolutionary set of beliefs that supported equality for women and democratic change while women in the rest of the world were still suffering in virtual slavery. This notion of Islam as a revolutionary movement has its roots in apocalyptic texts, and resonates with other voices from the modern world, both reformist and traditionalist, but it would be misleading to suggest that their interpretive strategies are identical. Whereas Mernissi and the reformers are challenging elitist control of the tradition, and opening up new interpretive possibilities, traditionalist extremists like Osama bin Laden are closing down and restricting interpretation.

Reformers find both inspiration and variety of opinion in the medieval texts; extremists find only their own perceptions.

There is perhaps no clearer counter-example to Osama bin Laden than Muhammad Abduh (d. 1905), one of the most important figures in recent Islamic history. Respected by both secular and religious authorities, Abduh transcended many of the divisions in Egyptian society of the late nineteenth century. As Grand Mufti of Egypt, Abduh held a position of power with the monarchy and with the British government. He used that power to help reform al-Azhar into a modern religious university, and he was instrumental in laying the foundations for Cairo University as a secular institution.

Abduh's book, *The Theology of Unity*, is another version of sacred history, but his starting point is neither the birth of the Prophet nor the creation of the world. Rather, he begins with a rational defense for the existence of God. Using the language of Muslim philosophers before him, he discusses God's attributes and his essence and sees God as the "originating cause" of all creation, the only being who is not contingent on some other cause but is himself "necessarily existing" (Abduh 1964: 44). By beginning in this way, Abduh seeks to portray Islam as a thoroughly rational religion.

Abduh freely admits the fact of warfare during the Prophet's lifetime, but emphasizes God's purposes in this warfare over human involvement.

> Like other religions, Islam began with its message. But it encountered a quite unprecedented enmity on the part of those who in their perversity oppressed the truth. No prophet had such antagonism or faced such humiliation as Muhammad ... The different religious sects inhabiting the Arabian peninsula and neighboring areas joined forces against Islam to root it out and strangle its message. It was a case of the strong against the weak, the wealthy against the poor. Islam in its steadfast self-defence had nothing to rely on save its inherent truth, pitted against error and the light of its guidance in the darkness of falsehood, to bring it to victory ...
>
> They waged war against the superior enemy and overcame them, for all their vast numbers, strength and advanced equipment. When the distresses of war were spent and sovereignty passed to the victor, Islam treated the vanquished with kindly gentleness, allowed them to maintain their religions and their rites in security and peace. They gave them protection and safeguarded their possessions, as they did their own people and their property, levying for this service a slight tax on their incomes according to stipulated rates. (Abduh 1964: 142–3)

Abduh uses much the same set of facts as does al-Tabari. But al-Tabari portrays the ill treatment of the Prophet as a crime that deserved to be punished. The view of war espoused by the Khazraj tribe is one of apocalyptic fury that might well never end. In contrast, Abduh sees the Prophet as an innocent, persecuted for simply preaching the truth. The early battles and the wars of conquest were only undertaken in self-defense, and against great odds. Victory was neither sought nor desired, but when it was thrust on the Muslims, they ruled in justice. This account of history fits into Abduh's overall claim for Islam as the most rational and most socially just of religions. After detailing the ways Islam removes racial and economic differences, he states:

> There is no important aspect of good conduct in which [Islam] has not brought a new lease of life—nothing essential to the social fabric it has failed to enjoin. As we have shown, it brings together for mature man, freedom of thought, intellectual independence of action, and thus integrity of character, enhancement of capacity and a general quickening of intention and achievement. Whoever reads the Qur'an rightly will find new impulse and initiative and unfailing treasure. (Abduh 1964: 140)

As different as Abduh's portrayal is from that of al-Tabari, they both place jihad into the past, seeing this sort of God-ordained warfare as something belonging to a specific historical moment in sacred history. Speaking from within a state controlled by the British government, Abduh is simply appealing for the right of self-determination, not calling for another revolutionary war.

After Abduh's death, however, British and French control over the Middle East only increased. In response, the Ottoman Empire allied itself with the axis forces of Italy and Germany in World War I. The results of that alliance were disastrous for the region, and the Empire was forcibly split into British and French spheres of influence. Egypt did not win full independence until the officers' revolution of 1952 that put Gamal Abd al-Nasir into power, and Algeria did not win independence from France until the bloody wars of independence in the 1960s. Nearly every Islamic nation in the world was born in the twentieth century out of some colonialist history, and many had pro-Western governments installed and maintained by Europe and the United States.

Part of this colonialist legacy can be seen in the legal institutions of these new nations, most of which have been borrowed from Britain, France, and other European countries. Calls for a "return to Islamic law" may sometimes be seen, therefore, as calls for local control over history and for self-determination. Such legitimate concerns are exploited by revolutionary extremists, like Osama bin Laden, who tap into popular discontent with military autocracy.

We know much more about bin Laden's thought in recent years, due to some excellent scholarship;[8] much insight can be gained, for example, from a 1998 declaration that he made along with other radical leaders.[9]

That declaration is important for several reasons, notably its claim that the killing of Americans is an "individual duty," incumbent on each and every Muslim. As al-Shafi'i noted earlier, such a claim goes against both the Qur'an and the Sunna of the Prophet, which define jihad as a duty on the collective community. By making jihad an individual duty, bin Laden is leaving conventional interpretations and condoning individual terrorist acts.

Further, bin Laden cloaks these new interpretations in a unique reading of Islamic history, one that both portrays the Prophet as a single-minded warrior and also describes the current situation in apocalyptic terms. By comparing bin Laden's readings with those of the traditional sources, we can understand the extremist nature of his rhetoric. For example, the declaration begins in good Islamic fashion with invocations of God and the Prophet:

> Praise be to God, who revealed the Book, controls the clouds, defeats factionalism, and says in His Book: "But when the forbidden months are past, then fight and slay the pagans wherever ye find them, seize them, beleaguer them, and lie in wait for them in every stratagem (of war)"; and peace be upon our Prophet, Muhammad Bin-'Abdallah, who said: "I have been sent with the sword between my hands to ensure that no one but God is worshipped, God who put my livelihood under the shadow of my spear and who inflicts humiliation and scorn on those who disobey my orders."[10]

In this short passage, the whole history of Islam is being manipulated in obvious, and also some less obvious, ways. War is portrayed as God's preferred means of spreading monotheistic beliefs, and that fighting is encouraged with citation of specific means. The war and the warlike stance are to be maintained until the whole world is subdued. Further, the Prophet is portrayed as conceiving his mission and indeed his whole livelihood in similar terms, with God actively supporting his every move. Missing, of course, are quotations from the Qur'an urging believers to incline toward peace (such as 8:61: "If they incline to peace, you should too!"), and the Prophet's preoccupation with peace treaties, state-building, and equitable treatment of both Muslim and non-Muslim.[11]

Far subtler is the manipulation of the Arabic sources. First, the translation consistently chooses the most warlike interpretations of the Arabic: "fight and slay" is chosen over the more accurate "fight," and "pagan" is chosen over "polytheist." The latter choice is important, since this verse refers explicitly to the polytheistic Meccans, and not to non-Muslims in general. Further, the verse is cut off in the Arabic text, before its important concluding section: "but if they repent, perform the prayer and pay alms, then let them go their way; surely God is most-forgiving and compassionate" (Qur'an 9:5).

The hadith of the Prophet is even more problematic. First, this hadith is unknown in the great medieval collections. The most important collection (Bukhari) only records the second half of the hadith, which reads quite differently when translated alone and more accurately: "My livelihood was placed under the shadow of my spear, and humiliation and scorn have been placed on those who oppose my orders" (Ibn Hajar 1986: 6:115). Even this hadith is questionable according to the standards set by medieval scholars, since the last transmitter before Bukhari (Abu Munib al-Jurashi) is unknown.[12] If we also disregard the classical sources, the English is still misleading; a better translation of the Arabic would be: "I have been sent with the sword while the hour is upon me, until God alone is worshipped."

The apocalyptic reference here to the Hour of God's Judgment is mirrored in the next paragraph of bin Laden's declaration, which describes the American presence on Saudi Arabian soil as "crusader armies spreading in it like locusts, taking over its land, eating its riches and wiping out its plantations." After a list of American crimes, the declaration culminates in an appeal to drive these armies from Muslim lands and to liberate the al-Aqsa mosque in Jerusalem and the Ka'ba in Mecca.

Through this careful manipulation of sources, bin Laden is able to suggest, against all evidence to the contrary, that individual acts of terrorism can actually be seen as ways of rehearsing sacred history. Apparently, some of the 9/11 hijackers were influenced by just this argument, as evidenced by a letter found with Muhammad Atta's belongings. This letter is striking in its use of religious devotional language, and the author seems to be convinced that his action was equivalent to those of the Prophet and his companions.[13] Of course, those actions were roundly condemned by all major Muslim authorities, both because of the wanton killing of innocent human beings and also because suicide is strictly prohibited in Islam.[14]

What Osama bin Laden demonstrates here is the power of that original sacred narrative to stir passions and foment social change. Were it not for the quotations of Qur'an and Prophetic hadith and the allusions to apocalyptic events, his call to "kill Americans everywhere" would come across as the ravings of a lunatic. But those quotations lend a substantial veneer of authority to his writings, so much so that many who have only a cursory knowledge of Islamic history have been fooled. This is, I would argue, precisely his purpose. By referring to sacred history in this manner, and by making donations to orphanages and other religious charities, bin Laden is making a claim on the heart of the Islamic tradition, attempting to present his extremist ideas as those of the mainstream.

Conclusion

It would be easy to conclude from this discussion that history does not matter, only its manipulation. After all, the same set of events seems to yield widely divergent interpretations: feminist versus militant; spiritual versus rational. Yet such a conclusion would be rash for two reasons. First, religious history does concern itself with real events that did, in fact, happen. Whatever interpretations may arise, they must always be in conversation with the evidence as preserved in manuscripts, archaeological sites, and other sources. We can use this evidence to identify bin Laden's construction of history as so extreme as to be nearly unrecognizable. Gone is the Prophet's distinction between the lesser and the greater jihad, and missing too are Abu Bakr's rules of engagement: "Do not kill women or children . . . Do not destroy an inhabited place." We can also compare the classical sources and criticize bin Laden's citation of Prophetic hadith, and complete his quotations from the Qur'an.

Second, interpretations do not happen in a vacuum but in the ongoing discussions of a community. For instance, martyrdom is an important subject for Islam, as it is for many other religious traditions, but bin Laden confuses suicide missions with martyrdom, a distinction that is clearly maintained in the classical sources.[15] The larger Muslim community has responded to bin Laden's constructions of history by censuring him and denouncing attacks organized by Al Qaeda; in responding in this way, they are reasserting their construction of sacred history as the norm.

Modern Muslim interpreters of history all struggle to have their version accepted as defining the new norm. In so doing, they implicitly recognize the power of sacred history to transform and revolutionize the community, as well as to express the community's most profound hopes and desires. When we read the history of another religion, we are joining that process. The more we learn, the more complex our picture of that religion will become, and the better we can discern pious exhortations to join the "Greater Jihad" from devious attempts to describe the killing of innocents as a religious act. Further, we can distinguish methods of interpretation that maintain an ongoing exploration of the classical sources from those that would purport to give us a singular definition of the truth. In these important ways, then, scholars of religion can take an activist stance, providing a useful analysis of religious movements while steering clear of both advocacy and cultural relativism.

It is interesting to note that despite all the fear of terrorism and of Muslims, Muslim immigration to the United States continues unabated. That mosque in Newburgh that I mentioned is growing, and the congregation has doubled in size since 2001. They have also, however, changed their name from the Mosque of the Greater Jihad to the Mosque of Ikhlas. Like jihad, *ikhlas* is a complex and important religious word; evoking the notions of faithfulness and devotion, it is the title of one of the most important chapters of the Qur'an. It seems to me that this move, from jihad to *ikhlas*, from struggle to faith, is a message of hope from that small congregation, a statement of their place, well woven into the fabric of American life.

Notes

1 Like many narratives of the Prophet, this one is laden with mythical elements and cannot be taken as historical fact; it is, however, a good reflection of a genuine tendency within the religious tradition.
2 In emphasizing the narrative elements of religious history, I am following a recent trend among scholars to respond to literary theorists. Like Andrew Greeley (1996), for example, I am intrigued by the imaginative and creative aspects of religious story telling, but I am not ready to ascribe so much power to the audience. Rather, like Richard Davis (1997), I find that historical facts, texts, and images can also play a corrective and creative role in this dialogue.
3 For those interested in a theoretical discussion of this dynamic of meaning, see Brockopp 2005.
4 For an overview, see Sohail Hashmi 2003.
5 See, for examples, Johansen 1999; Abou El Fadl 2001.
6 For a fascinating account of al-Tabari's approach to history, see Tayeb El-Hibri 1999.
7 See, for example, Mohammed Fadel's 1997 article reviewing Mernissi and other modernist authors.
8 See, for example, the excellent collection of his writings, introduced by Bruce Lawrence, *Messages to the World: The Statements of Osama Bin Laden* (Lawrence 2005). The statement discussed here appears in that collection on pages 58–62.
9 Published in the newspaper *Al-Quds al-'Arabi* (London) in Arabic; February 23, 1998.
10 The translation used here is the one first made available on the Internet. The translator is anonymous but, as I point out, made specific choices that emphasize the bellicose stance of the declaration. A new, more accurate translation is found in Lawrence 2005: 59.
11 Beyond the description of warfare as the lesser jihad, the sources record 27 peace treaties negotiated by the Prophet. Delegations were sent to all towns in advance of the conquering forces, and most major cities, such as Mecca, Jerusalem, and Alexandria, were taken with very little bloodshed. The Qur'an also makes many statements urging peaceful negotiations, such as "The good deed is not equal to the evil deed; repel [the evil deed] with one that is better. And behold! The one against whom there was enmity will be as a loyal friend to you" (41:34). See also Qur'an 2:256, 5:32, 16:125, and 29:46.
12 See the discussion in Ibn Hajar al-Asqalani 1986 vol. 6: 115–16. Ibn Hajar notes that Ibn Hanbal does record a longer version which reads: "I have been sent with the sword while the hour is upon me, and my livelihood was placed under the shadow of my spear, and humiliation and scorn were placed on those who oppose my orders."
13 See Woodward's article, "In Hijacker's Bags, a Call to Planning, Prayer and Death," in the *Washington Post*, September 28, 2001.
14 For a collection of some responses maintained by Omid Safi, see http://groups.colgate.edu/aarislam/response.htm.
15 See, for example, my essay on "The Good Death in Islamic Theology and Law" (Brockopp 2003).

References

Abduh, Muhammad. 1964. *The Theology of Unity*. Trans. Ishaq Musaad and Kenneth Cragg. London: Allen and Unwin.

Abou El Fadl, Khaled. 2001. *Conference of the Books: The Search for Beauty in Islam*. Lanham, MD: University Press of America.

al-Shafi'i, Muhammad b. Idris. 1979. *Al-Risala*. Ed. Ahmad Muhammad Shakir. Cairo: Dar al-Turath.

b. Anas, Malik. 1951. *Al-Muwatta'*. Ed. Muhammad Fu'ad 'Abd al-Baqi. Cairo: Dar Ihya' al-Kutub al-'Arabiyya.

Brockopp, Jonathan. 2003. "The Good Death in Islamic Theology and Law." In *Islamic Ethics of Life: Abortion, War and Euthanasia*, edited by Jonathan E. Brockopp, 177–93. Columbia, SC: University of South Carolina Press.

——. 2005. "Theorizing Charismatic Authority in Early Islamic Law." *Comparative Islamic Studies* 1 (2): 129–58

Davis, Richard. 1997. *Lives of Indian Images*. Princeton, NJ: Princeton University Press.

El-Hibri, Tayeb. 1999. *Reinterpreting Islamic Historiography*. Cambridge: Cambridge University Press.

Fadel, Mohammed. 1997. "Two Women, One Man: Knowledge, Power, and Gender in Medieval Sunni Legal Thought." *International Journal of Middle East Studies* 29 (2): 185–205.

Greeley, Andrew. 1996. *Religion as Poetry*. New Brunswick, NJ: Transaction.

Hashmi, Sohail. 2003. "Saving and Taking Life in War: Three Modern Muslim Views." In *Islamic Ethics of Life: Abortion, War and Euthanasia*, edited by Jonathan E. Brockopp, 129–54. Columbia, SC: University of South Carolina Press.

Ibn Hajar al-Asqalani. 1986. *Fath al-bari*. 13 vols. Cairo: Dar al-Rayan li-l-Turath.

Johansen, Baber. 1999. *Contingency in a Sacred Law: Legal and Ethical Norms in the Muslim Fiqh*. Leiden: E. J. Brill.

Lawrence, Bruce, ed. 2005. *Messages to the World: The Statements of Osama Bin Laden*. New York: Verso.

Mernissi, Fatima. 1991. *The Veil and the Male Elite*. Trans. Mary Jo Lakeland. Reading, MA: Addison-Wesley.

Watt, W. Montgomery and M. V. McDonald, trans. 1988. *Muhammad at Mecca (The History of al-Tabari, vol. 6)*. Albany, NY: State University of New York Press.

Woodward, Bob. 2001. "In Hijacker's Bags, a Call to Planning, Prayer, and Death." *The Washington Post*, September 28.

12 The roots of public attitudes toward state accommodation of European Muslims' religious practices before and after September 11[1]

Joel S. Fetzer and J. Christopher Soper

May I suggest that the last thing our society needs at this moment is more schools segregated by religion? Before 11 September, it looked like a bad idea; it now looks like a mad idea.

Tony Wright (*Hansard* November 22, 2001)

My country, France, my fatherland, is once again being invaded, with the blessing of our successive governments, by an excessive influx of foreigners, notably Muslims, to which we are giving our allegiance . . . From year to year we see mosques sprouting up pretty much everywhere in France, while church bells are becoming silent because of a lack of priests.

French actress and animal-rights advocate Brigitte Bardot
(Agence France Presse 1996)

I see that Islam can represent an enrichment for social life. I think it could represent an even greater enrichment if people approached it with a more open mind . . . People just want to have their prejudices confirmed. No one is ready, really to listen or in any way to think a little differently . . . Especially on the topic "Women and Islam," Islam is reduced to the hijāb, polygamy, and inheritance law.

Maryam, a 37-year-old German convert to Islam
(Biehl and Kabak 1999: 108)

In functioning democracies, political elites ignore mass opinion at their electoral peril. Over the last two decades, the political appeal of such anti-immigrant—or even anti-Muslim—political parties as the British National Party, the French Front National, and the Dutch List Pim Fortuyn appears to have led governing parties to adopt harsher measures toward immigrants, many of whom are Muslims. Rather than be thrown out of office by anti-Muslim voters, mainstream politicians prefer to adopt moderate versions of the anti-immigrant or anti-Muslim platforms advocated by the extreme right (Geddes 2002). The 2007 election of Nicolas Sarkozy is an indication of this trend.

European states have long struggled with how best to integrate Muslim immigrants into historically Christian societies (Nielsen 1999; Ramadan 1999). While states vary in the extent to which they foster Muslim religious activities, popular antipathy to Islam sometimes limits their policy options. Determining the extent of opposition to state accommodation of Muslim religious practices and isolating the causes of such hostility have thus become all the more critical to West European politics.

Many scholars have studied Europeans' attitudes toward immigration policy (e.g., Hoskin 1991; Fetzer 2000). Very few micro-level data on public views of Muslims' religious rights even exist, however, and methodologically sophisticated, cross-national analysis of mass-level attitudes toward Muslims is virtually nonexistent. Following a brief description of overall European attitudes toward state accommodation of Muslim practices, we therefore intend to close this gap in the literature by conducting a multivariate analysis of our privately commissioned polls on Muslim rights and of several related surveys. Because Britain, France, and Germany have the largest Muslim populations, we focus on these three countries in our surveys and analysis.

Data and descriptive statistics

To measure public support for state accommodation of Muslims' religious practices, respondents in our three-nation, two-wave survey (Roper Europe 2001, 2002) were asked policy questions specific to their country. Ideally, we would have used a common question in the three countries to make the responses perfectly comparable. However, policy debate on state accommodation of Muslims' religious rights varies in the three nations. The issue at the forefront of debate in Britain is state aid to separate Islamic schools (Dwyer and Meyer 1995). For decades, the state has financed thousands of Anglican and Catholic schools and dozens of Jewish ones. Muslims argue that the state, which currently finances only a handful of Islamic schools, should provide aid to their institutions under the same conditions. In France, the most controversial issue has been students' wearing of the hijāb in state schools. After more than a decade of controversy, the French parliament in 2004 passed a law banning the hijāb in such schools, but the issue remains a political flashpoint (Fetzer and Soper 2005). In Germany, finally, the most debated issue has been whether to include instruction about Islam in state schools. While schools in some Länder provide such publicly funded religious instruction (Pfaff 2000), others do not.

In Britain, participants in our poll were surveyed about whether the government should

1   approve funding for more Islamic schools (labeled "expand" in figure 12.1);
2   limit its approval to those currently permitted (labeled "status quo"); or
3   cancel its approval ("restrict").

French interviewees indicated whether wearing the hijāb

1   should always be allowed in state schools ("expand");
2   should only be allowed during school breaks and other recreational times ("status quo"); or
3   should never be allowed ("restrict").

In Germany, finally, respondents stated that state schools should

1   provide instruction in Islam for every Muslim student who wishes to have it ("expand");
2   provide such instruction only where Muslim students make up a large proportion of the school ("status quo"); or
3   never provide such classes ("restrict").

As figure 12.1 indicates, public attitudes toward state accommodation of Muslim religious practices differ significantly in the three countries. French respondents are far less likely to support an expansive policy (17 percent) than are their British (32 percent) or German counterparts (62 percent). It is also interesting to note that in none of the countries did a majority of the respondents support the policy status quo, which further indicates that issues surrounding Muslims' religious rights are both unsettled and contentious in each of the countries. Two other relevant polls generally mirror our results. The 1995 SOFRES French National Election Study included an item on whether it was "normal" for "Muslims living in France" to have "mosques to practice their religion" (Boy and Mayer 1997: Annexe 4). Nearly half (43 percent) of the respondents disagreed with this statement. The 1996 German Social Survey (ALLBUS 1996) likewise asked respondents their views about including Islam in religion classes in the state schools. A plurality (40.3 percent) of western German interviewees believed that such instruction should be provided, 33.3 percent held that only Christianity should be taught, and 26.5 percent maintained that religion classes should be abolished altogether.

Theories of opposition to the political accommodation of Muslim religious practices

No one theory specifically attempts to explain public attitudes toward state accommodation of Muslim religious practices. There are, however,

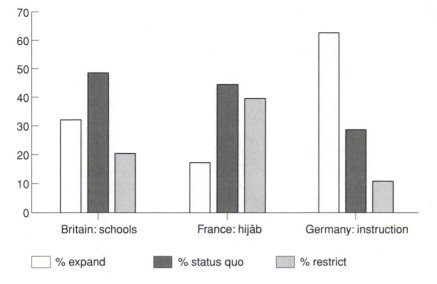

Figure 12.1 Public support for state accommodation of key Muslim religious demands in Britain, France, and Germany

a number of more general explanations of political behavior that may be applied to our inquiry.

Status as religious majority/minority

One theory that seems particularly relevant to our study is that of status politics, developed by Seymour Martin Lipset. Lipset (1981; see also Gusfield 1963) argues that status distinctions based on religion are often the basis for the political divisions in a society. The majority religion, often with the support of the state, subjects minority religions to various types of social and political discrimination. Minority groups respond by forming movements of religious defense, thereby bringing religious cleavages to the center of partisanship and political debate.

State policy in Britain, France, and Germany may advantage some churches and disadvantage Muslims and some other religious minorities in various ways. Mass public attitudes toward state accommodation of Muslim religious practices might reflect those policy choices. If this theory is correct, a person's religious identification should determine her or his attitude toward the political question of whether the state should accommodate Muslim religious practices. Religious minorities would favor an extension of state benefits to include Muslims, while members of the religious majority would oppose any further accommodation of Muslims' religious practices.

Duncan Macpherson (1997: 110) has hypothesized about such a mobilization among religious minorities in Britain. He suggests that the situation in

Table 12.1 Religious identification in Britain, France, and Germany

	Britain	*France*	*Germany*
Church of England	51.9		
Catholic	10.8	66.5	32.6
Lutheran or Reformed Protestant	2.2	1.9	39.8
Evangelical, Born-Again, or Free-Church Protestant	2.5		0.2
Methodist	3.1		
Baptist	1.3		
Muslim	2.3	3.5	0.8
Jewish	1.0	0.6	
Hindu	1.2		
Buddhist		0.2	
Other	4.7	1.4	1.5
No Religion	19.0	26.1	25.1
n	872	976	959

Source: Roper Europe (2001).

Note: Data weighted by demographic characteristics. Smaller religious groups may have been under-represented in this sample (e.g., Muslims and Jews in Germany).

which British Muslims found themselves at the end of the twentieth century was in many ways analogous to the social and political position of Roman Catholics in the last three-quarters of the nineteenth century. Given that they share "analogous experiences of exclusion and discrimination, of popular hostility and of intellectual disdain," it is quite possible that Muslims and Roman Catholics in Britain would join forces for political purposes.

As table 12.1 indicates, the religious majorities in the three countries are Church of England (Britain), Roman Catholic (France), and Lutheran or Reformed Protestant (Evangelische; Germany). Prominent religious minorities, on the other hand, include Jews, Hindus, Muslims, Buddhists, Baptists, Methodists, British and German Catholics, French Protestants, and British evangelical or German "free-church" Protestants.

As table 12.2 suggests, public opinion data do not generally support this religious-majority/minority theory. With the obvious exception of Muslims, religious minorities did not usually support the expansion of Islam in the schools. Conversely, our results do not confirm the hypothesis that the religious majority is significantly more hostile to such expansion.

The German sample in table 12.3 echoes our results in table 12.2; religious minorities showed no more support for Islamic instruction in state schools than did the majority.[2] In France, by contrast, Jews (b = 1.784, p < .10) and members of "other religions" (b = 1.373, p < .05) did support Muslims' right to build mosques.

Perhaps this slight difference in results between tables 12.2 and 12.3

Table 12.2 Determinants of support for Islam in the schools in Britain, France, and Germany

	Britain	*France*	*Germany*
Catholic	0.229		0.104
Lutheran or Reformed Protestant		0.058	
Evangelical, Born-Again, or Free-Church Protestant	0.865*		−0.537
Baptist, Methodist, or other Protestant	−0.094		
Muslim	2.537**	0.833**	0.107
Hindu, Jewish, Buddhist, or other religion	−0.242	−0.202	−0.397
No religion	−0.047	0.126	−0.030
Low support for church–state structure	−0.771**	−0.134	0.151
Medium support for church–state structure	−0.459*	−0.871	0.150
Female	0.393	0.168	0.204
Class			
A (Upper Middle)	−0.176	−0.529*	0.476
B (Middle)	0.044	−0.414	−0.130
C1 (Lower Middle)	−0.074	−0.297	0.192
C2 (Skilled Working)	−0.341	−0.124	0.737
D (Working)			
Income		0.048	0.065
Bac/Abitur		0.120	0.429**
Higher university degree		0.386*	0.039
Age	0.017**	0.023**	0.027**
Children	−0.071	−0.067	−0.317
Constant, restrict Islam in schools	−2.591**	−1.737**	−2.929**
Constant, maintain status quo of Islam in schools	−0.254	0.440	−1.105
n	695	811	738
pseudo R^2	0.111	0.065	0.086
χ^2	70.612**	47.097**	54.720**
df	16	16	17

* = $p < .10$. ** = $p < .05$.

Source: Roper Europe (2001).

Note: Estimates are ordered logit coefficients. Data weighted by demographic characteristics.

Table 12.3 Determinants of support for Muslim religious practices in France and Germany

	France	Germany
Catholic		
Active	0.484**	0.066
Nominal		0.192
Protestant	0.089	
Active		−0.342
Free-Church Protestant		−0.545
Other Christian		−0.590
Muslim	6.225	
Jewish	1.784*	
Other religion	1.373**	2.072**
No religion	0.252**	0.463**
Female	−0.123*	0.441**
Professional/managerial	0.215	0.420**
Manual laborer	−0.166	0.140
Non-paid worker	0.003	0.067
Income	0.068**	0.038
Bac/Abitur	0.730**	0.354
Higher university degree	0.851**	−0.104
Age	0.011**	−0.021**
Constant	−0.963**	0.103
n	3617	1305
pseudo R^2	0.123	0.122
χ^2	346.5**	125.1**
df	14	15

* = p < .10. ** = p < .05.

Source: 1995 SOFRES French National Election Study (France) and 1996 ALLBUS (Germany).

Note: Estimates are dichotomous logit coefficients. French data weighted by demographic characteristics.

stems from the different policies proposed. State funding for Islamic schools, Islamic instruction in state schools, or even allowing the wearing of the hijāb in public schools may all be plausibly viewed as state support for religion. Permission to build a mosque, on the other hand, does not imply state sponsorship of Islam. Religious minorities may be more likely to exhibit solidarity with one another on questions of religious liberty than on policies requiring explicit state encouragement.

Solidarity of the religious

Several other theories examine the effects of secularization on political behavior. Theories of culture wars (Hunter 1991), value conflict (Leege and Kellstedt 1993), and culture shift (Inglehart 1990) similarly claim that secularization undermines the political role of religion and poses a threat to religious groups who advocate religiously based public policy. The electoral impact has been a shift from political cleavages based on class to those based on lifestyle concerns. The result, particularly in the United States, has been political conflict around such cultural issues as abortion, gay rights, and the place of religion in public schools. The religious and political divide is not, however, between majority and minority faiths but rather between orthodox religionists of various traditions, who are culturally conservative, and secularists or religious liberals who are culturally liberal (Wuthnow 1988).

Given that large percentages of the population in each of the three countries in our survey claim to have no religion (19 percent in England, 26 percent in France, and 25 percent in Germany) secularism has clearly had an impact on the region. Religously orthodox elites are becoming increasingly aware that secularism threatens their social and political identities. Tariq Modood, a British Muslim, notes that "the real division of opinion is not between a conservative element in the Church of England versus the rest of the country, but between those who think religion has a place in secular public culture and those who think not" (Modood 1994: 72). Similarly, Leslie Newbigin, a British Christian, asserts "in our present situation in Britain, where Christians and Muslims share a common position as minority faiths in a society dominated by the naturalistic ideology, we share a common duty to challenge this ideology" (Newbigin, Sanneh, and Taylor 1998: 22).

If these theories are correct, the data should show a political coalition of secularists on the one hand and orthodox religionists on the other. Arguing that religion should be purely private, secularists should oppose the state accommodating Muslim religious practices. Religionists, on the other hand, ought to support Muslims out of a common conviction that the state should make room for the public expression of religious values.

The results for secularists ("No Religion") in tables 12.2 and 12.3 fail to support this theory, however. Nowhere were secularists more likely than the majority religious group to oppose state accommodation of Muslims' religious practices. In none of the three countries in our survey did the No Religion variable achieve statistical significance (see table 12.2). In table 12.3, moreover, being a secularist appears to have increased support for Muslims' practices (b = .252, p < .05 for France; b = .463, p < .05 for Germany).

Data from practicing or orthodox religionists, on the other hand, provide mixed support for this theory. In Britain, born-again Protestants, who are very likely to be religiously orthodox, did disproportionately agree with the expansion of faith-based schools to include Muslims (b = .865, p < .10; see table 12.2). Practicing Catholics in France likewise defended Muslims' right to build mosques (b = .484, p < .05; see table 12.3). In

Germany, by contrast, variables for Catholics or Evangelische Protestants who regularly attend religious services and free-church Protestants, who are likely orthodox, all failed to produce statistically significant results.

The data, in short, do tend to confirm the view that orthodox religionists have joined forces. It is too early to tell if this centripetal tendency represents the beginnings of the kind of political coalition of religious defense which Europe has seen in the past (Kalyvas 1996; Gould 1999). Secularists, however, do not appear to be rallying against Islam. Perhaps they do not view orthodox religion as enough of a political threat against which to mobilize.

Gender

Gender is another factor that might help to explain public attitudes toward state accommodation of Muslim religious practices in Western Europe. From the standpoint of some feminists, the Islamic faith oppresses women in various ways. They claim that certain passages from the Qur'an teach the inferiority of women, that Islamic laws of inheritance, marriage, and divorce favor males over females, that practices in some Muslim countries oppress women, and that patriarchal pressures and assumptions force Islamic women in Western countries into traditional gender roles. While French feminist Elizabeth Altschull, for example, believes that "all religions have their oppressive aspects toward women," she nevertheless concludes that "none [but Islam] has gone so far, is as systematic, or is as explicit about the inferior status of women, [a status] willed and created by God" (1995: 200). German scholar Ursula Spuler-Stegemann likewise labels the Shi'ah practice of "temporary marriage" (mut'ah) as "religiously legitimated prostitution" (1998: 193–4). Sallah Eddine Ben Abid (2000: 13) acknowledges that there has indeed been a revival in the practice of such marriages "in certain Muslim communities which have immigrated into Europe" (see also Heine 1997: 204–5). What is beyond dispute is that the role of women in Islam is a highly contested issue in Western Europe.

According to gender theory, public accommodation of Islam reinforces sexist models about the proper role of women. To the extent that Islam oppresses women, some feminists would claim, the state should not actively promote this faith by encouraging separate Islamic schools (Britain), allowing Muslim girls to wear the hijāb (France), or teaching about the faith in state schools (Germany). If this theory holds, women in the surveys should therefore disproportionately oppose these policies.

The data do not generally support this theory. No female variable in table 12.2 achieves statistical significance, and in the German ALLBUS sample (see table 12.3), women are significantly more supportive of Islamic instruction (b = .441, p < .05). The only result confirming gender theory is that for women in the French National Election Study, who are more likely to oppose mosque-building (b = –.123, p < .10).

What explains the fact that women are no more likely than men to oppose state accommodation of Muslims' religious practices? One set of explanations comes from some Muslim women, who argue that the Qur'an preaches the spiritual equality of women and men and that Islam is no more inherently patriarchal than other religious traditions. In a study of Islamic women in the West, Anne Sofie Roald notes that, "as in Christianity, where interpretations of biblical verses pertaining to women have been undergoing a process of change recently, in Islam a similar movement seems to be in progress" (2001: 296).

Similarly, many Muslim women argue that the wearing of the hijāb is a symbol of cultural identity, not a sign of women's oppression at the hands of men. While noting that "the early feminist lifting of the face-veil was about emancipation from exclusion," Fadwa El Guindi (1999: 184) asserts that "the voluntary wearing of the hijāb since the mid-seventies is about liberation from imposed, imported identities, consumerist behaviors, and resisting . . . Western dominance." That women in these three countries do not generally oppose state accommodation of Islam might suggest that they are just as likely to accept the claims of many Muslim women as they are to believe non-Muslim feminists about the effects of those policies on gender rights.

Social-class theory

An alternative theory focuses on social class. Scholars of immigration politics have demonstrated that members of the lower and lower-middle classes disproportionately oppose immigration and immigrant rights (Simon and Alexander 1993: 39–40; Fetzer 2000: 116–17), perhaps out of fear of economic competition with working-class immigrants. Because large percentages of migrants to Western Europe are Muslim, lower- and lower-middle-class respondents might plausibly oppose the accommodation of Muslim religious practices. Making life too comfortable for Muslim immigrants, such interviewees might argue, would encourage even greater numbers of Muslims to settle in Europe and compete economically with natives.

The data which we analyze, however, do not generally support this theory. Among respondents in our survey (see table 12.2), only professionals or managers from France produced a statistically significant estimate. This estimated effect, however, is in the direction opposite that predicted by social-class theory (b = -.529, p < .10). Rather than disproportionately supporting state accommodation of Islam, French professionals were more likely to oppose this policy. No occupation variable in the French National Election Study achieved statistical significance (see table 12.3). In the German ALLBUS, in contrast, professionals and managers were more supportive of Islamic instruction (b = .420, p < .05), thus confirming social-class theory.

These results for attitudes toward state accommodation of Muslim religious practices contrast with the findings of some studies of public opinion on immigration policy, which seem more likely to find class effects. It is possible that lower- or lower-middle-class respondents want to restrict immigration but do not necessarily make the connection between stopping further migration and making it more difficult for immigrants already in Europe to practice their religion. If so, this view is consistent with the policies of many states in the region, who are simultaneously acknowledging Muslims' religious rights but also drastically increasing the barriers to immigration by asylum-seekers or economic migrants (Lyall 2002).

Education

A number of studies have suggested that education has a liberalizing effect on political opinions (Jennings and Niemi 1981; Erikson, Luttbeg, and Tedin 1991: 154–9; Alwin, Cohen, and Newcomb 1992). Arguably, the liberal political position is for the state to accommodate Muslims' religious practices. Some scholars have advocated multicultural education in Western European countries on the ground that learning about other faiths would make people more tolerant and understanding of religious diversity (Nielsen 1999; Parekh 2000). If this theory holds, those with more education should be more likely to support Muslims' religious rights.

In almost all polls for which we have education data, our analysis confirms this explanation. In the French and German samples of our survey (see table 12.2), respondents with higher levels of education demonstrate greater support for allowing Muslim practices in the schools. In table 12.3, French holders of both the *baccalauréat* (b = .730, p < .05) and such advanced university degrees as the *maîtrise* (b = .851, p < .05) were substantially more sympathetic to Muslims' religious needs. In the ALLBUS, the effect of earning the German *Abitur* just misses reaching traditional levels of statistical significance (p = .108).

Views on church–state arrangements

The next theory looks at the relationship between mass attitudes toward the church–state arrangements in a particular country (i.e., the established Anglican church in Britain, separationist *laïcité* in France, and a dual, Evangelische/Catholic religious establishment in Germany) and popular support for the state accommodating Muslims' religious practices. We hypothesize that these different institutional church–state models socialize individuals to expect the state to accommodate religious groups in particular ways. Those citizens who favor the historically close ties between church and state in Britain and Germany may value state recognition of religion and therefore be more likely to see the benefits of extending that system to include Muslims. The French, by contrast, might oppose the wearing of the hijāb in public schools because of a strong preference for institutional *laïcité* and a strict separation of religion and public life.

To measure public support for existing church–state arrangements, respondents in the three countries in our survey were asked about the institutional model unique to each country. In Britain, the questionnaire asked about the Church of England's gradual accommodation of religious groups in areas such as education and membership in the House of Lords. French respondents indicated their level of support for the strict separation of religion and state (*laïcité*). In Germany, finally, interviewees voiced their agreement or disagreement with the system by which the state collects funds for churches that are publicly recognized (*Kirchensteuer*).

At least in France and Germany, however, the data provide no support for the mass-level version of our church–state-structure theory. French devotees of *laïcité* were no more likely to oppose the wearing of the hijāb than were those who rejected French separatism. German respondents likewise showed no propensity to link support for *Kirchensteuer* to sympathy for Islamic instruction in public schools. In Britain, on the other hand, opposing the Church of England's policy on non-established religious groups does appear to have increased hostility to the expansion of Islamic schools (b = −.771, p < .05).

September 11 attacks

The final theory is that the September 11, 2001 terrorist attacks in New York and Washington, DC affected Europeans' attitudes toward state accommodation of Muslims' religious practices. In the aftermath of the attacks, Western European governments became aware that many of the terrorists had lived in Europe, and that other radical Islamists were still in their midst (Waldmann 2002). In response, Britain, France, and Germany passed laws to crack down on domestic terrorists and further to restrict immigration and political asylum (Daley 2002).

In addition, the European Monitoring Centre on Racism and Xenophobia reported that Muslims across Western Europe had suffered increased hostility and physical attacks since September 11 (Allen and Nielsen 2002). In Britain alone, more than 300 assaults on Muslims were reported after the terrorist attacks (*The Guardian* 2002). Finally, a British public-opinion poll taken shortly after September 11 found that 26 percent of the population felt that Islam was a threat to Western values (Travis 2001).

If this theory is correct, public support for state accommodation of Muslims' religious practices in the schools should have decreased. In order to test this explanation, we had the identical policy questions from our July 2001 survey (Roper Europe 2001) added to a poll conducted in April of 2002 (Roper Europe 2002).

The data reported in table 12.4 partially confirm this theory. In Britain,

Table 12.4 Support for Islam in the schools before and after September 11

Responses (%)	Britain		France		Germany	
	pre-	post-	pre-	post-	pre-	post-
Expand	31.8	28.0	16.7	14.4	61.6	55.8*
Status quo	48.4	46.4	44.5	44.4	27.9	32.4*
Restrict	19.9	25.6*	38.8	41.2	10.5	11.8
n	756	777	951	1014	950	928
Muslim	2.3	0.8*	3.5	3.0	0.8	0.2
n	872	896	976	1031	959	956

Source: Roper Europe (2001, 2002).

Note: Data weighted by demographic characteristics. * = statistical test for independence of pre- and post- waves significant at the .05 level (see Wonnacott and Wonnacott
1985: 242).

support for abolishing state funding of Islamic schools increased from
19.9 percent to 25.6 percent, a statistically significant change. In Germany, support for always providing Islamic instruction fell from 61.6 percent to 55.8 percent, which is also statistically significant. The percentage
of French respondents who advocated banning the hijāb in public schools
also rose from 38.8 percent to 41.2 percent, though this difference fails
traditional tests of statistical significance.

It is also intriguing that the percentage of respondents who identified
themselves as Muslims fell in all three countries. Only in Britain was this
difference statistically significant, however. Given the increase in anti-
Muslim hate crimes and the intense public attention paid to Islamist radicals in the West, this apparent reluctance to acknowledge being Muslim
is not surprising.

Discussion

According to our analysis, the variables that best explain Europeans' support for the public accommodation of Muslim religious practices are education and religious practice. On the other hand, the data in this chapter
do not generally support explanations based on social class, gender, and
status as a religious minority. Exposure to a liberal-arts-style education
(e.g., in the German *Gymnasium* or French *lycée*) seems to increase support for public accommodation of Muslim religious practices. Students
who have reached this educational level have likely learned about cultures other than that dominant in a particular country. Perhaps those who
favor pro-accommodation policies, as we do, therefore ought to advocate
for multicultural education throughout the curriculum.

Our analysis also confirms that religiously active respondents do show solidarity with practicing Muslims. As Tariq Modood and others have argued, religionists perceive secularism as a common threat to their values. On the other hand, the data in this chapter do not support the second half of the solidarity-of-the-religious theory; secularists tend disproportionately to support state accommodation of Muslim religious practices. Our findings parallel those by Allport (1979: 449–53) on the curvilinear relationship between religiosity and racial or religious prejudice. In a predominantly post-Christian Western Europe, secularists may not feel threatened by a few orthodox religionists. Despite the apparent philosophical similarities between practicing Muslims and Christians, Muslims might be better served to join political forces with the large number of pro-multicultural secularists than with the small band of orthodox Christians.

The events of September 11, 2001, have affected popular attitudes toward European Muslims. In all three countries in our before-and-after surveys, respondents were less likely after September 11 to support the accommodation of Islam in state-run schools. In France, however, this decline in support did not achieve statistical significance. Nonetheless, interviewees even in Britain and Germany did not become markedly anti-Islamic, only changing their propensity to oppose accommodation by a few percentage points. Moreover, respondents in Britain and Germany seem far more tolerant toward Islam than reports in the popular press might suggest. Even with the knowledge that some of the 9/11 terrorists lived in Germany and Britain, German respondents remain overwhelmingly supportive of Islamic instruction in state schools, while most British interviewees continue to endorse state funding of Islamic schools. At least in Germany and Britain, politicians might thus consider policies that recognize the genuine religious pluralism in the region without having to worry about widespread public hostility to such programs.

Finally, our data do not seem to confirm a micro version of our church–state theory. At a popular level, the church–state structures, which are so important for shaping elite attitudes and public policy in these three countries, do not appear to determine individuals' views on state accommodation of Muslim religious practices. Perhaps as Converse (1964) might suggest, the Islam-related attitudes of European elites—who are more likely to strive for ideological consistency—are much more constrained by their country's particular church–state arrangement than are the views of ordinary citizens.

Notes

1   The writers are grateful for research support from the Society for the Scientific Study of Religion, the German Marshall Fund of the United States, the American Political Science Association, Pepperdine University, and Central Michigan University. This chapter was originally published as an article in volume 42 of the *Journal for the Scientific Study of Religion*, and we are thankful to the editors and publisher (Blackwell) of this journal for

permission to reproduce the piece here. We are also indebted to the many respondents in Britain, France, and Germany who were interviewed for this chapter. The opinions and analysis contained in this work are nonetheless solely those of the authors. This essay is part of a larger project on state accommodation of Muslim religious practices, which was published by Cambridge University Press as *Muslims and the State in Britain, France, and Germany*.

2   Although the independent variable "Other Religion" is statistically significant and strongly pro-expansionist (b = 2.072), this classification likely includes a majority of Muslims. Unfortunately, the 1996 ALLBUS grouped all non-Christian religions into a single category.

References

Agence France Presse. 1996. "Brigitte Bardot dénonce le 'débordement islamique' en France." Wire service "informations générales." April 26.

ALLBUS [Allgemeine Bevölkerungsumfrage der Sozialwissenschaften]. 1996. German Social Survey. Cologne: Zentralarchiv für empirische Sozialforschung.

Allen, Christopher, and Jørgen S. Nielsen. 2002. *Summary Report on Islamophobia in the E.U. after 11 September 2001*. Vienna: European Monitoring Centre on Racism and Xenophobia.

Allport, Gordon W. 1979. *The Nature of Prejudice*. Reading, MA: Addison-Wesley.

Altschull, Elizabeth. 1995. *Le voile contre l'école*. Paris: Éditions du Seuil.

Alwin, Duane F., Ronald L. Cohen, and Theodore M. Newcomb. 1992. *Political Attitudes Over the Life Span: The Bennington Women After Fifty Years*. Madison, WI: University of Wisconsin Press.

Ben Abid, Sallah Eddine. 2000. "The Sharia Between Particularism and Universality." In *Islam and European Legal Systems*, edited by Silvio Ferrari and Anthony Bradney, 11–30. Dartmouth, NH: Ashgate.

Boy, Daniel, and Nonna Mayer. 1997. *L'électeur a ses raisons*. Paris: Presses de Sciences Po.

Biehl, Frauke, and Sevim Kabak, eds. 1999. *Muslimische Frauen in Deutschland erzählen über ihren Glauben*. Gütersloh: Gütersloher Verlagshaus.

Converse, Philip E. 1964. "The Nature of Belief Systems in Mass Publics." In *Ideology and Discontent*, edited by David Apter. New York: Free Press.

Daley, Suzanne. 2002. "Europe Wary of Wider Doors to Immigrants." *The New York Times*, October 20.

Dwyer, Claire, and Aristide Meyer. 1995. "The Institutionalisation of Islam in the Netherlands and in the United Kingdom: The Case of Islamic Schools." *New Community* 21: 37–54.

El Guindi, Fadwa. 1999. *Veil: Modesty, Privacy and Resistance*. Oxford: Berg.

Erikson, Robert S., Norman R. Luttbeg, and Kent L. Tedin. 1991. *American Public Opinion*, 4th edn. New York: Macmillan.

Fetzer, Joel S. 2000. *Public Attitudes Toward Immigration in the United States, France, and Germany*. New York and Cambridge: Cambridge University Press.

Fetzer, Joel S. and J. Christopher Soper. 2005. *Muslims and the State in Britain, France, and Germany*. New York and Cambridge: Cambridge University Press.

Geddes, Andrew. 2002. "The Borders of Absurdity and Fear." *The Times Higher Education Supplement*, May 24.

Gould, Andrew C. 1999. *Origins of Liberal Dominance: State, Church, and Nineteenth Century Europe*. Ann Arbor, MI: University of Michigan Press.

The Guardian. 2002. "From Scholarship, Sailors and Sects to the Mills and the Mosques." *The Guardian* (London), June 18.

Gusfield, Joseph R. 1963. *Symbolic Crusade: Status Politics and the American Temperance Movement*. Urbana, IL: University of Illinois Press.

Heine, Peter. 1997. *Halbmond über deutschen Dächern*. Munich: List Verlag.

Hoskin, Marilyn. 1991. *New Immigrants and Democratic Society: Minority Integration in Western Democracies*. New York: Praeger.

Hunter, James Davison. 1991. *Culture Wars: The Struggle to Define America*. New York: Basic Books.

Inglehart, Ronald. 1990. *Culture Shift in Advanced Industrial States*. Princeton, NJ: Princeton University Press.

Jennings, M. Kent, and Richard G. Niemi. 1981. *Generations and Politics: A Panel Study of Young Adults and Their Parents*. Princeton, NJ: Princeton University Press.

Kalyvas, Stathis N. 1996. *The Rise of Christian Democracy in Europe*. Ithaca, NY and London: Cornell University Press.

Leege, David C. and Lyman A. Kellstedt. 1993. *Rediscovering the Religious Factor in American Politics*. Armonk, NY: M. E. Sharpe.

Lipset, Seymour Martin. 1981. *Political Man: The Social Bases of Politics*, expanded edn. Baltimore, MD: Johns Hopkins University Press.

Lyall, Sarah. 2002. "When Asylum Seekers Knock, Europe is Deaf." *The New York Times*, June 20.

Macpherson, Duncan. 1997. "Papists then and Muslims now." In *University Lectures in Islamic Studies*, edited by Alan Jones, 109–26. London: Altajir World of Islam Trust.

Modood, Tariq. 1994. "Establishment, Multiculturalism and British Citizenship." *The Political Quarterly* 65 (1): 53–73.

Newbigin, Leslie, Lamin Sanneh, and Jenny Taylor, eds. 1998. *The Secular Myth*. London: SPCK.

Nielsen, Jørgen S. 1999. *Towards a European Islam*. London: Macmillan Press.

Parekh, Bhikhu. 2000. *Rethinking Multiculturalism: Cultural Diversity and Political Theory*. London: Macmillan Press.

Pfaff, Ulrich. 2000. "Islamische Unterweisung an den Schulen in Nordrhein-Westfalen." *epd-Dokumentation* 2: 42–4.

Ramadan, Tariq. 1999. *To be a European Muslim*. Leicester: Islamic Foundation.

Roald, Anne Sofie. 2001. *Women in Islam: The Western Experience*. London and New York: Routledge.

Roper Europe. 2001. *Religion and the State I*. Leatherhead, Surrey, England: RoperASW Europe Ltd.

——. 2002. *Religion and the State II*. Leatherhead, Surrey, England: RoperASW Europe Ltd.

Simon, Rita J. and Susan H. Alexander. 1993. *The Ambivalent Welcome: Print Media, Public Opinion and Immigration*. Westport, CT: Praeger.

Spuler-Stegemann, Ursula. 1998. *Muslime in Deutschland: Nebeneinander oder Miteinander?* Freiburg: Herder.

Travis, Alan. 2001. "Attack on Afghanistan: ICM Poll." *The Guardian* (London), October 12.

Waldmann, Amy. 2002. "How in a Little British Town Jihad Found Young Converts." *The New York Times*, April 24.

Wonnacott, Ronald J., and Thomas H. Wonnacott. 1985. *Introductory Statistics*. 4th edn. New York: Wiley.

Wuthnow, Robert. 1988. *The Restructuring of American Religion: Society and Faith Since World War Two*. Princeton, NJ: Princeton University Press.

13 Buddhist perspectives on terrorism

Martin T. Adam and Wayne Codling

This essay concerns Buddhism and terrorism; in particular it is meant to express possible understandings of the latter from a vantage point representative of the former. While the topic of terrorism is certainly one that calls for clear and rational discussion, it also requires sensitivity to the emotional dimension of the realities under consideration. In what follows an attempt has been made to balance theoretical argument with contemplations born from practice-based experience. In this connection I have asked Mr. Wayne Codling, a meditation instructor in the Soto Zen tradition, to provide an afterword to my reflections.

I have limited my own discussion of Buddhist theory to certain core doctrines originally formulated in India and attributed by the tradition to the Buddha. An attempt to infer the relevance of these early ideas to the topic of terrorism is made only after they have been examined. The study proceeds by exploring some non-Buddhist perspectives that I believe help to bring out relevant features of the Buddha's teachings.

Buddhism and nonviolence (Martin T. Adam)

In 1998, while studying at the Central Institute of Higher Tibetan Studies in Sarnath, India, I had the opportunity to attend a question-and-answer session on Buddhism, presided over by the Institute's director, the Venerable Samdhong Rinpoche. At one point a young American student had asked Rinpoche, "If you had to sum up the essence of the Buddha's teachings in a few words what would you say?" The reply was immediate: "*ahimsā*." One word. Nonviolence.

I was genuinely surprised at this reply. The student, it seemed to me, was asking for some explanation as to that which is distinctively Buddhist. The doctrine of nonviolence, by contrast, is common to many religious traditions; it is today associated with Mahātma Gandhi and Martin Luther King Jr. every bit as much as the Buddha. The response didn't add up.

On the other hand, Samdhong Rinpoche was well known as an advocate of nonviolent Gandhian methods of civil disobedience (*satyāgraha*), especially in the context of Tibet's ongoing struggle for political liberation. This suggested the possibility of a connection, which I was missing.

Upon deeper reflection I began to suspect that there was a problem with the original question. After all, wasn't Buddhism opposed to the very idea of "essence"? Isn't lack of "essence" or "nature" (*nisvabhāva*) precisely the point of the Mahāyāna Buddhist doctrine of "emptiness" (*śūnyatā*)? According to this teaching, nothing possesses an underlying essence or independent existence. Every so-called individual "thing" (dharma) is actually a transitory event, arising and ceasing in mutual interdependence (*pratītyasamutpāda*) with every other thing/event—including the very minds that create and define them in the first place. The phenomena we call "Buddhism" are no exception. They too are empty. Emptiness is basic and it would seem to preclude the possibility of an essence for Buddhism.

And yet perhaps Rinpoche hadn't wished to enter into such an esoteric discussion. He may have found it more appropriate to choose a simpler, more immediately comprehensible doctrine. But why *ahimsā*? As a scholar, if I take his response at face value, this question concerning essence becomes "How, precisely, are we to understand the relationship between nonviolence and emptiness?"

Morality

As an academic trained in the Western philosophical tradition I have inherited a number of assumptions and attitudinal stances from which my enquiries generally proceed. Not the least of these is the basic Aristotelian understanding that in seeking out the essence of a thing one must be seeking out that which makes it unique, that which separates it, conceptually, from other things. There is a great deal to be said for this assumption, but clearly, in the context of the Buddhist tradition at least, it is questionable. Similarly dubious, as we have seen, is the ontological notion of essence as an "independent reality" or "unchanging substratum." How then might we make sense of the idea of *ahimsā* as the essence of Buddhism?

The Sanskrit word *ahimsā* has many possible translations. Literally "non-harm," *ahimsā* was probably first clearly articulated as a religious ideal by Vardhamāna Mahāvīra (599–527 BCE?), the great Jain teacher and older contemporary of the historical Buddha. The principal credo of the Jains is well known: "*ahimsā* is the highest religion (or duty, dharma)."[1] A similar preeminence is expressed in the Hindu tradition as well, for example in the Yoga school. Jainism and Yoga were both important influences in the formation of Gandhi's conception of nonviolence. These traditions place *ahimsā* first on the list of precepts to be lived by. Certainly, Buddhism is not alone in emphasizing an ideal of gentleness and concern for the welfare of living beings.

Of course, important differences do lie in the details of the respective traditions' conceptions of *ahimsā*. Jains, for example, subscribe to a much more comprehensive conception of "living beings" towards which their concern extends—including objects most non-Jains would consider inanimate. They have, as well, set out a much stricter code of conduct in order to minimize the possible harm one might do (e.g., gently sweeping the ground before one in order to avoid stepping on insects). A large part of the psycho-spiritual impetus behind this code lies in the idea that even unintentionally injurious actions have a negative karmic impact on the agent who performs them. They are instances of *himsā* (harm), and, if committed, future suffering for the agent is sure to follow.

For the Buddha, on the other hand, intention (*cetanā*) is the key determinant of the karmic consequentiality of actions performed. Inadvertently injuring a creature is regrettable, but does not carry with it any negative karmic repercussions for that specific effect. Of conduct that results in injury, it is only those actions that are intentionally harmful that bring such consequences. Like Mahāvīra, the historical Buddha subscribed to the view that the morally positive and negative actions (karma) that one performs respectively result in happy and painful experiences. But in the Buddha's moral discourse, the concept of action can be distinguished from that of mere behavior; an action is conceived in terms of the mental state motivating its performance, not in terms of its results: "It is intention that I call karma; having formed the intention one performs acts by body, speech and mind."[2] Without a motivating intention a given behavior does not constitute action *per se*. Thus the agent, so-called, does not bear moral responsibility for the results of that behavior. Those results are not relevant to whatever karmic fruit may arise from the conduct. From the point of view of intention such behavior cannot be considered either *himsā* or *ahimsā*.

Thus, to take an example, the same outward behavior that from a Jain perspective would be described with the sentence: "Ananda killed an ant without meaning to" might be given the following Buddhist analysis: "Ananda was walking. Without meaning to, an ant was stepped upon. It died." For Jains this event is clearly a case of killing, which is to say, *himsā*. For Buddhists the matter is not so clear-cut. To describe the act as an act of killing would require both the intention to kill as well as the death of the ant. While members of the Buddhist tradition do sometimes loosely employ the language of "harm" in reference to the objective effects of an action, the predication of *himsā* or *ahimsā* has traditionally been considered to turn on the subjective component of intention.[3]

Thus in general there is a contrast in the semantics of *himsā* and *ahimsā* in these two faiths, and certain English translations of the word seem more appropriate to one than the other. Those that initially point towards the objective component of the effects of one's activities on others seem to more clearly fit the Jain perspective (e.g., non-injury, non-killing). Translations that initially point towards the inner subjective state of mind that serves as the motivating cause of one's actions fit more comfortably with the Buddha's teaching (e.g., non-harmfulness, nonviolence, love).

This difference is connected to concrete divergences in practice and, as we will see, differences in ontology. In the Buddha's teaching, a person may only be faulted for accidentally injuring another sentient being on the grounds that he or she has been inattentive or careless, but she cannot be faulted for being harmful. The flaw, if there is one, lies in the lack of awareness characterizing the agent's intentional state (i.e., being inattentive), not in its degree of benevolence. Thus, in general, followers of the Buddha adopt a pragmatic, middle way when it comes to questions of practice and restraint of action. In the Jain tradition, because action *per se* is so potentially harmful, both to others and to oneself, it is to be avoided as far as this is possible. In the Buddhist tradition too, a certain restraint of action is considered integral to the religious life—both as a means of preventing harm and as part of the path of cultivating the awareness that leads to awakening (enlightenment, *bodhi*). One is to remain aware of one's environment, avoiding injury to others whenever one can. But balancing such considerations is a realistic recognition that one must engage in a wide variety of everyday activities in order to reach the final goal. Both traditions agree on the general principle that one should avoid injury to other creatures to the "greatest degree possible"; but they differ on where to draw the line. In seeking to do the "least possible harm" the two faiths understand "possibility" differently.

Not surprisingly, the differences between the two faiths with respect to *ahiṃsā* extend to their respective metaphysical understandings of the nature of karma and its operations within cyclical existence (*saṃsāra*). The Jain tradition holds to a materialistic conception of karma as a kind of sticky matter, the impure particles of which accrue to, or give a "color" to, the pure underlying self (or life-monad, *jīva*). Karma blocks the natural radiant light of omniscience inherent to the self; it binds that self to future rebirth. Physical, vocal, and mental activities all have the effect of attaching karma to the self (Dundas 1992: 98). Thus even unintentional actions have a negative karmic impact. By contrast, as we have seen, the Buddhist tradition regards karma as the intentional component of bodily, vocal, and mental actions. Furthermore, karma is conceived of as carrying its own momentum; rather than requiring an unchanging non-physical subject or self in which to inhere, it is part of a changing, impermanent mental continuum. There is no conceptual need to postulate an underlying permanent self.

In spite of such differences it is important to notice some very general understandings that the two religious perspectives share. Both subscribe to the view that a feeling of sympathy and gentleness towards living beings forms a necessary part of the path that leads to liberation. Both hold that malevolent intentions towards others are harmful to the subject who entertains them and that this is so irrespective of whether such intentions are acted upon. Both agree that it is worse for the agent if these intentions are acted upon. Thus, for both, it is assumed that some actions are objectively worse than others.

The reason it is important to articulate such underlying assumptions is for what they indicate regarding the deeper worldview at work. Clearly the cosmological vision of the Buddha, like that of Mahāvīra, encompasses a notion of the objective law-governed operations of karma. Put another way, we can say that the Buddha subscribed to a commonly held Indian viewpoint that accepted the existence of an objective moral order or natural law (dharma) at work in the unfolding of worldly events.

Connected with this notion of moral law is the idea of purity of action. Pure actions have positive results in experience. Impure actions, such as those motivated by intent to harm, have negative effects. This can be seen in the very first verses of the Buddhist *Dhammapada*, which clearly capture this idea of lawful regularity in the moral sphere, while at the same time bringing out the importance of the mental component of action.

> Mind precedes all mental states. Mind is their chief; they are all mind-wrought. If with an impure mind a person speaks or acts, suffering follows him like the wheel that follows the foot of the ox. (*Dhammapada* 1)

> Mind precedes all mental states. Mind is their chief; they are all mind-wrought. If with a pure mind a person speaks or acts, happiness follows him like his never-departing shadow. (*Dhammapada* 2)

Thus the Buddha held that purity of mind is conducive to happiness. Impure mental states were considered obstructive to this goal; they lead to suffering (*duḥkha*). In Buddhist vocabulary, pure mental states and actions are described as *kusala*, a word that may be best translated as either "wholesome" or "skillful" (see Harvey 2000: 42–6). As for impure states and actions, these were described with the word *akusala*, "unwholesome" or "unskillful." Of these translations, "skillful" suggests an end lying outside the action itself; "wholesome" on the other hand suggests a *telos* contained within, or identical to, the action itself. In Buddhist soteriology the end, happiness, may be equated with liberation or awakening. Thus in the Buddhist understanding *kusala* conduct both leads to and embodies the highest human good. This double implication, however, is lost in translation.

Classically, *akusala* actions are formulated in terms of "three unwholesome roots" or "three poisons." The presence of these impure motivations in one's mind bars one from the awareness that sees reality as it is (*yathābhūtam*).[4] The three are greed, hatred, and delusion (*lobha, dveśa, moha*). Their wholesome opposites are non-attachment, loving-kindness, and wisdom. These qualities both lead to and constitute awakening.

Of the three poisons, it is delusion (*moha*) that is generally considered the fundamental human problem. Buddhism, like Jainism, holds to a soteriology of liberating awareness or wisdom (*jñāna, prajñā*). When delusion is completely removed, liberation is achieved. Delusion does not merely indicate an absence of knowledge, but rather the presence of mistaken views that function to obscure one's awareness of the way events actually occur. Thus these obscurations are cognitive, while those associated with greed and hatred are emotional in nature. Of the cognitive obscurations the most fundamental is the mistaken view that accepts the existence of an independent permanent self. It is only on the basis of a deeply rooted attachment to this false idea of "self" that the emotional obscurations of greed and hatred can arise. If this basic disorientation is removed, so too are the twin possibilities of self-centered craving and antagonism towards so-called "others."

Actions marked by the three poisons are seen as unskillful in the sense that they lead to future suffering, both for the agent and for others. It is important to recognize, however, that in the Buddhist view such actions are not impure because of their negative results, but rather the reverse (Harvey 2000: 49). They bring negative karmic results on account of a quality that they actually possess, namely, the impure, unwholesome mental quality of an intention marked by the presence of one or more of the three poisons. Some actions are wholesome, sharing in the quality of awakening; some are not. Thus in spite of the anti-essentialist dimension of his teachings, the Buddha recognized that practically speaking there is an "objective" way that actions may be characterized in respect of the quality of awakening. Actions have "natures"—albeit transitory, interdependently arising ones. Among the terms that may be correctly and usefully employed to describe them are "pure" or "impure," "awakened" or "unawakened," as the case may be.[5]

Thus the idea that there exists an objective moral law (dharma) operational in the universe is both clear and commonplace in the discourses of the Buddha. The effort to understand and abide by this law in one's personal moral conduct (*śīla*) is considered essential to the attainment of awakening. The path leading to awakening involves training oneself to be nonviolent in thought, word, and deed. The conduct of a person who has completely purified the mind, and thereby attained liberation, will thereafter embody this moral law without effort (Harvey 2000: 44). Nonviolence is thus viewed as a natural, spontaneous expression of the highest spiritual realization. The intent to harm, on the other hand, is an expression of hatred, which is necessarily based on delusion. Such hatred is simply not possible for a person who realizes the emptiness of self and other, who truly sees the interdependence of beings.

The Buddhist tradition asserts that this highest of realizations is, in the last analysis, ineffable. Words can only point us towards that "emptiness" which must finally be known in experience. Nonviolence, on the other hand, is the concrete and active expression of this highest experiential knowledge. Whereas the realization of a Buddha might only be imagined, his actions can be plainly seen.

The middle way taught by the Buddha is a way of being and acting in the world, a way that aims to free sentient beings from unwholesome action. In this light it does not seem so implausible to suggest the principle of *ahimsā* as the most fitting candidate for the essence of the Buddha's teachings. It is this moral sensibility that guides Buddhists in everything they do.

Gandhi and Buddhism

Gandhi's views on *ahimsā* may be of some aid in shedding light on the teachings of the Buddha. Arguably the greatest exponent of nonviolence since Mahāvīra and the Buddha, he echoed their sentiments by identifying morality as the essence of religion itself (Gandhi 1982: 14). In the spirit of Buddhist anti-essentialism I now propose to briefly explore this possibility.

Gandhi once addressed an audience of Theravādin monks, chiding them (rather mischievously one suspects) for their view that the Buddha did not believe in God. "[The Buddha] emphasized and redeclared the eternal and unalterable existence of the moral government of the universe. He unhesitatingly said that the Law was God Himself" (Gandhi 1950: 272). Whatever one might make of Gandhi's historical claims concerning the Buddha's declarations, the implications of his point are worth considering. If there really is a moral principle of dharma operational in the universe, does it matter whether we call it God? When dealing with such a principle, do not the words we use matter less than the actions that flow from its realization?

Yet Gandhi himself usually exercised some caution in this area, identifying the highest principle with "Truth" (*satya*) rather than "God" (Gandhi 1950: 247). For Gandhi "Truth" signified a near-universal value. Even atheists, he argued, accept Truth as the goal of their considerations. Those who do not even believe in Truth, he considered lost (1950: 153).

It should be clear that Buddhists do not fit into the latter, nihilistic, camp; some vision of objective truth or "a way things are" definitely inspires those who have chosen to walk on the Buddhist path. On the other hand it is equally true that when Buddhists discuss the final nature of things they do not employ the word "God." With all its connotations of an eternal, non-dependent nature, there appear to be irresolvable logical problems associated with any such idea. But "truth" itself is not an objectionable term from a Buddhist perspective. The word does not necessarily carry with it any substantival connotations; it simply suggests that there is "a way things are" or "a way events occur." This way can be realized and accommodated in action, if not finally captured in words.

Depending on the context, the final truth in Buddhism may be identified with any one of a number of placeholders: emptiness, no self, interdepend-ence, the middle way, and so on. Interestingly, it is also sometimes given the appellation "*dharmakāya*" or "body of the dharma." Aside from referring to the truth of emptiness, this term also clearly suggests the idea of objective moral law (dharma).

The idea that the highest realization contains an essential moral dimen-sion is, of course, entirely consistent with Gandhi's views. Gandhi adhered to the idea of a moral sensibility that is the natural, human expression of the Truth. This is *ahimsā*. It is the effort to embody this state that leads to the realization of the Truth. And from this realization, in turn, *ahimsā* effortlessly flows. Thus for Gandhi the two are scarcely distinguishable:

> *Ahimsā* and Truth are so intertwined it is practically impossible to disentangle and separate them. They are like the two sides of a coin, or rather of a smooth un-stamped metallic disc. Who can say, which is the obverse, and which is the reverse? (1950: 251)

And yet Gandhi maintained the distinction: "Nevertheless *ahimsā* is the means; Truth is the end. Means to be means must always be within our reach, and so *ahimsā* is our supreme duty" (1950: 251).

This does not mean that a realized person could never knowingly hurt another or destroy a life, but rather that he could never be motivated by an intention marked by selfish interest or by hatred in doing so. Thus, a strict Jain interpretation of *ahimsā* as "not killing in any circumstance" is rejected by Gandhi (1950: 227–32). According to Gandhi, violence in the sense of the destruction of life is unavoidable in this world (1950: 232). There are instances in which the best course of action is to kill (e.g., in certain cases of mercy killing). It is, however, impossible to define the general conditions of such unavoidability. There is no formula for cal-culating these (1950: 207–9). One should attempt to do the "least harm possible," on a case-by-case basis (1950: 194). In his own written explo-rations of *ahimsā*, Gandhi vacillates on whether to call unavoidable kill-ing *himsā*. What counts, in the last analysis, is the agent's subjective state of non-attachment (1950: 231–2). Lack of attachment to the results of one's actions means lack of self-interested motive in undertaking them. A genuine lack of self-interested motive means acting out of a realization of the highest Truth or Self which is identical in all beings.[6] With such a rec-ognition, selfish intent and hatred become impossible. Thus for Gandhi, as for the Buddha, a pure, non-attached, "selfless" intention is considered the key factor relevant to the predication of nonviolence to any particular action.

These points are worth exploring with some care. In response to Jain criticisms, Gandhi acknowledged the apparent counter-intuitiveness of describing an act of intentional killing as an instance of *ahimsā*; he even went so far as to suggest that the language of *ahimsā* could be dropped in describing such conduct, so long as the correctness of the action was conceded (1950: 228). But, in general, he maintained the language of *ahiṃsā* even for such cases. In so doing, a negative understanding of *ahiṃsā* as "refraining from injury or killing" was displaced by a positive conception of *ahiṃsā* as a mental quality of selfless goodwill, of pure, universal love (1950: 186, 252). If this is one's understanding, the apparent absurdity is lost.

For Buddhists, as for Gandhi, a genuine realization of *ahiṃsā* implies a virtue that goes beyond a mere refraining from injury or killing. Just as the term *himsā* indicates something more than the objective occurrence of injurious effects, the term *ahiṃsā* indicates something more than a mere absence of such effects. The Buddhist tradition recognizes that a person who has advanced on the path acts lovingly, out of a basic compassionate orientation towards all beings seen in their suffering. Genuine *ahiṃsā* is thus understood positively; it does not merely indicate the absence of harmful intent, but in addition the actual presence of compassion. This compassion is the natural expression of spiritual awakening; it is likened to the feeling a mother has towards her own suffering child. This doctrine is especially developed in the Mahāyāna tradition, wherein great compassion (*mahākarūā*) displaces *ahiṃsā* as the central ethical term.

As is the case in Gandhi's ethical reflections, there are instances in specific Mahāyāna texts where, under exceptional circumstances, certain advanced spiritual beings, Bodhisattvas, are described as engaging in "compassionate killing."[7] Such killing is undertaken when the Bodhisattva psychically sees that there is no other way to stop a more damaging action from occurring. It is undertaken not only with the intent to minimize the suffering of potential victims, but also, importantly, out of a loving consideration for the would-be perpetrator who would suffer the karmic repercussions of the actions if he or she were to succeed in his or her attempt.[8]

And yet such passages are rare. It is interesting to note that they always involve Bodhisattvas (beings on the way to awakening), and never Buddhas (fully awakened beings). The Buddha is never depicted as engaging in acts of compassionate killing. There seems to be a deep intuition within the Buddhist tradition that the nature of full awakening precludes the possibility of taking life, even with the best, most loving of intentions.

This parallels some of Gandhi's intuitions regarding the nature of spiritual realization. To act with love in one's heart, with a selfless concern for the well-being of others foremost in one's mind, implies a negation of self-interest and hatred as motives. The closer one approximates a realization of Truth, the more effortlessly nonviolence comes to characterize one's actions—the more willing one is to take suffering upon oneself for the benefit of others. At points Gandhi even seems to suggest that a genuinely realized yogi could never purposefully kill another being (1950: 194–5). Something in the nature of the sage's realization would seem to preclude this as a live possibility. Perhaps this is because it is unnecessary.

According to Gandhi, the love of an awakened being possesses a super-natural force capable of subduing even ferocious wild beasts, a view that finds clear parallels in the Buddhist scriptures.[9]

Meditation

Although it is clear that Gandhi did speculate on the nature of Truth and its realization, he also maintained an attitude of humility in acknowledging the limitations of the human intellect. He seems to have regarded the question of Truth as best tackled "directly" in a non-speculative manner. Thus throughout his life he undertook numerous "experiments" in living aimed at a realization of the Truth within his own lived experience. This process of embodying or actualizing the Truth he viewed as nonviolence itself. It is our highest duty (dharma) and distinctive of our very humanity. In terms of interpersonal conduct it can be understood as requiring humility and an honoring of the other. It also entails honesty, including a willingness to acknowledge one's own faults. Such outward honesty pre-supposes an "inward honesty" or self-awareness, a firmness in determination to observe one's mental states without self-deception as to their actual nature. This implies a concentrated effort to stick to the Truth (*satyāgraha*) as opposed to viewing oneself through the distorted lens of complimentary self-images. In Buddhist terms, this can be seen as par-alleling the practice of "mindfulness meditation" (*smrtyupasthāna*, Pali: *satipatthāna*). A necessary aspect of this meditation is a willingness to see and acknowledge the three poisons at work in one's own mind (Nyanati-loka 1972: 166). This awareness naturally leads to conduct free from the poisons, which is to say, moral conduct.

Wisdom

In both the Gandhian and Buddhist traditions it is commonly understood that a person who is yet on the path to spiritual realization experiences the qualities of wisdom (the realization of emptiness, awakening, truth) and morality (nonviolence) as separate but progressively reinforcing. For a realized being they are no longer separate.

One of the obvious dangers of undertaking comparative analyses lies in the possibility of distorting the objects of comparison in order to find points of similarity. After all, Gandhi spoke in terms of both God and the Self. The Buddha did neither. The realization of God and the Self cannot be equated with the Buddhist realization of emptiness and no-self—or at least not without emptying the discussion of all literal meaning. But per-haps, in this context, this is precisely the point. In their final visions both point beyond words directly to the realm of compassionate action in the here and now.

The Buddha was not unique in teaching that the actualization of the noblest human potential precludes the possibility of violent action. Like Gandhi he considered such conduct to be possible only on the basis of a deluded, non-realized state. Basic to this ignorance is a deeply ingrained sense of "self" which images itself standing in ultimate opposition to "others." Skillful action discourages this sense of division. In this light perhaps the essential point to understand concerning the path taught by the Buddha is not that which differentiates it from other religious teachings, but that which it shares with them. Identifying *ahimsā* as the essence of Buddhism may thus be taken as itself an instance of the principle in action.

Transition

Acts of terrorism involve the intention to harm. As we have seen, from a perspective based on the Buddha's teachings harmful actions may be analyzed as involving various degrees of greed, hatred, and delusion. Actions motivated by greed, for example, may not be principally aimed at harming others so much as profiting oneself. Yet in the process, often enough, this pursuit generates conditions in which other beings are exploited, injured, or even killed. In some cases those who reap the benefits remain oblivious regarding such effects, innocent of the implications of their actions. But such ignorance is commonly only partial, accompanied by feelings of discomfort and, in many cases, considerable rationalization. Certainly this is a familiar enough criticism of the present-day leaders of state governments and multinational corporations, as well as the individuals who support and invest in them.

Self-centered conduct based on willful insensitivity can generate resentment and hatred in the minds of those who are harmed, just as much as conduct that is openly cruel. In both kinds of case, retaliatory acts of violence can result. Often these acts target individuals who are "guilty" only by way of association or group membership (e.g., nationality, religious affiliation). It is such deliberately harmful action that is usually labeled terrorist. It is characteristic of such conflict that each side views the other as the aggressor, the "real" terrorist. From a Buddhist perspective, however, the label is not the most important thing. According to the Buddha's teachings, any action that involves the intention to harm is deluded and immoral.

From a Buddhist perspective, what counts in the end is the inner spiritual condition of the agent. This consideration can be understood in terms of the absence or presence of the three poisons. Are the agent's intentions characterized by feelings of loving kindness towards those affected by their actions? Or are they marked by hatred and anger? Is the motivation one of generosity—the sincere wish for others' well-being? Or is it one of self-centered craving and the desire for power? In the Buddhist understanding, such negative mental states can only occur in a basic context of ignorance and delusion. It may be difficult to judge the nature of subjective states that belong to others—just as it is often difficult to clearly see one's own. But in the Buddhist tradition it is understood that this question pertains to objective matters of fact. With practice, it is possible to see the mind more clearly. Human beings have the unique capacity to remove delusion and bring about a nonviolent condition within. Such change both leads to, and in itself constitutes, the establishment of greater peace in the world.

Afterword by Wayne Codling

Though logic and common sense mitigated against any thought that the waves of gratuitous violence visited upon Europe and the Middle East were likely to pass us by, North Americans have only recently become terrorist-conscious. Despite several examples of domestic violence, it is the 9/11 events that have forced a direct confrontation with militant Islamic fundamentalists.

What causes terrorism? President Bush explains this very simply: "they hate us for our freedom," it's "good versus evil."[10] His rhetoric represents a viewpoint which accepts as axiomatic that "we" are hated, feared, or oppressed because of our proximity to the true God. This analytical mode finds purchase within Christianity and Islam; both tolerate a certain militant devotion to a deep belief that Destiny lies completely beyond time itself. Both valorize martyrdom and holy war. Both espouse a morality that justifies inflicting harm and nurturing a harmful intent as long as "we" are in the right. Each of these two religious histories is replete with examples. To say this in another way, morality within these religions is tethered to a notion that, ultimately, "It is better to be right than to be kind." Fundamentally, what is at stake in these traditions is Eternity, an unchanging heaven or unceasing hell. The gate to heaven opens in response to certainty and righteousness. Doubt and sinfulness open the gate of hell: simple, straightforward, and devastating. The morality that flows from such a notion is distinguished as a "meticulous" morality because it has at its base such a high component of fearfulness (*metus* = Latin for fear). We fear fear, as an earlier American president observed.

With due deference to the ambiguity of the term "terrorist" (Nelson Mandela, for example, was condemned as a terrorist), this paper attempts to look at terrorism as a tactic with some moral basis; how it might affect life in the West and how we might properly respond to what is effectively a new threat. President Bush is correct in identifying religion as having a causative relationship with the problem of terrorism, but the triumphal moral sensibility that he exemplifies is a major obstruction to a solution. Our tormentors are intelligent, energized, and possessed of a level of commitment available only to those who are responding to a "call." It is beyond "duty" and even "doctrine." To answer this call leads naturally to willingness, even eagerness to die. That is truly terrifying in an adversary. Additionally, militant Muslims assume, almost universally, that Western society today is in moral decline, defined and led by immoral or, at best, amoral people.

What if President Bush were a fundamentalist Buddhist instead of a born-again Christian? How might he approach the problem of terrorism from the *pratītyasamutpāda* point of view? *Pratītyasamutpāda* is the Buddhist vocabulary of causation. It means "co-dependent arising" or "interdependent co-arising" and represents how Buddhist thinkers, not having recourse to a Creator God, discuss the limit or initiation of the chain of cause and effect. Within this milieu, a "poison" is the religious equivalent of "sin." Unlike a "sin," a poison is not a violation of an external code of behavior; it is an activity that interacts with everything else (*dharmas*) in ways that are unwholesome and harmful. The antidote to the poisons is *ahimsā*. Delusion, like hatred and greed, is called a poison because it is invariably harmful, often supporting an arrogant and bullying certitude.

Terror as a weapon is not uncommon in the history of human conflict. When we are terrorized from without, we react convulsively like a frog that has found itself suddenly in hot water. Savage attacks have us reflexively dismantling all our cherished societal ideals and political freedoms. We feel forced into a corner. In order to protect our "freedom" we must become ever more repressive, ungenerous, and adversarial; the very conditions which foster internal instability and external hostility. Fear is the vehicle that can deliver the triumph of the Hobbesian vision of human life and society. The "war of all against all" assumes the inevitability and thus the rightness of brutality. From a Buddhist point of view, it is remarkably foolish and shortsighted to create or permit situations of alienation to the point where individuals and collectives have no stake in the status quo and no reason to sacrifice for the common good. Whole segments of society trapped between nothing to lose and nothing to gain; a perfect culture for anti-social reflexes. It's just not wise to conduct yourself this way.

Buddhist morality is different. It might be summarized as something like "It is better to be kind than to be right"—a reflection of the essential importance of *ahimsā* and a reversal of the meticulous assumptions regarding the kindness/rightness dyad of morality. Since it is axiomatic that no act of terrorism is without harm, the scrupulous morality of Buddhism can provide no sustenance for the impulse to inflict fear and retaliation, no matter how alienated, frustrated, and hopeless a situation might have become. There would quite likely be much sympathy and understanding, but always with that poised awareness of cause and effect that sees ill will (hatred) as a spiritual poison. The morality that develops from this divergent ideation is a "scrupulous" morality, denoting a moral code that is generated mostly from within; a weighed, measured, internally empowered sense of propriety.

Delusion or ignorance is the most interesting and "Zen" of the three poisons because it denotes a causal relationship between real, physical events and an absence of some kind. In Buddhist thought, delusion and ignorance are a little bit different. Ignorance is what you don't know, while delusion means that what you do know just is not so. But experientially these different things are invariably concomitant and in practice synonymous. This understanding of cause and effect is applicable both to individual and collective entities because these are not independent things. Indeed, in a conceptual universe governed by interdependent co-arising there could be no ultimately independent entities. How would a Buddhist moral sense differ from our normative morality and in what way would understanding this help us deal with international terrorism?

Borrowing Dr. Adam's illustration, even if Ananda's slaughtering of the ants is unintentional, there will still be karmic fruit from the action. Karmic consequences need not be seen as proceeding wholly from the "sin" of killing. For example, Ananda might experience an enhanced awareness of where he places his feet. Lacking this awareness can be seen as the root cause of the demise of ants. Thus, it is not quite correct to interpret the "karma as intention" doctrine as a moral loophole, because all unintended consequences are a result of ignorance. This is probably the seed understanding that leads the meditation-centered strains of Buddhism, such as Zen, to regard enlightenment (however conceived) as always an available option, not a distant goal. Failure to opt for the enlightened response is the result of not knowing it is available; which is to say, a failure to see things as they actually are. The exemplars of enlightenment, called Buddhas, are incapable of harm only in the sense that they are aware of pervasive Buddha-nature. And the vow of *ahimsā*, enacted and spoken at the very initiation of the path to Buddhahood, is the foundation that makes the ability to see things as they actually are a wholesome thing. Modern Buddhism recognizes two ways to relate to the ability to see things as they actually are. For the original Buddhists, enlightenment provokes an effort to cease rebirth through a radical minimalization of personal negative karma. This is the exemplar of the Arhat. Mahāyanists, on the other hand, respond with the Bodhisattva vow; to remain within the cycle of rebirth until and in order to help all beings attain the final repose of enlightenment. In Buddhist history, although the contending visions represented by the Arhat vow and the Bodhisattva vow have occasionally fueled acrimony, there are few, if any, incidences of warfare or destruction that result from these two interpretations of the path. Why? Because the scrupulous morality of *ahimsā* has no concept of "holy war."

Can a so-called scrupulous morality support or allow behavior equivalent to what is implied by "holy war"? I would argue that it can, and the equivalent moral action is very significant. Early in 1963 a Buddhist monk named Thich Quang Duc set himself on fire on a busy Saigon street. He sat in meditation posture and remained silent and composed while his body burned. In the days following Quang Duc's suicide, several other

Buddhist monks did the same thing. In each case, witnesses were horrified at this sight. The impact of the self-immolations was worldwide and very nearly changed the course of history. Indeed this act has been admired as the only effective response to the terrorist tactics employed by the US-supported Diem regime. Quang Duc and the others rallied the cowed population by strengthening a more liberal, generous, and accommo-dating view of governance. It was precisely because these monks were known to have so assiduously practiced *ahimsā* that this act of harm-ful intent was so powerful. Even while their bodies burned, these monks did everything they could to minimize the terrible effects of proximity to such an act. As Mahāyanists, they never abandoned their Bodhisattva vow and they made every effort to act intentionally and not in ignorance. They were not completely successful, but even so the salient effect of the manner of their deaths was to slow and almost halt the rapidly advanc-ing dogs of war. How different this application of suicide is from the idea of taking as many lives with you as possible. Furthermore, it should be noted that these monks were leaders of the peace movement, prominent government critics. They could have, but they did not, recruit younger people to die so dramatically. One does not see the leaders of terrorist factions today offering themselves as sacrifices. In the Buddhist under-standing of these things, only someone with a deep understanding of the vow of "not-harming" could harbor even a remote possibility of using their death as a tool for political purposes.

A Buddhist analysis of the appropriate historical response to terrorism would include taking an unsentimental look at the actual situation and locating our causative involvement in its fruition. Buddhism is above all something that one does: it is a path, a way. It is called the Middle Way, which is defined initially as avoiding "falling into extremes." The middle way requires suspending extreme judgments such as "good" and "evil," which is almost impossible to do but is nevertheless necessary. In meditation one learns how to do this. Even if brief, such moments of equipoise can bring a constructive influence to competitive living. These moments of equipoise or non-comparative awareness are as regenerative as the poisons are harmful. The middle way is to construct an inclusive way of thinking about and reacting to the exigencies of life and living. The Buddhist path uses meditation to intentionally bring composure into our everyday mind. The middle way suggests a need to emphasize and establish a scrupulous reflex with much less reliance on our meticulous ordering of things. A scrupulous response requires composure. Our chal-lenge is to find a response to terrorism that meets the near-term needs of security and defense without completely eliminating any possibility of a long-term solution (other than annihilation). Buddhist meditation might well be a tremendous asset in attempting to walk this razor edge. The vocabulary of the middle way is particularly useful because it emphasizes the importance of the relationship between extremes of dualistic thought rather than the absorption of the extremes into "one" or the choosing of one extreme over the other. Zen especially emphasizes the "not one, not many" vocabulary.

It is natural for a frog, tossed into hot water, to panic in its struggle to get out; just as it is in the nature of a frog to adapt to a slow heating of its environment even unto death. Individually and collectively we behave rather like the frog, but with this issue of worldwide and unrelenting terrorism, long-term survival requires a far more measured and scrupulous reaction. It has to be obvious that there can be no winner in the usual, triumphal sense of that word. As long as most of us think that rightness will triumph, there is very little hope that this new era of terrorism will be over soon. But, if we take the "kill 'em all and let God sort it out" approach, which some have already suggested, then we will have entered an immoral world which cannot sustain human life, for morality is an environmental necessity for human society. That is why the spiritual response to this must be renewal, and we must resist the impulse to indulge in moral judgment. The whole clamor to claim the "right" is the problem, not the solution. The spiritual value of renewal eschews any notion of a non-inclusive human destiny.

Do the militant fundamentalists have a point? Has our moral habitativeness been degraded? There is some reason to be concerned. Today our leaders, our defining classes, aspire only to blamelessness and inspire mostly cynical self-interest. Only the faintest traces remain of the noble convictions that once suggested that the status quo involved something worth dying for. The terrible and revealing irony is that our young die anyway. It is claimed that suicide is the third leading cause of death for young people in the West.[11] It seems many of our children prefer an ignoble and anonymous suicide to the future we lay before them. How much more attractive would suicide be in Islamic communities where despair and desperation can be directly redeemed by a meaningful and admired death?

We have allowed ourselves to be led gradually to this weakened state primarily through ignorance and delusion. The source of our vulnerability is not simply an asymmetric conflict with Evil but rather arises in consequence of the meticulous ethic. If we are to survive this attack, we need to find a voice that can impel a cohesion equivalent to that experienced among those who have responded to a call; a voice that can renew a feeling of being a part of, or an heir to, something worthy. Such a voice will have to come from some source other than the current religious, social, intellectual, or politically empowered elites. The voice of our religious traditions can scarcely be heard over the outrage of widespread abuse scandals. The voice of our political leadership is less and less concerned or able to exert authority without coercion and division. The exemplars of capitalism steal everything in sight the moment regulations are relaxed.

This terrorism from without is a major test of our basic civilization.

One of several, actually, but we undertake this test as an increasingly factionalized society; the factions set to squabbling with each other over crumbs of wealth like seagulls on a tourist beach. But we can, if we want to, find a voice that speaks from our better natures. That collective voice starts with each individual and can be reliably cultivated in the stillness of Buddhist meditation. *Ahiṃsā* assumes that, since "our" better natures are similar to "their" better natures, we need only act from our better natures to give ourselves a chance for survival.

Notes

1 "*ahiṃsā paramo dharma*"; see Dundas 1992: 160.
2 *Anguttara Nikāya* iii 415. Quoted in Gethin 1998: 120.
3 There is an ambiguity here, which we will have occasion to return to below. At this juncture, for purposes of comparison we merely identify the traditions' predominant manners of discourse concerning violence and non-violence. In fact, both traditions recognize the possibility of the other perspective. While Buddhists will occasionally speak of harm in "objective" terms, independent of intention, for members of the Jain tradition there is an important sense in which nonviolence refers to the "subjective" state of a *jīva* (life) completely purified through practice.
4 This is described in terms of three general characteristics of existence: suffering, impermanence, and lack of self. See Nyanatiloka 1972: 197.
5 This objective aspect of the Buddha's moral thinking is sometimes misunderstood or glossed over by modern Western interpreters of Buddhism. The idea of the ultimate lack of an independent nature, or emptiness, is often mistakenly considered to imply the view that there are no correct descriptions of conventional reality. The implication is that moral values are either subjective or culturally relative. But this is a non sequitur. For although it is true that events and actions may be seen, from an awakened perspective, as "empty" of any ultimate independent nature, such emptiness does not preclude their having a definite nature on the level of interdependent *samsāric* reality.
6 "The man who lives in the atman, who has subdued the demons in him and mastered the senses; who sees himself in all creatures and all creatures in himself, will make no distinction between relations and others. He will live ever as a servant of all, and will partake only of what remains after others have had their share. Of such a person it can be said, *kurvannapi na lipyate*, that he works, but is not bound by the effects of karma" (Gandhi 1993: 151).
7 As the only means to stop a mass murder from occurring, for example. Such cases are fruitfully discussed in Harvey 2000: 135–40.
8 Such are considered acts of self-sacrifice; it is understood that the Bodhisattva will suffer some negative karmic consequence for any deliberate act of killing, in spite of his good intent. See Harvey 2000: 136–7.
9 See Gandhi 1950: 232, Ñāṇamoli 1992: 262–4. At a minimum the exclusion of the possibility of intentional killing by a Buddha may suggest recognition of the danger of providing a scriptural basis for this kind of "calculation-based" action. The potential folly of such a course is clear. The wisdom of adhering to a negative formulation of the central moral principle is equally obvious.
10 See remarks by President Bush, September 20, 2001, at http://www.whitehouse.gov/news/releases/2001/09/20010920-8.html, and September 25, 2001, at http://www.whitehouse.gov/news/releases/2001/09/20010925-1.html.
11 See, for example, http://www.cdc.gov/ncipc/dvp/Suicide/youthsuicide.htm.

References and further reading

Adam, Martin T. 2005. "Groundwork for a Metaphysic of Buddhist Morals: A New Analysis of *Puñña* and *Kusala*, in Light of *Sukka.*" *Journal of Buddhist Ethics* 12: 62–85.

Clayton, Barbara. 2006. *Moral Theory in Śāntideva's Śikṣāsamuccaya: Cultivating the Fruits of Virtue.* Abingdon, Oxon and New York: Routledge.

Cousins, L. S. 1996. "Good or skilful? *Kusala* in Canon and Commentary." *Journal of Buddhist Ethics* 3: 136–64.

Dhammapada. 1986. Bangalore: Maha Bodhi Society.

Dundas, Paul. 1992. *The Jains.* London: Routledge.

Gandhi, Mohandas K. 1950. *Hindu Dharma.* Ahmedabad: Navajivan Publishing House.

——. 1982. *An Autobiography or The Story of My Experiments with Truth.* London: Penguin Books.

——. 1993. *The Bhagavadgita.* Delhi: Orient Paperbacks.

Gethin, Rupert. 1998. *The Foundations of Buddhism.* Oxford: Oxford University Press.

——. 2004. "Can Killing a Living Being Ever Be an Act of Compassion? The Analysis of the Act of Killing in the Abhidhamma and Pali Commentaries." *Journal of Buddhist Ethics* 11: 168–202.

Harvey, Peter. 2000. *An Introduction to Buddhist Ethics.* Cambridge: Cambridge University Press.

Keown, Damien. 1992. *The Nature of Buddhist Ethics.* London: Macmillan.

Ñāṇamoli, Bhikkhu. 1992. *The Life of the Buddha.* Seattle, WA: BPS Pariyatti.

Nyanatiloka. 1972. *A Buddhist Dictionary: Manual of Buddhist Terms and Doctrines.* Colombo: Frewin and Co.

Premasiri, P. D. 1976. "Interpretation of Two Principal Ethical Terms in Early Buddhism." *Sri Lanka Journal of the Humanities* 2 (1): 63–74.

14 Discussion

Historical and social reflections

Michel Desjardins

The overwhelming response in Canada immediately following the event now known as "9/11" was shock and horror, combined with deep sympathy for Americans who had lost family and friends. After several days of blanket US media coverage of this tragedy, the Canadian response became more complex and ambivalent. In newspaper editorials and discussions around the water coolers the common refrain was: "Can Americans not at least appreciate why some people in the world would hate them, given the horror they continue to inflict on the world, and given their ongoing, blinkered support for Israel?" Those critical comments later increased when America attacked Afghanistan, and they spiked with the invasion of Iraq. Currently, many Canadians consider America to be the greatest threat to world stability, a view shared by a large segment of the world's population.

Canadians also tend to consider the American Christian Right an American rather than a Christian phenomenon. Jerry Falwell, for example, was called an "American Fundamentalist" by many Canadians (there were less polite expressions) when two days after 9/11 he said: "I really believe that the pagans, and the abortionists, and the feminists, and the gays and the lesbians who are actively trying to make that an alternative lifestyle . . . all of them who have tried to secularize America—I point the finger in their face and say 'you helped this happen.'" The fear in Canada is not that "Christianity" is on the march to control the world, but that a re-Christianized America is intent on dictating to others how they should lead their personal and public lives. The Catholic Archbishop of Riga, who considers homosexuality a "sexual perversion" and urged Latvians to take to the streets to oppose the Gay Pride parade in June 2007, is an anachronism in a twenty-first-century Europe, but a Bush administration influenced by similar beliefs is a far more significant threat to human rights around the world, including the principles enshrined in the Canadian Charter of Rights.

In short, America is currently terrorizing the world to an extent that far surpasses anything that minority Muslim groups have done and will be able to do in the foreseeable future. Young Canadians especially are troubled by an America that seems out of touch with its egalitarian, humanistic principles. Conversations I have had over the last several years with my colleagues in the humanities and social sciences across Canada consistently raise the same point: gut-level anti-Americanism is rampant among our university student population, and many of us struggle with how to prod students to develop more sophisticated arguments for whatever position they choose to take on this matter.

In order to create a greater degree of balance and complexity, my conversations with students on this topic usually note that "America" can be quite distinct from "Americans"—particularly the many Americans that I know, respect, and love. To that I add stories about my own positive experiences in America, with Americans. As I write these words, my eldest son is about to graduate with a doctoral degree from an American university, having spent the last six years of his life getting a superb education, in one of the most progressive cities on the planet, supported by American largesse. Our entire family is thankful for that experience. Most Canadians have stories like this to tell, and many of us feel as welcomed in rural South Carolina as we do on the Saskatchewan prairies. Our America does not resemble the America that struts its way across the world stage.

Replace "America" and "Americans" with "Islam" and "Muslims" and you have the range of issues commonly discussed by scholars of religion, including those in this section of the book. In reviewing their positions, I will start by imaginatively considering what their chapter might cover were they discussing America instead of Islam.

Jonathan E. Brockopp might point to clear historical precedents for America's practice of taking what it wants by force, but he would then situate this violent trajectory within a more pervasive insistence on freedom and democracy. In dealing with Islam, Brockopp's position is courageous. Scholars of Islam today, anticipating an audience that feeds off negative impressions of this religion, often insist, rather disingenuously, that any violence done in the name of Islam misrepresents the tradition; they know, or at least should know, that violence is an intrinsic part of Islam—as it is intrinsic to every religion and every other human construct. To sanitize Islam is to patronize it, to remove it from the world. Brockopp, though flirting with this idealized view of Islam, traces the connections between jihad and violence to the core of the tradition, including some of the main commentaries. In the end, he insists that the greater jihad, the "struggle with one's own evil inclinations," has been the central Islamic view, and that bin Laden's use of religious texts to support violence misrepresents the tradition that he professes to model.

Martin T. Adam and Wayne Codling, in another context, might argue for considering Sweden and Canada as better examples of countries that promote freedom and democracy. Their essay explores Buddhism as an alternate form of religious expression, in the context of Jain and Gandhian parallels. Adam and Codling's interpretation of Buddhism, including their stress on *ahimsā*, or nonviolence, will not surprise scholars of Asian religions, but in the context of this book their (mainly) implicit comparison to Islam and other monotheistic religions is certainly a refreshing challenge. "What if President Bush were a fundamentalist Buddhist instead of a born-again Christian?" Adam finally asks. The answer is clear; in Codling's words: "the scrupulous morality of Buddhism can provide no sustenance for the impulse to inflict fear and retaliation no matter how alienated, frustrated, and hopeless a situation might have become."

Were they examining America, Joel S. Fetzer and J. Christopher Soper might explore citizen responses to US corporate spread in their countries—e.g., the possible sale of Coke in Syria and Iran, or the expansion of the North American Free Trade Agreement (NAFTA) for Canadians and Mexicans. Here, Fetzer and Soper review and analyze the results of surveys they conducted in some European Union countries before and after 9/11. Their sociological study queried British participants about state aid to separate Islamic schools in Britain, French participants about students' wearing of the hijāb in French state schools, and German participants about the addition of instruction about Islam in German state schools. The results are sometimes predictable (e.g., heightened negativity towards Islam after 9/11), but each reader will certainly find data to challenge their current assumptions. Moreover, scholars of religion who believe that education should make religion more publicly acceptable will likely take heart in one finding: "Exposure to a liberal-arts-style education . . . seems to increase support for public accommodation of Muslim religious practices."

One might imagine Mark Juergensmeyer exploring America's response to growing anti-Americanism—a response that includes increased American military activity around the world, and a refusal to abide by the rulings of the International Court of Justice and NAFTA tribunals when they do not suit American interests. His chapter addresses Islam's response to increasing Western secularism—a response that in some cases takes the form of terrorist acts, done to generate media events and place religion back on the world stage. Basing his analysis on his well-known and much respected comparative work on religion and violence, Juergensmeyer argues that these terrorist acts make sense when understood as global responses to secular nationalism, and (echoing the Bush administration) notes that terrorist acts are likely to remain with us for a very long time: "The postmodern religious rebels such as those who rally to the side of Osama bin Laden are therefore neither anomalies nor anachronisms . . . [T]hey exemplify currents of thinking and cultures of commitment that have risen to counter the prevailing modernism."

What needs to be remembered in reading these four valuable studies is that there is currently no Islam without America: both are in the process of extending deep roots inside the other, and throughout the world. We also need to remember that neither Islam nor America is fixed. Imagining them to be static entities ignores the diversity they contain, and the ongoing change that necessarily defines all human life. Finally, we should remember that the world encompasses more than Islam and America: there are other religious and political traditions, other models of being human, and other possibilities for promoting peace.

Pedagogical and
professional reflections

15 Teaching Islam through and after September 11

Towards a progressive Muslim agenda

Omid Safi

I miss September 10, 2001.

On September 10, the world was still filled with great injustice, untold beauty, and immense suffering. But it was a world that as a scholar of Islamic studies, I felt equipped to handle, to comment upon, and to teach about. All of that changed at about 9 a.m., Tuesday morning, September 11, 2001.

As a human being, as a parent, as a professor of Islamic studies, and as a Muslim, my heart keeps on breaking since September 11. I have needed time to grieve those who perished on September 11, and yet there would be no time to grieve. I have moved from grieving the innocent civilians of New York, DC, and Pennsylvania to grieving the innocent civilians of Afghanistan who have been killed in the US bombing of Afghanistan, to grieving the devastating bloodshed in Iraq going on for many years, to now anxiously anticipating the next cycle of violence, most recently in Iran. So much violence, so much pain, and no time to grieve. From that first morning, and literally every day and every night since then, I have been asked to somehow explain how anyone could have committed the atrocious actions of 9/11. As the only faculty member on a college campus whose main expertise is the Islamic faith, I have felt the burden to speak and speak again.

I have no "explanations." There is no justification. None. No matter what the political differences that others may or may not have with US foreign policy, nothing can ever justify the taking of 3,000 innocent lives. That act was cruel, barbaric, inhumane, and I would add, against the very principles of Islamic teachings. Since that terrible Tuesday, I have spoken about the Islamic tradition, the Muslim world in postcolonial times, and US foreign policies to a whole host of groups ranging from rural churches to urban mosques and synagogues, peace conferences, TV and newspaper reporters, and academic organizations. All too often, I have been the lone Muslim in our local area in addition to being the lone "expert" on Islamic studies. Time and again I have cautioned my audience—and myself—about the dangers of tokenism, reminding most of all myself that my perspective represents only myself, not the one billion plus Muslims all over this planet. Still, speaking out and writing have been among the few ways I have had to attempt to bring some sense of healing into this so fractured world. For this chapter, I would like to share some thoughts and reflections, based on my experiences as a self-identifying progressive Muslim who was at the time of 9/11 privileged to be teaching Islam at Colgate University, an elite liberal arts college located in a rural setting in North America. (I have since moved on to teaching Islamic studies at the oldest public university in the United States, the University of North Carolina at Chapel Hill.)

Teaching Islam on Tuesday morning, September 11, 2001

On Tuesday morning of 9/11, I was scheduled to teach two classes. My first class, an introduction to religion, started at 8:30, and ended at 9:45. Unknown to us, safely locked away in the confines of a beautiful class-room, was that at 8:45 and 9:03 a.m. Eastern time, two planes had hit the World Trade Center. My second class, called Experiencing Islam, started at 9:55. Given the quick ten-minute turnaround time between the two classes, I was busy checking with the students from my first class to see if they had any questions about the lecture, and going over my lecture notes for the second class. That day we were scheduled to talk about the significance of prayer (*salat* or *namaz*) in Islam. To prepare students for that discussion, I had brought in a CD of the call to prayer (*adhan*) to play for the students. As the students came into the class, they were greeted with the peaceful sound of the call to prayer. That would be perhaps the last bit of peace in that day, indeed the last bit of peace for many weeks and months to come.

One of my students, Cat, came in with a disoriented look. She was one of the "cool" kids in my class, with a remarkable combination of smarts and detached sophistication. Yet on this morning, she was clearly disheveled, disturbed, and disoriented. She came up to me and asked me if we could turn on the radio. Puzzled, I inquired why. She told me that she had heard a plane had had an accident at the World Trade Center in New York. I still remember my first thought upon hearing that. I imag-ined a small one-person propeller plane, dangerously—perhaps even comically—dangling off the roof of the World Trade Center. Not for one second did I, and I suspect anyone else who heard that brief description, imagine the grave suffering we would soon witness.

Still, for some reason that I could not explain at the time, I felt that we as a class should find out exactly what had happened. We could not pick up the radio signal in our classroom, and given the general level of agita-tion, I asked my student to accompany me to the student center, where there was a large-screen TV. On the way to the student center, I stopped for a quick second at a computer cluster, and checked cnn.com, to see if there were any news updates. Instead of bringing up the page instantan-ously as it usually did, the Internet stalled. I quickly checked abcnews.com and bbc.com. No page came up, just the blasted "Internet Explorer" icon turning and turning endlessly. That was my first indication that something drastic was wrong, that millions of people all over the country were also checking the news. I still remember the sensation of my heart sinking in my chest.

On our way to the student center, we had already heard that it was not one, but two planes that had hit the World Trade Center. Immediately, I remember having a most uneasy feeling in my stomach. One plane could be an accident. Two planes must be a plan, a sadistic plan. I had the nauseating feeling that it might have been a terrorist attack.

Right before entering the student center, I ran into a student who was at the time the president of the Muslim Student Association. As one of eight Muslim students (out of a population of 2,700 undergraduates) on our none-too-diverse campus and the only student on campus who covered her hair, she stood out easily. She came up to me, and said softly, painfully: "al-salamu 'alaykum. I pray to God that it was a white redneck who did this."

She did not elaborate, and she did not have to. For Muslims in America, and for teachers of Islam, more words were not needed. In spite of what it may seem like, her statement was not, I believe, a racist one. Simply put, as a 22-year-old she is old enough to have remembered the Oklahoma City bombing which claimed the lives of 168 people. She remembered the subsequent witch-hunt in which many Arabs and Muslims were persecuted before it was discovered that Timothy McVeigh and Terry Nichols were responsible for that heinous crime. Of course the fact that a pair of paramilitary, right-wing Christian Caucasians were found to be responsible for that crime did not mean that all Christians, all whites, or even all young white male right-wing Christians with a crew-cut were somehow going to become targets of hate crimes. No, in that case it was understood that the crime was somehow that of a small cluster of hateful minds and hearts, and it did not represent the collective will of others who may have looked like them or followed the same faith as them. That, ultimately, is what I believe that student was trying to say. She prayed that it was someone who would be held individually responsible for it, not a whole people. Not another witch-hunt. Not another set of hate crimes against Muslims. That, of course, is precisely what would follow in many places.

As a class we went inside the student center, and joined the dozens of others who were gathered around their TV. I stood with my students, watching in utter horror the pain and suffering that was unfolding before us. By the time we got there, the south tower had already collapsed. At 10:28, we saw the north tower fall before us, and the infernal tower of ashes spread all over Manhattan. There were over 200 people in that room, and I have never before or since heard it so quiet. What I have not mentioned yet about my students is that in general, Colgate students are a very privileged bunch who come largely from well-to-do backgrounds. A high percentage of them come from within a one-hour radius of New York City. Many of their parents work in the financial district of New York City. For many of them, the inferno that we were witnessing was none other than the offices of mom and dad.

There were some payphones in the back of the room, and I walked with my students, my friends, as they feverishly tried to call their parents. I stood in silence, with my arm around them, as they tried repeatedly—and failed—to reach their loved ones on overburdened and jammed phone lines. Amazingly, at these moments of great duress, these young souls patiently—and silently—took turns at the phones. Mostly, we sat in silence in front of the TV, watching the vision of hell on earth unfold before our eyes.

After a couple of hours, I left to go home. Partially because I had seen all I could bear, and partially because I felt that I should be home, to protect my family, just in case . . .

Reflections on Islam, at the community level

In reflecting back on the events of September 11 and its aftermath, I have usually recalled that when you stir something, two things can rise to the surface: the scum, and the cream. The events of 9/11 have stirred the soul of this great nation and our local community, and as a result both the scum and the cream have risen to the top. The "cream" of responses around the US is obvious and well documented: the immediate acts of the ultimate sacrifice by the firefighters and police officers at the World Trade Center, the courageous sacrifice by the passengers on the flight over Pennsylvania, the selfless acts of generosity from so many, etc. Those sublime moments have been extensively reported by others and the mainstream media, and I will only applaud them again. There have also been less enlightened moments of deep-seated prejudice rising to the surface, scum-like, in the form of thousands of hate crimes against American citizens of Arab ancestry or Islamic faith, or those that have simply "looked like" the above. These have gone much less noticed, and I believe that it is part of my task as a teacher of Islamic studies to call attention to them. Of the first two known casualties of the hate crimes after 9/11, neither victim was in fact Muslim. The first was a Sikh man in Arizona, whose only crime was having brown skin and wearing a turban. In the eyes of his murderer, if it is brown and it wears a turban, it must either be Osama bin Laden or someone a lot like Osama. The second victim was a Christian Egyptian, a Copt. Hate did not take time to get its victims exactly right.

In the weeks following 9/11, the Council on American Islamic Relations (CAIR) reported 1,717 cases of hate crimes against American Muslims.[1] The crimes ranged from police and FBI intimidation (224 cases), hate mails (315 cases),[2] discrimination in school (74 cases), airport profiling (191 cases), discrimination in the workplace (166 cases), death threats (56 cases), bomb threats (16 cases), physical assault and property damage (289 cases), and the largest number, public harassment (372 cases). There were, tragically, 11 death cases.[3] As anyone with experience in matters of reporting harassment or rape knows, it is not unusual for only 10 percent to 30 percent of cases to ever be reported. The actual number of hate crimes was easily in the thousands.

I was not exactly sure what to count on here in our small town of 2,100 residents after the tragedy. It is not and has not been easy being Muslim in such a small, largely homogenous place in upstate New York. (Yes, I do have visions of Kermit the Frog's "It's not easy being green" dancing through my head as I write these words.) For much of my time at Colgate, I was the only Muslim member of the faculty, my family the only Muslim family in Hamilton, and my son Jacob (aka Ya'qub) the only Muslim child in Hamilton Central School. Out of a population of around 2,700 university students, there are usually around eight Muslim students on Colgate's campus. It is hard to sustain a sense of a spiritual community when the numbers are so small. In my capacity as the advisor to these few Muslim students on campus, we had a meeting on the night of 9/11, to talk about what the campus reaction might be, and what to do in case any of the students on campus were targets of hate crimes. Perhaps the most powerful moment for the Muslim students on campus came that Friday, during a day of communal prayers. The chaplain, Nancy De Vries, organized a session where our president Jane Pinchin, Rabbi Michael Tayvah, and a number of administrators attended the Muslim prayers on the first Friday after 9/11. Standing shoulder to shoulder with the Muslim students, their silent support spoke more eloquently than any words could have. The message was clear: we will emerge through this chaos as one community. No one shall be left behind.

One of the realizations that I have had post-September 11 has been about the extent to which this small university community has become an intimate community for me. The support that colleagues and students have shown my family and the Muslim students has been nothing short of spectacular. Our kind neighbors left their front porch light on for quite a few days, so that we would be more comfortable when the frightening darkness of night time would come. One Hamiltonian neighbor brought us a beautiful basket of flowers. Our rough and tumble neighbor Charlie, he of the bald head and the heart of gold, told my wife Holly that if anyone gave her a hard time, she should go get him, and he would "kick their behind" (except he didn't use the word "behind"). One of the most meaningful aspects of our life post-9/11 has been getting to know many of our friends in the local churches and Jewish communities better. It is encouraging to know that the small size of our university and small town allows such face-to-face, human-to-human, and heart-to-heart encounters.

I know that many who live in larger, more impersonal settings have not been so fortunate.

The response of Colgate and Hamilton has been part of the "cream" that has risen to the top after 9/11. I am so proud of the way that we dealt with this unimaginable tragedy on campus. The response started from the day of the attacks, when many students gathered in the student center to watch those hellish scenes unfold in front of us. The next day, we met early in the morning with the first-year students, then with the students in each of our departments. Early in the afternoon three professors, including myself, addressed the entire campus body of approximately 3,000 people. Standing in the shadows of the chapel, I remember looking across the gathering of the whole Colgate community and seeing not a faceless crowd, but here a Tushar and there a Nicole, here a Matt and there a Khatera, here a Courtney and there a Nasheed. I recall the familiar faces of students and colleagues who were as full of pain and suffering and confusion as I was. I remember the humanity, anger, and compassion, and yes even pain and fear, in each other's eyes.

It was, for me, a powerful and difficult moment, to teach something about Islam in the midst of all the pain. I talked about the pain that we were all feeling, the numbness, and the confusion. I talked about the calls that were already being heard to punish people responsible for the attacks, whoever they might be. I called for us to pause and give ourselves time to grieve, time to bury our dead, and comfort one another. I called on us to proceed with justice, and not to confuse justice with revenge. I also talked about Islam. I talked about the fact that we need to take time to figure out who exactly is responsible for this hideous action, and bring them to justice. I also stressed that the actions of 9/11 cannot in any way be reconciled with the highest ideals of the Qur'an, the ones that state if anyone saves a single human life, it is as if they have saved the life of all of humanity; the ones that state that if one takes a single human life, it is as if they have taken the life of all humanity (Qur'an 5:32). I reminded them that to most Muslims, the actions of those who might claim to have undertaken the hideous actions of 9/11 in the name of Islam were as incongruent as the claims of KKK supporters to base their message of hate on Christian teachings are to most Christians. All traditions have their zealots. I reminded them of the poem by Sa'di, the thirteenth-century Persian poet:

> The Children of Adam are members of one body,
> made from the same source.
> If one feels pain,
> the others cannot be indifferent to it.
> If you are unmoved by the suffering of others,
> you are not worthy of the name human being.
>
> Sa'di, *The Rose Garden*

And in what would be the first of many difficult public statements, I told the campus body that I hold them accountable to a higher standard than that displayed by President Bush in a speech on TV the night before. The President had stated that we must "hunt down the faceless enemy." I reminded all of us that one could not hunt something that is faceless, unless one is willing to stoop to the level of persecution and witch-hunt. We first had to identify those responsible for this horrific crime, and then hold them and only them responsible for it, not an entire block of humanity.

Perhaps from someone else, someone with a longer history of political activism, those statements may not have seemed so shocking. But I had spent the better part of the past ten years avoiding radical political statements. As an Iranian-American who had lived through the 1979 revolution and the decade-long Iran–Iraq war, I had long ago decided to eschew overt public political talk. My scholarly research had largely consisted of the metaphysical speculation of premodern Muslim mystics (Sufis), an area that I had hoped would allow me to safely avoid the political intrigues of the Muslim world and that of the Muslim world vis-à-vis the West. That luxury (if it ever really existed, which I now seriously doubt) evaporated on September 11, 2001. On that Sunday, we had a memorial service for the 16 members of the Colgate family who perished on September 11. The memorial service featured a reading from the Qur'an, alongside that of passages from the Hebrew Bible and New Testament.

Imam or Islamicist?

Another very difficult role that many of us, as teachers of Islamic studies, are being asked and will be asked to play is to somehow be a liaison between the Muslim students' organization and the administration. Let me add that not all of us who are asked to take on such a role are Muslim. Let us remember that the overwhelming majority of MSAs around the country do not have a figurehead in charge that would correspond to the Jewish rabbi, or Protestant chaplain. Increasingly, many such organizations, including the one at Colgate, are put under the chaplain's office or the office of religious life. Part of what makes this an awkward arrangement for many of us, no doubt, is that the scholars of Islamic studies on campus are being asked to speak "devotionally" alongside Christian ministers and Jewish rabbis, and even lead joint prayer services. Many of us are not used to seeing ourselves in such "minister" roles, and some of us have even spent a good bit of our lives distinguishing between academic study of a subject and a confessional practice of it. As the years since 9/11 have gone on, the toll of this ministerial role alongside the endless public speaking—in conjunction with the still monumental academic burden of producing first-rate scholarship—has weighed heavily on many of my colleagues. The burden of being it all has led to divorce among far too many of my friends in this field.

I also feel that way, and a few times I have felt that people did expect me to become "Imam Omid," offering pastoral care. That is not a role that I have always been comfortable with, but it seemed to me that in these grave times it was more important to have some words of compassion and reason to share. I have no desire to become "Imam Omid," but perhaps I can speak from an academic perspective as a human being— who happens to be Muslim and is terribly concerned both about this catastrophic human tragedy and the cycles of violence that it has unleashed.

The Study of Islam Section web page

Much like myself, many of the colleagues who teach Islamic studies are situated in small, isolated, rural locations. Ideally, these are some of the very experts who at this crucial time would seek to explain things to the wider public. But how do you get the collective wisdom and voice of these people together? How do you make it publicly known and accessible? Even on the very day of 9/11, it was clear to me that we had to act publicly, quickly, carefully, and compassionately. With the non-stop news coverage, there had to be a way of getting a more reasonable, careful voice out into the public. As for myself, I know that being situated in rural upstate New York, there was not a great deal that I could do in terms of accessing national news media. So the answer seemed clear: a web page.

I started the Study of Islam Web Response to 9/11 web page literally on the night of 9/11. It went up on September 12. When I started the web page, I had no idea that it would eventually reach some 172 countries, and over 115,000 viewers. If I had, I would have picked an easier URL than http://groups.colgate.edu/aarislam/response.htm!

The goals of the web page were modest: put online the response from the American Academy of Religion Study of Islam section, add a few basic statements from various Muslim spokespersons, and include calls for mutual understanding and patience in these very difficult times. There was one other element that I knew from the start: it had to have pictures. I wanted to include pictures of Muslims and others from around the world sharing their grief and sympathy with those of us who have lost loved ones here. After 9/11, CNN repeatedly showed the same disturbing footage of 10–12 Palestinians dancing in the streets. While CNN certainly has the right to show that footage, I have wondered many times why they have not shown the pictures of a million Palestinian children standing for five minutes of silence to honor those who perished on 9/11. I wonder why they have not shown prayer vigils and peace rallies that took place in Muslim countries ranging from Indonesia to Bangladesh to Iran.[4] I wonder why they have not fully documented the statements from leading Muslim scholars and organizations condemning the terrorist attack. Why show that same disturbing footage ad nauseam? Is it because psychologically we want to think that the rest of the world hates us? In many ways, I specifically envisioned the Study of Islam web page as an antidote to the hyper-patriotic, "It's us against the rest of the world" tone of much of the mainstream media's coverage of the tragedy and its aftermath.

Another theme was also clear to me, and it was one that in the days to come would earn the web page both praise and criticism. Again, as a response to the deafening clamor calling for blood and war, I wanted to highlight voices (Muslim and non-Muslim) that were seeking nonviolent options first, voices like the 1987 Nobel Peace Laureate Oscar Arias who stated: "It is essential that justice be done, and it is equally vital that justice not be confused with revenge, for the two are wholly different."[5] The response to the web page overall has been phenomenal, and almost overwhelmingly positive. Perhaps the greatest indication of its success was that we had no way of disseminating the information on this page apart from relying on folks to pass it on to their friends and students. This they did, and at a rate we could not have foreseen. There were stories on the site in a number of national news media, including the *New York Times* (Stille 2001). The folks from the *Chronicle of Higher Education* also did an extensive interview about the page.

There were, of course, a few negative comments here and there. The negative feedback was almost evenly divided: half of it was from people who were convinced that Islam was a fanatic religion, full of hatred for the rest of humanity. No amount of statements from the Qur'an or Muslim leaders condemning the 9/11 attacks would change their minds. (Why let facts get in the way? They just complicate things . . .) The other set of responses were from extremist Muslims who objected to my inclusion of statements of peace from such luminaries as Gandhi, Martin Luther King, Jr., and the Dalai Lama. One such extremist called Gandhi a "godless Hindu," and objected to my inclusion of Gandhi's "An eye for an eye, and the whole world goes blind"!

Perhaps the more controversial aspect of the web page came about when the US government started the military campaign against Afghanistan. I felt that it was important to document the civilian casualties in this campaign, and give an accurate picture of the duress facing the transplanted and homeless millions of Afghanis. Many people who contacted me objected to what they felt was the "unpatriotic" nature of criticizing the war effort in Afghanistan. From my perspective, however, it was completely consistent with my stance against the hideous actions of 9/11. In both cases, I have attempted to uphold the non-negotiable sanctity of human life, all human life all over this small planet. American lives are sacred, as are those of Afghanis. With the ever-expanding nature of the so-called "war on terrorism," I have found myself gradually being more and more of an anti-war activist, and a defender of civil liberties. (Some of my thoughts on these matters appear in Safi 2002.) I have also included pictures on the site of the Afghani civilians who became victims of the "war on terrorism" even though they were in no way responsible for the actions of 9/11.[6] I don't think that most Americans realize that by now at least as many, and I would suspect more, civilian casualties have been caused in Afghanistan than the number who perished in the States on September 11. Yet their deaths are largely relegated to a footnote on the "war on terrorism." The loss of their lives is buried under vile euphemisms such as "collateral damage," and we are told to understand that war is a messy business and there will be some innocent loss of life. I seriously doubt if anyone who lost a loved one on 9/11 would be consoled by such callous words.

On the web page, I also highlighted the plight of the approximately 6 million Afghani refugees. It was concern for the welfare of these civilians that led the UN Human Rights commissioner, Mary Robinson, to call for a pause in the US-led air strikes against Afghanistan to allow vital aid to be taken in. She had stated that the pause was needed to enable humanitarian agencies to gain access before winter sets in (October 12, 2001).[7] Needless to say, her plea and others like hers were not heeded.

Zayn Kassam has indicated the collaborative efforts that went into producing the joint statement from the Study of Islam section, and I will not duplicate her work here (see Kassam 2002; the statement was reprinted in a special section of the journal *ARC*). What needs to be added is the way in which the Study of Islam LISTSERV and e-mail discussions quickly became a haven of sanity and support for the scholars of Islamic studies around North America. My favorite unofficial joke was, "Have you hugged your Islamicist today?" They did all look like they could use a hug! More seriously, we talked about everything ranging from what various Islamic legal sources might have to say about issues of suicide and martyrdom, to strategies in handling newspaper and TV interviews, to how to manage the incredible pressures that all of us felt during the forthcoming weeks and months. Without the friendship, wisdom, intellectual resources, spiritual fellowship, and emotional support of friends spread far and wide, this isolated, lonely Islamicist would not have made it through the fall of 2001. This gives me an opportunity to discuss the pressures that most of us, particularly those of us who were the sole person on a college campus to represent the Muslim world and/or Islam, were under at this time.

The pressures of responding to 9/11

The collective weight of making sense of all the non-sense approached a crushing level at times. I was trying to maintain my duties as a husband and a father to our two children. I was teaching an overload of courses, three each semester. As a junior faculty member, I was in that crucial stage of alchemically transmuting my long and unwieldy dissertation (nicknamed "cure for insomnia") into a readable (translation: publishable) manuscript. In addition to those, I took on what felt like a never-ending barrage of interviews. At its height—or worst, depending on one's perspective—that meant about four hours of phone interviews per night. A colleague in the department—who was concerned about the impact this would have on my teaching and scholarship, and prospects for tenure—suggested that I keep track of them, to be able to offer them as evidence of community service, an important category for tenure at our college. I lost track after about 150 interviews.

Part of the problem is with our rural location, part of it with the way that the academy has systematically neglected Islam and the Muslim world. Our college is located in rural upstate New York. The closest college to us, Hamilton College, does not have an Islamicist. Cornell University is about an hour and a half away. Syracuse University is about an hour away.[8] Going in other directions, one can go for about two or three hours to the north or east before getting to another university with a full-time person trained in Islamic studies. At times, it has felt like every church and every reporter from those areas without an Islamicist had my home phone number on their speed-dial. Needless to say, it put a great deal of pressure on my family life, teaching, and scholarship.

In terms of my own college, the days past September 11 also demonstrated how the Muslim world was one of the biggest gaps across our curriculum. We did not have scholars at the college whose primary area of expertise was in some of the areas most necessary: history, political science, anthropology, women's studies, etc. This created a particularly difficult situation, as I have been adamant that it is not enough to simply look to an ethereal, idealized notion of "Islam" to understand the context for 9/11. One must be able to situate groups like Al Qaeda in the context of other violent movements that adopt—or steal, depending on your perspective—religious language. Some of these movements are covered in Mark Juergensmeyer's valuable work *Terror in the Mind of God* (2001). Lastly, I have argued that it was vital for us to understand the long history of colonialism and imperialism in these parts of the world, which have directly fuelled the rise of anti-colonial and then postcolonial movements. I have insisted that our discussions include a historical component that situates Al Qaeda in the network of violent postcolonial movements in the Muslim world. "Islam," I have emphasized, was one and not necessarily the most important framework needed to make sense out of the non-sense of 9/11.

On jihad

In spite of the above, what everyone wanted to talk about, of course, was *jihad*. Like "karma" and "nirvana," the term jihad seems bound to be absorbed into mainstream American parlance, even if like those two previous terms its popular understanding was perhaps a great distortion of the original meaning.

Many TV commentators (and political scientists) have been naively translating the term as "holy war." Jihad, like many other terms in religious traditions, is a complex and contested term (for one take on the evolution of the concept of jihad, see Peters 1996; cf. Brockopp in this volume). The original meaning of the term, as it is used in the Qur'an, is not "holy war" but merely "struggle" and "striving" for a cause. In the Qur'an, the believers are told to "struggle" in the path of God using their own souls and possessions (see, e.g., Qur'an 8:72, 9:20, 9:41, and 9:88, where the believers are described as those who do struggle in the path of God with "their possessions and their souls"). There are other words in the Qur'an that mean "fight" (such as *qital*; see, e.g., 2:216, 2:246) and even "war" (*harb*; see, e.g., 2:279), but jihad certainly does not primarily mean war, and even less so "holy war" (something of an oxymoron to my own ears, having lived through the vicious Iran–Iraq war in my childhood). Prophet Muhammad himself is said to have stated that there are two types of jihad, the "greater" jihad that is against one's own selfish tendencies, and the "lesser" jihad that is against injustice and oppression in the society. This is how the overwhelming majority of Muslims have historically understood the term jihad.[9]

One of the distinguishing features of war in Islamic law is that it is recognized practically as a human phenomenon that all societies engage in. Since all societies fight, the perspective of expositors of Islamic tradition has been to at least have humanity fight in a restrained manner. To not have such restrictions, from this perspective, would simply result in even greater chaos. As the Qur'an states: "Fight in the path of God those who have begun a fight against you, but do not transgress the limits. Indeed God does not love the transgressors" (Qur'an 2:190). These limits have been clearly identified through the example of Prophet Muhammad and enshrined in Islamic law (*Shari'a*): One is not allowed to kill civilians, not allowed to kill women and children, not allowed to kill the elderly, not allowed to kill animals, cut down trees, or poison a water well.[10] There is simply no way that the killing of 3,000 innocent civilians could ever be justified under Islamic law.

The term "jihad," like the term "crusade" in the history of Christianity, has been and continues to be invoked by a wide range of political figures to justify their own ideological agendas. Ayatollah Khomeini called for a jihad against Iraq, Saddam Hussein called for a jihad against the US. As one American Muslim intellectual has quipped, now every Tom, Dick, and Abdullah is calling for jihad. The ambiguity of terms like "jihad" and "crusade" is that they are open to interpretation—and thus abuse.[11] Jihad may be legitimately undertaken to fight injustice and oppression. In fact, this is how many of the social movements that have fought sexism and racism in Muslim societies have justified themselves. Naturally, though, we also have situations where demagogues invoke jihad to support their own causes, just as in the history of Christianity we have the call for crusade being used to support all types of dubious causes.

So, what does Islam *really* say?

Since 9/11, one of the most common experiences of all of us who teach Islamic studies has been facing the earnest question: "So, what does Islam *really* say about violence?"[12] The questions are usually well intentioned. There is a sincere plea for us to muster all of our scholarly authority to unequivocally state that there is no relationship whatsoever between the beautiful teachings of Islam and the hateful words and deeds of Osama bin Laden. Faced with such questions, and the brevity of the time and space to go into depth, many of us have found our initial reactions to be that of "Islam is a religion of peace." As with many of my colleagues, I also found myself repeating such statements in the first few days after 9/11. And yet, for some reason, this simplistic response has left a not altogether satisfactory feeling behind—at least in my own mind.

Had I not spent the better part of my own training and teaching trying to avoid grand generalizations? Had we not worked so hard to critique orientalist assumptions and essentializations that described Islam as a religion of law, of unity, of the "Semitic mind," of the "Arab mind," of every other "single-key" explanation? Have we not strived to emphasize the historical, cultural, and intellectual diversity of the Islamic experience? While it is understandable that at such a time of crisis we would find refuge in "Islam is a religion of peace," I yearned to rise above that nicety and find a framework for deeper, more honest, more difficult, and perhaps more truthful conversations.

Beyond apologetics

Not surprisingly, this meant an immediate departure from the language of apologetics. Let me try to be clear here. I consider myself someone who was not just born into a Muslim cultural heritage, but makes a choice every morning to dedicate myself to a life of Submission to the Divine, based on the guidance of the Qur'an, the example of Muhammad, and later Sufi teachers. At a fundamental level, I do believe that the Islamic tradition offers peace, both in the heart and for the world at large (when the Islamic imperatives for social justice are implemented).

Part of the challenge of those first few months after 9/11 has been coming to terms with a forthright and intellectually honest reality that recognizes that there are many ways of talking about religion. Two of them seem to have gained prominence in the post-9/11 world. One level is a normative, theological way, when self-designated (or selected) representatives speak with the weight of authority, and feel perfectly entitled to make statements like "the Catholic faith states . . .," "the Jewish faith teaches us that . . .," and of course, "the Islamic faith states . . ." The other way of talking about religion is more historical, less theological, and more people-centered. The followers of this perspective might state: "This Jewish group practices the following ritual, while other Jewish groups practice otherwise . . ."; "These Muslim groups hold this interpretation of jihad, while their interpretations are opposed by the following groups . . ."

I find myself increasingly on the side of the second way of talking. While there are times and places that the majority of Muslim scholars have formed a clear enough consensus (*ijma'*) on issues so as to allow us to speak of near unanimity, on other issues—precisely those that many non-Muslims would be interested in hearing about—there have been and continue to be a wide range of interpretations and practices among Muslim scholars and communities. I see it as my task as an Islamicist not to bury the differences among Muslims in the interest of 30-second spots. I think it is imperative on us to demonstrate the spectrum of interpretations, particularly in dealing with the "difficult" issues (gender constructions, violence, pluralism, etc.).

Furthermore, I find myself being less and less patient and satisfied with "Islam teaches us" language. Islam teaches us nothing. Prophet Muhammad does. Interpretive communities do. One could argue that God does, through the text of the Qur'an. But even in the case of texts, there are human beings who read the texts, interpret them, and expound their meanings. Even in the case of the Prophet, our encounter with the Prophet is driven by different (and competing) textual presentations of him. In all cases, the dissemination of divine teachings is achieved through human agency. To drive this message home, I usually offer this intentionally irreverent comment to my students: Islam does not get up in the morning. Islam does not brush its teeth. Islam does not take a shower. Islam eats nothing. And perhaps most importantly for our consideration, Islam says nothing. Muslims do. Muslims get up in the morning, Muslims brush their teeth, Muslims shower, Muslims eat, and Muslims speak.

Is this just semantics? I do not believe so. My experience, at the level of both devotional and academic communities, has been that many people simply ascribe their own (or their own community's) interpretations of Islam to "Islam states," and use such authoritative and authoritarian language as a way to close the discussion. And closing discussions is something that we can no longer afford at this point.

Islamic studies and politics after 9/11

So, where do we go from here? What is our task in teaching Islam after 9/11? What social and political ramifications does the teaching of Islamic studies have today?

I will not presume to speak on behalf of anyone other than myself. Some have suggested that part of our mission should be pointing out the examples of *tolerance* towards non-Muslims in the Islamic heritage, and also instilling *tolerance* towards Muslims in our students. I beg to differ. I am not interested *per se* in teaching "tolerance." Allow me to elaborate: the root of the term *tolerance* comes from medieval toxicology and pharmacology, focusing on how much poison a body could "tolerate" before it would succumb to death. I refuse to participate in a system that conceives of its own civilization as the privileged host into which knowledge about the "other" is incorporated as a foreign object or parasite. Our task, I believe, should somehow be grander than finding out how much knowledge of all the disenfranchised and marginalized groups we can *tolerate* before it kills us! Rather, I see our mission as nothing short of the grand task of full engagement with the complexities of humanity, defined not based on the norms of any one civilization, but globally. Part of this mission consists of undertaking a more critical examination of our position in the world, particularly given our place of privilege and prominence. If we are to have any hope of getting anywhere resembling peace, that examination needs to include both the greatest accomplishments of all civilizations, and also a painful scrutiny of ways in which our place of privilege has come at a great cost to others. It means a critical study of not just our subject matters, but also of our own selves, and our own communities.

As for me personally, this has also meant being more outspoken not just as a scholar of Islamic studies with a particular fondness for premodern Sufi love poetry, but also as a modern (and yikes, even postmodern) self-identifying Progressive Muslim spokesperson and activist. Since 9/11, I have worked with other progressive Muslims in the United States and beyond to articulate a historically accurate, non-idealized, now challenged, now challenging, view of Islam with the uncompromising emphasis on social justice, equality, and pluralism. One of the first fruits of these conversations is the volume *Progressive Muslims*, in which fifteen contemporary Muslim intellectuals (all of whom are also teachers of Islamic studies) talk frankly about challenges facing Islam and Muslim communities today. It is our assertion that just as interpretations of Islam have been part of the problem in the past and today, new progressive interpretations of Islam can and should be part of the solution (Safi 2003).

The fluid boundary between being a professing Muslim and a Muslim professor (to excuse the pun) is one that has been receiving a great deal of attention in religious studies, albeit usually in the case of other religious traditions. I would state that my own approach is informed by recent developments in feminist hermeneutics, anthropology, and postcolonial studies. I refuse to stand on the mythical "cloud of objectivity" and pretend that my own view is somehow naively impartial and completely objective. Of course I do take my role in presenting different aspects and interpretations of Islam quite seriously: in my classes the students will encounter the Islamic experience as interpreted by Sunni 'ulama, Sufi mystics, philosophical pundits, political theorists, devotional hymnists, film makers, court poets, contemporary feminists, and Shi'i scholars. While presenting these manifold faces of Islam to them, I also see it as the intellectually honest step to position my own perspective as that of a self-identifying progressive Muslim who speaks out again sexist, racist, and classist practices in Muslim societies and the US. It is from such a perspective that I have spoken out against the hideous actions of those who brought so much suffering to New York, DC, and Pennsylvania on 9/11, and that I continue to speak out against the unchecked exertion of US power in response to 9/11, first in Afghanistan, and then Iraq. My experience over the last few years has been that most of my students respect the above, so long as I continue to be consistent in critiquing not just the US, but also Muslim societies for similar sins. In addition, many of them want to see not just a "deconstruction" of existing practices, but also a viable, compassionate, pluralistic alternative being proposed.

Islamic studies beyond "Clash of Civilizations"

We live in a world that some would see as doomed to an inevitable "Clash of Civilizations," to recall Samuel Huntington's trite and clichéd analysis of post-Cold War politics (Huntington 1993; see also his book length treatment of this theory in Huntington 1996). Even as other scholars have offered devastating critiques of the above theory, Huntington and his ilk continue to find a receptive audience both in the State Department and in the larger public. Let us remember that one of the most recent titles on Islam to end up on the best-selling list was the regrettable *What Went Wrong? Western Impact and Middle Eastern Response*, written by none other than the noted critic—less generous souls might say hater—of modern Muslims (read: Arabs), Bernard Lewis. In fairness to Lewis, he is an avid admirer of the subtlety and complexity of premodern Muslim society. It is, rather, in the Muslim encounter with modernity that Lewis repeatedly falls back on descriptions like "poor," "weak," "ignorant," "disappointing," "humiliating," "corrupt," "impoverished," etc. All of the above adjectives are simply from one page (2002: 151) of *What Went Wrong*! Lewis, who gave the very phrase "Clash of Civilizations" to Huntington, has been bandying his worn out thesis of "the Roots of Muslim Rage" for decades now, and has yet again found a new audience for his ideas (Lewis 1990). The very last paragraph of Lewis' *What Went Wrong* starts with this sentence: "If the peoples of the Middle East continue on their present path, the suicide bomber may become a metaphor for the whole region . . ." (Lewis 2002: 159). In reading Lewis' verdict, one cannot help but wonder if in the first few years of the twenty-first century any other group of humanity apart from Middle Easterners/Muslims would be described as a whole by being represented by a suicide bomber. One can only imagine the outrage that would be felt and heard from many corners if instead of talking about Middle Easterners (read: Muslims), one had described all Chinese, all Africans, all women, all Jews, or all Hindus in such a derogatory fashion. I have recently published a detailed critique of the "Clash of Civilizations" theory, and I invite readers to have a look at it (Safi 2006).

Faced with the clout, prestige, and access to media and print of the Huntingtons and Lewises of the world, what is one Islamicist at a liberal arts college in a rural corner of upstate New York to do?

In 1967, Martin Luther King, Jr., published a monumental essay titled *Where Do We Go From Here: Chaos Or Community?* Dr. King ended this essay by stating: "We still have a choice today: nonviolent coexistence or violent coannihilation" (King, Jr., 1986: 633). I too believe that we as members of one humanity, as North Americans, and as members of the academy, have a choice. I pray that we may have the courage to heal this fractured world. That healing process is one that for me by necessity has an intellectual and academic component. My part in contributing to the healing is through teaching Islamic studies. I refuse to reduce the complexity of the heritage of the Muslims' encounter with the Divine simply to "history," "philosophy," "metaphysics," or even "theology." For me, the key challenge of teaching Islamic studies is the same now as it was before September 11, 2001; it is only heightened now. The challenge is to position Islamic studies as the empathic engagement with human beings in their quest to find ultimate meaning in God, one another, and the cosmos. It is to bring our own humanity, whether as a progressive Muslim professor or non-Muslim student, to the engagement with fellow members of the human race. Human beings must remain at the center, with all of their humanity, aspirations for beauty, and gross imperfections. Can we live up to the challenge laid forth to us by Prophet Muhammad and the Persian poet Sa'di, to envision all of us as members of one body, to feel the pain of another as our own? Perhaps only then we will be worthy of the name human being.

In conclusion, I would like to end with two statements from two of the luminous souls who are proudly displayed on the Study of Islam Response to 9/11 web page. Their words sum up everything I would like to say, and then some. The first is a letter from His Holiness the Dalai Lama to President Bush after 9/11, and the second a statement from Martin Luther King, Jr.

> I am confident that the United States as a great and powerful nation will be able to overcome this present tragedy.
>
> The American people have shown their resilience, courage and determination when faced with such difficult and sad situations.
>
> It may seem presumptuous on my part, but I personally believe we

need to think seriously whether a violent reaction is the right thing to do and in the greater interest of the nation and people in the long run.

I believe violence will only increase the cycle of violence.

But how do we deal with hatred and anger which are often the root causes of such senseless violence?

This is a very difficult question, especially when it concerns a nation and we have certain fixed conceptions of how to deal with such attacks. I am sure you will make the right decision.

With my prayers and good wishes,

Yours sincerely,

The Dalai Lama

The ultimate weakness of violence is that it is a descending spiral, begetting the very thing it seeks to destroy.

Instead of diminishing evil, it multiplies it . . .

Through violence you may murder the hater, but you do not murder hate.

In fact, violence merely increases hate . . .

Returning violence for violence multiplies violence, adding deeper darkness to a night already devoid of stars.

Darkness cannot drive out hate; only love can do that.

Reverend Dr. Martin Luther King, Jr.

And Towards God We Are Ever-Returning (Qur'an)

Notes

1 http://www.cair-net.org. The number is derived from the figures given as of February 8, 2002.
2 While perhaps all of these numbers are vastly underreported, I can personally vouch that the number of hate mail cases was of an exponentially higher number than that reported by CAIR. Due to the various discussion groups that I am on, in the one week after 9/11 alone, I (and everyone on those groups) had received approximately 1,300 pieces of hate e-mail. These ranged from simple exclamations: "Why did you people do it? What had they done to you?" to specific threats against our families, some even threatening to pave the street with our blood.
3 http://www.cair-net.org/htm/bycategory.htm.
4 One of the pictures that elicited the most feedback was that of the impromptu peace rally in the streets of Tehran, complete with that most wonderful of traditions, a candle light vigil. See "Expressions of Grief and Sympathy in the Arab and Muslim World" http://groups.colgate.edu/aarislam/response. htm. How ironic that a short few weeks later, President Bush alienated many

of the same Iranians who marched to show their support for victims of 9/11 when he branded Iran part of the "axis of evil," a remark which clearly did not take into consideration the support of the majority of Iranians for the progressive President Khatami. Khatami has for years been calling for a respectful dialogue with the West.

5 Oscar Arias' statements were featured on a web page titled "The Peacemakers Speak," at http://www.thecommunity.com/crisis/.

6 It is important to point out that such civilian casualties continued long after the most intense period of bombing in late fall and winter of 2001. In the first days of July 2002, American planes looking for Al Qaeda bombed an Afghan wedding party, killing 48 women and children. See http://www. nytimes.com/2002/07/08/international/asia/O8VILL.html.

7 The BBC and European press covered the human cost of this war much more honestly and sympathetically than CNN, which largely abdicated its independent journalistic integrity and responsibility to ask critical questions by simply becoming a mouthpiece for the State Department. See BBC's "Millions at Risk" (http://news.bbc.co.uk/hi/english/world/south_asia/newsid_1598000/1598797.stm).

8 Exacerbating the matter of the paucity of experts on Islamic studies has been the fact that many Islamicists have been understandably reticent to speak publicly about such complicated issues, particularly when their analysis might include criticisms of US foreign policy as part of a larger discussion. With the passing of the so-called PATRIOT bill and other erosions of civil rights, many experts on Islamic studies—particularly the many who are not US citizens—have been rightly concerned that in these hyper-patriotic times, any criticism of the US government might lead to their deportation. The effect of such draconian measures on college campuses is discussed in the AP report: "College Staff Find Chilling Free Speech Climate" (http://www.indy-bay.org/news/2001/10/106371.php).

9 One has to admit that some later jurists did collapse jihad to the external layer of fighting in the external realm. However, their impact was always balanced by the injunctions in the Qur'an (discussed above) on one hand, and the Sufi prioritization of the inner jihad on the other.

10 For one such set of limitations, see al-Misri 1994: 603–4. Al-Misri's description of the rules of jihad conforms mostly, though not completely, to the above list.

11 Thus the uproar in the Muslim world when in the days after 9/11, President Bush unwisely described the American response as a "crusade." While the President perhaps intended a meaning along the lines of a "valiant effort," to many Muslim ears the term crusade still has the connotation of an aggressive, Christian attack against Muslims. Or was that a Freudian slip?

12 For a highly sensitive and intelligent discussion of the complicated discourse of violence and Islam see Lawrence 1998.

References and further reading

Abou El Fadl, Khaled. 2001. *Speaking in God's Name: Islamic Law, Authority, and Women*. Oxford: Oneworld.

Al-Misri, Ahmad ibn Naqib. 1994. *'Umdat al-Salik*, trans. Nuh Ha Mim Keller as *Reliance of the Traveller: A Classic Manual of Islamic Sacred Law*. Beltsville, MD: Amana Publications.

Huntington, Samuel. 1993. "Clash of Civilizations." *Foreign Affairs* 72 (3): 22–49.

——. 1996. *The Clash of Civilizations: Remaking of World Order*. New York: Simon and Schuster.

Juergensmeyer, Mark. 2001. *Terror in the Mind of God: The Global Rise of Religious Violence*. Berkeley, CA: University of California Press.

Kassam, Zayn. 2002. "September 11, 2001 and Islam." *ARC: The Journal of the Faculty of Religious Studies, McGill University* 30: 185–9.

King, Jr., Martin Luther. 1986 [reprinted 1991]. "Where Do We Go from Here: Chaos or Community?" In *A Testimony of Hope: The Essential Writings and Speeches of Martin Luther King, Jr.*, edited by James M. Washington, 555–633. San Francisco: Harper San Francisco.

Lawrence, Bruce. 1998. *Shattering the Myth: Islam Beyond Violence*. Princeton, NJ: Princeton University Press.

Lewis, Bernard. 1990. "The Roots of Muslim Rage." *The Atlantic Monthly* 266 (3, September): 47–60.

——. 2002. *What Went Wrong? Western Impact and Middle Eastern Response*. New York: Oxford University Press.

McCutcheon, Russell T., ed. 1999. *The Insider/Outsider Problem in the Study of Religion: A Reader*. London: Cassell.

Mottahedeh, Roy. 1996. "The Clash of Civilizations: An Islamicist's Critique." *Harvard Middle Eastern and Islamic Review* 2 (2): 1–26.

Peters, Rudolph. 1996. *Jihad in Classical and Modern Islam*. Princeton, NJ: Markus Wiener.

Sa'di. 1997. *The Rose Garden (Gulistan)*. Trans. Omar Ali-Shah. Reno, NV: Tractus Books.

Safi, Omid. 2002. "Being Muslim, Being American Through this Absurd 'War on Terrorism.'" In *Taking Back Islam: American Muslims Reclaim Their Faith*, edited by Michael Wolf, 67–75. Emmaus, PA: Rodale Press.

——. ed. 2003. *Progressive Muslims: On Justice, Gender, and Pluralism*. Oxford: Oneworld.

——. 2006. "I and Thou in a Fluid World: Beyond 'Islam versus the West.'" In *Voices of Islam: Voices of Change*, edited by Omid Safi, 199–222. Westport, CT: Praeger.

"Statement from the Steering Committee, Section for the Study of Islam, American Academy of Religion." *ARC: The Journal of the Faculty of Religious Studies, McGill University* 30: 181–4.

Stille, Alexander. 2001. "Islam Experts Off on a Wild Ride, Willing or Not." *The New York Times*, November 10. Online at http://query.nytimes.com/gst/fullpage.html?res=9402EED81738F933A25752C1A9679C8B63.

16 Islam within the context of higher education*

Zayn Kassam

During a 2003 panel discussion on "Religion and Higher Education: Disciplinarity and Social Justice," my colleagues discussed why every student should have the opportunity to learn about religion, and what we try to do in the religious studies classroom. For my part, I wanted to talk more specifically about Islam within the context of higher education. As many must have felt most keenly over the past few years, the need for intelligent discourse on Islam and Muslims has never been more critically felt than since 9/11. Our campuses have struggled with ways to cope with the trauma collectively felt by our students, our colleagues, and our nation. My colleagues who teach Islam in institutions of higher learning all across the United States and Canada were invited by religious organizations, by high schools and colleges, by the media, by their own institutions, and by neighbors to explain Islam, explain terrorism, explain jihad, explain why "they" hate "us," and explain what it is about their religion that incites people to engage in such unspeakable acts as we saw carried out in New York and Washington on September 11, 2001.

According to a religious studies survey published in *Religious Studies News*, at the Bachelor's degree level, only 26 percent of religious studies departments offer courses in Islam—the comparable figure for Judaism is 30 percent, for Christianity 96 percent; while at research universities, the figure goes up to 66 percent for Islam, 85 percent for Christianity, and 86 percent for Judaism. Consequently, teaching Islam or, for that matter, Judaism to undergraduates does not appear to be a priority for 75 percent of undergraduate departments in religion, while at research universities, courses offered in Judaism and Christianity top those offered in Islam by about 20 percent. Recall the world statistics for the numbers of

---

* *Editors' note*: The following essay was originally given as an oral address for the Association of American Colleges and Universities in Seattle, Washington on January 24, 2003, within a session on "Religion and Higher Education: Disciplinarity and Social Justice" organized by Susan Henking. The oral tone of the address has been largely retained in this published version.

adherents: Christians, Catholic and Protestant together, make up a little over 2 billion or 33 percent of world population; Muslims account for 1.2 billion or 20 percent, while Jews account for 18 million or less than 1 percent of the world population. The primacy given in research to Judaism makes sense given that both Christianity and Islam base their sacrality on the Hebrew Bible. One could also argue that the 5 percent lead for courses in Judaism over courses in Islam simply acknowledges that although numerically Jews and Muslims are about the same in this country (roughly 6 million), Jews have been here longer and are better established both within and outside the academy. The same data, cut somewhat differently, show that 51 percent of public institutions of higher learning offer Islam, 64 percent offer Judaism, 86 percent offer Christianity; private non-sectarian figures are comparable, with slightly higher numbers for Judaism, and private Catholic and Protestant institutions are, understandably, much higher for Christianity and much lower for Islam and Judaism.

The point of sharing all these statistics with you is that while there is some expertise on Islam and Muslims at our institutions of higher learning, there needs to be more, much more. In the face of all the measures that have been enacted on the civic front as well as with the pursuit of the so-called war on terrorism, it is extremely critical that we continue to engage in critical discourse about issues pertaining to Islam, Muslims, and our relations with the Muslim-majority societies. Those faculty members at our institutions with expertise on Islam and Muslims have continued to do their utmost to step up to the plate. All my colleagues in Islamic studies and in religious studies generally, as well as in politics, history, international studies, media studies, Asian studies, and women's studies, have reported how intense the months following 9/11 have been for them as they are called upon by diverse constituencies to teach the history and background as well as current developments in the war on terrorism. I suggest, then, that administrative support for faculty development with respect to Islam and the Muslim world is critical for our institutions to continue to train students and to act as community resources. It is vital for us to engage in informed discourse about areas of the world to which we are connected by our foreign policy, our trade, our military action, our development efforts, and our cultural interaction. In addition to thinking about whether it is now time to push efforts for hiring in Islamic studies, it is also possible to engage in other kinds of efforts. For instance, in what seems now a somewhat prescient move, I represented Pomona College in a collaboration with Claremont Graduate University, one of our sister Claremont Colleges, to apply in the summer of 2001 for an NEH Focus Grant to bring three specialists in different facets of Islamic studies to our campuses in order to have a workshop with both undergraduate and graduate faculty in religious studies. The aim here was to enable religious studies faculty trained in specializations other than Islam to introduce cognate Islamic materials into their courses by way of comparison, showing resonances and differences while working toward larger understandings of how religions go about addressing particular issues. One can imagine how dynamic and useful these workshops were as they took place during the spring semester following 9/11.

What does a religious studies class have to do with critical, informed discussions of our current geopolitical situation? Such a question is quite valid to raise. Religious studies as a field has undergone a remarkable change from early in the twentieth century when much of the work of religious studies was concerned with theology, philosophy, and credal formulations with some attention paid to ritual and myth.

In recent years, religious studies has perhaps become one of the few disciplines in which true interdisciplinarity takes place, as the study of a religion entails examining religious theologies, philosophies, histories, rituals, myths, institutions, mystical beliefs and behaviors, its arts and cultural expressions, all within the context of the peoples professing that faith. We no longer debate the question of Truth with a capital T, but rather ask an assortment of questions: how do people in a particular context and in a larger cultural configuration understand the truth? What relation does their expression of what they think is the truth bear with the social and political and economic realities they face? How do they define and deal with the Other, how do they engage moral and philosophical issues, how do they interpret their sacred texts in order to either maintain the status quo or to challenge it? How do they ritually express transformations in understanding? How do postmodern and feminist challenges get met? How does religious language become an instrument of political power and how do religious institutions maintain power politically, socially, economically?

Thus, in my classes, and in the classes of my colleagues in Islamic studies, teaching Islam is not about trying to convert students to Islam. Many may remember the furor that occurred when Michael Sells' translation and commentary on selected verses in the Qur'an was adopted as an entering class reader for discussion purposes. One of the key criticisms was that some people felt it was akin to brainwashing our kids in Islam. Such criticism does not appreciate fully what it is that we do in the academy when we teach about religion. Rather, as I have outlined, the goal in our classes is to develop in students critical thinking skills with respect to any body of knowledge. My Muslim students report that they understand much better the history of their tradition and are able to see that their normative understanding is only one way in which to grasp the huge and complex diversity of Muslim traditions. They also come away able to see the political and social conditions under which some key theological doctrines were developed, and the ongoing impact of these. For instance, they are able to appreciate why a woman who veils is expressing her piety, but also how that veiling represents, in some parts of the world, a political statement of difference from Western cultural hegemony, and in other parts of the world, an imposed rule of piety for a program of Islamist ambitions for state power. My non-Muslim students report that they understand much better how deeply orientalist discourse is embedded in our media reportage of Muslim peoples, often masking the real issues at stake, and how patriarchy and struggles for power are as endemic to the Muslim world as they are in North America, yet under very different conditions and expressed in very different ways. They also come away being able to think critically about the material preconditions necessary for democracy and civic society, and see how religion, economic realities, political discourse, and society all shape and influence each other.

It is now a truism that to study the Other is really in some ways to study oneself, by contrast, by comparison, and often in relation. Since 9/11 another key development that is worthy of attention is the politicization involved in the act of teaching about Islam and Muslims. The terror, grief, and destruction that our nation witnessed on 9/11 were caused by acts that are inexcusable, morally reprehensible, and for which the perpetrators must be held accountable. At the same time, the response to the simple question, "Why do they hate us?" is anything but simple. Indeed, it is an extremely complex set of responses, responses that demand that we think and act intelligently, with forbearance, and for the long term. There are no short-term solutions such as "let's bomb them out of existence." Historians, political scientists, and Mideast experts such as Howard Zinn, Chalmers Johnson, Joel Beinin, and others have pointed to our foreign policy as in part implicated in the creation of political groups within the Islamic world that are, to put it mildly, unhappy with us; others have weighed in with the observation that the Israeli–Palestinian conflict needs better brokering toward peace; and still others have suggested that the oil-wealth enabled export of the Saudi form of Islam, dubbed Wahhabism, provided the ideological fervor that lay behind the attacks— after all, not only is the bin Laden construction empire responsible for the erasure of most of the historical sites connected to Muhammad, the prophet of Islam, but the executors of the 9/11 tragedy were overwhelmingly Saudi in origin and ideology, as are the ideologues of the Taliban. None of these three explanations in themselves (our foreign policy; the Mideast situation; Wahhabism) are sufficient in understanding the complex factors at play that led to 9/11. In bringing some of these complexities to public discourse as we attempted to address the trauma caused by 9/11 on our campuses and within our communities, we came under attack almost immediately by the organization headed by Lynn Cheney, wife of Dick Cheney. That organization, the American Council of Trustees and Alumni, in its report on November 11, 2001 (www.goacta.org), identified academics as the weak link in the war on terrorism, implying that academics were being unpatriotic—indeed, Pomona College was named as one of the institutions of higher learning on that list, an honor we shared with Brown, Haverford, Rutgers, MIT, and others too numerous to be mentioned here. While it was my colleague, Jerry Irish, who teaches philosophy of religion and ethics, and not myself who was the specific person intended, you can imagine how difficult and challenging it became to speak the truth gathered from one's many years of training and analysis—because who, in these difficult and grief-filled times, wants to be accused of not being patriotic?

If Lynn Cheney's organization was reacting to the responses that implicated our foreign policy, then another organization called Campus Watch responded with its own damning attack on academics who dared to suggest that the Israeli–Palestinian conflict needs to be better understood from both sides. Campus Watch, created by Martin Kramer and Daniel Pipes, called upon students to report their professors for inciting anti-Semitism by criticizing Israeli government policies and actions toward the Palestinians. While it is one thing to hate the Jews, who have suffered immeasurably over the centuries and most recently in that blight on the collective human conscience, the Holocaust, it is quite another to be prevented from speaking out against some of the excesses of the Israeli government and military against Palestinians on charges of anti-Semitism. To be silenced on these issues ignores both the data and the plight of the Jews, Christians, Muslims, and secularists who together make up the peoples in the region. In fact, those speaking out against Israeli government policies include Jewish activists and academics in the US and in Israel, as well as Israelis and Palestinians who have banded together both inside and outside Israel and the Palestinian territories in protest of suicide bombings and other acts of violence on the one side, and the curfews, land-clearing for building more settlements, and military aggression on the other.

The third challenge to academic discourse about the issues connected to Islam and Muslims comes from the directive from John Ashcroft's office that now requires, if requested, academic institutions to report on their students from countries on the terrorist list. What courses they took, when and where. Will courses they take on Islam or Mideast history and politics, or engineering or chemistry, all become equally suspect in case this information is used to disseminate militant fundamentalist Islamic thought and action, or build nuclear facilities, or create chemical weapons of mass destruction? What about the critical importance of education as a facilitator of social change, as a developer of critical thinking skills in the advancement of society, as an enabler of human dignity in the long march away from human suffering?

The point of these challenges is that 9/11 has clearly highlighted the important role that institutions of higher learning can play in bringing intelligent discourse to the table, to the media, to our community organizations, to our policy makers, to the international constituency that is our students. At the same time, the deeply rooted fear and mistrust of Islam and Muslims—something that goes back at least to the Crusades—continues to resurface in the form of organizations that seek to undermine the key work of critical thinking, analysis, and teaching that we do, by using silencing tactics that label academics unpatriotic or anti-Semitic (and let me just briefly mention here that many of the academics labeled anti-Semitic are themselves Jews).

In light of the subtitle of that 2003 panel, "Disciplinarity and Social Justice," I wish to advance the notion that we are not doing our patriotic duty by caving in to challenges to the academy's mandate of examining even the hardest, toughest issues intelligently, fairly, and strategically. As educators in higher education, we must continue to follow this mandate even if that means examining our foreign policies, our understanding of and relations with others, critically, carefully, and constructively, to determine how we can create international engagements that result in "win–win" situations, rather than simply assuring our access to resources and to markets for our goods at the expense of supporting dictatorships that undermine the democratic freedoms we hold so dear. Further, I believe we inadvertently collaborate in the rise of anti-Semitism in many parts of the Muslim world when we continue to squash intelligent debate, analysis, and examination of the Israeli–Palestinian situation as well as our own role within it. This a role that includes facilitating, through our financial and military aid programs, the repressive policies that continue to sustain the context for Palestinian violence and continue to ensure support for militant arms of Palestinian political groups. And finally, we are severely compromising our ability to further the development of Muslim societies when students from Muslim countries are afraid or denied the ability to study at our institutions, in order to learn how we create and sustain a civil society. Through their participation in our academic institutions, students from Muslim-majority societies learn the essential critical thinking skills that will help to develop their own societies in combating hunger, in creating liberal educational institutions, and strong social institutions that do not need to take recourse to militant Islamic ideologies to put bread on the table. Much of this process can be done in partnership. To this end, I believe that as administrators and as educators, we also need to equip our home-grown students to rise to the global challenges they will face when they take up their positions as contributing members to a world in which they represent currently the strongest nation on earth.

17 Thoughts on being a scholar of Islam and a Muslim in America post-9/11

Amir Hussain

I begin my chapter in memory of Balbir Singh Sodhi, the Sikh gas station owner from Mesa, Arizona who was murdered on September 15, 2001, the first fatality of the hate crimes following the terrorist attacks on September 11.

I teach Islam as an associate professor in the Department of Theological Studies at Loyola Marymount University in Los Angeles (LMU). Born in Pakistan, I moved to Canada at the age of four with my family. All of my education, kindergarten to PhD, was in Canada. My doctoral dissertation at the University of Toronto was on Muslim communities in Toronto. In 1997, I was hired at California State University, Northridge (CSUN), where I taught until I moved to LMU in 2005. I have been living in the United States since 1997.

For the last while, the song that I keep playing over and over again is "Pacing the Cage," by the Canadian singer-songwriter Bruce Cockburn (I should point out that it is a common trait of Canadians living abroad to obsessively mention other Canadians). Bruce wrote the song while he was in Philadelphia, and the last verse is, sadly, appropriate:

> Sometimes the best map will not guide you
> You can't see what's round the bend
> Sometimes the road leads through dark places
> Sometimes the darkness is your friend
> Today these eyes scan bleached-out land
> For the coming of the outbound stage
> Pacing the cage
> Pacing the cage. (Cockburn 1996)

Events in the year after 9/11

On the evening of Monday, September 10, 2001, I led a session for my course on death and dying in the world's religions. As it was the second meeting of the course, I was still introducing students to the topic. For that particular class, I had asked students to answer the following question:

"What object, film, song, piece of music, art, or writing helps you to understand death?" My own contribution to the discussion was Lou Reed's song, "Magic and Loss," from the CD with that same title released in 1992. The CD and the title song were occasioned by the death of two of his closest friends. In my mind, Reed is synonymous with New York City. The song ends with the line: "There's a bit of magic in everything and then some loss to even things out."

The next day, I was awakened by a telephone call from a friend in the early morning, insisting that I turn on the television. I turned it on, and watched the horrors of 9/11 on my TV screen. My first thoughts were about my friends in New York City, including an editor who lives a few blocks away from the World Trade Center. I went into the office so that I could email those of my friends that I could not reach by telephone. It took me most of that day to confirm that my friends were still alive. During that day I was contacted by our provost, who put together a small committee to deal with the issues arising at my university from these events. We canceled classes that afternoon. The following day, I urged our provost to hold a memorial on our campus, which we did on Friday, September 14.

Jon Brockopp, Zayn Kassam, and Omid Safi have all described in this volume reactions in the immediate aftermath of 9/11. We saw a tremendous increase in the messages to the LISTSERV for the Study of Islam section of the American Academy of Religion. We were all called upon to make numerous presentations to various community groups.

A year later, I found an essay by Mark Slouka to be the best in attempting to understand the impact of what had happened:

> . . . I believe, to put it plainly, that last year's attack was so traumatic to us because it simultaneously exposed and challenged the myth of our own uniqueness. A myth most visible, perhaps, in our age-old denial of death.
>
> Consider it. Here in the New Canaan, in the land of perpetual beginnings and second chances, where identity could be sloughed and sloughed again and history was someone else's problem, death had never been welcome. Death was a foreigner—radical, disturbing, smelling of musty books and brimstone. We wanted no part of him.
>
> And now death had come calling. That troubled brother, so long forgotten, so successfully erased, was standing on our porch in his steel-toed boots, grinning. He'd made it across the ocean, passed like a ghost through the gates of our chosen community. We had denied him his due and his graveyards, watered down his deeds, buried him with things. Yet here he was. He reminded us of something unpleasant. Egypt, perhaps.
>
> This was not just a terrorist attack. This was an act of metaphysical trespass. Someone had some explaining to do . . . (Slouka 2002: 36)

Let me, at this point, shift to a discussion about Muslim concerns in North America in the first year after 9/11. In doing so, it is important to remember that many Muslims in North America are a postcolonial people; that is, immigrants who have a history with the legacies of empire. Mohammed Arkoun, a leading Western scholar of Islam, describes the intersection of colonialism and human rights with respect to Muslims: "The colonial adventure ended badly. It is difficult to speak to a Muslim audience today about the Western origin of human rights without provoking indignant protests. We must not lose sight of the wars of liberation and the ongoing, postcolonial battle against Western 'imperialism' if we want to understand the psychological and ideological climate in which an Islamic discourse on human rights has developed in the past ten or fifteen years" (Arkoun 1994: 109).

In the United States, African-Americans form an important minority community. For many African-Americans, due to the history of slavery and racism in the United States, there is sometimes an understanding of America that parallels that of non-White immigrants. The majority of North American Muslims are "Brown" (at least 25 percent African-American, 35 percent South Asian, and 33 percent Middle Eastern), and so American Muslims are automatically marginalized by the racism that is present here in America. As members of a religious minority, they are further marginalized. Of course, many other factors contribute to Muslim identity in North America. There are questions of religious affiliation. Is one a Sunni or a Shi'i? Is one a member of the Ahmadiyya, a Muslim group that is proscribed in Pakistan? Is one a member of the various Sufi orders that are found in North America? Is one a member of the working class, or does one have a higher socio-economic status? Can one pass as "White," or does one's ethnicity prohibit this?

There are also a great many questions of representation, especially the question of who "represents" Muslim interests in North America. There is a wide variety of groups claiming to speak for North American Muslims. Some of them are in competition with each other to claim an (or "the") authentic voice of Muslims. One thinks, for example in Canada, of the struggle between the Canadian Islamic Congress and the Muslim Canadian Congress. In November 2004, the Progressive Muslim Union of North America was launched to the acclaim of many Muslims, and the concern of many others. Those of us who teach about Islam have to talk about these issues of representation. On my web page, for example, I have the following disclaimer to a list of North American Muslim groups: "This list includes links to various groups who consider themselves to be Muslim. I make no judgment about their Islam, but I understand that others may be all too willing to do this."[1]

As North Americans, many Muslims have learned and adopted popular North American notions of equality and justice. As Muslims, many North Americans have similar notions, rooted for example in the Qur'anic verse about God being with the "oppressed on the earth" (28:5). As North American Muslims, we may therefore be doubly shocked or scandalized when the secular North American environment does not live up to its universalist values.

Many North American Muslims also perceive a double standard against Muslims. This perception increased following the attacks on September 11, 2001. The Council on American–Islamic Relations (CAIR) released its seventh annual report on the status of Muslim civil rights in the USA on April 30, 2002, some seven months after the attacks (CAIR 2002). The report detailed the 1,516 complaints that CAIR received, a three-fold increase from the previous year. Some 2,250 people were affected by these complaints. What was most troubling for CAIR was that the majority of the complaints involved various levels of government: "Of all the institutional settings tracked by this report, the largest number of complaints involved profiling incidents at airports or those at the hands of government agencies, especially the INS, FBI, and local law enforcement authorities" (CAIR 2002: 11).

While the signing into law of the Patriot Act on October 26, 2001, and the passenger profiling at the nation's airports, did not target only American Muslims, many North American Muslims were concerned by these two developments. I have had my own experiences with such ethnic targeting (see Hussain 2005). Of greater concern were the estimated 1,200 Muslims who were detained, the 5,000 Muslim foreign nationals who were "voluntarily" interviewed, and the three Muslim charities (Holy Land Foundation for Relief and Development, Global Relief Foundation, and Benevolence International Foundation) that were closed by the federal government. Many American Muslims perceived that they were being targeted by their own government. This was particularly galling for the American Muslims who had voted for George W. Bush in the 2000 presidential election, precisely because he had spoken out against the "secret evidence" that was often used against Muslims. For many American Muslims there was a sense that they did not have the basic human rights that were given to other Americans, that while they considered themselves American, they were not considered as such by their own government.

Events in the years after 9/11

Having mentioned something of the events of that first year post-9/11 let me turn to a discussion of more recent events. There has been a great deal written about the scholar as public intellectual. For myself, I prefer a different term, the scholar as citizen. I have taught in both state and private universities in California. Regardless of whether I receive direct funding from the State of California, I have an obligation to the state and its citizens. For me, it is important to reach different audiences. I reach some in my classes, others with the scholarly writing that I have done. Yet, I reach a far greater number of people with my editorial pieces in newspapers, or my work with various local and national media. My students do not know me from my scholarly writing, but they recognize me from their great signifier: they have seen me on television on the History Channel or on the local news, or on *Politically Incorrect with Bill Maher* or *The Tavis Smiley Show*.

I mention this because I think it signals a shift for some of us as academics. Most of us work in universities (even my own, which sees itself as much as a teaching institution as a research institution) where peer-reviewed journal articles and scholarly monographs are the coin of the realm. I have been fortunate to have many of those, and I recognize the value of "serious" scholarship. But I also understand the need to get our work "out there," to people who do not have the ability to take our courses or read our scholarly prose (with all of its own conventions of style and jargon). And I am also under no illusions. I am sure that no more than 50 people have read any of my scholarly pieces, but a million or so have read my work in the *Los Angeles Times*, and several million have seen me on television. I get far more email about op-ed pieces in the newspaper than I have ever received about a scholarly article. To be sure, if all of my publishing were in the local newspaper, then I would not consider myself a very good academic. Yet, I would argue that I am not being a socially responsible academic if I fail to try to put some of my work out to the general public. In the case of Islam and Muslim communities, it is all the more important to get my work out to the widest possible audience.

Post-9/11, many of us have made curriculum changes. I used to start with a standard historical introduction that introduced the Qur'an and the Prophet Muhammad. I now have students start by reading a book that describes how the news media construct reality (Postman and Powers 1992). Most of my students get their information about Islam and Muslim lives from television, so I think it is important to begin with how the television news works. I also use a videotape of Bill Moyers interviewing Jon Stewart and talking about *The Daily Show with Jon Stewart*. My students are admirers of Stewart's work, and agree with me that the "fake" news that he presents is much better than the "real" news. I have also had colleagues from local television stations come to my class to talk about ratings, and how important they are to the local news.

Having discussed media constructions of Muslim lives, I sometimes then move to something of a case study. In the American media, Palestinians—whether they are Muslim, Christian, or secular—are constructed as "Muslims." I next ask students to read a graphic novel (i.e., comic book) that describes something of the realities of Palestinian experience (Sacco 2001) and contrast that presentation with the ways in which Palestinians are perceived in America. There is a great advantage to using a comic book in class (aside from the reactions of students who are delighted or appalled to have a comic book on the reading list). Some students still think that a photograph is "objective," that it "tells the truth." They do not consider how it is composed. It is much easier to show this with drawings, where it is obvious that someone has made the drawing, and someone else might do it differently.

There has been a great deal of discussion among academics who teach Islam regarding our roles with the media. Personally, I prefer to work with print or radio journalists. Generally, I do not work with commercial television, but I will work with public television. My experience working with commercial television immediately after 9/11 soured me. It made me realize that it was all about entertainment, and not about education. It was all about trying to summarize complicated situations in eight-second sound bites. This is something that I refuse to do.

In addition to working with the media, many of us have been asked to work with various student groups on our campuses. Omid Safi's chapter offers a good discussion of these issues. There has been difficulty for many of our exchange students in border crossings and obtaining US visas. This has also been a problem for Muslim and non-Muslim faculty members. Two of the most famous recent cases, involving Tariq Ramadan and Yusuf Islam, will be discussed later in this chapter.

There has also been great concern about the monitoring of Middle East studies. At the time of writing this chapter, Bill HR 3077 ("to amend title VI of the Higher Education Act of 1965 to enhance international education programs") has been passed by the US House of Representatives and is currently before the Senate. That bill includes a provision for the creation of an "International Higher Education Advisory Board" to monitor academic work on Middle East studies.[2]

Changes have also occurred within the Study of Islam section of the AAR. This group used to be a small group of scholars who mostly talked only with one another. Now, it is a much larger group, and we are asked to reach out and talk to all sorts of people outside our group. One of our group, Carl Ernst, has written about his own recent experiences:

> . . . it still amazes me that intelligent people can believe that all Muslims are violent or that all Muslim women are oppressed, when they would never dream of uttering slurs stereotyping much smaller groups such as Jews or blacks. The strength of these negative images of Muslims is remarkable, even though they are not based on personal experience or actual study, but they receive daily reinforcement from the news media and popular culture. (Ernst 2003: xvii)

Ernst goes on to point out that in workshops on key issues in Islamic studies in 1992 and then a decade later, it was determined that "the real issue is to humanize Muslims in the eyes of non-Muslims" (Ernst 2003: xvii).

Much of our work in the Study of Islam section has been on how we rework our courses in light of students who now have a great deal of misinformation about Islam and Muslim lives from what they see on television or listen to on talk radio stations. We have also discussed how to handle our increased obligations (mentioned earlier in this chapter) to speak to various community groups about Islam.

Of course, this concern to humanize Muslims does not mean that we take an "everything is as wonderful as the perfume of roses on the wind" attitude towards the very serious problems that exist within Muslim communities. We need to discuss issues such as gender discrimination, religious arrogance and intolerance, violence, etc. However, we also need to make clear that many people see these problems as the only reality of Islam, and are unaware of the richness and beauty that exists as well.

Post-9/11 came the invasions of Afghanistan and, later, Iraq. What was interesting on the CSUN campus was that student opposition to these wars did not come from our Muslim students. Instead, it predominately came from our Central American students, many of whom have experienced American imperialism in their own lives in places such as Nicaragua or El Salvador. There was also a connection with Japanese Americans, who were the first to stand beside Muslim Americans post-9/11.

As mentioned earlier, there has been concern about certain Muslims not being allowed entry into the US. In the case of Cat Stevens/Yusuf Islam, if it were not so chilling, it would be funny. Jon Stewart said it best on *The Daily Show with Jon Stewart*: "in the war on terror, we finally got the guy who wrote 'Peace Train.'" Yet, coming on the heels of the revocation of Tariq Ramadan's visa to begin a tenured professorship at Notre Dame, it is part of a larger and more worrisome trend.

As one of a group of Muslim academics that teaches about Islam, I have always been outspoken against violence and terrorism. I have personally been involved in peace and justice groups since I was a university student. After the horrible attacks on September 11, 2001, I was one of a group of Muslim scholars who contributed to a book entitled *Progressive Muslims* (Safi 2003). This was our attempt to answer the question, "Where are the voices of moderate or progressive Muslims?" It is crucial for us to provide our voices, voices which might be silenced in our countries of origin, or would have been silent here in North America in past decades.

The US government has claimed to want to enter into dialogue with "progressive" or "moderate" Muslims. However, the policy of the government, especially the recent exclusions of Muslims from the United States, leads me to worry. In the case of Tariq Ramadan, the two major relevant academic groups (I am a member of both), the Middle East Studies Association and the American Academy of Religion, wrote a joint letter protesting the decision to revoke his work visa. In that letter, they wrote: "Denying qualified scholars entry into the United States because of their political beliefs strikes at the core of academic freedom." The American Association of University Professors has also taken up the cause.

In such cases, there has been no explanation given. Just the broad and vague reference to "security concerns." I also find that troubling. One of the things I admire about the United States, and why I chose to emigrate here and choose to live here, is the rule of law. But here, there are no charges. Just things done in secret. With the case of Yusuf Islam, I have only heard allegations, not any proof. Yes, Cat Stevens did convert to Islam, changing his name to Yusuf Islam. When he converted, he joined a rather conservative group of Muslims. Not knowing any different, when they told him that music was "un-Islamic," he hung up his guitar. Later, he learned that this was an extreme opinion and began to record again. The same with the controversy over Salman Rushdie. In 1989, at Kingston University in London, Yusuf was asked about the death sentence. He gave the stock answer about the traditional punishment for apostasy being death. At no time did he say that Rushdie *should* be killed. Of course, this statement was misquoted in the papers the next day. I have an interest in this issue, as part of my PhD dissertation was on the controversy over *The Satanic Verses*, and I published an article about it in the *Journal of the American Academy of Religion* (Hussain 2002).

Yusuf Islam has worked tirelessly for causes of peace and justice. He has built a respected Islamic school. He did fundraising for Bosnian orphans. And while risking the obscenity of comparing suffering, he let us remember that some 7,000 Bosnian Muslims were murdered (by Christians) in 1995 in Srebrenica. That is about two and a half times the number of people murdered on 9/11.

After 9/11, Yusuf expressed his shock and horror. His op-ed piece, "They Have Hijacked My Religion," was one of the most moving things that I read during those first days after the attacks. He donated a portion of his royalties to the charity established to support the families of 9/11 victims.

There seemed to be several "charges" against Yusuf Islam in the media. First, that Israel denied him entry. Without getting into Israeli politics, let us just say that in the past few years, Israel has denied many American citizens, who are not terrorists, entry. They were on humanitarian or peace missions, and were turned back. At no point were they denied re-entry into the United States nor were they charged with any crime or jailed. And of course, being denied entry to Israel—as far as I know—does not automatically deny one entry to the United States.

The second charge was that he gave money to a terrorist organization, possibly Hamas. To this charge, all that I can say is: show me the proof. If he gave money to a terrorist organization, then I can see why he should have been denied entry. But an allegation is not proof.

As with the case of Tariq Ramadan, there seems here to be no room for alternative views, or dissent. The first time that I was in Israel, in 1988,

I had the great privilege of sitting in on a seminar at the Shalom Hartman Institute. This is a high-level think tank for rabbis. The theme for that seminar was "Can Israel and the Jewish people survive without discussion and dissent?" The seminar raised a theme common to rabbinical studies and medieval Islam, where respected teachers would quote opposing viewpoints before giving their own. Sadly, that was no longer the case. Now it is not "here are the views of my respected opponents and then my own views," but "here are my views, the only ones that are right."

Where was the room for the freedom of expression that again is a hallmark of the United States? Do I agree with everything that Yusuf has said? Of course not. But I do not know what I gained by being denied the opportunity to enter into dialogue with him.

Many American Muslims also see a double standard when it comes to "contentious dialogue" and Islam. Alan Dershowitz, perhaps the most famous lawyer in America and a professor at Harvard University, has publicly spoken in favor of the use of torture to extract information from suspected terrorists. Nathan Lewin, a prominent Washington attorney, has called for the execution of the family members of suicide bombers. And American Muslims are left to wonder, if prominent American lawyers can call for the use of torture and the execution of innocent civilians—and remain respected partners in the civil conversation—isn't there an obvious double standard for Muslims?

And what of those American Muslims who have taken stands against terrorism and fanaticism? Will we be next? Will we say something that someone in authority does not like? Will innuendo and allegations undo decades of work that is open in the public record for all to see? Have we not walked this path before in America? Don't we know where that road leads?

Where we go from here

Let me conclude this chapter with some thoughts on Islam and Muslims in America. In trying to understand recent events, I was reminded once again about the relationship between "Narrative" and "History." I am aware that the Latin and Greek roots, respectively, of both words have to do with the telling of stories. The knowledge of established historical facts may disappear quickly, but the narratives that are constructed from that history develop great force and help to shape our lives. Let me give my own example of what I mean by this. In 2004, I watched with great interest the state funeral for former President Ronald Reagan. The Reagan Presidential Library is some 15 miles from my house; so many of the events were very close to home. Reagan was the first US President during my "adult" life. As such, I remember well certain incidents about his presidency. The ones that remain most clear in my mind are his handling of the air traffic controllers' strike; the policy that for the purpose of school lunches, "ketchup is a vegetable"; the social implications of the closing of mental institutions when he was California's governor; and the Iran–Contra scandal. Reagan also helped to arm the Afghanis in their war against the Soviet invasion, and spoke of the *mujahideen* as "freedom fighters." That, for me, was the Reagan of history. Yet in watching the funeral, I was amazed to hear pundits talking about him as "the greatest president of the twentieth century." That was the Reagan of narrative, the one that some people remember. They spoke of his single-handedly ending the Cold War, as if Mikhail Gorbachev never existed. His state funeral was replete with military honors (21 gun salutes, horse and caisson, military pallbearers, etc.), even though he did not serve in World War II (I understand, of course, that one of his titles as president was "commander in chief," but it was still odd to see a head of state who wasn't a military man given full military honors). There was no talk of events from his presidency coming back to the modern world. No reference to the Book of Hosea, about sowing the wind and reaping the whirlwind when it came to Afghanistan or Iraq. Mahmood Mamdani has an excellent new book on this topic (Mamdani 2004). In that book, Mamdani writes about how Reagan and the Cold Warriors of his administration helped to arm and train the *mujahideen* in what was the largest covert operation in the history of the CIA. Jihadists were recruited from much of the Muslim world, and trained in camps across Pakistan and Afghanistan to fight against the Soviets. It was this policy of bringing together, training, and arming Muslim radicals that would lead to the Taliban and, indirectly, 9/11. There seems to be a collective amnesia about these events among some Americans, including those in positions of authority. The next time I teach my religion and film course, I will show my students *Rambo III* and see how they interpret it some 20 years later. For those unfamiliar with the Rambo trilogy, that one was set in Afghanistan, with Rambo being recruited to help the *mujahideen* in their fight against the Soviets.

With regard to the power of narrative, people are, by now, familiar with the phrase "the clash of civilizations." It was brought into current usage in a very influential article by a political scientist at Harvard University, Samuel P. Huntington (1993). He later expanded his article into a book, *The Clash of Civilizations and the Remaking of the World Order* (Huntington 1996). Most recently, he has updated the thesis. In that new version, *Who Are We? The Challenges to America's National Identity*, the clash is not between White American Protestants of European descent in the United States and Brown Muslims (Huntington 2004). Instead, it is between White American Protestants of European descent in the United States and Brown (mostly Catholic) Latino/as. For Huntington, there is always an "other" to White Protestant America, and whether that "other" is Muslim or Catholic is not important to his argument or rhetoric.

The best refutation of Huntington's thesis is by another Harvard professor, the historian Roy P. Mottahedeh (2003). Mottahedeh is best known for his magisterial book *The Mantle of the Prophet: Religion and Politics in Iran* (2000), which I consider to be the best one-volume introduction to contemporary Iranian history. Mottahedeh wrote that book while at Princeton University, and he describes how he came to write the book, after a visit to Princeton by an Iranian religious scholar (a mullah) who had been educated in the traditional way at a seminary in the city of Qom:

> I asked my friend about his early education: How did one study to become a mullah? He told me that in the Shiah seminaries such as those in Qom a student began by studying grammar, rhetoric, and logic. From that moment I knew I wanted to write this book.
>
> Grammar, rhetoric, and logic comprise the trivium, the first three of the seven liberal arts as they were defined in the late classical world, after which they continued to constitute the foundation of the scholastic curriculum as it was taught in many parts of medieval and Renaissance Europe. So basic were the subjects of the trivium that people who had passed on to more advanced levels of learning considered an elementary knowledge of all three commonplace and therefore of little importance; hence our word "trivial." I realized (and subsequent study confirmed) that my friend and a handful of similarly educated people were the last true scholastics alive on earth, people who had experienced the education to which Princeton's patrons and planners felt they should pay tribute through their strangely assorted but congenial architectural reminiscences of the medieval and Tudor buildings of Oxford and Cambridge. (Mottahedeh 2000: 8)

That quote gives the lie to the simple dichotomy of "Islam" and "the West," and the simplistic worldview of the "clash of civilizations." It is mullahs in Iran who are getting the traditional liberal arts education, not undergraduates in Princeton. It is those mullahs, moreover, who are reading Aristotle, and thereby weakening the case for distinct, pure "civilizations."

In debunking Huntington's thesis, Mottahedeh made a comparison between the ways Catholics were viewed in America in the past, and the ways in which Muslims are viewed in the present:

> In America, the distrust of Catholicism seems only to have died with the election of John F. Kennedy as president in 1960. In 1944 the most distinguished American Protestant theologian of his time, Reinhold Niebuhr, lamented the chasm "between the presuppositions of a free society and the inflexible authoritarianism of the Catholic religion." To distrust the ability of sincere Catholics to be true democrats seems as quaint and fanciful to us at the end of the twentieth century as will seem, in a generation, our present distrust of the ability of sincere Muslims to be true democrats. (Mottahedeh 2003: 140)

As someone who now teaches in a Jesuit university where half of my students are Catholic, the comparison is a personal one for my students. They are too young to remember a time of anti-Catholic prejudice, but conversations with their parents and grandparents provide insight for them.

A newer phrase in contrast to the "clash" is the "dialogue of civilizations," which President Khatami of Iran proposed. In 2001, the United Nations adopted the metaphor of "dialogue of civilizations" for worldwide discussions during that year. In addition to the metaphors of "clash" and "dialogue" there are also (as noted above) the metaphors of "Islam" and "the West." I do not like the metaphorical contrast of "Islam and the West." To me, this is unhelpful, and presents "Islam" and "the West" as mutually incompatible. Instead, I prefer the phrase "Islam in the West." First, this phrase acknowledges the reality of Muslims living in the West. Islam is, of course, a "Western" religion, sharing deep roots with Judaism and Christianity. Muslims are also a strong presence in "the West." Islam is the second-largest religion in Canada, Britain, and France, and may well be the second-largest religion in the United States. Secondly, the phrase "Islam in the West" recognizes the entwined heritage of Islam and the West. The West as we know it would not be what it is without the contribution of Muslims (as well as the contributions of many other peoples, to be sure). The danger of presenting Islam as "Islam and the West" (within a clash or a dialogue) is the generalization and subsequent obfuscation of what is actually a complicated, multicultural social and historical dynamic.

One aspect of Muslim contributions to the construction of the West is in literature. María Rosa Menocal published a groundbreaking book in 1987, *The Arabic Role in Medieval Literary History*. In that book, she talked about a derivation for the English word "troubadour" (in Provençal "*trobar*") from the Arabic word *taraba*, meaning "to sing": "*Taraba* meant 'to sing' and sing poetry; *tarab* meant 'song,' and in the spoken Arabic of the Iberian peninsula it would have come to be pronounced *trob*; the formation of the Romance verb through addition of the *-ar* suffix would have been standard" (Menocal 1987: xi).

So the tradition of troubadours, playing guitar and singing love poetry, which is a hallmark of medieval European society, has deep roots in the Islamic world. In the contemporary world, one of the best modern troubadours is Richard Thompson, himself a British convert to Islam now living in the United States.[3] That challenges our easy assumptions, our simple dichotomy between "Islam" and "the West," when we consider that one of the best guitar players in the world is a Muslim. Of spirituality in music, Richard has said in an interview on his web page: "Music is spiritual stuff, and even musicians who clearly worship money, or fame, or ego, cannot help but express a better part of themselves sometimes when performing, so great is the gift of music, and so connected to our higher selves. What we believe informs everything we do, and music is no exception." I often play my students a recording of his song, "Shoot out the Lights." The particular version that I play is a live recording with Richard on guitar and Danny Thompson (no relation despite the common surname), another British Muslim convert, on bass. The song, which most people take to be about a relationship gone wrong, was actually written about the Soviet invasion of Afghanistan.

Conclusion

Let me end this chapter with these final thoughts. María Menocal described another important connection between Islam and the West:

> In the destruction of the whole of the magnificent National Library and other major collections in Sarajevo several years ago, in 1992, it now appears one very significant book was rescued, the famous manuscript called the Sarajevo *Haggada*. A Haggada is of course a prayer book that is, appropriately, the collection of prayers to be said on Passover, on the eve of exodus, but despite its name this gorgeous and elaborately illuminated manuscript, considered the best of its kind anywhere in the world, and much treasured by Jews everywhere, is not "Sarajevan" at all, nor "merely" Jewish, but rather "Spanish." And what can "Spanish" possibly mean, what do I mean it to be that is so different from what it seems to be in most other uses of this and other "identity" tags? Made in Spain in the late thirteenth century, it is, to put it most reductively, one of the many reflections of a Jewish culture that flourished and had its Golden Age, the Golden Age, precisely because it adopted the virtues of exile and found its distinctly impure voice within an Arabic culture that was expansive and promiscuous and often exilic itself. It was thus altogether fitting that the precious object, the book that inscribes the story of the exile from Egypt, was carried out of Spain by members of the exiled Sephardic community in 1492: and remained, for the better part of the subsequent five hundred years, well-protected and cherished inside the Ottoman Empire, itself a remarkable example of the great good of empires, which learn how to absorb and tolerate and intermarry "identities," and which became, after 1492, the place of refuge of most Sephardic Jews and of many Andalusian Muslims. But the manuscript had to be rescued once again, during World War II, and it was when a Muslim curator in Sarajevo, attached as most Muslims are to the memory of Spain, saved that Spanish Haggada from Nazi butchers.
> ... Surely, the morals of the story are perfectly clear: to understand the richness of our heritage we must be the guardians of the Haggada— the Muslim librarian who was not an Arab, of course, but who in

saving the manuscript was fulfilling the best of the promises of Islamic Spain and Europe—and we must be the translators who reveal the exquisite ambivalence and sometimes painful conflict of identity of Judah Halevi, whose poetry is sung in so heavy an Arabic accent, and we must be the guardians and defenders of the interfaith marriage between the Christian girls who sang in corrupt Romance and the refined poets of the Arab courts, which is left inscribed, as a passionate and great love, in the *muwashshahat*. We must, in other words, reject the falsehoods of nations in our work, and reveal, with the exquisite Ibn 'Arabi, the virtues of what he more simply calls love. "My heart can take on any form," he tells us, and then he simply names those temples at which he prays, the temples that inhabit him: the gazelle's meadow, the monks' cloister, the Torah, the Ka'ba. These are the temples whose priests we need to be, if we are to understand what any of this history is about, and it is only in them that there can be any future understanding of the complex "identity" of Europe in the Middle Ages. And almost undoubtedly in its present and future as well. (Menocal 2003: 269–70)

This is the virtue of exile, the great good that secularism brings. Remember, however, that "secular" does not mean without religion. When we say, for example, that America is a secular society, we do not mean that it is a non-religious society. Indeed, by any measure, America is one of the most religious countries in the world, certainly much more "religious" than Europe. Instead, what we mean is that there is no official state religion.

It is in secular North America where I work, a Muslim scholar of Islam in a Catholic university. It is here where Muslims are trying to live out the poetry of their ordinary lives in all of the splendid diversity that those lives are lived. It is here, we hope, that we can be seen as full participants in our societies and not as threats to the common good. Again, this does not mean that we are naïve or silent about the problems in our communities. We cannot see ourselves as innocent victims, and shift the blame for our internal problems to outsiders. We need to deal with the social and ideological problems such as hunger, abuse, discrimination, etc. that are part of any society. We need to address the alarming conservatism among some Muslims, whose ahistorical and non-contextual readings of Islam allow for misogyny and violence against Muslims and non-Muslims. We as scholars can provide different alternatives, different narratives to give meaning to our lives and allow us all to be fully human.

As a Canadian, I have made a conscious choice to live in the United States. Technically, that makes me an émigré and not an exile. But as an émigré, as a Canadian of South Asian background, what Americans call a "person of color," as a scholar whose calling is to find words for complex identities, what Americans call an "intellectual," and now especially as a

Muslim in post-9/11 America, the metaphor of exile deepens my compassion and clarifies my work. With his usual brilliance, Edward Said wrote this about the condition of exile: "Most people are principally aware of one culture, one setting, one home; exiles are aware of at least two, and this plurality of vision gives rise to an awareness of simultaneous dimensions, an awareness that—to borrow a phrase from music—is *contrapuntal*" (Said 2002: 186). Perhaps this is the best descriptor for those of us who teach Islam, especially those of us who are Muslim. We live contrapuntal lives.

Notes

I am indebted to Michel Desjardins, Tazim Kassam, Pat Nichelson, Bruce M. Sullivan and Philip Tite for their help in various incarnations of this chapter. I also honor the blessed memory of my teachers, Willard Oxtoby and Wilfred Cantwell Smith.

1   My web page is available at: http://bellarmine.lmu.edu/theology/amir/.
2   Information on HR 3077 can be found on the following web page: http://thomas.loc.gov/cgi-bin/bdquery/z?d108:h.r.0377.
3   For more information, see his web page: http://www.richardthompson-music.com.

References

Arkoun, Mohammed. 1994. *Rethinking Islam: Common Questions, Uncommon Answers*. Trans. Robert D. Lee. Boulder, CO: Westview Press.

CAIR. 2002. *Stereotypes and Civil Liberties: The Status of Muslim Civil Rights in the United States, 2002*. Available online at http://www.cair-net.org/civilrights 2002.

Cockburn, Bruce. 1996. "Pacing the Cage." From the music CD *The Charity of Night*. Rykodisc.

Ernst, Carl W. 2003. *Following Muhammad: Rethinking Islam in the Contemporary World*. Chapel Hill, NC: University of North Carolina Press.

Huntington, Samuel. 1993. "The Clash of Civilizations." *Foreign Affairs* 72 (3): 22–49.

——. 1996. *The Clash of Civilizations and the Remaking of the World Order*. New York: Simon and Schuster.

——. 2004. *Who Are We? The Challenges to America's National Identity*. New York: Simon and Schuster.

Hussain, Amir. 2002. "Misunderstandings and Hurt: How Canadians Joined World-Wide Muslim Reactions to Salman Rushdie's *The Satanic Verses*." *Journal of the American Academy of Religion* 70 (1): 1–32.

——. 2005. "Reflections on Exile." *Amerasia Journal* 30 (3): 17–23.

Mamdani, Mahmood. 2004. *Good Muslim, Bad Muslim: America, the Cold War, and the Roots of Terror*. New York: Pantheon Books.

Menocal, María Rosa. 1987 [reprinted 2004]. *The Arabic Role in Medieval Literary History: A Forgotten Heritage*. Philadelphia: University of Pennsylvania Press.

——. 2003. "The Myth of Westernness in Medieval Literary Historiography." In *The New Crusades: Constructing the Muslim Enemy*, edited by Emran Qureshi and Michael A. Sells, 249–87. New York: Columbia University Press.

Mottahedeh, Roy P. 2000. *The Mantle of the Prophet: Religion and Politics in Iran*. New edn. Oxford: Oneworld.

——. 2003. "The Clash of Civilizations: An Islamicist's Critique." In *The New Crusades: Constructing the Muslim Enemy*, edited by Emran Qureshi and Michael A. Sells, 131–51. New York: Columbia University Press.

Postman, Neil and Steve Powers. 1992. *How to Watch TV News*. New York: Penguin.

Sacco, Joe. 2001. *Palestine*. Seattle, WA: Fantagraphic Books.

Safi, Omid, ed. 2003. *Progressive Muslims: On Gender, Justice, and Pluralism*. Oxford: Oneworld.

Said, Edward W. 2002. "Reflections on Exile." In *Reflections on Exile and Other Essays*, Edward W. Said, 173–86. Cambridge, MA: Harvard University Press.

Slouka, Mark. 2002. "A Year Later: Notes on America's Intimations of Mortality." *Harper's Magazine*. September: 34–43.

18 Discussion

Pedagogical and professional reflections

Susan E. Henking

Entering the conversation anew/again: religion, religious studies, higher education

For those of us who teach (about) religion in the United States, everything changed on September 11, 2001. Or did it? I know I thought the same thing before, when the first Gulf War started and when the Oklahoma City bombing happened. More recent challenges including shootings at Virginia Tech, the ongoing war in Iraq, and homophobic, racist, and sexist politics enacted globally and locally on my own home campus; each raise significant questions for me: How can I teach? How can I sustain my belief in the transformative power of higher education not just for individuals but also for the social order? Both the immediate horror of such moments and the force of gradually eroding cynicism make teaching difficult. Just as, after each death of an individual family member, friend or loved one, I vow to remember the inevitability of loss and live more fully, more lovingly, more consciously, so each tragedy—like each challenge to hope (whether gradual or sudden)—calls me to a renewed pedagogical responsibility (Henking 2006). So, too, September 11, 2001 (and this despite its widespread misuse as a rhetorical tool among Americans to marshal obedient, unreflective, and thus uncritical patriotism). The drama of social change, including social injustice targeted at particular groups, reaches into our classrooms and our hearts, in the form of both structures of oppression and, equally, opportunities for agency as teacher/scholars and as citizens.

As Omid Safi has put it in this volume, "I miss September 10, 2001." That world was "filled with great injustice, un-told beauty, and immense suffering." But the context of injustice, beauty, and suffering changed around 9 a.m. Eastern Standard Time the next day—and it has changed even more as the American government has pursued political, legal, and military actions which, indeed, "shock and awe." Safi, and the two other authors whose essays are collected here, Zayn Kassam and Amir Hussain, raise issues particular to teaching Islam in US higher education post-9/11; while each evokes many feelings and thoughts, my response will connect their reflections to part of what we share—the academic study of religion understood broadly and the challenges facing all scholar/teachers in the twenty-first century. In focusing on particular connections, I seek not to obliterate the specificity of Muslim scholars and/or scholars of Islam but to consider the ways that specificity contributes to a renewed understanding of US higher education for the twenty-first century as well as the academic study of religion as pedagogical practice and as theory. Put another way, I ask: what can I learn from these teacher/scholars with whom I share much and yet who differ from me significantly? What can I offer from where I stand that contributes to the hope of a wider form of what Safi calls "intimate community"? Doing so, for me, leads me back to higher education, to the academic study of religion, and, finally, to the classroom.

Themes in higher education

Let me begin with higher education most broadly, focusing on the situation in the United States because our three authors teach in various sectors of the landscape of American higher education. Several themes raised in these essays seem particularly pertinent today. These include: (1) academic freedom; (2) the public role of intellectuals; (3) the nature of liberal education; (4) the entanglement of our self-understanding with our understanding of "the other"; (5) the relevance of emotions—pain, grief, and joy—to the teaching and learning which are central to the mission of higher education; and (6) the question "for whom?" While these themes are entangled in both lived experience and conceptually, I will focus on them sequentially.

For many denizens of higher education in the United States, "academic freedom" with its complex extension of speech rights beyond those of the first amendment to the special freedoms and responsibilities of academia is significantly at risk today (see Doumani 2006; Gerstmann and Streb 2006). As phrased by the American Association of University Professors in their 1940 Statement of Principles on Academic Freedom and Tenure:

1   Teachers are entitled to full freedom in research and in the publication of the results, subject to the adequate performance of their other academic duties; but research for pecuniary return should be based upon an understanding with the authorities of the institution.
2   Teachers are entitled to freedom in the classroom in discussing their subject, but they should be careful not to introduce into their teaching controversial matter which has no relation to their subject. Limitations of academic freedom because of religious or other aims of the institution should be clearly stated in writing at the time of the appointment.
3   College and university teachers are citizens, members of a learned profession, and officers of an educational institution. When they speak or write as citizens, they should be free from institutional censorship

or discipline, but their special position in the community imposes special obligations. As scholars and educational officers, they should remember that the public may judge their profession and their institution by their utterances. Hence they should at all times be accurate, should exercise appropriate restraint, should show respect for the opinions of others, and should make every effort to indicate that they are not speaking for the institution. (http://www.aaup.org/AAUP/pubsres/policydocs/1940statement.htm)

Where did these notions come from? What is their history? While I can only hint at answers in these remarks, I would note that academic freedom is a concept that arose in 1915 as John Dewey and Arthur Lovejoy responded to the radically changing landscape of US higher education in the late nineteeth and early twentieth centuries, including the 1900 removal of Edward A. Ross from Stanford University. Mrs. Leland Stanford was not pleased with Ross' views on immigration and employment practices associated with the railroad industry—and he was fired. This moment, many argue, was crucial to the history of higher education. This is the origin myth for tenure and for academic freedom, both defining features of the American professoriate. And yet, critical reflection on this mythic incident points in many directions; Ross' views have been construed as racist, for example (the immigrants whose arrival he deemed un-American were Chinese railroad construction workers), and thus our understanding of academic freedom is situated in a particular loaded ideological, political, and global economic context from its very origins. How one focuses on this situatedness—while strongly rejecting today's infringements on (and misuses of) academic freedom and, indeed, on freedom more broadly—is centrally important. As Robert Bellah's book *The Broken Covenant* long ago warned, America is simultaneously a site of freedom and broken at its core; our founding documents embrace an aspiration for universal freedom while perpetrating racist and sexist laws. And the aspiration can become the basis for critiquing our own failures—and thus calls us to social change. So too, perhaps, with academic freedom. That academic freedom is both an aspiration, and potentially broken at its core, is difficult to face when the Patriot Act and everyday experiences make evident the targeting of Muslims and of dissidence more broadly. That the university is centrally entangled in both the hope of freedom and its brokenness is revealed in recent cases of infringement on academic freedom as well as higher education's ongoing relationship with the military and the commodification of knowledge. Invoking academic freedom thus invokes our hope and our brokenness.

Academic freedom is, of course, directly related to the public role of intellectuals in the United States, including those roles that public events after September 11 impose upon scholars of Islam and/or Muslim scholars. While not all intellectuals are academics, many are. And, while not all intellectuals (whether academics or not) operate equally directly in civil society, the mythic isolation of the scholar/teacher in American history exists in tension with our public responsibilities as citizens, knowledge producers, and knowledge disseminators. For many of us, the current political denigration of dissent, the specter of American empire, and the wider history of American anti-intellectualism (Hofstadter 1966) are directly connected with our (often changing) understandings of the public role of the professoriate. If dissent is unacceptable and intellectuals are defined through critical inquiry, to be an intellectual risks being read as un-American—and this despite constitutional and mythic equations between dissent and American aspirations to freedom. (These risks, perhaps, explain today's burgeoning literature on the public intellectual.) Amir Hussain thus joins a wider conversation when he draws on the language of the scholar as citizen, emphasizing the public role of scholarly and other writing, speech, and teaching. Moreover, Hussain reminds us of the entanglement of American higher education with the ongoing question of who counts as American—and thus with assimilation, integration, separation, and segregation, struggles which remain as relevant and as volatile today as when Edward Ross raised his critique of the use of Chinese immigrants to build railroads. In this context, Hussain finds the scholar/citizen to be obligated to the state—and to his or her fellow citizens, arguing that citizenship is not merely about rights but also about responsibility. In offering such arguments, Hussain and others remind us of the ways in which higher education—and the work of "scholar citizens" within it—is not merely a private good (gaining students, for example, for more stable economic futures) but also a public good, a good *necessary to democracy*. That both public educational institutions and private colleges contribute to that public good merits reiteration in 2008.

In addition, these three authors remind us of the contemporary importance of the particular form of education called liberal education, including its role in the dissemination both of accurate information, as over against misinformation, and of the skills of historical inquiry, comparison, and critical thinking. As Zayn Kassam puts it: "It is now a truism that to study the Other is really in some ways to study oneself, by contrast, in comparison, and often in relation." This is, indeed, the public good of higher education today. Or it should be. Such study—embedded in such a liberal education—will also, our three authors argue, push us beyond the parochialism of everyday life to investigate the scandalous rejection of shared values which confuses individual perpetrators with their social group. As Hussain notes, historical and comparative reflection requires us to remember both the historic connection of liberal education to Islam, for example, as well as nineteenth- and twentieth-century (not to mention twenty-first-century) American histories of inclusion and exclusion in higher education, which can act as signals of our limitations, our ideals, and our capacity for change.

There is, of course, more to what these authors render visible regarding higher education for the twenty-first century. By pointing to the pain, the grief, and indeed the joy and beauty of the world around us, these authors reinforce late twentieth-century calls to complicate epistemologies which bifurcate fact and value, life and work, normative and descriptive, politics and scholarship. Read through the lens of contemporary politics, Safi, Kassam, and Hussain jointly argue that simplistic wholism is as risky as simplistic binarism, thereby asking us to face squarely today's renewed challenge to steer between the Scylla of undue certainty and the paralyzing Charybdis of uncertainty (see Marris 1996). They offer their lives and the lives of their colleagues as reminders of the teacher/scholar as human, in the many specificities of their situations. And this despite the trenchant and important critique of humanism affirmed in postmodern discourses. Safi's poignant words are centrally important: "as a human being . . . my heart keeps on breaking . . ."; putting it another way, he writes:

> I refuse to participate in a system that conceives of its own civilization as the privileged host into which knowledge about the "other" is incorporated as a foreign object or parasite. Our task, I believe, should somehow be grander than finding out how much knowledge of all the disenfranchised and marginalized groups we can *tolerate* before it kills us! Rather, I see our mission as nothing short of the grand task of full engagement with the complexities of humanity, defined not based on the norms of any one civilization, but globally.

This is not a challenge we can meet alone. Nor can we rush into community easily. (For a critique of the notion of community, see, for example, Bounds 1997.) As these authors imply, part of what demands our ongoing attention is who counts as part of a community and how this defining question is entangled with who counts as teacher/scholar and what the mission of American higher education is for the twenty-first century. This is truly a critical time and a grand task.

Themes in the academic study of religion

Pursuing this grand task—along with negotiating the complications of tolerance and the public/private divide—requires critical historical engagement with the place of religion in American history. This is not always obvious. And yet, this very point undergirds the arguments of Hussain, Kassam, and Safi. (On tolerance, see helpful discussion in Jakobsen and Pelligrini 2004. On the historical relation of religion and higher education, see Henking 2004 and Reuben 1996. On the relation of public/private in the US see, e.g., Hammond, Machacek, and Dazur 2004.) Indeed, their essays make evident that just as the shifting context of higher education shapes our ability to comprehend religion, so too the shifting context of religion affects higher education. After September 11, at least three important tensions that have characterized the (history of the) academic study of religion in the United States have become newly critical. Each receives attention from our three authors.

First, the history of the academic study of religion has been characterized by a tension between one form of inquiry, often labeled theological or apologetic, and another that emphasizes "methodological atheism" (Berger [1969] 1992), variously labeled religious studies or the scientific study of religion. Sometimes understood as mutually exclusive and often as polar opposites, both "theology" and "religious studies/scientific study of religion" are, in their dominant Western forms, a product of the hegemony of Christianity and especially Protestant Christianity (see, e.g., Fitzgerald 2003; King 1999; Masuzawa 2005). In this way, even secular forms of academic inquiry regarding religion emerged in the context of a *particular* secularization and are, thus, post-Christian (see in this regard, Jakobsen and Pelligrini 2000). In challenging the organization of higher education in the US, therefore, these authors also ask us to consider what the academic study of religion is, not merely in a world after September 11 but in a world where Islam exists. Or, in a world where not all secularisms follow Christianity and some may follow Islam. In this, our three authors renew and extend Wilfred Cantwell Smith's argument in *The Meaning and End of Religion*—requiring us to (re-)consider how the fractures in our field continue to index Christian hegemony. What might this mean for how we understand and undertake the academic study of religion, they ask. And, like Smith, they ask us to consider as well the difficult dilemma of engendering social justice.

This problematic connects to the tension between the vocation of the professor of the academic study of religion and what Safi, for example, labels the ministerial (or, in the particular case of Muslim scholars, imam) role. The challenge thus faces us all: as professors of the academic study of religion in the twenty-first century, how can and will we *care*—for our students, for the world we live in, for ourselves? While the need to address the first of these tasks may be particularly visible given the dramatic demographic changes among our students (see Eck 2002), all three are critical professional and human challenges in the twenty-first century. The separation of science as a vocation and politics as a vocation advocated by Weber, for example, emerges as more complex once vocation, profession, and professoriate are understood as more fully situated practices in this newly complex, secularizing, globalizing, and religiously resurgent world.

Undergirding this tension is another: that regarding what counts as religion. Here, the work of Wilfred Cantwell Smith is again relevant. So too is the question of violence. Is religion inherently violent? (See Girard 2005 or Selengut 2004.) And how does re-conceiving the notion of religion, and situating it as a product of a particular Western history (Asad

1993), require us to re-conceive its opposite(s)? Are secularism and secularization potential goods? How must we understand them in today's age of empire? Are "religious" and "secular" mutually exclusive?

In these questions, a final tension appears: that regarding the mission of the academic study of religion. While this is, in part, a restatement of the tension between religious studies and theology, it is a broader issue as well. In the time after September 11, we must ask: What is religious studies for? What is theology for? What is the aim of the academic study of religion? With Wilfrid Cantwell Smith—and many others—these three authors call for peace, for social justice, for the role of knowledges in creating and sustaining a better world. Thus, they call for a public mission for the academic study of religion. In this, they call not for theology. Nor do they call for religious studies or the scientific study of religion. They do not ask that scholars of religion bifurcate themselves, but that we live in novel ways. They call for a new phenomenon entirely, emerging from the ambiguity and uncertainty of our time, a new professoriate pursuing a new academic study of religion. Imagining this new pursuit is our challenge. And it lives most, perhaps, in our roles as teachers.

In the classroom

These essays remind us of a critical point regarding the classroom: its walls are permeable. Like students and like faculty, staff, administrators, and others whose lives are lived in the wider context of higher education, classrooms are part of the world in which we live. Classrooms are part of history. While we may have been tempted by the notion of the academy as a site of withdrawal, by the cynicism of the marketplace, the undue privatization of higher education, or the allure of a utopian imaginary, these essays remind us of the academy as a site of engagement and the world as a site where, using Safi's metaphor, both cream and scum rise to the top. In this, Hussain, Kassam, and Safi challenge us to construct anew the intimate communities of higher education and the academic study of religion.

References and further reading

Asad, Talal. 1993. *Geneaologies of Religion: Disciplines and Reasons of Power in Christianity and Islam*. Baltimore, MD/London: Johns Hopkins University Press.

Bellah, Robert. 1992. *The Broken Covenant: American Civil Religion in a Time of Trial*. 2nd edn. Chicago: University of Chicago Press.

Berger, Peter. 1992 [1969]. *The Sacred Canopy: Elements of a Sociological Theory of Religion*. New York: Anchor.

Bounds, Elizabeth M. 1997. *Coming Together/Coming Apart: Religion, Modernity and Community*. New York: Routledge.

Doumani, Beshara, ed. 2006. *Academic Freedom After September 11*. New York: Zone Books.

Eck, Diana. 2002. *A New Religious America: How a "Christian Country" Has Become the World's Most Religiously Diverse Nation*. San Francisco: Harper San Francisco.

Fitzgerald, Timothy. 2003. *The Ideology of Religious Studies*. New edn. Oxford: Oxford University Press.

Gerstmann, Evan and Matthew Streb. 2006. *Academic Freedom at the Dawn of a New Century: How Terrorism, Governments, and Culture Wars Affect Free Speech*. Stanford, CA: Stanford University Press.

Girard, Rene. 2005. *Violence and the Sacred*. New edn. London: Continuum.

Hammond, Phillip E., David W. Machacek, and Eric Michael Dazur. 2004. *Religion on Trial: How Supreme Court Trends Threaten the Freedom of Conscience in America*. Walnut Creek, CA: AltaMira Press.

Henking, Susan. 2004. "Religion, Religious Studies and Higher Education: Into the 21st Century." *Religious Studies Review* 30 (2, 3): 129–36.

——. 2006. "Difficult Knowledges: Gender, Sexuality, Religion." *Spotlight on Teaching* 21 (4, October): viii.

Hofstadter, Richard. 1966. *Anti-intellectualism in American Life*. New York: Vintage.

hooks, bell. 1994. *Teaching to Transgress: Education as the Practice of Freedom*. London/New York: Routledge.

Jakobsen, Janet R. and Ann Pelligrini. 2000. "Dreaming Secularism." *Social Text* 18 (3): 1–27.

——. 2004. *Love the Sin: Sexual Regulation and the Limits of Religious Tolerance*. Boston, MA: Beacon Press.

King, Richard. 1999. *Orientalism and Religion: Post-Colonial Theory, India and the "Mystic East."* London/New York: Routledge.

Marris, Peter. 1996. *The Politics of Uncertainty: Attachment in Private and Public Life*. London/New York: Routledge.

Masuzawa, Tomoko. 2005. *The Invention of World Religions: Or, How European Universalism Was Preserved in the Language of Pluralism*. Chicago: University of Chicago Press.

Reuben, Julie A. 1996. *The Making of the Modern University: Intellectual Transformation and the Marginalization of Morality*. Chicago: University of Chicago Press.

Selengut, Charles. 2004. *Sacred Fury: Understanding Religious Violence*. Walnut Creek, CA: AltaMira Press.

Smith, Wilfred Cantwell. 1991 [1962]. *The Meaning and End of Religion*. Reprint edn. London: Augsburg/Fortress.

Aesthetic reflections

19 Seeing what is missing

Art, artists, and September 11

Maureen Korp

What makes a place sacred? Miracles? Rituals? Memories? What makes an art sacred? Myth? Memories? Intention? Liturgy?

I began to think about "ground zero," the World Trade Center site, as sacred ground, as a sacred place, on a sunny Friday afternoon—September 14, 2001. Walking up to Parliament Hill that day for Ottawa's commemorative ceremonies, my neighbor startled me with her question: "Will they build there?" she asked. "Do you think they will ever build at the World Trade Center site again?"

My answer was abrupt, dismissive: "Of course. Land in New York is expensive. They'll build. Clear the rubble and build."

That week I had been going through the motions—saying and doing expected things. Lacking sleep (who could sleep?), I located friends, family, answered questions, offered advice, explained the historical background, sorted news reports, counseled my students, looked for friends . . . Truthfully, I do not remember much about any of this. Part of me was not of this time or this place. I was derailed. Dropped off somewhere near the edge of aphasia. At odd moments, I could hardly speak.

Parliament Hill I remember clearly, however. My neighbor and I stood on the east side of the lawn. The light was brilliant. The air softened by a light breeze. Light seemed to cradle us there, in that place, in the silence. A hundred thousand people stood in ritual silence for three minutes. No larger number had ever before gathered on the hill. We dispersed quietly. I carried home a memory of light and silence.

A month later I went to New York City to see old friends. Meryl Taradash is a sculptor. She works in metal, creating large, wind-driven mobile work, usually for public sites. Arriving at her apartment, I knocked on the door. Meryl opened it, took me by the hand, and led me directly into the living room. "Look," she said, "look at my windows." The large windows were covered with a fine, light brown, delicate tracery. "It looks like lace," I replied, "What is it?"

"It's ash, ash from the site," Meryl whispered. "It blew here that day. I cannot clean the windows."

"Of course not," I said. "It's a witness."

Meryl went to close a window. The wind had shifted. I smelled something ugly and winced. "Yes. It's coming from the site," she said, "it's metal burning. The fires are burning seven stories down. You don't want to breathe it."

The morning of September 11, Meryl Taradash had watched the assault upon both towers from the windows of her Greenwich Village apartment. The apartment faces south and is on the 23rd floor.

A day or two later, I went over to Brooklyn to see artist Donna Henes. For more than two decades the Port Authority of New York and New Jersey sponsored and supported Donna Henes' public art performances at the World Trade Center. The artist's last performance at the twin towers was entitled "Keeping the Fires Burning for Peace: A Summer Solstice Sunrise to Sunset Vigil for Peace on the Planet 1999." In 1986, Henes's winter solstice performance of "Chant for Peace Chance for Peace" was part of an international radio simulcast which began in Australia and followed the sun around the earth. The artist's chant at the World Trade Center was simultaneously chanted by artists in India, Africa, Europe, and the United States. In New York City, the uplink to the satellite for the winter solstice performance was the golden angel atop the City of New York's Municipal Building on Chambers Street.

Donna Henes and I sat outdoors, enclosed by the low walls of her little roof garden. We were facing north to lower Manhattan. Smoke rose from the World Trade Center site. "Look," Donna said, "look at the smoke. It's white. It's always white. I keep asking, "What happens when so many souls leave their bodies at once? Do you know?"

I had no answer for her.

The wind shifted again as I walked to the subway. Burning metal, it claws the air. Acrid, vicious stuff. The next day I crossed the river and went to Hoboken to see filmmaker Julie Sloane. We had been roommates when we were students, then shared an apartment in New York City when we worked our first jobs. Julie was waiting for me on the train platform. She took me to the Hoboken, NJ pier where she and others had waited to assist with the dead and the injured, but there had been few bodies and fewer injured. My friend pointed across the Hudson River towards the Manhattan skyline and said, "It's located right in back of those two buildings. Do you see it?" I could see nothing. Just clouds. Ash. How can one see what is not there?

The light shifted, brightened. Flared. We both looked around to see why: where was the light?

The sun was filling windows with flame in that moment everywhere—windows on both sides of the river. Pink, yellow, white, rose, gold light shimmered on every reflective surface—the water, the fences, the buildings, the pier. Light on both sides of the river. New Jersey and Manhattan. A miracle, we marveled.

Later, with a map, I sorted it out. I think we saw a light bounce created

1 Naz Ikramullah, *City under Siege*, 1996. Collage and mixed media on paper, h. 23" × 36". Photo credit: © Naz Ikramullah, 1996, Ottawa.

2 Naz Ikramullah, *Lost Dreams*, 2002. Collage and mixed media on paper, h. 36" × 24". Photo credit: © Naz Ikramullah, 2002, Ottawa.

3 Marie-France Nitski, *Animal Encounters*, 2002. Enamel paint, oil pastels on metal and wood, h. 80" × 60". Photo credit: © Marie-France Nitski, 2002, Ottawa.

4 Audrey Churgin, *In Sight Recovered*, 1998. Pastel on paper, three panels, each panel, h. 60" × 36". Photo credit: © Audrey Churgin, 1998, Ottawa.

Plates 5–10 From *Think Different: Power and Decline of the New Economy* (Manhattan in March 2000), series, completed 2000. Chromogenic photograph on paper. Photo credit: © Hans J. Mettler, 2000, Ottawa: City of Ottawa Collection.

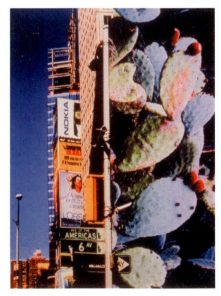

5 Hans J. Mettler, "Internet Expressway. Think Different. One Way"

6 Hans J. Mettler, "A New Century"

7 Hans J. Mettler, "Find Out How Much Oxygen Your Blood Can Hold"

8 Hans J. Mettler, "www.smashstatusquo"

9 Hans J. Mettler, "Hey, You Don't Have To Run Out"

10 Hans J. Mettler, "Absolute Carting"

11 Robin Campbell and Nina Handjeva-Weller. *Prayers for Peace*, 2001. Detail of Installation, Honen-In Temple, Kyoto, Japan, 2001. Photo credit: © Robin Campbell and Nina Handjeva-Weller, 2001, Kyoto.

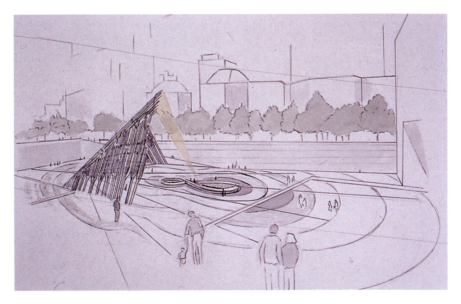

12 Meryl Taradash, Sundial Memorial Project: World Trade Center Memorial Site Competition, 2003. Ink on paper, h. 30" × 40". Photo credit: Photograph © William Schick 2003, New York City.

by the setting sun behind us, light reflecting off the buildings, bounced by the river, and baffled by the white clouds rising from the World Trade Center site. We were standing on the shoreline where the Hudson River runs almost N–S.

May 30, 2002, the recovery and clean-up efforts at the World Trade Center site came to an end. Nearly 1.7 million tons of rubble had been carted from the site and taken to the Fresh Kills landfill on Staten Island (Leith 2002: A12). Before any of the debris is discarded, what can be saved is sifted and sorted, identified, catalogued, then set aside to be incorporated into memorial settings. Of the nearly 3,000 who died on September 11, nothing has been found and identified of nearly 1,700 (Anonymous 2002: 18). There is only ash.

I do not know what happened to the much photographed standing cross that stood at the site itself—the large cross created when one I-beam was hurled with such force it pierced another at right angles. In October 2002, after the site had been cleared of rubble and debris, the cross was still there at the site. When I pointed to it, a police officer replied with a tired, deep anger, "Yes. It's here. We wouldn't let them take it away."

Much remains unfinished. Uncounted. Unsorted. Not understood.

Misunderstood. Including this: not all the dead were Americans. The people who died on September 11 at the World Trade Center site came from all over the world—from 92 different nations (Lower Manhattan Development Corporation 2003). One cloudless Tuesday morning they got up out of their beds and headed off to work. They disappeared. Their ashes, lighter than air, blown everywhere.

Sacred ground and myth

"Will they build there again?" my neighbor had asked. Yes. I am sure of that, but the idea disturbs me because the complex, symbolic dimensions of the site are not yet well understood. In this place, there are more than commercial, political, and national interests to be reckoned with. It is too soon to build.

The site is holy—consecrated not by virtue of the slaughter of 3,000, but because so many who died, died with their hands extended to help another. The people who jumped from the towers were seen holding hands as they leapt together. The emergency workers who climbed the stairs—climbed twenty, thirty, forty flights of stairs with heavy equipment. How was that humanly possible?

Stories were soon told of how people had died (Whitney 2002). A Franciscan priest died because he did not leave one of the towers when ordered to exit. Instead, he continued giving the Last Rites to a dying rescue worker. Both were pinioned in falling debris. When the priest's body was found, firefighters carried it to a nearby church and laid it upon the altar. Mychal Judge had been their chaplain. He was the first person known to have died that day. Another group of survivors told of being shoved down the tower stairs by a retired soldier. He cadence-counted the flights of their descent. When spirits flagged and people despaired, the soldier responded by singing Welsh mining songs, singing them loudly. All kept moving, and all reached safety. Richard Cyril Rescorla is credited with saving 2,700 people by marching them down the stairs. He himself died when he turned around and went back into the tower stairwell to look for other hesitating souls. Rescorla was the director of security for Morgan Stanley.

So many of the stories told of September 11 are mythic, highly symbolized, and sacramental. Each story has the same locale: the World Trade Center site. Telling and retelling the stories of these deaths imbues the place where the deaths occurred with meaning. For many people, the World Trade Center site has become a public holy ground—holy not through death, but through the miracles, witness, and rituals engendered by that day; and public because we saw it. We saw again and again on our television screens the imagery of two airplanes ramming into the twin towers, and their subsequent collapse.

Identification of the World Trade Center site with sacrifice and sacrament strengthened further during the early days of the clean-up period. People protested the removal of a large pyramidal remnant of the towers' facade. The shard, backlit against white clouds of steam, ash, and smoke, had been photographed so often it became the iconic image of that day. The symbolic associations were destruction and the city rising, reborn; and, for many, the standing shard was an image of faith.

Holy ground requires appropriate behaviors. The public, for example, intuitively understood the firefighters' claim that they and only they could give ritual witness and ceremony to each and every broken bit of firefighter found in the rubble (ABC News 2002). When the professional clean-up crews wanted the firefighters off the site, the public protested. Outcome? The firefighters stayed until the ground was swept clean.

It was no surprise then when the first architectural designs proposed by the developer for the site were greeted with loud cries of dismay and criticized for being too "commercial." They were. The designs were soon withdrawn.

Building on sacred ground

The World Trade Center site, like all sacred places, can be described in physical terms (see Korp 1997). Sacred places have boundaries which set them apart—this place, and not that place. There is something within that centers the site, something within to provide a focal point. Moreover, the pathway to the point of entry is one which facilitates focused awareness—perhaps by being a path that is a straight-line ascent or, in the case of the twin towers, a path traversed by turning the corners of city blocks, by climbing stairs, or by being majestically lifted by escalator and elevator from trains underground. All of these approaches to the site combined to create a dramatic sense of expectation, heightened awareness, and, in other words, a sense of "domain"—here, all the world is centered, in this place, for this moment.

The rebuilding of the World Trade Center site has begun. The master site plan architect is Daniel Libeskind. The architect designing the tallest of the several proposed buildings is David Childs, lead designer for the renowned architectural firm of Skidmore, Owings and Merrill. The developer, Larry A. Silverstein, chose Childs to deliver the final plans. Silverstein and Childs first met to plan the rebuilding of the World Trade Center a mere two days after the collapse of the twin towers (Iovine 2003).

The symbolism proposed in Libeskind's architectural design is narrowly nationalistic and political. The tallest building will be called the "Freedom Tower." It is a glass tower (one assumes for "freedom" and "transparency") 1,776 feet high. The number references the year a confederation of breakaway British colonies in North America signed a pact—"Declaration of Independence"—to separate from the British Crown. The building's architectural design, therefore, relies upon a symbol associated only with American civil religion. Those who were killed that day in September 2001 came from 92 different nations. They were not murdered because they had rebelled against the British Crown.

There were two earlier installations at the World Trade Center site, each in its way more sensitive to the site than a building whose pinnacle is a superfluous broadcasting antenna. On March 11, 2002, six months after the destruction of the twin towers, two beams of light were thrown high into the air to be light memorials for those killed in the towers. The light beams replicated the ghost image of the towers the *New York Times Magazine* had used for its cover, Sunday, September 23, 2001.[1] Unfortunately, there was only one perspective from which the two beams of light could be seen clearly that March—across the Hudson River, east of the site itself. North or south of the site, the two light beams blurred and diffused into one glow.

The light display lasted a month. The second effort to build at the site was less tentative. The City of New York erected "viewing" platforms at the perimeter of the excavation site. Nomenclature matters here because people sometimes speak of a wake as a "viewing." A wake is that most intimate vigil the night before a funeral when family and friends may see the body of the dead one more time. Traditionally, if possible, the coffin is kept open. In the morning when the coffin is closed, the interment rituals begin. The City's platforms were not labeled "WTC Observation Areas." It seems to me, the City intended that people who wanted to visit the site should behave as if they were standing vigil with the dead.

From the earliest of times, we have acknowledged the dead. Our histories of ancient civilizations are constructed from the study of burial places. Our oldest stories everywhere are about those who were alive before even then. Miracles, rituals, and memories are our pathways to lands of the dead. The dead must be acknowledged, witnessed, not just viewed. But how? Others in other places and times have asked the same question. One of the most beautifully conceived memorials to the dead is in Romania.

Brâncuşi's WWI memorial at Târgu Jiu

Constantin Brâncuşi's WWI memorial at Târgu Jiu, Romania, encompasses the entire town from the bridge over the river in the west to the hilltop on the eastern side of town. In his architectonic program for the memorial, the artist combined his own deeply felt, Romanian Orthodox religious beliefs with the well-known—to Romanians—local lore of the Maiastra, the golden "soul bird."[2]

The artist's conception is a narrative map with markers—sculptural elements—that chart a W–E movement of the souls of the dead. The story begins at the river's edge where the townsfolk (the children, the women, and the old, crippled, and maimed) had defended the town against an invading German force in 1916. Leaving the riverbank, the artist traces the movement of the souls of the dead along a straight line east into a small park, by way of the *Table of Silence*, through the *Gate of the Kiss*, along the Avenue of Heroes with its Church of the Heroes, and clear to the other side of the town. Here, the dead carried by the Maiastra fly to the top of the golden *Endless Column* at the crown of the hill. There the dead are reborn in the light of the rising sun.

Brâncuşi's WWI memorial complex at Târgu Jiu is little known in the West as a citywide architectonic program having linked components. Also little known is this note: Brâncuşi's *Table of Silence* was initially called by the artist the "table of the hungry" (Brezianu 1999: 170, note 4). We hunger for a last moment, a last word, a last touch, for something of that lost person, just one more time. Something. One more time. All the bargaining in the world cannot bring back the dead no matter how often their names are invoked.

The Târgu Jiu memorial complex was designed and built in the space of three years. It was dedicated October 27, 1938. Constantine Brâncuşi's work commemorates those who had died more than 20 years earlier. Three weeks before the dedication of the memorial, German troops invaded Czechoslovakia. The Second World War was about to begin. It would be followed by the Cold War standoff. Any chance for the Târgu Jiu memorial to become known in the West disappeared. Today, the best-known war memorials for the dead are probably François Rude's frieze *La Marseillaise* (Paris, Arc de Triomphe, 1792) and Maya Ying Lin's *The Vietnam Memorial* (Washington, DC, 1983). Lin is one of the members of the World Trade Center memorial committee.

The WTC memorial

Once the architects were commissioned to begin building at the World Trade Center site, an international competition opened for a memorial to those who were killed. The rules, devised by the Lower Manhattan Development Corporation, were complex: the artists' designs should acknowledge individually all who were killed on September 11; should provide quiet areas for all site visitors; should provide private, set-aside areas for mourners of the dead; should make visible the towers' "footprints"—the two squares where the towers used to be—and, lastly, should acknowledge those who were killed in an earlier truck bombing at the World Trade Center on February 26, 1993. Six died in 1993, many more were injured. The guidelines of the competition emphasized the importance of arriving at a design with an international orientation—one that acknowledged that those who died on September 11 came from all over the world, from 92 different countries. Essentially, artists were asked to design a graveyard for ashes and unidentified human remains, a graveyard to be built in the middle of a business and cultural complex.

Registration for the competition opened April 28, 2003, ending a month later. One month after, June 30, the artists' submissions were due. There were 5,201 submissions, each one presented anonymously on regulation-sized posterboard.

Somehow, in the next ten weeks, the jury of 13 identified a finalists' slate of eight submissions.[3] November 19 the designs of eight finalists were announced to the public.

The slate selected was not strong, not even to the eye of the jury. Some did not want the selection shown to the public at all (see Collins and Dunlap 2004). Their caution was well advised. The public did not like the designs very much either. What were the problems? Multiple.

No stories are told in any of the designs. The designs are interchangeably featureless. That is the greatest fault. Any of the eight might be built anywhere, whatever size the calamity to be memorialized. Not one of the eight acknowledges the day or date of death; not one makes use of any of the carefully collected shards from the site. Were the artists reluctant to incorporate relics into the design? To acknowledge the date—September 11—by which the destruction is known worldwide?

There are other problems, too. Each of the eight designs is technically sensitive and complex to operate. Each design relies upon high-maintenance design features, including moving parts and images—all to be operated by computers.

Is there any religious content? Yes, somewhat. The symbolism appears to be a watery gruel of Roman Catholicism swirled with a dollop of Mahayana Buddhism. There are, for example, "altars" in several designs. One of the eight submissions proposed an altar for each and everyone killed (and the hijackers?). Some of the designs included set-aside areas for "votive lights" and places where visitors might "light candles." Other submissions suggested there be "offering paths" and "sanctuaries." In all eight designs, light is an important feature of the design, but the light usually specified is artificial light (except for the candles).

How could such a weak slate be drawn from more than 5,000 submissions forwarded from all over the world?[4] In their effort to avoid presenting a politicized, narrowly nationalized "American" monument, perhaps the selection committee lost their way in the thicket of so many submissions. Nonetheless, the committee pressed on and cobbled together a decision. Michael Arad's design *Reflecting Absence* was selected. The committee's decision was announced January 7, 2004.

In the January version of Arad's submission, architect Michael Arad is joined by Peter Walker, a prominent landscape architect of national reputation. They revised *Reflecting Absence* substantively, adding in such elements as deciduous trees and an underground museum where relics of the site can be shown to visitors. The Arad–Walker plan retains the prominent topographical feature of Arad's initial submission. The towers' footprints are configured as sunken pools of cascading water. At street level, the pools of water are hidden in a 16-acre grove of trees.

Reflecting Absence is an elegant design. Herbert Muschamp, preeminent architecture critic for the *New York Times*, argues subtly for the revised Arad–Walker proposal (Muschamp 2004). He likens the two cascading, sunken pools of *Reflecting Absence* to the myth of Narcissus and his double—the "pairing of our inner and outer worlds."

Perhaps Muschamp is right. Perhaps these sunken pools are that mythic possibility of time and life come round again, but I do not know if we are able to look into such empty spaces. I fear the pools will soon ice over because they also suggest a watery grave—not metamorphosis, not renewal. Are the absent dead here "deep-sixed"—to invoke sailor's jargon for a burial at sea? I hope not.

Truthful witness

The earliest responses by artists, musicians, and actors were public events, such as fundraising concerts and appeals. Prayer was needed, too. In Wakefield, Québec, members of the Wakefield United Church created a flower petal mandala. The parishioners used the last blooms from their summer gardens in a memorial ritual designed and led by Wakefield artist c.j. fleury—not a member of the church—at the request of Giselle Gilfillan, the minister. Thinking back to her own role that evening, the artist wrote, "The way the minister folded the mandala activity into the larger—and I might add—highly symbolic event was really an honour. Art was being used so beautifully. I have been touched—and healed—by that in a very special way" (fleury 2003). Making the mandala was the centerpiece of the church's memorial ceremony for the September 11 dead.

Some artists attempted to recreate the imagery of destruction literally

—of towers being hit, people falling, warplanes in the sky. These attempts were doomed at the outset. The artists' skills could carry them no further than illustration. Few artists are able to depict a horrific scene and transcend it. Pablo Picasso could and did in his painting *Guernica*, 1937. The focal point of Picasso's composition is a *pièta*—an anguished mother holds her dead child. Picasso had painted quickly, feverishly when he learned of the bombing of Guernica, a small Basque fishing village. The Guernica bombardment was the first time a civilian population had ever been terror-bombed.

Many who were murdered September 11 died by chance. They might have been somewhere else. A series of chance events in their lives had brought them to the World Trade Center that day. Art, however, alters chance. That is its genius. Art establishes connections through time— Picasso's *Guernica* is linked to any image of an anguished mother holding her dead child. Looking at art is, for the viewer, a confrontation with the same moment when the artist stood back from the work and said, "That is it; I cannot do it any better." That is why, in a sense, looking at an artist's work, really looking into the artist's work, collapses time—if the looking is done carefully enough. The viewer sees the artist's work with the critical, show-me eyes of the artist.

In Naz Ikramullah's collages, the compositions, at first glance, appear to be romantic views, souvenirs, of the ancient marketplaces, mosques, and walled cities of her South Asian heritage. They are not. A second look usually reveals something more perilous—for example, a figure with machine gun, hiding in a doorway. Look even closer, there may be ghosts in the compositions. For more than ten years, Ikramullah has been depicting scenes of violence underscored by religion in her lithographs and collages. In *City under Siege*, 1996, for example (see plate 1 in plate section), the ghost that rises from the ruins of the ancient city is a young woman—her hair wild, arms spread wide, disoriented. She is blindfolded. The city has been bombed to rubble.

Naz Ikramullah, born in England and educated in England and Canada, is an observant Sunni Muslim of South Asian heritage. In response to the contextual events of September 11, the artist created *Lost Dreams*, 2002 (see plate 2). It is a vertically organized collage (h. 24" × 36"). The colors are mostly secondaries—soft greens, oranges, and violets. Ikramullah's composition combines the winter streets of Karachi with those of Kandahar, and winter scenes of Canada with imagery of the *mujahideen*. The linchpin of the composition is an area shaped like an inverted *tau* cross. Here Ikramullah inserted a scene drawn from a photograph of what she calls an "Arab cemetery." Rising from the cemetery scene is a spare outline in white against black. It is the figure of a *mujahid*. In the lower left-hand corner, the viewer may see a second figure. This one is of a small woman who wears a blue dress with modest décolleté. Her hair is short, uncovered, and she appears to be watching the viewer. Her head is bent in sorrow. The woman appears "Westernized." In the entirety of the composition, however, the woman in the corner is eclipsed by the composition's central imagery of the *mujahideen* in winter.

Marie-France Nitski, born in France, schooled in South America and Canada, is another artist with superb night vision. She, too, "sees" uncommonly well in the dark, around corners, and into boggy, hidden places. For years, in the tradition of the European CoBrA artists, Nitski's paintings have told the stories of folkloric animals and beings. These are creatures that inhabit mythic worlds. They are also ones the artist sees in her dreams and in the woods around her house. In 1999 two new figures entered her visual design field—the "lost blue angel" and the "red angel." In the aftermath of September 11, Nitski's visual field became crowded with refugees and displaced creatures—dogs and fish, ravens, turtles, little girls and lost angels, red and blue.

Animal Encounters, 2002 (see plate 3), is large (h. 80" × 60") and painted on panels of sheet metal and wood because the artist built it to last. Nitski's colors are bold—red, yellow, blue enamels and oils. The composition, in theory hieratic, is frantic—not at all stately. In the center, a wild-eyed, naked little girl is standing. She has run and run and is now stopped, her arms flung out, fingers hyper-extended in fear, her lips drawn back into a grimace. A fish, a dog (with angel wings), a snake, all try to comfort her. The little girl cannot be calmed. Inchoate fear has rendered her dumb. She runs, terrorized, as terrorized as the little girl who ran naked into the roadway—My Lai 4, Vietnam, 1968. *Animal Encounters* has tossed them all—child, friendly dog, wild beast—into a thundering vortex of terror and entrapment.

We were never, any of us, more entrapped, more fearful, than when we were children. Tens of thousands of people did escape the twin towers of the World Trade Center. Their ways out were passages of fear so intense that the only comparison possible is one that hearkens back to childhood.

Prediction and prophecy

Artist Audrey Churgin was born in New York City, resettling in Canada in 1970. In her work, Churgin often includes imagery of her two children. *In Sight Recovered*, 1998 (see plate 4), is a large triptych: the dimensions of each panel are h. 60" × 36". The medium is pastel: the colors the artist uses are black, white, and a multitude of greys. In each of the three panels, two children are visible. They stand together and apart: a boy, a girl, one older, one younger. Both are very young. There is a doorway, it opens, the children do not go through it. The hallway extends, the dark deepens. All of our fears are grounded by those we knew as children when we were afraid of the dark. It is hard to look into fear.

When Churgin finished the triptych in 1998, she put it away, unframed.

Nearly four years later, she pulled it from storage and had it framed. *In Sight Recovered*, 1998, had never been shown before. The artist had held it back, knowing all the time that it was "powerful, one of my best," as she wrote (Churgin 2002). Now, she wanted others to see it.

In the wall-sized imagery of *In Sight Recovered*, the artist knew she had made a truthful image of what it must have been like inside the towers for those who were there as we learned from the descriptions written by those who found their way out of the towers. Churgin's visual imagery matches their descriptions.

How is that possible?

Not often, but sometimes, an artist's work—at least in hindsight—appears to have been predictive of events that occurred later. Artists are artists, in part, because they are sensitive to their milieux. Some, not many, have both talent and insight. Their antennae are uncommonly sensitive. They "read" their surroundings as text to be decoded for hidden meaning. If *In Sight Recovered* appears prophetic, it is because of the artist's talent for insight and the circumstances of chance.

The best artists do not make art as a form of self-expression and personal therapy. That is the public's most common, and most hurtful, misconception about art and artists.

Think Different: Power and Decline of the New Economy (Manhattan in March 2000), a series of six photographs by artist Hans Mettler, is predictive by insight and by intention. Mettler's photographs were taken early in March 2000 in and around Wall Street. The series was completed in 2000 and exhibited in January 2001, at the Ursula Wiedenkeller Gallery in Zurich, Switzerland. The scenes selected by the artist for the *Think Different* series are typical of the New York financial district at the height of the "dot.com" bubble. People hurry down the streets through an urban environment of billboards urging them to run even faster into a new era, a new economy, a "globalized" world (was it ever a cube?).

Deeply disturbed by what he saw in that March 2000 visit to New York City, Hans Mettler digitally combined six New York street photographs with six photographs of succulents, cacti, and other garishly colored plants he photographed in the collections in the Montreal Botanical Gardens. Each of Mettler's photo-collaged images reads as a visual jeremiad.

The street photographs are of billboards, posters, traffic signs—all exhorting the viewer harshly to "think different." The first image of the series declares—by billboard and traffic sign—"Internet Expressway. Think Different. One Way" (see plate 5). In the bottom half of the photograph is a congestion of coleus leaves, "protesting," the artist says (Mettler 2003a).

The second image from the series identifies a corner of 6th Avenue, also known as "Avenue of the Americas" (see plate 6). Billboard fragments announce: "A new century, dream" and ask, "Will you be . . . if it happens . . .," the rest of the query lost in the corner's turn. The right half of the image is crowded with prickly pear cactus, its fruit droplets, bloodied, the cacti colored watery blue and green.

The billboard centered in the third image asks "Find Out How Much Oxygen Your Blood Can Hold" (see plate 7). On the right side of the building with that billboard we see tall refinery towers, flaming, burning off noxious gases. The bottom half of the image is of vegetation, thickly planted. It is an aquarium, one rotting with algae and seaweed.

The viewer's already high tension level jumps sharply with the fourth of the *Think Different* series (see plate 8). A billboard covers the entire side of a building. It shows businessmen, in suits, proceeding solemnly through a wasteland. Their ties are aflame. Smoke is everywhere. The billboard text reads "www.smashstatusquo.com." Cacti with long, long needles are advancing from below upon the scene.

In the fifth image, Mettler photographs the subway entrance for the "Chambers Street Station World Trade Center" (see plate 9). Here, the traveler is admonished to "enter at Liberty or Vesey St. between Church & W. Broadway." Above, a blue billboard with a weirdly armored figure reads, "Hey, you don't have to run out." Tumbling pell-mell, however, out of the underground are soft, furry, grey and yellow maggots. They are not maggots. They are succulents, curved like feeding maggots.

In the sixth and final image, "Absolute Carting" (see plate 10), a black dump truck carries debris away. Large, red-veined leaves pile up. "The plants will survive," the artist comments, "they can live without us" (Mettler 2003a).

When Hans Mettler exhibited the series in 2000, he wrote in his artist's statement accompanying the portfolio:

> The virtual world is invading our lives with incredible speed and bogus realism, generating a new myth of Aldous Huxley's "brave new world." In this series, for which all the photographs were taken in 2000 in New York City's borough of Manhattan, I want to showcase the blatant manifestations of the new economy and its impact on society . . . a warning of the evil that will befall us . . .

In three of the images in the *Think Different* series, the sky is visible; the sky is an intense blue, not a cloud in it. That is the sky we remember we saw on September 11, 2001. There are no people on the streets in Hans Mettler's photographs, only the plants that can grow in blasted, destroyed places.

Hans Mettler was for many years a journalist working in print, radio, and television media in Europe before becoming a professional artist in 1991, and relocating to Canada in 1995. He holds a PhD in European Studies and Ecology. In other words, the artist's eyes are wide open and his scientifically trained judgment astute. The gift of prophecy? How can one account for that? The artist's trip to New York in 2000 should have been an ordinary visit because he had been there before. What had changed? Mettler can say only, "I had the feeling 'this is going to stop, this is going to end'" (Mettler 2003b).

There is no satisfaction in having this sort of visionary skill. Predictive insight is, in fact, a burden, as artists admit. Hans Mettler notes quietly: "I did that series [*Think Different*] one year before and it's still disturbing my mind" (Mettler 2003c).

Liminality, silence, and memory

The artist bargains for truth, for insight, for vision, so does the mystic, the saint, the prophet. In his prayers, three times daily, Rabbi Irwin Kula chants the last words recorded on telephone answering devices on September 11 (Kula 2002). Left messages. The words are words of connection: "Honey, something terrible has happened, I don't think I'm going to make it." "I love you." "Tell the children I love them." "Mama, I love you." The last words are poems, breathe in, breathe out, their rhythms an inspiration, the same sounds going out ritualistically into the air, shaping the air, the words of a rabbi's prayer.

Religious silence is a discipline. It is not inchoate. The Buddhist speaks of "becoming mindful," of finding your "Buddha Mind," as Shunryu Suzuki describes (Suzuki 1970). From Japan, Canadian artist Robin Campbell wrote soon after September 11:

> The image of the people hurling themselves from the burning building has stayed with me . . . Michelangelo's figures falling anguished into hell and at the opposite extreme [I see] the Buddha diving serenely off the cliff to feed the starving tigers below. Considering a juxtaposition of images . . . all pretty raw. (Campbell 2001)

Three installations followed. In each one Robin Campbell, working with Nina Handjeva-Weller, deepened her understanding of the initial liminal vision. The first installation using the teachings of this imagery was one month after September 11. A group of artists working in Kyoto, including dancers and musicians, Japanese and foreigners alike, organized an exhibition and performance entitled: "The Healing of the World post 9/11." For this event, the two artists' installations included images of four meditating Buddhas. In front of each sculpture (see plate 11), they placed a mandala, formed of a circular pattern, multiplying and drawing into mandala images of people murdered on September 11 and people fleeing chaos. The design's inspiration is found in Shingon Buddhism.

One year later, the two artists used the mandalas they had collaged from the published imagery of September 11 and transformed them into halos for a second set of five Boddhisatvas. This installation was exhibited in a Buddhist temple—Honen-In, Kyoto. Each of the Boddhisatvas is accompanied by offerings and a wooden altar to the earth. Each Bod-dhisatva holds a small image of the planet earth in her hands. The whole installation is entitled *Prayers for Earth*.

In 2003, the monks of Honen-In invited the artists back to work again at their temple. *Paradise Realms for Other Species* is the two artists' larg-est installation to date. It incorporates sculpture, painting, and ceramics. The Boddhisatvas' halos are now altar screens and fans, symbols of silence and motion. The imagery of people falling from the towers on Septem-ber 11 is fully subsumed in the compassionate gestures of the Jizo Bosatsu. This Boddhisatva's compassion extends to all beings, "but especially to children and small animals," Robin Campbell writes (Campbell 2003). Miraku Bosatsu is a Boddhisatva of vision, paired to Kokuzo Bosatsu, the Boddhisatva of practical wisdom. All three Boddhisatvas are, Campbell writes further, "personifications of the qualities necessary to bring peace to this world, to realize paradise here" (Campbell 2004).

Robin Campbell's practice of Buddhism began as an artist in Montreal. The more she worked in her studio, the more the artist learned from silence. In silence, time stretches, then compresses, then is nothing. In silence our hearing, sight, all our senses become more acute. In silence the material is sometimes suffused with light, and transfigured, if not transformed. Swiss artist Paul Klee, using only small dots and lines, created a vibrantly hopeful world in his small painting entitled *The Light and Much Else*. Klee finished the painting in 1931. A few years later, Constantin Brâncuşi began to work on the Târgu Jiu memorial.

Both Klee and Brâncuşi have inspired Canadian artist Barry Strasbourg-Thompson. In his paintings the artist walks along shorelines where the islands are scarcely visible against the weight of the sky above, the seas surrounding, and the pull of the tides of memory. Aquatic animals might nest here, but this is not a dwelling land for humans. On full moon nights, the tides run particularly high, and the bugs bite hard. Yet even here there is an implicit order, a balanced division of day and night, nothing lost or diminished.

A year after September 11, Strasbourg-Thompson selected work from two series of paintings on silence—half created before September 11, half following. The paintings were large, often painted on wood with the wood grain visible. The surfaces of the paintings were usually divided into proportions consistent with the Pythagorean measures of the golden section. The paintings suggested something else could be seen if one were quiet enough and waited patiently enough.

Barry Strasbourg-Thompson's exhibition was entitled *On Silence*. It opened in Ottawa, September 11, 2002. There were more than 20 paint-ings and sculptures—all of it disciplined, spare work, some of it fearful, despairing. And then, as promised, balance can be and was obtained, in silence.

One must be silent to remember. To become engaged with imagery is to cross time and culture, to enter into the soul of another and to see with the eyes of another.

In conclusion

A few months after September 11, I began asking artists, "What did you do to get through that first hard week?" The answers I heard began to fall into patterns or clusters—silence, nature, ritual, cause, and loss. Then the patterns reformed into religious categories—prediction and prophecy, description and witness, silence and light . . . shimmering, pellucid, insight.

The answers to my questions are heard and seen in the voices and finger-pointings of those who think visually. Filmmaker Julie Sloane, who waited to help with the wounded on the pier at Hoboken that night, is today a founding member of the Cantigas Women's Choir of Hoboken. They are an advocacy group, using song to sing for those "whose voices need to be heard." The choir have just released their first recording.

Artist and healer Donna Henes walked around her Brooklyn neighborhood a lot in the aftermath of September 11. She called this time her "walk your talk pilgrimage," and, as she wrote in her quarterly newsletter:

> There is an intense white light, an inner glow that is now emanating from the people of New York City. We have risen to an unthinkable occasion and we like ourselves for doing so. (Henes 2001)

Henes continues organizing her seasonal ritual performances—although her sites and sponsorships have changed. The American Indian Community House and the National Museum of the American Indian of the Smithsonian Institution stepped in to pick up the slack left by the loss of the artist's World Trade Center ritual space.

In the wake of September 11, much of the New York art world seems fed up with the trash talk, which had earlier dominated the contemporary art scene. There is no time left to be amused by a postmodern pastiche, or be distracted by a theory-burdened, but content-less, art. A hunger is emerging for beauty, clarity, a disciplined art. Beautiful paintings, sculpture, photographs are now found in the most important New York galleries. They were always there, but now they are visible.

Meryl Taradash has always made beautiful, elegant metal sculpture. Following September 11, the City of New York offered a public site for one of her large installations; a cancer center in New Jersey took another; and a hospital in Virginia yet another. Collectors and patrons are beginning to find their way to her Brooklyn studio. Encouraged by this attention, the artist pulled together a design team and made a submission to the World Trade Center Memorial competition.[5]

The artist's *Sundial Memorial Project* was not one of the eight finalists selected. Its posterboard presentation (see plate 12) was perhaps too modest to attract the attention of the judges; there were, after all, more than 5,000 entries. Nonetheless, unlike those that were selected as finalists, Meryl Taradash's design is practical, simple, and clear of concept. There are no mechanical moving parts, no computerized functions, no underground caverns, no altars and candles.

The heart of the Taradash design is the sun and the shadow of the sun measured by a large sundial. The reckoning point of the sundial, its gnomon, is designed by the artist as an element constructed from the latticework shard that survived the towers' destruction. The sundial's analemma—that figure of infinity cast by the sun's shadow over the course of any year from any fixed noon line—is the site of the memorial's mass grave. In the artist's design for the memorial, the dead are shadow calibrations grouped by birth month and year along the edge of the analemma. Their ashes would be placed in the two center sections of the analemma. The words "analemma" and "gnomon" mean "to reflect" and "to know."

To reflect and to know are tasks an artist accepts in order to work truthfully. Artists are courageous beings, those who are religious visionaries. We do not think of them in these terms, but we might. The best are vision-driven; they risk much. American sculptor Louise Nevelson, one of the most important of our time, said of her art, and of being an artist:

> I think it's [art] as important as any religion . . . You're given a gift to fulfill. You didn't bargain for happiness; you bargained for something else. You bargained for revelation. You bargained for a closer concept of reality. And you bargained for your own sanity, I think, half the time. You're really right down with the elements. (Louise Nevelson, quoted in Streeter 1961: 32–3)

The elements of art (as in religion) are light, and silence. That much we could hang onto at the World Trade Center site if nothing more were built there. All we really need is a walkway or two upon cleared ground so people could walk quietly. The miracles, rituals, and memories are already present. For now, that could be enough.

Notes

1   The *New York Times Magazine* cover image, September 23, 2001, was entitled, "Phantom Towers." Paul Myoda and Julian LaVerdiere conceived the memorial image. The image itself was created digitally by the newspaper staff by manipulating a photograph by Fred R. Conrad, also of the *New York Times*.

2   See Korp 2002. In Romania, tales of the Maiastra, drawn from ancient pre-Christian belief, have been folded into Christian burial customs.

3   Each submission was given two months and an honorarium of as much as $130,000 to translate their posterboard submissions into professionally built

maquettes and models. November 19, 2003 the designs of eight finalists were announced to the public as reported by Collins and Dunlap 2004.

4   Seven of the eight selected proposals presented on posterboards were designed with color-saturated, computer-drawn images. Those boards would stand out in any group of boards with hand-drawn designs, no matter how skillfully drawn. Designs on hand-assembled poster boards may have slid from view given the pressure upon the jury to winnow so many submissions in so little time.

5   The author advised Meryl Taradash on her submission of the *Memorial Sundial Project* to the 2003 memorial competition organized by the Lower Manhattan Development Corporation.

References

ABC News, Nightline. 2002. "Ground Zero: Crime Scene, Recovery Site, Hallowed Ground." Broadcast November 3.

Anonymous. 2002. "A Stillness at Ground Zero." *Newsweek*, June 16: 18.

Brezianu, Barbu. 1999. *Brâncuşi in Romania*. Bucharest: Editura ALL.

Campbell, Robin. 2001. Personal communication (e-mail) with author, September 28.

——. 2003. Personal communication (artist's note) with author.

——. 2004. Personal communication (e-mail) with author, February 28.

Churgin, Audrey. 2002. Personal communication (e-mail) with author, January 9.

Collins, Glenn and David W. Dunlap. 2004. "The 9/11 Memorial: How Pluribus Became Union." *The New York Times*, January 19 (available online: www.nytimes.com/2004/01/19/nyregion/19MEMO.htm).

fleury, c.j. 2003. Personal communication (e-mail) with author, August 13.

Henes, Donna. 2001. "Always in Season." *Autumn Equinox Peace Special*, no. 12.

Iovine, Julie V. 2003. "The Invisible Architect." *The New York Times*, August 31: AR17.

Korp, Maureen. 1997. *Sacred Art of the Earth*. New York: Continuum.

——. 2002. "Brâncuşi at Târgu Jiu: The Local Context of his WWI Memorial." In *Art Remembers: Conference Proceedings, School of Visual Arts 16th Annual National Conference, New York, October 23–25, 2002*. Romania: Romanian Academy of Art.

Kula, (Rabbi) Irwin. 2002. Interview for *Frontline*: "Faith and Doubt at Ground Zero." Broadcast WPBS Television, Watertown, NY, September 3.

Leith, Sam. 2002. "You Never Get Closure On This." *Ottawa Citizen*, May 30: A12.

Lower Manhattan Development Corporation. 2003. Guidelines, World Trade Center Site Memorial Competition.

Mettler, Hans. 2003a. Classroom lecture, Carleton University, Ottawa, November 19.

——. 2003b. Personal communication (interview notes, Ottawa) with author, August 20.

——. 2003c. Personal communication (telephone) with author, August 13.

Muschamp, Herbert. 2004. "Strong Depth of Emotions and No Frills in 2 Footprints." *The New York Times*, January 15 (available online: www.nytimes.com/2004/01/15/nyregion/15muschamp.htm).

Streeter, Tal. 1961. "Six Sculptors in America." Unpublished MFA thesis, University of Kansas.

Suzuki, Shunryu. 1970. *Zen Mind, Beginner's Mind*. New York: Weatherhill.

Whitney, Helen, producer. 2002. *Faith and Doubt at Ground Zero*. Written by Helen Whitney and Ron Rosenbloom. 120 minutes, VHS, 2002. Broadcast PBS, Watertown, NY, *Frontline*, September 3.

Concluding reflections

20 Religion, violence, and the pursuit of truth

Bryan Rennie

I once quipped that the academic attempt to define postmodernism was the indefatigable in pursuit of the indefinable (1996: 231). Now, older and more cautious, I am inclined to think that this condition is more widespread, affecting not only postmodernism, but possibly all academic vocabulary. "Religion," as is widely recognized in the field, is not a thing, it is a word, the use of which serves a variety of purposes for the user. It is not, that is to say, a natural sort signifying a known, invariant, and closed class of objects and events in the physical world. But then, even "violence" is not precise. When does play or sport slide through "horse-play" into violence? When does protective custody or paternal restraint become violence? When is legitimate punishment violence? When does the struggle to be obedient to the will of the merciful and compassionate Allah become "holy war"? Add to this already potentially chaotic mix the loaded concept of truth and we have a linguistic "three body problem" in which the trajectory of each term perturbs not only the trajectory but the very constitution of the others in a wildly complex interaction. That said, it is at least possible to suggest some relations, complex though they may be, between these terms as they might usefully be conceived.

Evidently, to attempt to force all of the contributions to this volume to speak with a single voice and to fit a single pattern would be to betray the principles of a "postmodern historiography" as I tried to outline it in a 2003 review essay in *Method and Theory in the Study of Religion*. Rather, the voices of our contributors and those of our subjects remain distinct and unique. Some speak from the academic study of religion, some from within one or another religious tradition, some infuse politics with theology, and some strive to maintain the objectivity of the social scientist. However, there are some underlying commonalities, and one is that the terror underlying all these essays can be seen as the terror of history itself. When terrorist activity explodes into our lived experience, the actual violently betrays the ideal. We see, not only in the essays in this volume, but also in their subject matter, the constant attempt to reconcile and re-integrate the actual, history, the empirical, with the ideal, the conceptual. Religious forms of expression—chiefly language, but also, as

Maureen Korp's important essay shows, all the other arts of expression—maintain the continuity of these two worlds: what is encountered in lived experience and what we believe to be. Religious expression gives some empirical form to what we believe to be in a way that seeks to reconcile our physical experience with that belief. The effort to do so truthfully, or at least convincingly, often leads to convoluted and desperate—sometimes violent—expressions, especially, of course, in situations in which the actual diverges most violently from the ideal, in which history most brutally belies our cherished ideals.

The question of truth, as I say, is anything but simple. The term "truth" is one of the more polysemic and indefinable terms in language—and one of the most rhetorically powerful reifications of all. That which we take to be true is always that which is finally most convincing and most effectively motivating. Although some would argue for a sharp and qualitative distinction between the actually true and the merely convincing, it is difficult, at the limits, to maintain that distinction or to analytically determine what constitutes it. The fact remains: that which I take to be true is identical to that which is most convincing to me, and what people take to be true is that upon which they are motivated to act. Truth, as in the true lines of a well-constructed building, the true flight of the arrow to its target, the true friend, might be seen as the point of intersection of the actual and the ideal. I avoid saying that in truth the actual "corresponds" to the ideal. Correspondence theories of truth have, quite deservedly, come under withering fire from philosophical analysts: in truth "correspondence" is a mysterious relation; at best an unknown, at worst a viciously circular tautology in which truth is the characteristic of statements that correspond to actual affairs and correspondence is the characteristic of true statements.

In this context, it is always salutary to remember that truth is a characteristic of expressions, not of states of affairs, and what we see in reactions to terrorism is the attempt to restore the harmonious relation of actual experience with cherished notions via expressions that seek to give substantial form to the ideal when that relation has been deliberately and violently disrupted. Both secular and religious rhetoric seeks to provide an experience—aesthetic in the literal sense of being empirically apprehended—that allows some coherent response to the actual and to the ideal simultaneously. There is, of course, a modernist tendency to insist that the actual, the empirical, the historical, *is* the real and that the ideal, the conceptual (what Hans Küng calls "vision") is not real, or is significantly *less* so. This is, I have long contended, a historically and culturally local notion which does not stand under the scrutiny of the history of religions (Rennie 1996: especially 103–6). Apart from the problem that modernist programs stand squarely on problematic ideal terms (being, time, truth, reality) it is also the case that for most human cultures, some non-empirical sacred has served as the real, the true. For

Plato the world of ideal forms was more real than the empirical realm, and for apocalyptic traditions such as Christianity and Islam the wish of the believer is to see God's kingdom come, on earth as it is in heaven. That is, observably and factually through much of human history and across most human cultures, people have valued the conceptual above the historical and have thus been motivated to act as much, if not more, by the ideal than by the actual. If, as David Hume argued, "no is implies an ought" (*A Treatise of Human Nature*, 3.1.1) then we simply cannot be motivated by the historical and the actual *without* the operation of the ideal to translate the former into meaningful conditions eliciting a comprehensible response.

The historical is liable to sudden, violent, and unexpected change. The ideal, on the other hand, is something that is relied upon to be invariant. Confronted with a world of unpredictable change, we respond with expressions of the cosmos as a reliable order with predictable dynamics. Occasionally our attempts to reconcile the two become fraught and tenuous, and each tradition reconciles them in its own internally variable ways. The history of religions illustrates how the unanticipated irruptions of history require the creative evolution of religious ideas. The most notable example, of course, being the Exile in Babylon and the near-extinction of the Hebrew culture, which called forth a great period of religious creativity.

However, a crucial question becomes whether or not the agenda revealed by any such creative act is narrowly self-serving in the sense that it derives benefit for one group through damage to another. One might see this question as religious—the divine will demands altruism and charity— or as entirely pragmatic—actions occasioning harm to others provoke retaliation and thus increase rather than reduce violence. The example of those who sought "the authentic heart" of Islam (see McCutcheon's essay) seems quite clear—they sought to establish as authentically obedient to the will of the divine the irenic, peaceful, pacifistic tendencies of that religion over its potentially martial elements, and thus their agenda seems less obscurantist than morally laudatory. It is self-serving only in the sense that the self is identified with the whole human race. Although I agree that "assuming that the spheres named as religion and politics are ontologically distinct realms" (McCutcheon this volume) is both unwarranted and a suspect rhetorical strategy, on the other hand, any attempt to emphasize the divinity of peace should be welcome.

One thing that connects many of these essays is this kind of rhetorical strategy. They themselves are attempts to harness the effective power of expression, but they are, hopefully, ones which struggle to prioritize the element of truth as the finally most effective rhetorical device of all. The recrudescence of religion as a political power (of course, it never really went away, although it was fairly challenged by modernism and secularism) is a continuation of the "linguistic turn" recognized by Richard

Rorty, leading to a "rhetorical turn" in the late twentieth century—and this itself merely seeks to restore the common condition of humanity. When Mark Juergensmeyer, for example, states that "politics have become religionized . . . [w]orldly struggles have been lifted into the high proscenium of sacred battle," the history of religions tells us that, in fact, they always were. The spheres of religion and politics are not, after all, ontologically distinct. This point is forcefully made in Norman Cohn's admirable *Chaos, Cosmos and the World to Come*. Warfare was invariably portrayed in the ancient world as the sacred duty to defend against the forces of chaos, and "what we have called a religious world-view could just as well be called a political ideology, and the theologians who created and elaborated it could just as well be called political propagandists" (1993: 18).

The myths, rituals, doctrines, and all other aesthetic expressions, all the visual and verbal arts of institutional religion, contribute hugely to effective rhetoric. And it can be effective for good or ill. Hence the dissatisfaction felt, for example, by Omid Safi, who cannot be easily comfortable with the "simplistic" response that "there is no relationship whatsoever between the beautiful teachings of Islam and the hateful words and deeds of Osama bin Laden." Religious rhetoric, like logic, is used both before and after the event—both to promote and to justify actions. It seems extremely unlikely that those who respond to the rhetoric of religion to motivate and to justify their, and their community's, actions will suddenly begin to respond instead to the alternative rhetoric of academic reason, much less to some logical-positivist and historicist arguments. Indeed, it might even be suggested that extreme claims for and initiatives towards radical historicism could be suspected as significantly weakening the irenic case and as one of the principal reasons for the failure of academic reason and the return to overtly religious rhetoric. This is a case in which one can only continue to fight fire with fire, so that the religious rhetoric (or, if you prefer, theology) of Riswold, Küng, and Wink, which discourages and condemns violence, will continue to be one of the most effective ways of limiting the damage done by alternative religious rhetoric that encourages and justifies violence.

This is not a hopeless acquiescence and declaration of powerlessness and it is certainly not an abandonment of the modernist pursuit of factual accuracy. On the contrary, the claim is that religion as a traditional institution does not justify violence. The narrowly self-centered and self-serving rhetoric of "chosen rightness, certainty, and the will of God" (to quote Caryn Riswold) seems finally to be outweighed by the rhetoric of compassion, mercy, and real justice foundational to institutional traditions (and perhaps natively human, as Omid Safi argues). The rhetorical abuse of tradition which does not recognize this must finally collapse, undermined by self-contradiction, inhumanity, and hypocrisy. The promotion of the in-group (the group with which any speaker identifies) as somehow inherently superior, deserving of special privilege, and thus worthy of promotion at the expense of other competing groups, appears simply untrue. In religious terms, it denies the compassion of Allah, or rejects the love of God, or invokes the ineluctable processes of karma, and so on. In non-religious language, it promotes and perpetuates a cycle of destructive violence.

When I was fortunate enough to be in Durban, South Africa, in 2000 for the Congress of the International Association for the History of Religions, I simply assumed that the black South African population would still be violently embittered against whites because of their oppression under apartheid for almost 50 years. I was somewhat astonished, on the contrary, to be greeted hospitably and warmly by black people (being from northern Britain, I'm about as white as they come). I did not fail to take the opportunity to ask about this and, although I do not want to over-simplify a complex and painful situation, a rather straightforward picture emerged. Many locals told me that "Mr. Mandela taught us" that the whites were not bad people; it was, rather, a bad political situation, and one that could be addressed. On further investigation it began to appear that the process of "truth and reconciliation" seemed to have grounded, as it were, the potentially lethally destructive backlash of anger and resentment of blacks against whites.[1] The Truth and Reconciliation Commission was created when apartheid ended in 1994, and the nation faced the challenge of healing divides rooted in 48 years of violent oppression. It is one of the most effective demonstrations I have seen that before we can hope for the reconciliation of past violence we have no choice but to face the truth of its origins and dissemination. It is a commonplace in literature on US race-relations, especially in the writings of minority scholars, that until white America truthfully recognizes its self-advancement by means of the oppression of indigenous and minority peoples, any lasting reconciliation remains a distant dream.

Gerrie Ter Haar, in the introduction to her and James Busuttil's edited volume on religion and violence (2005), as well as referring to the South African example gives a comparable example from Liberia where

> some charismatic churches . . . use the ritual means at their disposal to re-integrate child-soldiers into the community . . . [they] give public testimony of the often horrific acts they have committed during the civil war. Such testimonies assume the character of public confession, providing enormous psychological relief to these young people [assisting them to] effect a change of life [and re-integrating them into the community, although their] anti-social deeds cannot easily be forgotten and forgiven. (2005: 24)

In the same volume Mark Gopin also emphasizes truth, disclosure, and accuracy as crucial for success in any peace-making initiative (pp. 45–8) and Jan Van Butselaar gives another example, comparable to the Truth and Reconciliation Commission, of the importance of honesty in the process of peace-making. In the process of "reconciling memories" in Northern Ireland, "responsibility is accepted, and forgiveness of sin sought" (Van Butselaar in Ter Haar and Busuttil 2005: 149, quoting Falconer). Here the proximity to the Christian doctrine of reconciliation is explicit: one must repent before one can be forgiven, but the process is surely a human universal. It is hardly possible to forgive the unrepentant, and the unconfessed wrong is less likely to be reconciled. The truth must be faced for the wound to be healed. However, before the truth can be told, the truth has to be known. One more example is the group of Christians in Rwanda two years after the genocide of 1994, who gathered to formulate the "Detmold Confession," "in which they admitted their guilt and promised to work for reconciliation" (Ter Haar and Busuttil 2005: 152). All these examples show the need for both personal honesty and accuracy of information concerning events that are all too prone to be misrepresented by the guilty parties, *even to themselves*. The need for accurate and impartial scholarship, devoted primarily to the production of statements which are enduring in their agreement with lived experience, is an indispensable part of the peace process.

The speakers and writers of the religion academy, if they are motivated primarily by the academic desire to correctly and accurately describe past and present cultural developments—including the relations mediated through religious behavior and language—would seem to be an indispensable medium through which to recover that truth. News media and politicians have clearly vested interests that do not necessarily focus on truth above all. As I have said, the very notion of truth is one of extreme philosophical complexity, but suffice it for now to define it as that which appears most authentically convincing without any determination by narrow self-interest: that conclusion at which all investigators are liable finally to arrive irrespective of the cultural determination of their perceptions.

When Ram Puniyani, a retired professor of biomedical engineering from the Indian Institute of Technology, edited his *Religion, Power and Violence: Expression of Politics in Contemporary Times* (2005) on the interaction of religion and violence in the recent history of India, he included academics and intellectuals, mainly social scientists, omitting historians of religion. The resulting volume is admirable and the specific case of religion and violence in India is very instructive indeed, but this omission makes its mark. Professor Puniyani, for example, states that "tritheism" is an "intermediate phase of transition from polytheism to monotheism" (2005: 34), and another contributor, Jawaid Quddus, despite his otherwise valuable insight, states that the Romans banned the practice of Christianity in Palestine and expelled the Jews from Jerusalem in 70 CE (pp. 93–4), and that the Crusaders ransacked Solomon's Temple (p. 104). Specific expertise in the history of religions has a significant role to play in avoiding such inaccuracy. The scholars of religion who contribute to our present volume represent the Western academy of religion more broadly and can help both in ascertaining the truth and in formulating the rhetorical strategies that will promote its irenic effect.

No scholar has much of a contribution to make without the whole institution of higher education. Unless we are allowed to speak, and more, unless we are heard with respect, our insights, words, data, and expertise mean little. With remarkable consistency, not only the theologians, theoreticians, philosophers, and methodologists, but also the sociologists, political scientists, and secular humanists in this volume as well as in Puniyani's and Ter Haar and Busuttil's, all agree that religion is not the cause of violence. Puniyani, for example, asks, "Is it religion or deeper economic interests of the US and elite sections of Indian society who are masquerading their imperial and hegemonic ambitions under the cover of religion?" (Puniyani 2005: 14), and he approvingly cites Quddus, that "socio-economic circumstances lead to this phenomenon [violence] and not religion *per se*" (p. 21). Ter Haar states that "it is not religion, but migration, regional and international, that is the truly controversial issue of politics worldwide . . . In none of these cases should religion be mistaken for the real issue. The real issue is the pressure to share resources with others" (Ter Haar and Busuttil 2005: 15). In the same work Chandra Muzaffar argues that

> Religious doctrine and practices, however different they may be, have seldom given rise to actual conflicts . . . Difference in doctrine and ritual may at times create a certain social distance between religious communities. They may, on occasion, impede social interaction. But they do not in themselves, and this must be emphasized over and over again—cause conflict. (Muzaffar in Ter Haar and Busuttil: 58)

However, such is the rhetorical power of religion that it is all too easy to use it to convince people that this is not the case; that some specific religion *is* the culprit (some *other* religion, naturally). In our day, of course, Islam is seen as the guilty religion *par excellence*. A close inspection of the history and the data gives another impression—the violence and oppression perpetrated on the Muslim world by the West has provoked the current retaliation. As Jonathan Brockopp puts it, "[n]early every Islamic nation in the world was born in the twentieth century out of some colonialist history, and many had pro-Western governments installed and maintained by Europe and the United States." But who has the time to make that inspection and to sort out sometimes unpleasant and self-deprecating truths from the emotionally satisfying and self-serving misinformation?— especially when elite groups have a vested interest in satisfying and serving their listeners. In a situation in which voters in the United States seem more inclined to vote for a politician because he lacks an adequate vocabulary than because he possesses one, anti-intellectualism rather than respect for learning seems poised to carry the day. In the sensitive times and positions in which we as members of the academy of religion find ourselves, it is crucial that we now comport ourselves with the utmost honesty and integrity in order to justify whatever respect we may earn from the populace, who are our students.

In Ter Haar and Busuttil's volume, Sarto Esteves gives an instructive example: "The people are made to believe, by constant, endless repetition . . . that millions of Dalits, Hindus, Adivasis, etc., are being converted every day and soon the Hindus will be reduced to a negligible minority and that Christians will be the majority community in India!" (p. 285). In fact, the percentage of Christians in India fell slightly from a mere 2.35 percent in 1951 to 2.21 percent in 2001 (p. 285). This is indicative of the effect that misinformation can have, and how effective it can be in the absence of accurate and reliable education. This may be an extreme example but it can be easily compared to repeated use of the image of a clash between the Christian West and the Arab-Muslim world, which "has become so much part of the political ideology of the West that it reinforces the idea that religion itself is a root cause of the numerous violent conflicts in the modern world" (Ter Haar and Busuttil 2005: 4–5). This despite the considerable weight of scholarly evidence to the contrary.

One might even suggest a role for the scholar of religion, as for all scholars and members of the academy, comparable to the system of checks and balances characteristic of Western democracy. It is often claimed that the judicial, legislative, and executive branches of government serve to balance and restrain one another in the best interests of the people as a whole. However, without an implicit fourth arm, the educational branch, motivated primarily by a desire to uncover unbiased truth and a belief that this "truth" is of greater value than any other undertaking, then even democracy—*especially* democracy—is liable to corruption and self-destruction by misinformation, ill-education, and the misleading rhetoric of those who subordinate accuracy to their own ends. I can only hope that with the preceding discussion of what I intend by "truth" it will be realized that I do not assume any inerrant access to it by which some limited group may derive absolute power. The academic branch must be checked and balanced reciprocally by the legislative, judicial, and executive. Furthermore, the truth *about* the truth (and Andersen's edited volume by that title remains commendable reading) should serve to check itself—the understanding of truth as a characteristic of expressions that have certain homologies with lived experience, that cohere with other true statements, and that are pragmatic instruments in the promotion of human agendas, actively supports a view of truth as limited, plural, and polymorphous.

From the social sciences an analysis such as that of Joel Fetzer and Christopher Soper in this volume clearly demonstrates that it is much easier to generate plausible hypotheses than it is to substantiate them, and intuitively obvious hypotheses are frequently incorrect. If nothing else, this indicates our dependence on such careful statistical analysis to differentiate between and substantiate some of the numerous conflicting hypotheses that are suggested by the same initial data. Puniyani points out that the statistical data often totally refute the concoctions of those who promote violence (Puniyani 2005: 24), but, unless the statistical data are accorded the respect they deserve, the purveyors of the easy, superficial, or stirring concoction will move the larger audience. Statements such as "the United States was founded on Christian principles," or "fundamentalism is a return to the original sense and meaning of our tradition," become credible through simple repetition, but they are not simple truths and are open to complex interpretations. The members of the religion academy have a very significant role in assuring that the voting body of Western democracies have an accurate and informed position—an indispensable element of truth and reconciliation is truth.

One truth that the United States might perhaps benefit from is that others do not feel the same sense of violation that many Americans speak of in connection with 9/11 (see, for example, Mark Slouka's essay quoted in Hussain's chapter). I do not personally know anyone killed, nor even anyone who had a relative killed, nor does the idea that someone can bomb my home country strike me as surprising. September 11 is a rather disembodied, archetypal event—for me, as for many non-US natives. Although reading Maureen Korp's account of the ash from the twin towers that had settled on her friend's windows, the smell of the burning metal, no one can deny the sheer emotional power associated with the event. But the emotional focus on this event as if it were one of history's greatest evils, justifying almost any retaliation, should give us pause. Consider the concomitant hijacking of the term "ground zero" to describe the bombing. My father, a British soldier involved in the Korean conflict in the early 1950s, was stationed in Japan and took photographs of what I came to know, very early in my life, as "ground zero": the atomic bomb site in Hiroshima. Estimates vary from 145,000 to 103,000 people—almost all civilians—who lost their lives at that ground zero. Today a web search for "ground zero" with no further parameters will turn up nine out of ten hits for the World Trade Center bombing and misses Hiroshima entirely. How did the site of the twin towers usurp the name applied to the site of the Hiroshima bombing with more than 30 times the casualties? Because 9/11 is more local, more recent—because it has more media interest and more rhetorical weight—because it is closer to the lived experience of a certain audience. The truth may not be comfortable but it is the *raison d'être* of the academy that the truth is worthy of pursuit and finally instrumental in the promotion of human peace.

When Caryn Riswold raised the question of whether or not terrorism can be "defeated," I was led to ask whether or not this is an appropriate metaphor. One can defeat an opponent in a conflict, be it war, wrestling, or a chess game, and one may be said to defeat, for example, a disease. But is the metaphor appropriate there, either? One more accurately *cures* a disease and perhaps it is more appropriate to seek a cure for terrorism. This would imply that the whole terminology of the so-called "war on terrorism" is fundamentally misguided and counter-productive (although it is clearly very effective rhetoric) because it will not contribute to a cure. As Mark Juergensmeyer points out, "the absolutism of war makes compromise unlikely." So the so-called "war on terrorism" might be likened to attempting to cure a disease by beating the symptoms with a stick. The formulation of truths in the hope of the reconciliation of conflicting groups has more chance of effecting a cure than does beating the symptoms with a stick. But these truths will have to be consonant not only with our empirical experience but also with the ideal formulations of our manifold religious traditions.

Note

1   See Piet Meiring (1999), and note that recently Pumla Gobodo-Madikizela, who served alongside Archbishop Desmond Tutu as one of ten members of South Africa's Truth and Reconciliation Commission, has been on the world lecture circuit talking about this unprecedented experiment in peace and justice.

References and further reading

Andersen, Walter Truett. 1995. *The Truth About the Truth: De-confusing and Re-constructing the Postmodern World*. New York: Putnam.

Assefa, Hizkias, and George Wachira. 1996. *Peacemaking and Democratisation in Africa: Theoretical Perspectives and Church Initiatives*. Nairobi: East African Educational Publishers.

Avalos, Hector. 2005. *Fighting Words: The Origins of Religious Violence*. Amherst, NY: Prometheus Books.

Cohn, Norman. 1993. *Chaos, Cosmos and the World to Come: The Ancient Roots of Apocalyptic Faith*. New Haven, CT and London: Yale University Press.

Cooper, Barry. 2004. *New Political Religions, or an Analysis of Modern Terrorism*. Columbia, MO: University of Missouri Press.

Coward, Harold, and Gordon S. Smith, eds. 2004. *Religion and Peacebuilding*. Albany, NY: State University of New York Press.

Eagleton, Terry. 2005. *Holy Terror*. New York: Oxford University Press.

Ellens, J. Harold, ed. 2004. *The Destructive Power of Religion: Violence in Judaism, Christianity, and Islam*. 4 vols. Westport, CT: Praeger.

Falconer, Alan D. and Joseph Liechty, eds. 1998. *Reconciling Memories*. Dublin: Columba Press.

Gaddis, Michael. 2005. *There Is No Crime for Those Who Have Christ: Religious Violence in the Christian Roman Empire*. Berkeley, CA: University of California Press.

Gopin, Mark. 2000. *Between Eden and Armageddon: The Future of World Religions, Violence, and Peacemaking*. New York and London: Oxford University Press.

Hoffman, R. Joseph, ed. 2006. *The Just War and Jihad: Violence in Judaism, Christianity, and Islam*. Amherst, NY: Prometheus Books.

Lincoln, Bruce. 2003. *Holy Terrors: Thinking About Religion after September 11*. Chicago: University of Chicago Press.

Marty, Martin E. 2005. *When Faiths Collide*. Malden, MA: Blackwell.

Meiring, Piet. 1999. *Chronicle of the Truth Commission: A Journey Through the Past Present, into the Future of South Africa*. Vanderbijlpark: Carpe Diem Boeke.

Puniyani, Ram, ed. 2005. *Religion, Power and Violence: Expression of Politics in Contemporary Times*. New Delhi and Thousand Oaks, CA: Sage Publications.

Rennie, Bryan. 1996. *Reconstructing Eliade: Making Sense of Religion*. New York: State University of New York Press.

——. 2003. "Religion after Religion, History after History: Postmodern Historiography and the Study of Religions." *Method and Theory in the Study of Religion* 15 (3): 68–99.

Sills, Chip and George H. Jensen, eds. 1992. *The Philosophy of Discourse: The Rhetorical Turn in Twentieth-Century Thought*. 2 vols. Portsmouth, NH: Boynton.

Steffen, Lloyd. 2003. *Demonic Turn: The Power of Religion to Inspire or Restrain Violence*. Cleveland, OH: Pilgrim Press.

Ter Haar, Gerrie and James Busuttil, eds. 2005. *Bridge or Barrier: Religion, Violence and Visions for Peace*. Leiden and Boston, MA: Brill Academic Publishers.

Index